FESTIVAL AND SPECIAL EVENT MANAGEMENT

SECOND EDITION

WITHDRAWN

JOHNNY ALLEN

WILLIAM O'TOOLE

IAN McDONNELL

ROBERT HARRIS

Second edition published 2002 by
John Wiley & Sons Australia, Ltd
33 Park Road, Milton, Qld 4064

Offices also in Sydney and Melbourne

First edition 1999

Typeset in 10.5/12 pt New Baskerville

© Johnny Allen, William O'Toole, Ian McDonnell,
  Robert Harris 2002

National Library of Australia
Cataloguing-in-Publication data

Festival and special event management.

  2nd ed.
  Includes index.
  ISBN 0 471 42182 0.

  1. Festivals — Management. 2. Special events —
  Management. I. Allen, Johnny. II. McDonnell, Ian.
  Festival and special event management

394.26068

Cover and internal images: © 2001 PhotoDisc Inc.
and Coo–ee Picture Library

Printed in Singapore by
Kyodo Printing Co (S'pore) Pte Ltd

10 9 8 7 6 5 4

PREFACE

Each year in January, February and March, events occur in New South Wales and Victoria that dominate the media, fill airline seats and hotel rooms, colour the streets, and help shape the identity of their host cities all year round.

The Sydney Gay and Lesbian Mardi Gras was born out of a street march and protest against police discrimination in Sydney's Oxford Street in 1978. It quickly grew into a celebration attracting interest well beyond the gay community, as it captured the spirit of cheeky extroversion and in-your-face hedonism of Sydney. The original Mardi Gras street parade has now grown into the month-long Sydney Gay and Lesbian Festival, which the organisers justifiably tout as the largest gay and lesbian event in the world. It has become a major community event, as gay clubs and societies, travel agents, hairdressers, costume designers, dancers and satirists combine to put on the city's biggest annual street parade and party. A crowd estimated at more than 500 000 people lines Oxford Street to view and cheer the parade, which is followed by an all-night dance party at Fox Studios.

Organisers have not been slow to tout the event's economic and tourism significance to Sydney. An economic impact evaluation study (Marsh and Levy 1998) revealed 7341 interstate visitors, 5190 international visitors and a total impact on the inner Sydney economy of just under $99 million. The festival is not without its detractors, most famously the Reverend Fred Nile, but it is an undeniable feature of Sydney's cultural life and international tourist profile.

Meanwhile, in almost the same time frame, Sydney's rival Melbourne plays host to a very different event, both in style and conception. The Australian Formula One Grand Prix was lured away from Adelaide in 1992 with the backing of then Victorian Premier Jeff Kennett, ambitious for his State to dominate the Australian events scene and for Melbourne to make its mark by hosting a major international event. It forms part of the international formula one racing circuit, with a global television audience of 500 million (Kyriakopoulos 1996).

The grand prix track has taken over a section of Albert Park on the edge of the city, which has not pleased everyone and has created a significant strand of community opposition to the event. However, the distinctive black and white check insignia of the race has dominated Melbourne's streets and restaurants for the event; in 1996, 154 000 spectators spilled out into the surrounding streets and suburbs of Melbourne. Overall, the event has been judged a success by the organisers, the public and the media:

> ■ Motor racing is quintessentially macho, loud and fast, with an abundance of ornamental women on hand. It is a celebration of the politically incorrect: precious fossil fuels are burnt by the gallon and the whole event is sponsored for the most part by tobacco companies and, this year, Melbourne's toll freeway project. Yet the crowd lapped it up, and the protestors, whose rallies outside the arena were overwhelmed by the enormity of the event, faded away without incident (Kyriakopoulos 1996). ■

A few weeks earlier, in mid-January, another event takes place in the northern New South Wales city of Tamworth. The Australasian Country Music Festival and Awards began in 1972 as an awards ceremony in Tamworth Town Hall. Locals still recall the days when a bell had to be rung outside in the street to round up a sufficient audience to stage the awards ceremony. The festival now attracts an estimated 50 000 visitors and contributes $40 million to the city's economy. For example, motels and restaurants on the New England Highway from Newcastle to the Queensland border share in the tourism bonanza. Attractions such as the Country Collection Wax Museum, Roll of Renown, Hands of Fame, the giant golden guitar and the guitar-shaped swimming pool demonstrate Tamworth's status as the country music capital of Australia. Recording studios, syndicated radio programs, and publications such as *Capital News* and the *Country Music Directory* help to support an economy based on country music. A series of monthly concerts, the Tamworth Country Theatre, caters for the busloads of tourists arriving throughout the year for the Tamworth country music experience. They even arrive at a guitar-shaped visitor centre. The organisers' original goal was to create an identity for an otherwise undistinguished town and to reverse the summer flow of Tamworth's residents to the coast. Through the dedicated and professional development of the event, they have certainly achieved these goals and, in the words of local festival observer Nick Erby, 'Tamworth now has a second Christmas every January'.

These three events, which are discussed in later chapters, illustrate in various ways the power of events to raise the profile of their host cities, attract visitors, deliver economic benefits and create jobs. They also illustrate the various origins of events, ranging from a community celebration growing out of protest, to an international event supported for political and economic ends. They all raise issues of costs and benefits, and of the impact on their host communities. They also serve as models for event management, development and marketing.

Festival and Special Event Management second edition examines these and other aspects of events in the Australian context. In part one, 'Event context', the reasons human societies create events and the events culture that has evolved in contemporary Australia are examined, as are the range and types of event and their impacts on their host communities, environment and economy. In part two, 'Event strategy', a methodology for the strategic management of events is illustrated by an examination of the processes involved in developing, planning, implementing and marketing events. The third part of the book, 'Event administration', examines sponsorship and other sources of funds, and provides guidance on budgeting and financial control mechanisms. Information is also provided on general administrative issues such as contracts, payments, taxation, insurance, copyright and risk management. Part four, 'Event coordination', covers such topics as operations, stage management, and the process of monitoring and evaluating events and reporting back to stakeholders.

The book is amply illustrated throughout with Australian case studies, which assist the reader to relate the theory of events management to the real world of events practice, with all its challenges, frustrations and rewards. The book provides the reader with both a tool for greater understanding of events management and a framework for planning and implementing events.

By its very nature, events management is a creative process, and by drawing on the body of knowledge in the field, it is hoped that the reader will in turn contribute to the future of this young and exciting industry.

REFERENCES

Kyriakopoulos, Vikki 1996, 'And the winner is . . . Melbourne', *The Bulletin*, 19 March, p. 86.

Marsh, I. & Levy, S. 1998, *Sydney Gay and Lesbian Mardi Gras: Economic Impact Statement 1998*, Sydney Gay and Lesbian Mardi Gras Ltd, Sydney.

ABOUT THE AUTHORS

Johnny Allen

Johnny Allen is Director of the Australian Centre for Event Management at the University of Technology, Sydney. He was Events Manager for the Darling Harbour Authority from 1989 until 1996 and has an extensive career in event planning, staging and management. Prior to his current position, he was the special events manager for Tourism New South Wales.

William O'Toole

William O'Toole has been involved in the creation and organisation of events for more than 20 years, primarily concert events and music festivals. He is currently researching the application of risk resilience to event organisation.

Ian McDonnell

Ian McDonnell is a lecturer in the Faculty of Business' School of Leisure, Sport and Tourism, University of Technology, Sydney where he teaches in the area of management and marketing of leisure and tourism services.

Rob Harris

Rob Harris is a senior lecturer and director of continuing professional education at the School of Leisure, Sport and Tourism at the University of Technology, Sydney. Rob has been involved in event management, training and research for the past six years, and has developed undergraduate, postgraduate and TAFE programs in the area. He is also a founding director of the New South Wales Festivals and Events Association and member of the editorial board of the academic journal, *Event Management*.

CONTENTS

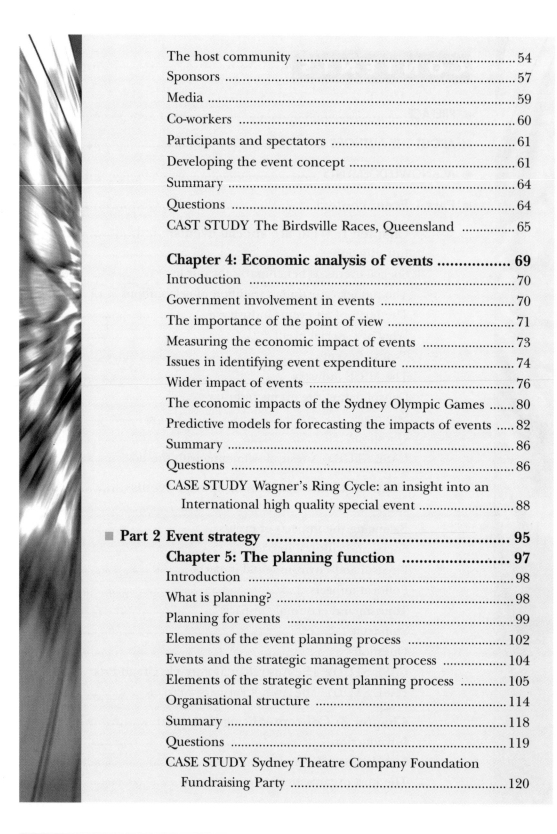

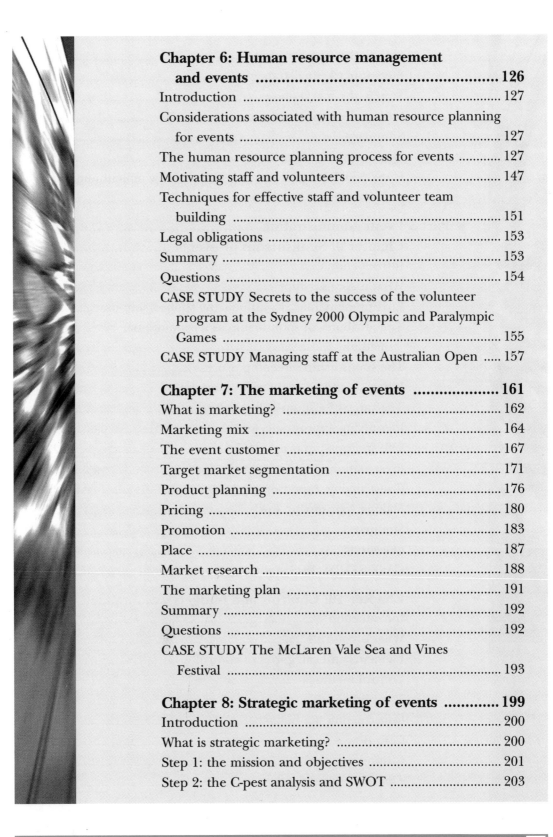

ACKNOWLEDGEMENTS

The authors and publishers wish to thank the following people and institutions for permission to reproduce material covered by copyright.

Figures

Figures 5.1 (p. 99), 6.1 (p. 128), 6.11 (p. 144), adapted from *Event Management and Event Tourism*, Donald Getz, Cognizant Communication Cororation, New York, 1997, pp. 76, 184, 194 respectively. Figure 5.4 (p. 116), by permission Tennis Australia 1997. Figure 6.4 (p. 134), R. Clark, *Australian Human Resources Management*, 2e, McGraw-Hill Book Company, Sydney, 1992, p. 236. Figure 6.8 (p. 140), © School of Volunteer Management, Sydney, 2001. Figure 6.9 (p. 141), Bradner 1997, p. 75, in T. Connors (ed.), *The Volunteer Management Handbook*, John Wiley & Sons, New York. Figure 6.12 (p. 147), Peach and Murrell, 1995, in T. Connors (ed.) *The Volunteer Management Handbook*, John Wiley & Sons, New York. Figure 6.14 (p. 149), adapted and reprinted by permission of *Harvard Business Review*, from Herzberg 1968, 'One more time: how do you motivate employees?', Sept.–Oct., 1987, p. 112. Figure 7.1 (p. 167), Middleton, N. T. C., 1994, *Marketing in Travel and Tourism*, 2e, Butterworth-Heinemann, Oxford, p. 67. Figure 7.2 (p. 169), Saleh and Ryan, 1993, 'Jazz and knitwear — factors that attract tourists to festivals', *Tourism Management*, August, pp. 289–97, reprinted by permission of Pearson Education Limited. Figure 7.3 (p. 174), Stanton, Miller and Layton, *Fundamentals of Marketing*, 3e, McGraw-Hill Book Company, Sydney, 1994, p. 97. Figures 7.7 (p. 179), 7.10 (p. 184), 7.12 (p. 191), Morgan, 1996, *Marketing for Leisure and Tourism*, Prentice Hall, London, reprinted by permission of Pearson Education Limited. Figure 7.9 (p. 183), reproduced from Lovelock, Patterson and Walker, *Services Marketing*, 2e, © Pearson Education Australia, 2001, p. 255. Figure 8.3 (p. 205), Porter, 1990, *Competitive Advantages of Nations*, Free Press, New York, © Pearson Education Inc. Figure 8.6 (p. 212), adapted from Booms and Bitner, 1981, 'Marketing Strategy and Organization Structures for Service Firms', in Donnelly, *Marketing of Services*, p. 47, American Marketing Association. Figures 8.5 (p. 210), 8.7 (p. 213), from *Marketing Strategy* by Paul Fifield. Reprinted by permission Butterworth-Heinemann. Figure 9.1 (p. 225), © Cognizant Communication, Crompton, 1994. Figure 9.4 (p. 234), Advance Energy. Figure 13.7 (p. 335) Woodford Folk Festival, 1997. Figure 13.8 (p. 336), Northern Rivers Folk Festival program. Figure 13.18 (p. 352), A. Volders, 1996, Port Fairy Folk Festival Audience Survey. Figure 15.4 (p. 400), Bureau of Tourism Research, Canberra.

Text

Table 4.1 (p. 81), by permission NSW Treasury and the Centre for Regional Economic Analysis, University of Tasmania, 1997. Event Profile, p. 100, New South Wales Centenary of Federation Committee. Table 6.1 (p. 151), Peach and Murrell, 1995, T. Connors (ed.), *The Volunteer Management Handbook*, John Wiley & Sons, New York. Table 7.3 (p. 170), D. Getz, *Festivals, Special Events and Tourism*, Von Nostrand Reinhold, New York, 1991, p. 85. Table 7.4 (p. 173), Morgan, 1996, adapted from *Marketing for Leisure and Tourism*, Prentice Hall, London. Reprinted by permission Pearson Education Limited. Table 7.5 (p. 174), Getz, 1997, *Event Management and Event Tourism*, Cognizant Communication Corporation, New York, p. 29.

Every effort has been made to trace the ownership of copyright material. Information that will enable the publisher to rectify any error or omission in subsequent editions will be welcome. In such cases please contact the Permissions Section of the publisher which will arrange the payment of the usual fee.

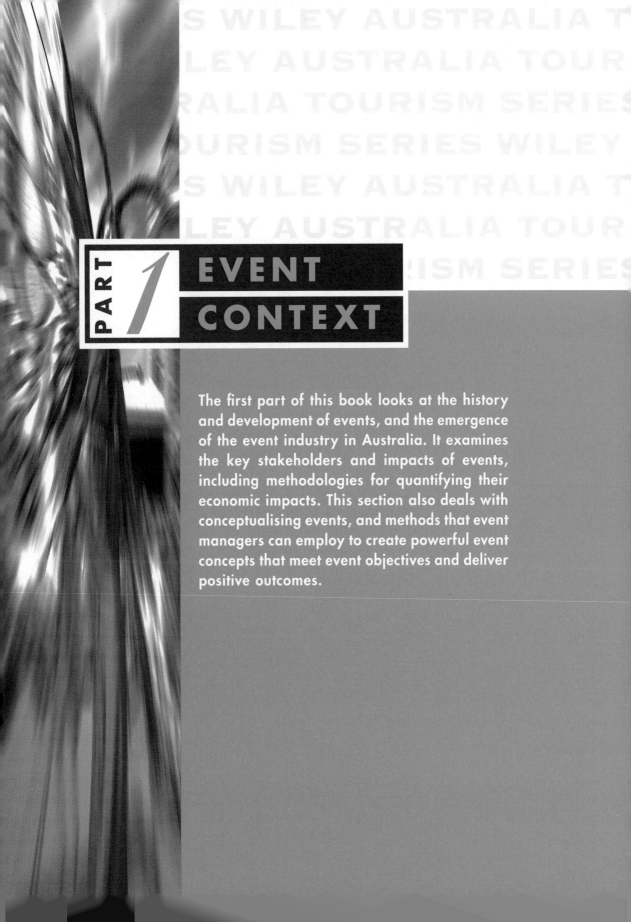

PART 1

EVENT CONTEXT

The first part of this book looks at the history and development of events, and the emergence of the event industry in Australia. It examines the key stakeholders and impacts of events, including methodologies for quantifying their economic impacts. This section also deals with conceptualising events, and methods that event managers can employ to create powerful event concepts that meet event objectives and deliver positive outcomes.

1

What are
special events?

LEARNING OBJECTIVES

After studying this chapter, you should be able to:

- define special events

- demonstrate an awareness of why special events have evolved in human society

- describe the role of special events in Australia, and the Australian tradition of special events

- describe the rise and effect of the community arts movement on special events

- understand the growth of State events corporations and the emergence of an events industry

- distinguish between different types of special events

- discuss the attributes and knowledge requirements of a special event manager

- describe the consolidation of the special event industry in Australia.

Historical events		Celebrations, festivals and events
Arrival of the First Fleet	1788	First Anniversary Day celebrations — Other States begin to celebrate their own Foundation days
Gold rushes 1850s	1850	
	1860	
	1861	First Melbourne Cup — Development of country show circuit
Federation	1901	Inauguration of Federation of Australia, Sydney — Company and trade union picnics Development of Australian Rules football
World War 1 1914–18	1914	
	1918	Development of surf lifesaving carnivals and test cricket matches; growth of Anzac Day
World War II 1939–45	1939	
	1945	
	1950	
	1954	Visit of Queen Elizabeth II
	1956	Melbourne Olympic Games — Growth of civic festivals
	1959	
	1960	First Adelaide Festival of the Arts
Australian involvement in Vietnam War 1962–72	1970	Early rock festivals
	1971	
Whitlam Government 1972–75	1972	First Tamworth Country Music Festival
	1973	Nimbin Aquarius Festival
	1974	Sydney Opera House opening
	1975	Community arts movement Multicultural festivals
	1976	
	1977	
	1978	First Gay and Lesbian Mardi Gras
	1979	
	1980	
	1981	
	1982	Commonwealth Games, Brisbane
	1983	
	1984	Victoria's Sesquicentenary — Australia's Bicentenary
1980s economic boom	1985	First Adelaide Grand Prix — Tall Ships visit
	1986	America's Cup defence, Fremantle — Opening of Darling Harbour, Sydney
	1987	First Maleny (later Woodford) Folk Festival
	1988	
	1989	Expo 88, Brisbane
	1990	First Aboriginal Survival Day concert, Sydney
	1991	First Gold Coast Indy
	1992	Opening of South Bank, Brisbane, and Southgate, Melbourne
	1993	
	1994	
	1995	
	1996	Australian Formula One Grand Prix moves to Melbourne
	1997	Opening of Crown Casino, Melbourne
	1998	Olympic Festival of the Dreaming
	1999	
	2000	New millennium celebrations and Sydney Olympic Games
	2001	Centenary of Federation celebrations
	2002	Goodwill Games, Brisbane
■ Figure 1.1 *Australian event time line*	2003	Rugby World Cup, Sydney — World Masters Games, Melbourne
	2006	Commonwealth Games, Melbourne

INTRODUCTION

Today events are central to our culture as perhaps never before. Increases in leisure time and discretionary spending have led to a proliferation of public events, celebrations and entertainment. Governments now support and promote events as part of their strategies for economic development, nation building and destination marketing. Corporations and businesses embrace events as key elements in their marketing strategies and image promotion. The enthusiasm of community groups and individuals for their own interests and passions gives rise to a marvellous array of events on almost every subject and theme imaginable. Events spill out of our newspapers and television screens, occupy much of our time, and enrich our lives. As we study the phenomenon of events, it is worth examining where the event tradition in Australia has come from, and what forces are likely to shape its future growth and development. As events emerge as an industry in their own right, it is also worth considering what elements characterise such an industry, and how the Australian event industry might chart its future directions in an increasingly complex and demanding environment.

SPECIAL EVENTS AS BENCHMARKS FOR OUR LIVES

Since the dawn of time, human beings have found ways to mark important events in their lives: the changing of the seasons, the phases of the moon, and the renewal of life each spring. From the Aboriginal corroboree and Chinese New Year to the Dionysian rites of ancient Greece and the European carnival tradition of the Middle Ages, myths and rituals have been created to interpret cosmic happenings. To the present day, behind well-known figures such as Old Father Time and Santa Claus lie old myths, archetypes and ancient celebrations. The first Australians used storytelling, dance and song to transmit their culture from generation to generation. Their ceremonies were, and continue to be, important occasions in the life of the community, where cultural meaning is shared and affirmed. Similarly in most agrarian societies, rituals were developed that marked the coming of the seasons and the sowing and harvesting of crops.

Both in private and in public, people feel the need to mark the important occasions in their lives, to celebrate the key moments. Coming of age, for example, is often marked by a rite of passage, other examples are the tribal initiation ceremony, the Jewish bar mitzvah and the suburban twenty-first birthday.

At the public level, momentous events become the milestones by which people measure their private lives. We may talk about things happening 'before the new millenium', in the same way that an earlier generation talked of marrying 'before the Depression' or being born 'after the War'. Occasional events — Australia's Bicentenary, the Sydney Olympics and the new millennium — help to mark eras and define milestones.

Even in the high-tech era of global media, when many people have lost touch with the common religious beliefs and social norms of the past, we still need larger social events to mark the local and domestic details of our lives.

THE MODERN AUSTRALIAN TRADITION OF CELEBRATIONS

In the cultural collision between Aboriginal people and the first Europeans, new traditions were formed alongside the old. Probably the first 'event' in Australia after the arrival of the First Fleet was a bush party to celebrate the coming ashore of the women convicts in 1788:

■ Meanwhile, most of the sailors on *Lady Penrhyn* applied to her master, Captain William Sever, for an extra ration of rum 'to make merry with upon the women quitting the ship'. Out came the pannikins, down went the rum, and before long the drunken tars went off to join the convicts in pursuit of the women, so that, Bowes remarked, 'it is beyond my abilities to give a just description of the scene of debauchery and riot that ensued during the night'. It was the first bush party in Australia, with 'some swearing, others quarrelling, others singing' (Hughes 1987, pp. 88–9). ■

From these inauspicious beginnings the early colonists slowly started to evolve celebrations that were tailored to their new environment, so far from Georgian Britain. Hull (1984) traces the history of these early celebrations, noting the beginnings of a national day some 30 years later:

■ Governor Macquarie declared the 26th of January 1818 a public holiday — convicts were given the day off, a ration of one pound of fresh meat was made for each of them, there was a military review, a salute of 30 guns, a dinner for the officers and a ball for the colony society. ■

This may have been the first festival celebrated by the new inhabitants of Australia. Although 'Anniversary Day', as it was known, was not to become a public holiday for another 20 years, the official celebration of the founding of the colony had begun with the direct involvement and patronage of the government that exists to this day. In contrast to government-organised celebrations, settlers during the nineteenth century entertained themselves with balls, shows and travelling entertainments as a diversion from the serious business of work and survival. The rich tradition of agricultural shows and race meetings such as the Melbourne Cup still survives today. The Sydney Royal Easter Show, after surviving from the mid-nineteenth century, is re-inventing itself today as 'The Great Australian Muster'.

At the turn of the century, the celebration of Australia's Federation captured the prevailing mood of optimistic patriotism:

■ At the turn of the year 1900–1 the city of Sydney went mad with joy. For a few days hope ran so high that poets and prophets declared Australia to be on the threshold of a new golden age ... from early morning on 1 January 1901 trams, trains and ferry boats carried thousands of people into the city for the greatest day in their history: the inauguration of the Commonwealth of Australia. It was to be a people's festival (Clark 1981, p. 177). ■

At the beginning of the twentieth century, the new inhabitants had come to terms with the landscape of Australia, and the democratic ritual of the picnic had gained mass popularity. This extended to guilds, unions and company workers, as demonstrated by the following description of the annual picnic of the employees of Sydney boot and shoe manufacturers McMurtie and Company, at Clontarf in 1906:

■ 'The sweet strains of piano, violin and cornet ... added zest and enjoyment to the festive occasion', said the Advisor. 'Laughter producers were also in evidence, several of the company wearing comical-looking hats and false noses so that even at the commencement of the day's proceedings hilarity and enjoyment was assured.' The enjoyment continued as the party disembarked to the strain of bagpipes, and the sporting programme began ... The 'little ones' were provided with 'toys, spades, balls and lollies'. The shooting gallery was well patronised, and when darkness fell dancing went on in the beautiful dancing hall. Baby Houston danced a Scotch reel to the music of bagpipes. Miss Robinson sang *Underneath the Watermelon Vine*, and little Ruth Bailey danced a jig.

At 8 pm, the whistle blew and the homeward journey commenced with 'music up till the last' and a final rendering of *Auld Lang Syne* as the *Erina* arrived at the Quay (Pearl 1974). ■

However, Australians had to wait until after World War II before a home-grown form of celebration took hold across the nation. In the 1940s and 1950s, city and town festivals were established, which created a common and enduring format. Even today, it is a safe assumption that any festival with an Aboriginal or floral name, and that includes a 'Festival Queen' competition, street parade, outdoor art exhibition and sporting event, dates back to this period. Sydney's Waratah Festival (later replaced by the Sydney Festival), Melbourne's Moomba, Ballarat's Begonia Festival, Young's Cherry Festival, Bowral's Tulip Time, Newcastle's Mattara Festival, and Toowoomba's Carnival of Flowers all date back to the prolific era of local pride and involvement after World War II. Moomba and Mattara both adopted Aboriginal names, the latter word meaning 'hand of friendship'.

Holding such a festival became a badge of civic pride, in the way that building a School of Arts hall had done in an earlier era, or constructing an Olympic swimming pool would do in the 1950s and 1960s. These festivals gave the cities and towns a sense of identity and distinction, and became a focus for community groups and charity fundraising. It is a tribute to their importance to communities that many of these festivals still continue after half a century.

Alongside this movement of community festivals was another very powerful model. In 1947 the Edinburgh Festival was founded as part of the post-war spirit of reconstruction and renewal. In Australia, the Festival of Perth (founded in 1953) and the Adelaide Festival of the Arts (founded in 1960) were based on this inspiring model. The influence of the Edinburgh Festival proved to be enduring, as shown by the resurgence of arts festivals in Sydney, Melbourne and Brisbane in the 1980s and 1990s.

By the 1970s, however, with the coming to power of the Whitlam Government and the formation of the Australia Council, new cultural directions were unleashed which were to change the face of festivals in Australia.

The Community Arts Board of the Australia Council, under the leadership of Ros Bower, developed a strategy aimed at giving a voice to the voiceless and taking arts and festivals into the suburbs and towns of Australia. Often for the first time, migrants, workers and Aboriginal people were encouraged to participate in a new cultural pluralism which broke down the elitism which had governed the arts in much of rural and suburban Australia. Sensing the unique cultural challenge faced by Australia, Bower (1981) wrote:

> ■ In terms of our national cultural objectives, the re-integration of the artist into the community is of crucial importance. Australia lacks a coherent cultural background. The artist needs to become the spokesman, the interpreter, the image-maker and the prophet. He cannot do it in isolation or from an ivory tower. He must do it by working with the people. He must help them to piece together their local history, their local traditions, their folk-lore, the drama and the visual imagery of their lives. And in doing this he will enrich and give identity to his work as an artist. The arts will cease to be imitative, or preoccupied with making big splashes in little 'cultured' pools. They will be integrated more closely with our lives, our history, our unique environment. They will be experimental and exploring forces within the broader cultural framework. ■

The 1970s saw not only the emergence of multiculturalism and the 'new age' movement, but also the forging of the community arts movement and a new and diverse range of festivals across Australia. Some examples of the rich diversity spawned by this period are the Aquarius Festival staged by the Australian Union of Students at Nimbin in northern New South Wales, the Lygon Street Festa in Melbourne's Carlton, the Come Out young people's festival held in alternate years to the Adelaide Festival, the Carnivale celebration of multiculturalism across Sydney and New South Wales and Sydney's Gay and Lesbian Mardi Gras. Festivals became part of the cultural landscape, and became connected again to people's needs and lives. Every community, it seemed, had something to celebrate and the tools with which to create its own festival.

THE BIRTH OF AN EVENTS INDUSTRY

Through the 1980s and 1990s, certain seminal events set the pattern for the contemporary events industry as we know it today. The Commonwealth Games in Brisbane in 1982 ushered in a new era of maturity and prominence for that city and a new breed of sporting events. The Commonwealth Games also initiated a career in ceremonies and celebrations for a former ABC rock show producer, Ric Birch, which led to his taking a key role in the opening and closing ceremonies at the Los Angeles, Barcelona and Sydney Olympics. The Olympic Games in Los Angeles in 1984 demonstrated that major events could be economically viable. They managed to combine a Hollywood-style spectacular with a sporting event in a manner that had not been done before, and would set a standard for all similar events in future. The production and marketing skills of the television industry brought the Olympics to an audience wider than ever before. Television also demonstrated the power of a major sporting event to bring increased profile and economic benefits to a city and to an entire country.

The entrepreneurs of the 1980s economic boom in Australia soon picked up on this, and the America's Cup defence in Perth and Fremantle in 1986–87 was treated as an opportunity to put Perth on the map and to attract major economic and tourism benefits to Western Australia. By 1988, there was a boom in special events, with Australia's Bicentenary seen by many as a major commemorative program and vehicle for tourism. This boom was matched by governments setting up State events corporations, thereby giving public sector support to special events as never before. In Brisbane, the success of Expo 88 rivalled the Bicentennial activities in Sydney, and Adelaide managed a coup by staging the first Australian Formula One Grand Prix.

The Bicentenary caused Australians to pause and reflect on the Australian identity. It also changed forever the nature of our public celebrations:

> ■ I would argue that the remarkable legacy of 1988 is the public event. It is now a regular feature of Australian life. We gather for fireworks, for welcome-home marches for athletes and other Australians who have achieved success. We go to large urban spaces like the Domain for opera, rock and symphonic music in our hundreds of thousands. The Sydney Festival attracts record numbers. The Gay Mardi Gras is an international phenomenon... Whatever the nature of debate about values, identity and imagery, one certainty is that Australians are in love with high-quality public events that are fun and offer to extend the range and experience of being Australian (McCarthy 1998). ■

The Bicentenary also left a legacy of public spaces dedicated to celebrations and special events and of governments supporting the social and economic benefits of such events. Sydney's Darling Harbour opened to welcome the Tall Ships on 16 January 1988, and provided the city with a major leisure centre. Darling Harbour incorporates dedicated celebrations areas, tourist attractions, a festival marketplace and convention and exhibition centres, all adjacent to the Sydney Entertainment Centre and the Powerhouse and National Maritime museums. Likewise, Brisbane's riverside Expo 88 site was converted into the South Bank Parklands, and Melbourne followed suit with the Southgate development on the Yarra River.

Whatever the economic causes of it were, the recession of the late 1980s and early 1990s put a dampener on the party mood and the seemingly endless growth of events. That is, until 4.27 a.m. on 24 September 1993 when those memorable words were spoken by International Olympic President Juan Antonio Samaranch: 'And the winner is... Sydney!'

It was said by many that the recession ended the day Sydney was awarded the Olympic Games of the new millennium. Certainly it meant that the events industry could once more look forward with optimism, as though the recession had been a mere pause for breath. Events corporations formed in the late 1980s and early 1990s started to demonstrate that economic benefits could be generated through special events. This led to competition between the States for major events, with the then Victorian Premier, Jeff Kennett, taking the Australian Formula One Grand Prix from Adelaide, the Australian Motorcycle Grand Prix from Sydney, and hosting, in Melbourne, the Three Tenors concert, the Bledisloe Cup and the Presidents Cup golf tournament. New South Wales fought back, with Sydney taking the AFI Awards from Melbourne and hosting the musicals *Showboat* and *The Boy From Oz*. Sporting and cultural events, always part of the landscape, had become weapons in an events war fuelled by the media. Australia approached the end of the twentieth century with a competitive events climate dominated by the Sydney Olympics, the new millennium and the Centenary of Federation celebrations in 2001. This enthusiasm for events looks set to continue well into the first decade of the new century with the staging of the Goodwill Games in Brisbane in 2001, the World Masters Games in Melbourne and the International Gay Games in Sydney in 2002, the World Rugby Cup in Sydney in 2003 and the Commonwealth Games in Melbourne in 2006.

EVENT PROFILE

International Festivals and Events Association

The International Festivals and Events Association (IFEA) promotes the networking and professional development of its members through a program of publications, seminars and conferences. Headquartered in the USA, it has affiliated groups in Europe, Asia and Australia. It produces a quarterly newsletter *Festivals*, a membership directory *Who's Who in Festivals*, and a range of publications on topics of interest to festival and event managers such as sponsorship, fundraising and creative festival ideas.

Festivals and Events Associations have been formed in most Australian States including New South Wales, Queensland, South Australia, Western Australia and Tasmania. IFEA conferences have been held in Adelaide in 1996, and Hobart in 1999. The NSWFEA staged a conference, New Millennium/New Nation, in Sydney in 1999, and a second conference, The Art of Celebration, in 2001. It organises regular meetings and forums for its members, and is currently devising a training and accreditation program for the events industry.

The stated objectives of the NSWFEA are:
- to promote and improve communication and cooperation between members and member organisations
- to promote the value of festivals and events to the community at large
- to provide opportunities for the development of skills for festival and event organisers by conducting workshops, seminars, conferences and regular network sessions
- to improve government awareness of the role of festivals in economic development, tourism and the arts by lobbying and representing members' views to government
- to facilitate the sharing and exchange of performers between festivals and events
- to establish and maintain a register of event organisers and their activities within NSW

Source: *International Festivals and Events Association 2000 and New South Wales Festivals and Events Association 1995.*

WHAT ARE SPECIAL EVENTS? ··································

The term '**special events**' has been coined to describe specific rituals, presentations, performances or celebrations that are consciously planned and created to mark special occasions or to achieve particular social, cultural or corporate goals and objectives. Special events can include national days and celebrations, important civic occasions, unique cultural performances, major sporting fixtures, corporate functions, trade promotions and product launches. It seems at times that special events are everywhere; they have become a growth industry. The field of special events is now so vast that it is impossible to provide a definition that includes all varieties and shades of events. In his groundbreaking work on the typology of events, Getz (1997, p. 4) suggests that special events are best defined by their context. He offers two definitions, one from the point of view of the event organiser, and the other from that of the customer or guest.

■ 1. A special event is a one-time or infrequently occurring event outside normal programs or activities of the sponsoring or organizing body.
2. To the customer or guest, a special event is an opportunity for a leisure, social or cultural experience outside the normal range of choices or beyond everyday experience. ■

Among the attributes that he believes create the special atmosphere are festive spirit, uniqueness, quality, authenticity, tradition, hospitality, theme and symbolism.

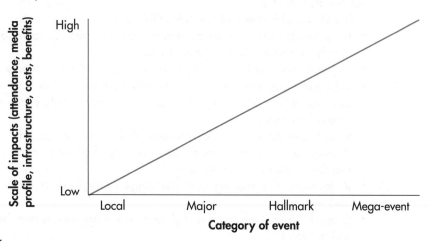

■ **Figure 1.2**
Categorisation of events

*T*YPES OF EVENT

Special events are often characterised according to their size and scale (see figure 1.2). Common categories are mega-events, hallmark events and major events, though definitions are not exact and distinctions become blurred. Events are also classified according to their purpose or to the particular sector to which they belong, for example, public, sporting, tourism and corporate events, which will be explored further in chapter 3. In this text, we will be examining the full range of events that are produced by the events industry, and we will use the term 'event' to cover all the following categories.

■ Mega-events

Mega-events are those that are so large they affect whole economies and reverberate in the global media. They include Olympic Games and World Fairs, but it is difficult for many other events to fit into this category. Getz (1997, p. 6) defines them in the following way.

■ Their volume should exceed 1 million visits, their capital costs should be at least $500 million, and their reputation should be of a 'must see' event . . . Mega-events, by way of their size or significance, are those that yield extraordinarily high levels of tourism, media coverage, prestige, or economic impact for the host community or destination. ■

Hall (1992, p. 5), another researcher in the field of events and tourism, offers this definition:

> ■ Mega-events such as World Fairs and Expositions, the World Soccer Cup final, or the Olympic Games, are events which are expressly targeted at the international tourism market and may be suitably described as 'mega' by virtue of their size in terms of attendance, target market, level of public financial involvement, political effects, extent of television coverage, construction of facilities, and impact on economic and social fabric of the host community. ■

By these definitions, the Sydney Olympic Games in 2000 was perhaps Australia's first true mega-event. The Melbourne Olympics in 1956 belonged to an earlier era of far less extensive media coverage and smaller television audiences, although in relative terms it may well qualify as a 'mega-event' of its era. Even Brisbane's Expo 88 was officially a 'B' class Expo, and events such as the Commonwealth Games in Brisbane in 1982 and the America's Cup defence in Perth and Fremantle in 1986–87 would struggle to meet Getz's criteria. Australia's Bicentenary celebrations in 1988, if taken as a national event, would probably qualify, as might the Centenary of Federation celebrations staged in 2001.

■ Hallmark *events*

The term 'hallmark events' refers to those events that become so identified with the spirit or ethos of a town, city or region that they become synonymous with the name of the place, and gain widespread recognition and awareness. Tourism researcher Ritchie (1984, p. 2) defines them as:

> ■ Major one-time or recurring events of limited duration, developed primarily to enhance awareness, appeal and profitability of a tourism destination in the short term and/or long term. Such events rely for their success on uniqueness, status, or timely significance to create interest and attract attention. ■

Classic examples of hallmark events are the Carnival in Rio de Janeiro, known throughout the world as an expression of the vitality and exuberance of that city, the Kentucky Derby in the USA, the Chelsea Flower Show in Britain, the Oktoberfest in Munich, Germany, and the Edinburgh Festival in Scotland. Such events, which are identified with the very character of these places and their citizens, bring huge tourist dollars, a strong sense of local pride and international recognition. Getz (1997, pp. 5–6) describes them in terms of their ability to provide a competitive advantage for their host communities:

> ■ The term 'hallmark event' is used to describe a recurring event that possesses such significance, in terms of tradition, attractiveness, image, or publicity, that the event provides the host venue, community, or destination with a competitive advantage. Over time, the event and destination become inseparable. For example Mardi Gras gives New Orleans a competitive advantage by virtue of its high profile. Stratford, Ontario, has taken its tourism theme from the successful Shakespearean Festival. Increasingly, every community and destination needs one or more hallmark events to provide the high levels of media exposure and positive imagery that help to create competitive advantages. ■

Examples in Australia might include the Sydney Gay and Lesbian Mardi Gras, the Australasian Country Music Festival at Tamworth, the Melbourne Cup and the Adelaide Festival, all of which have a degree of international recognition and help to identify the ethos of their host cities.

■ Major *events*

Major events are events that, by their scale and media interest, are capable of attracting significant visitor numbers, media coverage and economic benefits. Melbourne has developed the Australian Open tennis tournament and the Australian Formula One Grand Prix into significant annual major events. The Tall Ships visit, hosted by Sydney in 1988 and awarded to Hobart on the occasion of Bass and Flinders' Bicentenary in 1998, provided a focus on maritime heritage as well as attracting international prestige and media. Many top international sporting championships fit into this category, and are increasingly being sought after and bid for by national sporting organisations and governments in the competitive world of international major events.

Cultural events can also be contenders. The Victorian Government was keen to stage the Three Tenors concert in 1997, and major musicals such as *Phantom of the Opera* and *Cats* reap considerable tourism revenue for their host cities. Betty Churcher, the former director of the National Gallery of Australia, enhanced the reputation of the gallery and helped create a tourism bonanza for Canberra through the staging of 'blockbuster' exhibitions of works by Rubens, Turner and the Surrealists, among others. South Australia has hosted Opera in the Outback and Womadelaide, and Canberra has initiated the National Multicultural Festival, each place with an eye to positioning itself in the tourism market as well as in the arts world.

THE MICE INDUSTRY

Closely allied to the events industry, and often seen as a component of it, is the MICE industry (Meetings, Incentives, Conventions and Exhibitions). This sector is largely characterised by its business and trade focus, though there is a strong public and tourism aspect to many of its activities. Meetings can be very diverse, as revealed by the definition of the Commonwealth Department of Tourism (1995, p. 3):

> ■ all off-site gatherings, including conventions, congresses, conferences, seminars, workshops and symposiums, which bring together people for a common purpose — the sharing of information. ■

The MICE industry market is worth an estimated $7 billion per annum (Johnson, Foo & O'Halloran 1999). Two major events alone — the World Congress of Chemical Engineers in Melbourne in 2001 and the World Congress of Cardiology in Sydney in 2002 — are expected to attract 13 000 big-spending delegates to Australia.

Another lucrative aspect of the MICE industry is incentive travel, defined by the Society of Incentive Travel Executives (1997) (cited in Rogers 1998, p. 47) as 'a global management tool that uses an exceptional travel experience to motivate and/or recognise participants for increased levels of performance in support of organisational goals'. Australia's colourful and unique locations and international popularity as a tourism destination make it a leading player in the incentive travel market.

Last, but not least, exhibitions are a considerable and growing part of the MICE industry. Exhibitions bring suppliers of goods and services together with buyers, usually in a particular industry sector. They can be restricted to industry members, referred to as trade shows, or can be open to the general public. The International Motor Show, the Home Show and the Boat Show are three of the largest exhibitions in Sydney, each generating tens of thousands of visitors. Major convention centres in most Australian cities and many regional centres now vie for their share of the thriving MICE industry market.

CONSOLIDATING THE EVENTS INDUSTRY

The growth of events that serve a wide variety of purposes and agendas has led to the emergence of an events industry with its own body of knowledge, job opportunities and career paths.

Further indications of the emergence of an events industry, noted by Harris and Griffin (1997), are the formation of industry associations and the establishment of training courses and accreditation schemes. A number of industry associations have been formed that represent the various specialisations within the industry. Event managers should identify the association that best suits their situation and needs.

- The International Special Events Society (ISES) has established chapters in Sydney and Melbourne, and offers an exam-based accreditation as a Certified Special Events Professional (CSEP). ISES deals mainly with the corporate and business events area.
- The International Festivals and Events Association (IFEA) is more concerned with festivals and events produced for public entertainment and consumption. Individual associations exist in most Australian States, and membership in Australia offers affiliation with the US parent association.
- The New South Wales Festivals and Events Association (NSWFEA) organises industry gatherings and conferences, and is currently considering an accreditation scheme based on the IFEA American model.
- The Meetings Industry Association of Australia (MIAA) provides training for the industry, and runs a general industry accreditation program as well as a specialist accreditation program directed at meetings managers.

The Exhibitions and Events Association of Australia (EEAA) promotes the value of exhibitions as well as the professionalism of its members. It is currently considering an accreditation program.

Dedicated courses in event management are now provided by the University of Technology, Sydney, Victoria University in Melbourne, Southern Cross University in Lismore and State-based technical and further education (TAFE) bodies. These courses focus on the provision of training for professionals who are working in the event industry, and generally the courses cover event management, marketing and operations. Courses in events are also included in many tourism, leisure and hospitality programs in universities and private training colleges around the country.

Harris and Griffin (1997) developed a profile of the education levels and event experience of event managers through a survey of 113 event organisers in Sydney and regional New South Wales.

■ As a group, event organisers are relatively highly educated with 56% of those sampled holding a postgraduate, undergraduate or TAFE qualification. The level of event related experience possessed by the sample group was high with 50% having played a significant role in the organisation of an event attracting 10,000 or more people, with a similar number (45%) being involved in organising two (2) or more different types of events. ■

Perry, Foley and Rumpf (1996) described the attributes and knowledge required by event managers based on a survey of the views of 105 managers who attended the Australian Events Conference in Canberra in February 1996. Seven attributes were frequently mentioned, of which vision was listed as the most important, followed closely by leadership, adaptability, and skills in organisation, communication, marketing and people management. Knowledge areas considered most important were project management, budgeting, time management, relating to the media, business planning, human resource management and marketing. The graph in figure 1.3 shows some of the results of the survey. Respondents were asked to indicate how strongly they agreed or disagreed with a statement such as: 'An events manager requires skills in project management'. The numbers at the base of the graph show agreement and disagreement, with 1 being 'strongly disagree' and 5 being 'strongly agree'.

The results of this survey have also been incorporated into the planning of the postgraduate certificate in Events Management which is offered by Victoria University.

As the study and discipline of event management grow, a distinct body of knowledge that constitutes industry best practice is being codified and taught. As this grows hand in hand with accreditation, career paths in the industry are beginning to take form.

The emerging events industry, with its needs, challenges and opportunities, will be examined in the following chapters.

■ **Figure 1.3**
*Knowledge
required
by event
managers —
respondents
to survey*

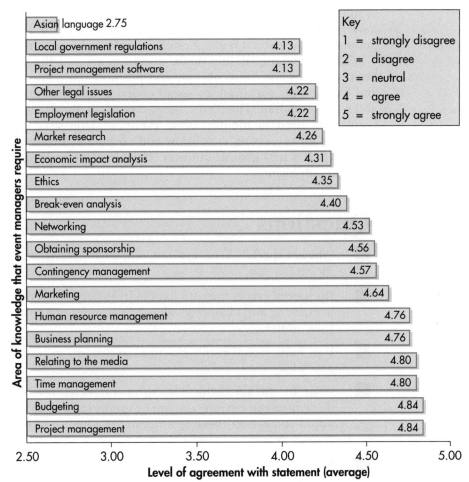

Area of knowledge that event managers require	Level of agreement with statement (average)
Asian language	2.75
Local government regulations	4.13
Project management software	4.13
Other legal issues	4.22
Employment legislation	4.22
Market research	4.26
Economic impact analysis	4.31
Ethics	4.35
Break-even analysis	4.40
Networking	4.53
Obtaining sponsorship	4.56
Contingency management	4.57
Marketing	4.64
Human resource management	4.76
Business planning	4.76
Relating to the media	4.80
Time management	4.80
Budgeting	4.84
Project management	4.84

Key
1 = strongly disagree
2 = disagree
3 = neutral
4 = agree
5 = strongly agree

SUMMARY

Special events perform a powerful role in society, and they have existed throughout human history in all times and all cultures. Aboriginal culture had a rich tradition of rituals and ceremonies prior to the arrival of the Europeans. The events tradition in modern Australia began in a primitive way with the arrival of the First Fleet, and developed through the late eighteenth and nineteenth centuries as the colony prospered and the new inhabitants came to terms with their environment. The ruling elite often decided the form and content of public celebrations, but an alternative tradition of popular celebrations arose from the interests and pursuits of ordinary people. During the twentieth century, changes in society were mirrored by changes in the style of public events. The post-war wave of civic festivals and arts festivals was strongly influenced by the community arts movement in the 1970s, along with multiculturalism and the 'new age' movement. Notions of high culture were challenged by a more pluralistic popular culture, which reinvigorated festivals and community events.

With the coming of the 1980s, governments and the corporate sector began to recognise the economic and promotional value of special events, and State events corporations spearheaded a new level of funding, profile and professionalism. The terms 'mega-events', 'hallmark events' and 'major events' are used to identify those events of large-scale significance and impact. With increasing expansion and corporate involvement, events are emerging as a new growth industry, capable of generating economic benefits and employment.

Questions

1. Why are special events created, and what purpose do they serve in society?

2. Do special events mirror changes in society, or do they have a role in creating and changing values? Give some examples to illustrate your answer.

3. Why have special events emerged so strongly in recent years in Australia?

4. What are the key political, cultural and social trends that determine the current climate of events in Australia, and how would you expect these to influence the nature of events in the coming years?

5. Identify an event in your city or region which has the capacity to be a hallmark event and give your reasons for placing it in this category.

6. What characteristics define an 'industry'? Using these criteria, do you consider that there is an 'events industry' in Australia?

7. Do you agree with the attributes and knowledge areas events managers believe they require? Create a list of your own attributes and skills based on these listings.

A festival swimming
with the tide!

River*festival* is a vibrant community-based celebration with strategic and ambitious long-term international aspirations. The rapid growth River*festival* has seen over the last three years can be attributed to its host city, Brisbane, and its natural icon, the Brisbane River. For generations Australia's River City had turned its back on this natural resource and its very existence. For an entire generation, architects seemed to have had a preference for designing buildings facing the street backing onto the river — rather than appreciating the extraordinary views of the winding Brisbane River.

Brisbane River history

Industry, agriculture, storm water, sewerage and bad land management practices all began contributing to the demise of the Brisbane River. The most recent of the major floods in 1974 created an unflattering public image of the river as some-thing that had to be endured rather than enjoyed and on occasions feared. This was a departure from a river that once sustained more than 5000 Aborigines of the Yugarabul language group who knew the river as mairwar, a river so beautiful and abundant that the Surveyor General of New South Wales, John Oxley, had no hesitation in recommending its shores as the site of the new northern penal settlement.

What happened over the first 175 years of European settlement is indicative of what has occurred to river systems worldwide. The once proud river became a perceived liability. It is at this point that visionaries, those who can see beyond that which seems obvious, are needed.

Brisbane is fortunate enough to benefit from the services of a few key vision-aries, none more important than the Mayor, Councillor Jim Soorley of Brisbane. The Lord Mayor commenced a push to stop extractive dredging, commissioned a fast catamaran ferry service (CityCats), encouraged surrounding councils and the State Government to address the many problems facing the river, including the collection of scientific data and information about the river system, and, perhaps the least obvious of all actions, the call for a river-based celebration.

As this initial concept of a river-based celebration was not adequately resourced in current budgeting, the 125th anniversary celebrations of Newstead House, the historic riverside residence of Queensland's first governor, was trans-formed from an event inwardly focused on past glories to a river-based cel-ebration with a futuristic outlook.

The inaugural Down by the River celebration was undertaken and proved an instant success as the Brisbane public warmed to a post-winter celebration with great food, wine and entertainment 'down by the river'.

Buoyed by the success of this trial the Brisbane City Council allocated funding to appoint a full-time production team and set about creating its very own Brisbane River Festival. Rather than begin planning for such a festival from scratch, a worldwide search was conducted seeking best management practices in successful festivals. This search revealed distinct trends in the importance of good quality food, waterfront celebration and an emerging trend of strategic celebrations designed to deliver on community-desired outcomes, and in a few unique cases these were environment-based outcomes.

It is not surprising that communities have been pairing celebration and festivity with desired change of popular beliefs and practices. This approach had not been widely embraced in Australia. At the time of researching, the then highly successful Stockholm Water Festival (1991–98) was the best case example for Brisbane's purposes. The founding general manager of the Water Festival, Caj Malmros, was invited to Brisbane to outline Stockholm's achievements. The importance of having Caj visit Brisbane was to ensure that he was able to personally deliver his message to every key decision maker in Brisbane as to the potential of what a river- or water-based festival could mean to the city of Brisbane. It is better for the uninitiated to hear the vision from someone with the authority of experience than to just to rely upon the potential of the vision alone.

It must be noted that most of those organisations who met with Caj Malmros have supported the Riverfestival since its inception and have continued their support to the present day.

Riverfestival begins

In September 1998 the inaugural Brisbane River Festival was staged and featured an over-ambitious program of eclectic river-based celebrations from walking (and eating) tours of Brisbane's finest riverside restaurants, a lunch on the Victoria Bridge for over 2000 patrons culminating in an event entitled Riverfire which set about exploding, with pyrotechnics, as many of the River City's architectural features as authorities would allow. The net result was 515 000 visitors and a seemingly new found public love affair with their river (table 1.1).

Riverfestival has continued to enjoy strong growth over the first three years of operation and this is likely to continue with the festival's linkage with the Goodwill Games Brisbane in 2001.

Riverfestival today

Riverfestival offers Brisbane an excitingly diverse range of deliverables with its potential yet to be fully realised. It has fast become the city's iconic annual celebration, attracting the attendance of 55 per cent of the region's population each year and enjoying a 95 per cent awareness rating after only three years of operation.

It offers the city a sense of identity as Australia's 'River City', strengthening its international profile as a destination. The annual International River Management Symposium is considered by the industry to be the most significant of its kind in Australia, in many respects leading the world in networking managed river systems and showcasing world's best practice in river management.

YEAR	ATTENDANCE FIGURES	BUDGET (CASH AND IN KIND)	MARKET RESEARCH ACHIEVEMENTS
1998	515 000	$2.1m	• 95% awareness
1999	788 000	$3.07m	• 88% population see advertising
2000	654 000 (reduced program from '99 to '00)	$3.78m	• 55% population attend River*festival* • 22% population aware of sponsors • 18% believe River*festival* means 'celebration for the river'
2001 (projected)	1 million	$4.95m	• extremely high satisfaction rating (4.5 out of 5) • up to 80% of population expected to attend event in 2001

The attendance of the world's best river managers each year offers the region access to the latest information and technology, an ability to compare first hand our progress of river management and techniques, as well as drive and secure the long-term agendas required to ameliorate our river system.

The River*festival*'s $100 000 International River*prize*, awarded in 1999 to Mersey Basin Campaign (UK) and in 2000 to the Grand River Conservation Authority (Canada), has afforded Brisbane extensive international recognition valued in the millions of dollars as well as invaluable long-term networks and partnerships.

A multi-layered approach designed to appeal to key target demographics within the Brisbane region as well as to an international forum on river management issues has led to River*festival*'s rapid growth and success to date. With continuing sound fiscal management and innovative artistic direction, the River*festival* tradition has a unique opportunity to continue to grow and strengthen for as long as the Brisbane River continues to flow through the city. As long as River*festival* remains linked to the city's greatest natural asset and continues to celebrate the diverse and relaxed lifestyle, it will have meaning and subsequently enjoy continued public support.

Sponsorship

River*festival* successfully acquired 53 sponsors in 2000 with the Brisbane City Council, Queensland Government and Channel 9 as primary funding providers. The increased support to be part of Brisbane's largest river and water celebration became evident after 1998 with an increase in sponsorship revenue in 1999 by 113 per cent. Satisfaction of their sponsorship support is also evident, with sponsors keen to increase the period of their contracts, and with repeat sponsorship each year.

Demographics

River*festival*'s primary target market is the 25–55 years, AB demographic within the greater Brisbane River region (including the Gold Coast, North Coast and Ipswich/Toowoomba regions). This primary target market has remained constant over the last three festivals and will continue to remain the key demographic. However, with improved awareness and programming of the River*symposium*, a secondary international target market is being targeted.

Organisational structure

River*festival* has a consultant-based production team (John Aitken Productions), River*festival* Pty Ltd-appointed staff and an appointed River*festival* Board (of 10–12 members) working closely as a team to achieve a successful result for the festival.

Volunteers are an integral resource within River*festival*. River*festival* requires about 50 volunteers annually to assist with front of house, logistics, marketing, administration, and so on.

Festival vision

Strength of vision that reflects community aspirations for self-expression and desired change, alongside sound long-term planning which runs well beyond political or commercial agendas of the day, are vital elements. Add to this unqualified support of a growing list of key community leaders, the recruitment of the best available expertise, the production team fostering a burning passion for the project, and communities and corporations are well on the way to achieving an event with great potential! This is the recipe for Brisbane's River*festival*.

John Aitken
Producer, Riverfestival

Questions

1 What roles should events play in current society?

2 What is the correlation between events franchised by the host community and those developed from the ground up? Do they both achieve different agendas and if so, what? Which is more valuable and why?

3 Are the enormous resources required to develop a grass roots event justifiable? How can such an event be held accountable over the short and long term?

4 What other agendas should events like River*festival* be embracing?

5 What are the potential pitfalls of the approach taken by River*festival*?

6 How does strong fiscal management sustain a good festival? What influence, if any, should fiscal management have on the artistic direction of a festival?

REFERENCES

Bower, Rosalie 1981, 'Community arts — what is it?', *Caper*, vol. 10, Community Arts Board, Australia Council, Sydney.

Clark, Manning 1981, *A History of Australia*, vol. 5, Melbourne University Press, Melbourne.

Commonwealth Department of Tourism 1995, *A National Strategy for the Meetings, Incentives, Conventions and Exhibitions Industry*, Australian Government Publishing Service, Canberra.

Getz, Donald 1997, *Event Management and Event Tourism*, Cognizant Communication Corporation, New York.

Hall, Colin Michael 1992, *Hallmark Tourist Events: Impacts, Management and Planning*, Belhaven Press, London.

Harris, Robert & Griffin, Tony 1997, *Tourism Events Training Audit*, prepared for Tourism New South Wales Events Unit, Sydney.

Hughes, Robert 1987, *The Fatal Shore*, Collins Harvill, London.

Hull, Andrea 1984, 'Feasting on festas and festivals', paper delivered to the Association of Festivals Conference at Caulfield Arts Centre, Victoria.

International Festivals and Events Association 2000, www.ifea.com (accessed 21 September 2000).

Johnson, L., Foo, L. M. & O'Halloran, M. 1999, *Meetings Make Their Mark: Characteristics and economic contribution of Australia's meetings and exhibitions sector*, BTR Occasional Paper No. 26, Bureau of Tourism Research, Canberra.

McCarthy, Wendy 1998, 'Day we came of age', *Sun-Herald*, 25 January, p. 46.

New South Wales Festivals and Events Association 1995, *An Invitation to Join New South Wales Festivals and Events Association* (membership brochure), New South Wales Festivals and Events Association, Sydney.

Pearl, Cyril 1974, *Australia's Yesterdays*, Readers Digest, Sydney.

Perry, M., Foley, P. & Rumpf, P. 1996, 'Event management: an emerging challenge in Australian education', *Festival Management & Event Tourism*, vol. 4, pp. 85–93.

Ritchie, J. R. Brent 1984, 'Assessing the impact of hallmark events: conceptual and research issues', *Journal of Travel Research*, vol. 23, no. 1, pp. 2–11.

Rogers, T. 1998, *Conferences: a Twenty-first Century Industry*, Addison Wesley Longman Limited, Harlow.

CHAPTER 2

The impacts of
special events

LEARNING OBJECTIVES

After studying this chapter, you should be able to:

■ identify the major impacts that events have on their stakeholders and host communities

■ explain how events can be used to strengthen community pride and values

■ anticipate the social impact of events and plan for positive outcomes

■ understand the management of crowd behaviour

■ describe the physical and environmental impacts of events

■ understand the political context of events

■ describe the ways that events can be used to increase tourist visits and length of stay

■ balance the economic costs and benefits of staging an event

■ demonstrate an understanding of the role of the event manager in balancing the impacts of events.

INTRODUCTION

Events do not take place in a vacuum — they touch almost every aspect of our lives, be it the social, cultural, economic, environmental or political. The benefits arising from these positive connections are a large part of the reason for the popularity and support of events. These benefits are increasingly well documented and researched, and appropriate strategies developed to enhance event outcomes and optimise their benefits. However, events can also have unintended consequences that can bring them to public prominence and media attention for the wrong reasons. The cost of event failure can be disastrous, turning positive benefits into negative publicity, political embarrassment and costly lawsuits. An important core task in the organising of contemporary events is the identification, monitoring and management of event impacts. This chapter examines some of the main areas impacted by events, and looks at strategies that can be employed by event managers to balance event impacts.

BALANCING THE IMPACTS OF EVENTS

Events have a range of impacts — both positive and negative — on their host communities and stakeholders (see table 2.1). It is the task of the event manager to identify and predict these impacts and then manage them to achieve the best outcome for all parties, so that in the balance the overall impact of the event is positive. To achieve this, all foreseeable positive impacts must be developed and maximised, and negative impacts countered. Often negative impacts can be addressed through awareness and intervention — good planning is always critical. Ultimately, the success of the event depends on the event manager achieving this positive balance sheet and communicating it to a range of stakeholders.

Great emphasis is often placed on the financial impacts of events, partly because of the need of employers and governments to meet budget goals and justify expenditure, and partly because such impacts are most easily assessed. However, the event manager should not lose sight of the full range of impacts resulting from the event, and the need to identify, describe and manage them. It is also important to realise that different impacts require different means of assessment. For example, social and cultural benefits play a vital role in calculating the overall impact of an event, but describing them may require a narrative rather than a statistical approach. Some of the complex factors that need to be taken into account when assessing the impacts of events are discussed in this chapter.

SPHERE OF EVENT	POSITIVE IMPACTS	NEGATIVE IMPACTS
Social and cultural	• Shared experience • Revitalising traditions • Building community pride • Validation of community groups • Increased community participation • Introducing new and challenging ideas • Expanding cultural perspectives	• Community alienation • Manipulation of community • Negative community image • Bad behaviour • Substance abuse • Social dislocation • Loss of amenity
Physical and environmental	• Showcasing the environment • Providing models for best practice • Increasing environmental awareness • Infrastructure legacy • Improved transport and communications • Urban transformation and renewal	• Environmental damage • Pollution • Destruction of heritage • Noise disturbance • Traffic congestion
Political	• International prestige • Improved profile • Promotion of investment • Social cohesion • Development of administrative skills	• Risk of event failure • Misallocation of funds • Lack of accountability • Propagandising • Loss of community ownership and control • Legitimation of ideology
Tourism and economic	• Destinational promotion and increased tourist visits • Extended length of stay • Higher yield • Increased tax revenue • Job creation	• Community resistance to tourism • Loss of authenticity • Damage to reputation • Exploitation • Inflated prices • Opportunity costs

(**Source:** *Adapted from Hall 1989*)

SOCIAL AND CULTURAL IMPACTS

All events have a direct social and cultural impact on their participants, and sometimes on their wider host communities as outlined by Hall (1989) and Getz (1997). This may be as simple as a shared entertainment experience, as is created by a sporting event or concert. Other impacts include increased pride, which results from some community events and celebrations of national days, and the validation of particular groups in the community, which is the purpose of many events designed for seniors and disabled people. This purpose was reflected in the mission statement of the Sydney Paralympic Games: 'to inspire the world by staging a Paralympic Games which sets new standards in excellence, enabling the athletes to achieve their best' (Sydney 2000 Paralympic Games 2000). Some events leave a legacy of greater awareness and participation in particular sporting and cultural activities. Others broaden people's cultural horizons, exposing them to new and challenging people, customs, or ideas. The Grand Australian Sumo Tournament, held in Sydney and Melbourne in 1997, introduced the Japanese Sumo tradition, with its strong religious and cultural associations, to Australian audiences. It went beyond the bounds of a sporting event, and became a genuine Japanese–Australian cultural exchange, with strong awareness levels in both countries. In the same year, the ceremonies for the handover of Hong Kong from Great Britain to China had great symbolic importance for these countries. World media coverage of the ceremonies provoked emotions ranging from pride to sadness, and from jubilation to apprehension.

Events have the power to challenge the imagination and to explore possibilities. A series of Reconciliation Marches around Australia in 2000 served to express community support for reconciliation with Aboriginal people, and to bring this issue powerfully to the attention of the media. In Sydney the march took the unprecedented step of closing the Sydney Harbour Bridge, providing a powerful symbolic statement of the bridging of the two communities, and placing additional pressure on the Australian Government to support the reconciliation process.

Research suggests that local communities often value the 'feel-good' aspects of hallmark events, and are prepared to put up with temporary inconvenience and disruption because of the excitement which they generate, and the long-term expectation of improved facilities and profile. A study by Soutar and McLeod (1989) of Fremantle residents' views of the America's Cup indicated that the event was perceived as improving the quality of life in Fremantle, and providing the foundation for long-term improvement in the city's fortunes. Most residents said they would like to see another America's Cup or similar event in Fremantle in the future. The Australian Formula One Grand Prix in Adelaide was also popular among residents; Arnold et al. (1989) reported that 'The Grand Prix in 1985 set Adelaide alive ... The spirit infected all of us, including large numbers of people who in "normal" times might be expected to be against the notion of this garish, noisy, polluting advertising circus'.

However, such events can have negative social impacts. Arnold et al. (1989) showed that in the five weeks around the 1985 Australian Formula One Grand Prix in Adelaide, there was a 34 per cent increase in the number of road accident casualties compared with the same period for the previous five years. Taking into account the rising trend of road accident casualties over those years, they calculated that about 15 per cent of these casualties were left unexplained, and suggested that they could be due to the off-track emulation of Grand Prix race driving.

The larger the event and the higher its profile, the greater the potential for things to go wrong, generating negative impacts. The Sydney Festival in 1992 was responsible for the sixtieth anniversary celebrations of the opening of the Sydney Harbour Bridge. Arrangements were made to close the bridge to traffic, and to invite the public to walk across it from either end and experience a concert to be held at the centre of the bridge. Unfortunately, no-one had foreseen the effect of two very large crowds converging simultaneously from both north and south, and the result was chaos. The event became a negative experience for the participants, and was not a success from the point of view of the organisers.

Events, when they go wrong, can go very wrong indeed. Consider the Toohey's World's Biggest BBQ that ran out of food, and the Christmas Day riots at Bondi Beach in 1995. More seriously, the world was shocked by the bombing incident at the Atlanta Olympic Games in 1996, the collapse of the bridge at the entrance to the stadium for the Maccabiah Games in Israel in 1997, and the tragic drownings during the Sydney to Hobart Yacht Race in 1998. Such events have far-reaching negative impacts, resulting not only in bad press but damage or injury to participants, stakeholders and the host community.

■ Managing *crowd behaviour*

Major events can have unintended social consequences such as substance abuse, bad behaviour by the crowd and an increase in criminal activity (Getz, 1997). If not managed properly, these unintended consequences can hijack the agenda, and determine the public perception of the event. It has been necessary for events as diverse as the Australasian Country Music Festival at Tamworth and the Bathurst 1000 motor race to develop strategies to handle alcohol-related bad crowd behaviour and protect their reputation and future. The case study at the end of this chapter examines the Australian Motorcycle Grand Prix at Phillip Island in Victoria and the successful strategies implemented to manage such unintended impacts.

Crowd behaviour can be modified with careful planning. Sometimes this is an evolutionary process. For example, the management of New Year's Eve in Sydney has seen a series of modifications and adjustments over successive years. The impact of crowd behaviour on residents in The Rocks in the early 1980s caused the Sydney Festival to move the timing of the fireworks display forward from midnight to 9.00 p.m. This resulted in families leaving the city after the end of the fireworks. However, teenagers and much of the general audience remained in the city until well after midnight, transferring some of the problems to areas such as Kings Cross and Darling Harbour. By the early 1990s at Darling Harbour teenage alcohol abuse was resulting in bad crowd behaviour, confrontations with police, injuries and arrests. The Darling Harbour Authority had its regulations changed to allow it to prevent alcohol from being brought into the venue, and modified its program and marketing strategies to create the expectation of a family-oriented celebration. The result was a turnaround in crowd behaviour, and a dramatic decrease in injuries and arrests. In recent years, Sydney City Council and its contracted New Year's Eve event organisers, Specktak Productions, have orchestrated simultaneous celebrations across the city in different locations. This allows crowds to be spread out instead of concentrated in one area, facilitating better crowd management and a reduction in behaviour problems. Other Australian events, such as the New Year's Eve celebrations at Bondi Beach and Byron Bay, have been similarly transformed. There has been a similar trend overseas with initiatives like the First Night Program of alcohol-free celebrations, which began in Boston and has been adopted by a wide range of communities. As a result of better crowd management and improved strategies, global celebrations of the New Millennium were largely reported as good-spirited and peaceful.

■ Community ownership *and control of events*

Badly managed events can also have wider effects on the social life and structure of communities. These can include loss of amenities owing to noise or crowds, resentment of inequitable distribution of costs and benefits, and cost inflation of goods and services that can upset housing markets and impacts most severely on low income groups, as outlined by Getz (1997). It follows that communities should have a major say in the planning and management of events. However, Hall (1989) concludes that the role of communities is often marginalised:

> ■ . . . In nearly every case study of hallmark events the most important decision of all, whether to host an event or not, is taken outside of the public arena and behind the closed doors of a private office or city hall. Indeed, often government may have no initial say as to whether to host an event or not, as with the winning of the America's Cup by Alan Bond in 1983. Therefore, public participation usually becomes a form of placation in which policy can only be changed in an incremental fashion and then only at the margins. The substantive policy decision, that of hosting the event, still remains. In this situation, public participation within the planning process becomes reactive rather than proactive. Instead of a discussion of the advantages and disadvantages of hosting events, public participation becomes a means to increase the legitimacy of government and developers' decisions regarding the means by which events should be held. ■

This makes it all the more important for governments to be accountable, through the political process, for the allocation of resources to events. Hall (1992) maintains that political analysis is an important tool in regaining community control over hallmark events, and ensuring that the objectives of these events focus on maximising returns to the community.

Allegations of corruption within the International Olympic Committee (IOC) and the scandal over ticketing strategies by the Sydney Organising Committee for the Olympic Games (SOCOG) are examples of the increasing pressure for transparency and public accountability in the staging of major events.

PHYSICAL AND ENVIRONMENTAL IMPACTS

An event is an excellent way to showcase the unique characteristics of the host environment. Hall (1989) points out that selling the image of a hallmark event includes marketing the intrinsic properties of the destination, and quotes the use of images of Perth's beaches, the Swan River and historic Fremantle in advertisements for the America's Cup, and the emphasis on the creation of an aesthetically pleasing environment in the promotion of Sydney's Darling Harbour.

However, host environments may be extremely delicate and great care should be taken to protect them. A major event may require an environmental impact assessment before council permission is granted for it to go ahead. Even if a formal study is not required, the event manager should carefully consider the likely impact of the event on the environment. This impact will be fairly contained if the event is to be held in a suitable purpose-built venue, for example, a stadium, sportsground, showground or entertainment centre. The impact may be much greater if the event is to be held in a public space not ordinarily reserved for events, such as a park, town square or street. Aspects such as crowd movement and control, noise levels, access and parking will be important considerations. Other major issues may include wear and tear on the natural and physical environment, heritage protection issues and disruption of the local community.

Good communication and consultation with local authorities will often resolve some of these issues. In addition, careful management planning may be required to modify impacts. In Sydney, the Manly Jazz Festival worked for several years to progressively reduce the traffic impact of visitors to the festival by developing a 'park and ride' system of fringe parking with shuttle buses to the event area. Many food and wine events have reduced their impact on the environment by using biodegradable containers and utensils instead of plastic, and selling wine-tasting souvenir glasses which patrons can take home after the event. Many event managers are discovering that such measures make good financial as well as environmental sense.

When staging large events, the provision of infrastructure is often a costly budget component, but this expenditure usually results in an improved environment and facilities for the host community, and provides a strong incentive for it to act as host. Brisbane profited from the transformation of the Expo 88 site into the South Bank leisure and entertainment precinct, and Sydney's available public space was enhanced when the 1988 Bicentennial celebrations caused derelict railway goods yards to be redeveloped, creating the Darling Harbour leisure precinct. Similarly, the Australian Formula One Grand Prix has given Melbourne a first-class motorsport venue, although some people argue that this has been at the cost of the public leisure amenity of Albert Park.

■ Waste management *and recycling*

Governments are increasingly using public education programs and legislation to promote the recycling of waste materials and reduce the amount of waste going to landfill. Events are targeted as opportunities to demonstrate best practice models in waste management, and to change public attitudes and habits. EcoRecycle Victoria and NSW Waste Boards have combined to create Australia's first fully integrated event waste management, recycling and education program. This is promoted through the seven steps to a waste wise event (see figure 2.1). Recycling equipment, standard signage and a comprehensive list of companies that provide waste management services and environmentally friendly products are provided to assist the event manager in implementing the program. NSW Waste Boards quote research that shows that 87 per cent of people support the introduction of recycling at public events, and that an astounding 95 per cent of event attendees believe that event caterers should be encouraged to use environmentally friendly packaging (NSW Waste Boards 1999).

For the event manager, incorporating a waste management plan into the overall event plan has become increasingly good policy. Community expectations and the health of our environment require that events demonstrate good waste management principles, and provide models for recycling. The waste wise event manager will reap not only economic benefits, but the approval of an increasingly environmentally aware public.

■ **Figure 2.1**
The seven steps to a waste wise event

Step 1 Commitment — become a waste wise event

Step 2 Packaging — select materials that reduce waste and litter and are easily recycled

Step 3 Equipment — match equipment to the packaging material used

Step 4 System — match a management system to the equipment and packaging used

Step 5 Standards — where appropriate use standard signs and equipment to reduce confusion

Step 6 Communicate — tell caterers, vendors and participants about your program before, during and after the event

Step 7 Evaluate — how effective was your waste wise program?

(**Source:** *NSW Waste Boards 1999*)

■ The Sydney Olympic Games *and the environment*

As the world's largest event, the Olympic Games provide both enormous challenges for managing environmental impacts and enormous opportunities for benchmarking and public education. These include environmental management systems for the design and construction of venues, and for the use of resources, transport and waste disposal involved in the staging of the Games.

Despite some historic initiatives, environmental issues were rarely addressed by the Olympic movement until the early 1990s. Arising from the watershed 1992 United Nations Conference on Environment and Development in Rio de Janeiro (The Earth Summit), the International Olympic Committee (IOC) and its International Federations and National Olympic Committees signed the Earth Pledge. This resulted in the environmental theme being included in the Olympic bid manual, and the environment being adopted as the 'third pillar' of Olympism after sport and culture in 1994 (IOC Commission on Sport and the Environment 1999).

In 1993 Sydney was selected to host the 2000 Summer Olympics on the basis of a bid that included a set of comprehensive environmental guidelines that were the most ambitious up to that time (Sydney Organising Committee for the Olympic Games 2000). They are expressed in ecologically sustainable development policies which include commitments to energy conservation; water conservation; waste avoidance and minimisation; air, water and soil quality; and the protection of significant natural and cultural environments.

In the planning and construction of Olympic facilities and the running of the Games, the guidelines committed Sydney to initiatives including:
• conduct of environmental and social impact studies
• minimisation of adverse impacts on Olympic sites and nearby residents
• protection of the natural environment or threatened ecosystems
• enforcement of environmental guidelines on suppliers and contractors
• concentration of venues in compact zones
• placement of all venues and the majority of training venues within 30 minutes travel from the Olympic Village
• use of energy efficient design and materials
• maximum use of renewable sources of energy
• water conservation and recycling
• best practice in waste reduction and avoidance
• use where practicable of non-toxic substances
• use of recyclable packaging and non-disposable cutlery and crockery at food outlets where possible
• use of recycling bins at all Games venues
• information transferred electronically where possible to conserve paper, supplemented by paper recycling procedures
• public transport as the only means of access by spectators to events at Olympic sites.

Green Games Watch 2000, the Earth Council and Greenpeace Australia were nominated as independent watchdogs to monitor and evaluate the implementation of the guidelines. Among the achievements of the Sydney Olympics were the use of advanced environmental technologies and systems including:
• solar-powered homes and services for the Olympic Village
• alternatives to PVC in building materials, electrical wiring, piping and so on
• innovative non-mechanical ventilation/cooling systems for sports facilities
• roof-top water-siphoning system for collecting and storing rainwater (IOC Commission on Sport and the Environment 1999).

In the area of waste management, the Sydney Games had targeted an 80 per cent diversion of waste from landfill, and had achieved 70 per cent (Lawson & Cole 2000). Given that the Atlanta Games had targeted an 85 per cent diversion and had achieved 50 per cent, this should be considered as a very positive result.

As this book went to press, final reports were not yet available on the Olympic environmental program. However, the Sydney 2000 Olympic Games seems to have left Sydney not just with a legacy of 'state of the art' sports venues, but with environmental management blueprints for the conduct of large scale events that will have important implications in the future.

$\mathcal{P}$OLITICAL IMPACTS

Politics and politicians are an important part of the equation that is contemporary event management. Ever since the Roman Emperors discovered the power of the Circus to deflect criticism and shore up popularity, shrewd politicians have had an eye for events which will keep the populace happy and themselves in power. No less an authority than Count Niccolo Machiavelli, adviser to the Medicis in the sixteenth century, had this to say on the subject:

■ A prince must also show himself a lover of merit, give preferment to the able and honour those who excel in every art... Besides this, he ought, at convenient seasons of the year, to keep the people occupied with festivals and shows; and as every city is divided into guilds or into classes, he ought to pay attention to all these groups, mingle with them from time to time, and give them an example of his humanity and munificence, always upholding, however, the majesty of his dignity, which must never be allowed to fail in anything whatever. ■

The Royal House of Windsor took this advice to heart, providing some of the most popular events of the last century with the Coronation of Queen Elizabeth II and the fairytale-like wedding of Prince Charles and Princess Diana. Australian Prime Minister Robert Menzies made good use of the public affection for the British royal family, with royal tours to Australia providing a boost to the popularity of his government. Successive Australian politicians have continued to use the spotlight offered by different events to build their personal profiles and gain political advantage. Former South Australian Premier Don Dunstan used the Adelaide Festival to create an image of Adelaide as the 'Athens of the South', and of himself as a visionary and enlightened leader. Sallyanne Atkinson used Brisbane's Expo 88 and successive Olympic bids to boost her mayoral profile. Former New South Wales Premier Neville Wran and colleague Laurie Brereton used the building of Darling Harbour to create an image of New South Wales as a go-ahead State, but critics at the time accused them of creating a monument to themselves. Former Prime Minister Bob Hawke bathed in the glory of Alan Bond's America's Cup victory. And continuing in the grand tradition,

Former Victorian Premier Jeff Kennett used a succession of events including the Australian Formula One Grand Prix, rugby's Bledisloe Cup and the Presidents Cup golf tournament to create an image of himself as a winner — and his rival, New South Wales Premier Bob Carr, as the loser — in the race for events. Prime Minister John Howard turned the Centenary of Federation celebrations to the benefit of his government by distributing grant funds through local federal members of Parliament.

Arnold et al. (1989) leave no doubt about the role of events in the political process.

■ Governments in power will continue to use hallmark events to punctuate the ends of their periods in office, to arouse nationalism, enthusiasm and finally, votes. They are cheaper than wars or the preparation for them. In this regard, hallmark events do not hide political realities, they are the political reality. ■

Governments around the world have realised the ability of events to raise the profile of politicians and the cities and States that they govern. Events attract visitors, and thus create economic benefits and jobs. This potent mixture has prompted governments to become major players in bidding for, hosting and staging major events. Brisbane built up a strong reputation with events such as the Commonwealth Games, Expo 88, the International Lions Convention, the World Masters Games and the Goodwill Games. Sharry (1997) describes how, with the coming of Super League, Brisbane grasped the opportunity to host the Super League Grand Final. Brisbane City Council commissioned a study by Griffith University that assessed the economic impact of the event to be worth over $7 million, leading it to decide that a serious bid should be made to host the Grand Final. The bid was first developed by staff of the ANZ Stadium, and refined through discussions with executives of Super League and the Brisbane Broncos. A week-long program of activities was planned for the lead-up to the match. This included a ball, a street parade, a city festival, a golf event, family activities at South Bank, an awards ceremony, breakfasts, and a civic reception. Plans were made to enlarge the capacity of the stadium with temporary seating, and an impressive multimedia bid presentation was commissioned. Brisbane's efforts were rewarded by hosting the Super League Grand Final, which set new benchmarks for the enhancement and packaging of major sporting events.

This increasing involvement of governments in events has politicised the events landscape, as recognised by Hall (1989).

■ Politics are paramount in hallmark events. It is either naïve or dupli[citous] to pretend otherwise. Events alter the time frame in which planning occurs and they become opportunities to do something new and better than before. In this context, events may change or legitimate [sic] political priorities in the short term and political ideologies and socio-cultural reality in the longer term. Hallmark events represent the tournaments of old, fulfilling psychological and political needs through the winning of hosting over other locations and the winning of events themselves. Following a hallmark event some places will never be the same again, physically, economically, socially and, perhaps most importantly of all, politically. ■

It is important to acknowledge that events have values beyond just tangible and economic benefits. Humans are social animals, and celebrations play a key role in the wellbeing of the social structure. Events can engender social cohesion, confidence and pride. Therein lies the source of their political power and influence, and the reason why events will always reflect and interact with their political circumstances and environments.

*T*OURISM AND ECONOMIC IMPACTS

Governments are increasingly turning to tourism as a growth industry capable of delivering economic benefits and job creation. Events in turn are seen as catalysts for attracting visitors, and increasing their average spend and length of stay. They are also seen as image-makers, creating profile for destinations, positioning them in the market and providing a competitive marketing advantage. This has led to the creation of a new field, known as event tourism, which Getz (1997) defines as:

■ 1. The systematic planning, development and marketing of events as tourist attractions, catalysts for other developments, image builders, and animators of attractions and destination areas; event tourism strategies should also cover the management of news and negative events.
2. A market segment consisting of those people who travel to attend events, or who can be motivated to attend events while away from home. ■

Government tourism bodies often consciously use events to position their destinations in the market. Key objectives of the Tourism New South Wales Events Strategy (1996) are to:
• position Sydney and New South Wales as the events capital of Australia and reinforce the brand of Sydney and New South Wales as defined by Tourism New South Wales in its marketing strategies
• develop and promote existing and new international calibre events for Sydney, which position it as a cultural capital of Asia and the Pacific
• capitalise on the opportunity provided by the Sydney Olympic Games to brand New South Wales as a unique lifestyle destination — a centre for sport, fitness and healthy lifestyle
• identify and develop events in regional New South Wales that express the cultural strengths of the State and serve as flagships for the promotion of regional tourism.

If events are to be effective in positioning their destinations in the market, they must strive for authenticity and the expression of the unique characteristics of their communities. Visitors want to do what local residents do, and experience the things that they enjoy about the destination. The New South Wales Tourism Masterplan (1995) argues that 'Those destinations that preserve, enhance and celebrate the things that set them apart and give them a meaning of their own, will produce a more rewarding visitor experience and a higher yield for the host community'.

Conversely, destinations that produce events solely for tourists, without meaning for their own communities, run the danger of the results being inauthentic and shallow. Exploitative or badly managed events with inadequate planning or facilities can damage the reputation of a destination.

■ Events *and seasonality*

A strong advantage of event tourism is that it can attract visitors in the low season, when airline and accommodation providers often have surplus capacity. Additional economic benefit is derived when visitors use what would otherwise be under-utilised tourism infrastructure. Getz (1997) describes the way that events can overcome seasonality by capitalising 'on whatever natural appeal the off-season presents, such as winter as opposed to summer sports, seasonal food and produce, and scenery or wildlife viewed in different places and under changing conditions'. He also notes that 'in many destinations the residents prefer the off-season for their own celebrations, and these provide more authentic events for visitors'.

Many Australian destinations have developed events to enliven off-season periods. Some examples are the summer program at Thredbo in the New South Wales snowfields, which has used jazz, blues and world music festivals to attract guests in the off-season summer months; and the Sydney Festival, which has transformed the traditionally quiet midsummer period in the city into a highlight of the events calendar.

■ Events enhance *the tourism experience*

Events can provide newness, freshness and change, which sustain local interest in a destination and enhance its appeal to visitors. Tourist attractions and theme parks incorporate events as a key element in their marketing programs. Movie World on the Gold Coast, Fox Studios and Darling Harbour in Sydney and Southbank in Melbourne all use extensive event programs to increase market profile and attract repeat visits. Getz (1997) notes the use of events by a wide variety of tourism attractions to animate and interpret their products.

> ■ Resorts, museums, historic districts, heritage sites, archaeological sites, markets and shopping centres, sports stadia, convention centres, and theme parks all develop programs of special events. Built attractions and facilities everywhere have realized the advantages of 'animation' — the process of programming interpretive features and/or special events that make the place come alive with sensory stimulation and appealing atmosphere. ■

■ Events as catalysts *for development*

An event can enhance the quality of life of a neighbourhood, by adding to its sense of place and residential amenity. Citywest Development Corporation, in charge of the redevelopment of Sydney's Pyrmont peninsula, commissioned an event strategy to position events as image-builders for the community. Likewise, Sanctuary Cove in Queensland used the Ultimate Event concert with Frank Sinatra to promote itself as the ultimate luxury real estate development in Australia.

Large events act as catalysts for urban renewal, and for the creation of new or expanded tourism infrastructure. The Melbourne Olympic Games in 1956 provided major facilities that contributed to the city's reputation as a sporting centre for several decades. Other examples are the provision of facilities at the port of Fremantle in Western Australia for the America's Cup defence in 1986–87, the Expo 88 site in Brisbane and the Homebush Bay site for the Sydney Olympic Games, all of which gained infrastructure development through hosting large-scale events. Hotel and facilities development, better communications and improved road and public transport networks are some of the legacies left by these events.

EVENT PROFILE

Australian Tourist Commission

The Australian Tourist Commission (ATC) is an Australian Government statutory Authority formed in 1967 to promote Australia as an international tourism destination. Its principal objectives are to:
• increase the number of overseas visitors to Australia
• maximise the benefits to Australia from overseas visitors
• work with other relevant agencies to promote the principle of ecologically sustainable development and raise awareness of the social and cultural impacts of international tourism in Australia.

The ATC promotes Australia to consumers and the travel industry in more than 40 countries. Its activities include consumer advertising on television and in print, public relations and information programs, and the coordination of Australian industry participation in international trade shows. It has made extensive use of events in its promotional campaigns, including maximising the tourism opportunities presented by the Sydney 2000 Olympic Games through media programs and alliances with global marketing partners.

The ATC's current marketing campaign, Brand Australia, aims to express the personality of Australia through images which depict the country's natural attractions, friendly people and the experience of an Australian holiday. The $150 million, three-year Brand Australia campaign will be seen by 300 million people in 11 countries. The Tourism Forecasting Council predicts overseas visitor numbers to grow by 7.3 per cent per year to around 5.1 million in 2001. Tourism is Australia's top export earner, generating $17 billion in export earnings in 1999 and accounting for 5.8 per cent of Australia's GDP. Tourism employs almost one million Australians (Australian Tourist Commission 2000).

■ Economic *benefits*

The strong growth of the festival and special event sector in Australia is part of a general economic trend away from an industrial product base to a more service-based economy. The expenditure of visitors, spread over travel, accommodation, restaurants, shopping and other tourism-related services, is just one way that a host community can benefit from an event. Events can also provide a boost to other areas of the economy. The construction industry — witness the construction boom that resulted from the Sydney Olympic Games — is often stimulated by the need for new or improved facilities to stage a major event. Employment and the local economy are temporarily boosted by the expenditure involved in staging an event. Thus whole mini-economies surround and work off the events industry.

The expenditure generated by events also circulates in the wider economy, creating flow-on impacts and benefits. This process, and methodologies for measuring the economic impacts of events, will be examined in the chapter on the economic analysis of events.

Table 2.2 summarises the economic benefits of a number of recent events in Australia. The results are not strictly comparable, as the methodologies for evaluating events vary widely. However, the table does demonstrate the considerable tourism and economic benefits that flow from major events.

■ **Table 2.2**
Comparative table of economic benefits of events

EVENT	TOTAL ATTENDANCE ('000S)	TOTAL VISITORS INTERSTATE AND OVERSEAS ('000S)	TOTAL EXPENDITURE INTERSTATE AND OVERSEAS VISITORS ($M)	IMPACT ON GROSS STATE PRODUCT (GSP) ($M)
World Cup of Athletics, Canberra 1985	46	10	7.8	18.8
Australian Formula One Grand Prix, Adelaide 1992	260	19	14.4	37.4
World Masters Games, Brisbane 1994	23*	18	27.5	50.6
World Police and Fire Games, Melbourne 1995	7*	9	11.5	21.7
Adelaide Festival, 1996	42	6	7.8	13.0–15.5
Sydney Gay and Lesbian Mardi Gras, 1998	500	12.5	37.0	41.4

* Figure stated is number of participants in event and does not count accompanying persons.

Events have the potential to provide niche development opportunities for city and State governments. As outlined in the case study on page 404, Tamworth has developed a year round strand of economic activity based on its positioning as the country music capital of Australia. In another example, Uekrongtham (1995) demonstrates that theatre can have a major impact on tourism and the economy with the 1992 Broadway theatre season worth US$2.3 billion to the economy of New York City, and the 1990–91 West End theatre season worth £114 million to the city of London. He quotes Tourism Victoria research which concludes that in two and a half years the *Phantom of the Opera* attracted 550 000 visitors worth at least $300 million to Melbourne. Auckland in New Zealand maximised the economic benefits of staging the America's Cup defence in 2000 by integrating its marine industry components and stakeholders through MAREX (Marine Export Group), placing its marine industry at the centre of a range of exciting developments (Davies 1996). Sydney used the staging of the Olympic Games to position itself as a centre of excellence for sport and healthy lifestyle (Tourism New South Wales 1995). Sydney's hosting of the Paralympic Games also opened up a niche market opportunity in sport for the disabled.

■ Valuing *events*

The high costs of staging major events has caused governments and event managers to examine the costs and benefits of events. Burns, Hatch and Mules (1986) reported on a survey of the economic impacts of the 1985 Australian Formula One Grand Prix in Adelaide. They estimated the tangible or measurable benefit–cost ratio at an upper bound of $23.630:7.520 million, and a lower bound of $24.806:6.571 million, or to put it more simply, from 3.1:1 to 3.8:1. After adjustment for a $5 million Federal Government grant to the event, they concluded that the benefit–cost ratio of money spent on the event was better than just about any other use of the money for the higher bound, and was beaten only by expenditure on communications, community services or public administration for the lower bound.

Extensive surveys of residents and business houses were carried out to assess the social, less tangible costs and benefits associated with running the event. Positive or 'psychic' benefits included a week-long carnival of fringe entertainments, the feeling that 'the whole world is watching' and the general air of excitement created by the media. Negative impacts included traffic congestion, noise, road accidents, vandalism, loss of amenity and possibly loss of business to those business houses near the circuit. Where possible, financial values were attributed to these social benefits and costs (see table 2.3). Social costs were measured at $9.426 to $12.026 million, and social benefits in excess of $28 million.

The researchers concluded that social costs did not appear to be significant in relation to the overall surplus of tangible benefits, and that all things considered, the Grand Prix was a successful hallmark event that produced significant social benefits for the State.

SOCIAL COSTS		SOCIAL BENEFITS
Traffic congestion (time lost)	$6.2m	Psychic income $28m+
Property damage	$0.026m	• general excitement
Increased vehicle thefts and		• good opinions of oneself
thefts from vehicles	n.a.	• extra shopping access
Noise	n.a.	• opportunity to have guests
Accidents	$3.2–5.8m	• home hosting opportunities
		• pleasure in 'experiencing' the event

■ Monitoring *long-term impacts*

Impacts that are calculated during the actual time frame of an event tell only part of the story. In order to form a full picture of the impact of an event, it is necessary to look at the long-term effects on the host community and its economy.

A study by Selwood and Jones (1991), four years after the America's Cup defence in Fremantle in 1987, gives some indication of the aftershock of this event. They point out that Fremantle's profile as a destination was greatly enhanced by the attention it received: in 1989 Fremantle was visited by 83 per cent of international visitors to Western Australia and 13 per cent of all international visitors to Australia (a higher proportion than in the year before the event) and was ranked as the State's leading tourist attraction. The city was left with a legacy of infrastructure and quality tourism developments that were either initiated or expedited by the event. The America's Cup had also placed Fremantle on the map of world sailing, making it a staging post for the Whitbread Round the World Race, and attracting the world's leading sailors to Perth on a regular basis for events such as the Australia Cup. The Francis Ford Coppola movie *Wind* was filmed in Fremantle, featuring five of the yachts that participated in the defence, along with another feature film, *The Great Pretender.*

On a wider level, the Western Australian EventsCorp, the first of its kind in Australia, grew out of the America's Cup office with the encouragement of the Western Australian Development Commission. This shows how organisations set up to stage an event can subsequently evolve to have a broad and continuing role in attracting visitors to a destination. With a brief to attract or initiate hallmark events for the State, it has already staged the 1991 and 1998 World Swimming Championships as well as a series of major events under the banner 'The Best on Earth in Perth'.

The study found that the America's Cup defence had accelerated development and hastened gentrification of Fremantle, but that this process had inevitably caused some social dislocation, and increased pressure on low-income earners. The influx of a range of new groups with different values into Fremantle created some tension. For example, for the period of the Cup defence, the licensing hours of waterfront pubs were extended to match international standards. This encouraged a flourishing of late night drinking and entertainment venues, which remained when the hours went back to normal. This created problems of disturbance and vandalism for local residents. The study concluded that the America's Cup defence had increased the levels of employment and economic activity in the tourist and heritage industries in Fremantle, and significantly improved the infrastructure of the city for the benefit of residents and visitors. However, the loss of the defence in 1987 had probably protected Fremantle from further development pressures fuelled by international capital, and allowed instead the steady long-term development of Fremantle's tourist industry.

SUMMARY

All events produce impacts, both positive and negative, which it is the task of the event manager to assess and balance.

Social and cultural impacts may involve a shared experience, and may give rise to local pride, validation or the widening of cultural horizons. However, social problems arising from events may result in social dislocation if not properly managed. Events are an excellent opportunity to showcase the physical characteristics of a destination, but event environments may be very delicate, and care should be taken to safeguard and protect them. Many events involve longer-term issues affecting the built environment and the legacy of improved facilities. Increasingly, environmental considerations are paramount, as shown by the comprehensive environmental guidelines which have been developed for the Sydney Olympic Games, in conjunction with Greenpeace, to manage their environmental impact.

Political impacts have long been recognised by governments, and often include increased profile and benefits to the host community. However, it is important that events fulfil the wider community agenda. Governments are attracted to events because of the economic benefits, job creation and tourism which they can provide. Events act as catalysts for attracting tourists and extending their length of stay. They also increase the profile of a destination, and can be designed to attract visitors during the low-season when tourism facilities are under-utilised. Large events also serve as catalysts for urban renewal, and for the creation of new tourism infrastructure. Events bring economic benefits to their communities, but governments need to weigh these benefits against costs when deciding how to allocate resources.

Questions

1. Describe some examples of events whose needs have been perceived as being in conflict with those of their host communities. As the event manager, how would you resolve these conflicting needs?

2. Describe an event with which you are familiar and which has been characterised by social problems or bad crowd behaviour. As the event manager, what would you have done to manage the situation and improve the outcome of the event? In your answer, discuss both the planning of the event and possible on-the-spot responses.

3. Select a major event that has been held in your region, and identify as many environmental impacts as you can. Evaluate whether the overall environmental impact on the host community was positive or negative, and recommend steps which could be taken to improve the balance.

4. Describe an event that you believe was not sufficiently responsive to community attitudes and values. What steps could be taken in the community to improve the situation?

5. Identify an event in your region which has a significant tourism component, and examine the event in terms of its ability to:
   (a) increase tourist visits and length of stay
   (b) improve the profile of the destination
   (c) create economic benefits for the region.

6. Select an event in which you have been involved as a participant or close observer, and identify as many impacts of the event as you can, both positive and negative. Did the positive impacts outweigh the negative?
   (a) What measures did the organisers have in place to maximise positive impacts and minimise negative impacts?
   (b) As the event manager, what other steps could you have taken to balance the impacts and improve the outcome of the event?

The Australian
Motorcycle Grand Prix

Picturesque Phillip Island has hosted a series of international Motorcycle Grand Prix events, from 1989 to the present. Best known for its Fairy Penguin Parade and seal colonies, the island also has a strong tradition of motor racing dating back to the 1960s. It provides one of the most spectacular backdrops for motor racing events in the world, with rolling green hills and rugged cliff faces plunging to the surf-swept rocks that face the Bass Strait.

Organising a large international event consisting of approximately 100 000 spectators, on a small island with a population of only 6500 residents, presents many challenges which require a great deal of planning and coordination to overcome. This planning occurs at State and local levels and involves tourism and event organisers, motorcycle associations, police, traffic, emergency and health services.

For this event, the 'tyranny of distance' is a major difficulty. Phillip Island is 120 kilometres south-east of Melbourne, approximately one and a half hours' drive. By road, the island is only accessible by a narrow two-lane bridge connecting it to the mainland, and it has very limited sea and air access. In addition, the island's patchwork of roads — sometimes congested through normal use during holiday periods — are ill-suited to the massive volumes of spectators commuting to and from the event. The event itself, which runs over a four-day period climaxing on the last day in the internationally televised 500cc race, attracts thousands of tourists who come either for the duration of the Grand Prix or to witness daily events. To efficiently move and accommodate these spectators requires a detailed and integrated traffic management plan and the establishment of temporary campsites for an additional 15 000 campers. A notable aspect of this planning has been the establishment of the Grand Prix Rally which allows many thousands of motorcycle enthusiasts to ride to the island in a convoy, complete with police escort!

Building positive relations between the police and the 'bikie' fraternity has also been an integral part of the event, given the poor history of similar events in other Australian States. A violence prevention plan has been developed, featuring close liaison with motorcycle associations, a community policing style, and the encouragement of 'bikie stewards' to allow for self-policing among the participants at various camping grounds and points of congregation.

To combat crowding at a few central sites on the island, temporary liquor outlets and entertainment were organised at different campsites, which enabled diffusion of participants to a range of smaller more manageable locations.

Another special feature of this event is the adoption of a public health approach, emphasising harm minimisation. Coordinated through the local San Remo Community Health Centre, health authorities have instituted the 'Ride Safe' health promotion campaign featuring the slogan 'Condoms — safest rubber on the island'. The campaign involves volunteers circulating through the crowd and a track-side caravan providing information, education and counselling on health related issues of HIV, hepatitis C, sexually transmitted diseases and drug and alcohol use.

These initiatives and others have ensured the prevention and management of a number of potential problems at the event, and have contributed to high levels of consumer and resident satisfaction with the Australian Motorcycle Grand Prix at Phillip Island.

Neil Mellor
Former Senior Research Officer
Turning Point Alcohol and Drug Centre
Victoria

Questions

1 If you were the public relations officer for the Australian Motorcycle Grand Prix, how would your public relations plan support the crowd control strategies developed for the event?

2 List the crowd behaviour and social issues discussed in the case study, and the strategies used to address them. What other issues might be involved in an event of this kind, and what strategies would you use to address them?

3 Identify an event that has existing or potential crowd behaviour problems. How might some of the principles developed at Phillip Island apply to this event? State the strategies which you consider to be the most useful, and explain how they would need to be modified to serve the particular conditions at the event.

The Avenel
Farmers' Market

The role of agriculture in the local economy and its relationship to rural tourism development is an important one. For some regions, the tourism profile is largely dependent upon the local agricultural product and a key issue for local government authorities is how to 'manage and package this tourism potential' (Rural Tourism Program 1998, p. 5). One way to accomplish this is to encourage the development and expansion of community events and festivals combined with an emphasis on locally grown produce.

Melbourne's annual Food and Wine Festival provides visitors with a range of special events that showcase the State's regional produce and cuisine. Events include the World's Longest Lunch held in 10 regional locations, 'A Day in the Country' providing a selection of winemakers' luncheons, as well as unique and rare wine tasting, and picnic races and entertainment events. Other activities complementing the variety of regional produce and tourism activities available in regional areas are pick-your-own fruit farms, roadside stands, and farmers' markets, field days, farm stays and farm visits.

One special event featuring local produce is the Goulburn Valley Vintage Festival held in northern Victoria, in the Shire of Strathbogie. The festival incorporates a series of events at various wineries in and around Nagambie (Mitchelton, Chateau Tahbilk, Traeger's and Plunkett's) and a farmers' market held at the rear of the Avenel Harvest Home Restaurant. The farmers' market is an annual event held in March each year and showcases the agricultural produce, wine, cuisine and selected value-added products created within the region.

A farmers' market is a market where the products and/or services are sold directly to the consumer by the producer (or farmer) and can be viewed as being an 'old institution being revived to fit new times' (Sommer & Wing 1980, p. 10; Marr & Gast 1995). A resurgence of interest in locally grown fresh produce has been identified in the United States through the introduction of farmers' markets, with a similar trend beginning to appear in Australia (Adams 1999).

The Avenel Farmers' Market is the initiative of a local restaurateur who identified an opportunity for building on and developing the Strathbogie region's evolving horticultural and agricultural profile. The market is seen as a way of showcasing and selling local produce and encouraging community participation, and draws visitors to the region to experience the local product. The market also provides tourism operators with an opportunity to package the event with other existing activities in the region. Some of the key issues considered in establishing and operating the farmers' market were the existence of a ready and reliable source of produce, consideration of the frequency with which the market is held, based on the availability of produce, and provision of facilities. The establishment of the market as an event also relied on the support of local government, industry and the farming community. To identify this level of support a survey of property owners within the shire was undertaken to determine the availability, variety and seasonality of produce, as well as to ascertain farmers' willingness to participate as siteholders at the market. The local community was also surveyed in order to gauge interest in attending the market and for purchasing local produce. The survey sought to establish both the supply and demand side of the event as part of the planning process.

A follow-up survey of siteholders and visitors at the market not only identified new forms of produce, value-added products (such as preserves) and the siteholders' preparedness to contribute to a joint marketing campaign, but also provided valuable information concerning visitor demographics and motivation, and the potential for repeat visitation. This, combined with expenditure levels and interest in other tourism activities, provided the organisers and local tourism authorities with insights concerning the market's potential to develop as a regular event and the prospects for packaging the event with other regional activities.

In its first year of operation (1998) the market had 17 siteholders selling locally produced goods to 300 visitors. In its second year the number of siteholders increased to 40 and visitors to 800. In 2000 there were 44 siteholders and over 1000 visitors to the market. The one-day farmers' market operated from 10.00 a.m. until 5.00 p.m. with visitors being charged a small entry fee. A sliding fee for siteholders was charged, with community groups paying less than the farm producer or industry operator. Each siteholder was provided with a trestle table and expected to bring their own tablecloths, decorations and shade umbrella. Siteholders were generally pleased with the level of sales and the majority indicated they would continue to participate in the event in future. Siteholders reported being satisfied with the location, management and provision of facilities at the market, although they expressed some concerns about the lack of signage and advertising.

Marketing and advertising of the event are important issues for the organising committee to address and although the market was promoted primarily to the local community, many residents remained unaware of its existence. A more targeted approach to advertising should be considered and strategies developed to attract both local and non-local visitors. Liaison with the local government authority concerning by-laws governing signage should also be undertaken.

The organising committee is continually monitoring the management and conduct of the event and is seeking methods to improve it. The timing of the event to coincide with the vintage festival was considered an important aspect in the development of an event for the region, and for fostering local community participation. Another objective of the organising committee was to increase the frequency of the market. However, the reliance on seasonal produce may limit this possibility. The creation of a seasonal produce calendar for the region is seen as one way to address this situation. Farmers may be encouraged to complement their existing agricultural/horticultural range of produce by introducing value-added products to compensate for any seasonal variability, or to introduce new boutique ranges of produce. The success of the event at this early stage depends very much upon its inclusion within a broader events program in the region, and upon participation by the local farming community. Moves to reschedule the vintage festival as has been suggested by the wineries may impact on the viability of the farmers' market. The implications for small community events and festivals need to be considered along with any restructuring of the event calendar. Events that rely on a synergistic relationship with other festivals and events during their infancy will be most at risk from any such restructuring.

Farmers' markets have the potential to encourage more tourists to regional Australia. A visit to a farmers' market could be promoted as a 'lifestyle' experience where the visit is part of a broader regional tourism experience with links to wine, arts and crafts, and the environment. Farmers' markets also have a strong educational component. One of the benefits of learning about farm produce is that it makes it easier for a visitor to know what to buy and provides a greater understanding and appreciation of how food is produced. Farmers' markets give individuals the opportunity to reconnect to their source of food, and encourage them to visit the source of production — regional Australia. Therefore, as well as the opportunity of developing food and wine packages incorporating the Avenel Farmers' market, there is also the opportunity to become involved in Tourism Victoria's network of regional food and wine trails, as well as in their strategic plan for food and wine event promotion.

Farmers' markets have the potential not only to entice visitors to regional locations, but also to encourage expenditure within the region. Local events and festivals can help to develop and promote the destination, create and reinforce a sense of place, offset seasonality, and encourage participation in a broader range of activities (Frew & Dore 2000; Walo et al. 1996; Ritchie 1996; Clarke 1999; Yoon et al. 2000).

Lyn Dore
La Trobe University

Questions

1 Identify the positive impacts of an event for a regional destination.

2 What benefits can be gained by scheduling an event to coincide with other festivals and events?

3 From the event description of the Avenel Farmers' Market, what do you think were the key stages in developing the event?

4 What other type of activities could be packaged with the Avenel Farmers' Market to promote a regional destination?

REFERENCES

Adams, Jane 1999, 'Market Forces: Farmers' markets thrive in the US but have not yet caught on in Australia, though it's only a matter of time', *Australian Gourmet Traveller*, August, pp. 113–114.

Arnold, A., Fischer, A., Hatch, J. & Paix, B. 1989, 'The Grand Prix, road accidents and the philosophy of hallmark events', in *The Planning and Evaluation of Hallmark Events*, eds G. J. Syme, B. J. Shaw, D. M. Fenton & W. S. Mueller, Avesbury, Aldershot.

Australian Tourist Commission 2000, http://www.atc.net.au

Burns, J. P. A., Hatch, J. H. & Mules, T. J. 1986, 'The Adelaide Grand Prix — The Impact of a Special Event', The Centre for South Australian Economic Studies, Adelaide.

Clarke, J. 1999, 'Marketing structures for farm tourism: beyond the individual provider of rural tourism', *Journal of Sustainable Tourism*, vol. 7, no. 1, pp. 26–47.

Davies, John 1996, 'The buck stops where? The economic impact of staging major events', paper presented to the Australian Events Conference, Canberra.

Frew, Elspeth & Dore, Lynne, 2000, 'Farmers' markets as special events: a case study of Avenel Farmers' Market', *Events Beyond 2000 — Setting the Agenda*, Australian Event Evaluation, Research and Education Conference, 13–14 July 2000. Sydney.

Getz, Donald 1997, *Event Management and Event Tourism*, Cognizant Communication Corporation, New York.

Hall, Colin M. 1989, 'Hallmark events and the planning process', in *The Planning and Evaluation of Hallmark Events*, eds G. J. Syme, B. J. Shaw, D. M. Fenton & W. S. Mueller, Avebury, Aldershot.

Hall, Colin M. 1992, *Hallmark Tourist Events — Impacts Management and Planning*, Belhaven Press, London.

IOC Commission on Sport and the Environment 1999, *Building a Positive Environmental Legacy through the Olympic Games*, International Olympic Committee, Lausanne.

Lawson, John & Cole, Stephen 2000, 'Performance and results of the Sydney 2000 Waste Management System', paper presented at the forum Lessons Learned — Medals Earned: Forum on Waste Management Performance at the Sydney 2000 Games conducted in Sydney in December 2000.

Machiavelli, Niccolo 1962 (1514), *The Prince*, trans. L. Ricci, Mentor Books, New York.

Marr, C. & Gast, K. 1995, 'A guide to starting, operating and selling in farmers' markets', in *Direct Farm Marketing and Tourism Handbook*, eds R. Tronstad & J. Leones, Department of Agriculture and Resource Economics, The University of Arizona, Tucson, Az., pp. 9–16.

New South Wales Waste Boards 1999, *Waste Wise Events*, Waste Boards NSW, Sydney.

Ritchie, B. W. 1996, 'How special are special events? The economic impact and strategic development of the New Zealand Masters Games', *Festival Management & Event Tourism*, vol. 4, pp. 117–126.

Rural Tourism Program 1998, *Cultivating Rural Tourism*, Cox Inall Communications Pty. Ltd, Victoria.

Selwood, John H. & Jones, Roy 1991, 'The America's Cup in retrospect — the aftershock in Fremantle', in *Leisure and Tourism: Social and Environmental Change*, eds A. J. Veal, P. Jonson & G. Cushman, Centre for Leisure and Tourism Studies, University of Technology, Sydney.

Sharry, Stephen 1997, 'A super win', *Australian Leisure Management*, vol. 1, no. 3, pp. 30–32.

Sommer, R. & Wing, M. 1980, 'Farmers' markets please their customers', *California Agriculture*, pp.10–12.

Soutar, Geoffrey N. & McLeod, Paul 1989, 'The impact of the America's Cup on Fremantle residents: some empirical evidence', in *The Planning and Evaluation of Hallmark Events*, eds G. J. Syme, B. J. Shaw, D. M. Fenton & W. S. Mueller, Avesbury, Aldershot.

Sydney Organising Committee for the Olympic Games, *Sydney 2000 — Environmental Guidelines*, http://www.olympics.com/enq/about/green/reports/index.html (accessed 20 September 2000).

Sydney 2000 Paralympic Games 2000, http://www.olympics.com/eng/paralympics/about_us/home.html (accessed 20 September 2000).

Tourism New South Wales 1995, *New South Wales Tourism Masterplan to 2010*, Sydney.

Tourism New South Wales 1996, *Events Strategy*, Sydney.

Uekrongthan, Ekachai (1995). *The Impact of Theatre on Economy and Tourism*, prepared for Cameron Mackintosh Pty Ltd.

Walo, M., Bull, A. & Breen, H. 1996, 'Achieving economic benefits at local events: a case study of a local sports event', *Festival Management & Event Tourism*, vol. 4, pp. 95–106.

Yoon, S., Spencer, D. M., Holecek, D. F. & Kim, D-K 2000, A profile of Michigan's Festival and Special Event Tourism Market, *Event Management*, vol. 6, pp. 33–44.

FURTHER READING

Giddings, Chris (1997). *Measuring the Impact of Festivals — Guidelines for Conducting an Economic Impact Study*, National Centre for Culture and Recreation Studies, Australian Bureau of Statistics.

Conceptualising
the event

LEARNING OBJECTIVES

After studying this chapter, you should be able to:

- identify the range of stakeholders in an event
- describe and balance the overlapping and conflicting needs of stakeholders
- describe the role of government, corporate and community sectors in events
- discuss trends and issues in Australian society that affect events
- understand the role of sponsorship in events
- develop partnerships with sponsors and the media
- identify the unique elements and resources of an event
- understand the process of developing an event concept.

INTRODUCTION

A crucial element in the creation of an event is the understanding of the event environment. The context in which the event is to take place will be a major determinant of its success. In order to understand this environment, the event manager must first identify the major players — the stakeholders and the people and organisations likely to be affected by it. The event manager must then examine the objectives of these major players — what each of them expects to gain from the event, and what forces acting on them are likely to affect their response to the event. Once this environment is understood, the event manager is then in the best position to marshal the creative elements of the event, and to shape and manage them to achieve the best outcomes for the event. This chapter examines the key stakeholders in events, and outlines some of the processes that event managers can use to produce creative and successful events.

STAKEHOLDERS IN EVENTS

As discussed in the previous chapters, events have become professionalised, and are increasingly attracting the support of governments and the corporate sector. One aspect of this growth is that events are now required to serve a multitude of agendas. It is no longer sufficient for an event to meet just the needs of its audience. It must also embrace a plethora of other requirements including government objectives and regulations, media requirements, sponsors' needs and community expectations. The successful event manager must be able to identify the range of stakeholders in an event and manage their individual needs, which will sometimes overlap and conflict (see figure 3.1). As with event impacts, the event will be judged by its success in balancing the competing needs, expectations and interests of a diverse range of stakeholders.

Mal Hemmerling (1997), architect of the Australian Formula One Grand Prix in Adelaide and former chief executive of SOCOG, describes the task as follows:

> ■ So when asked the question 'what makes an event successful', there are now numerous shareholders that are key components of modern major events that are looking at a whole range of different measures of success. What may have been a simple measure for the event organiser of the past, which involved the bottom line, market share, and successful staging of the event are now only basic criteria as the measures by other investors are more aligned with increased tourism, economic activity, tax revenues, promotional success, sustained economic growth, television reach, audience profiles, customer focus, brand image, hospitality, new business opportunities and investment to name but a few. ■

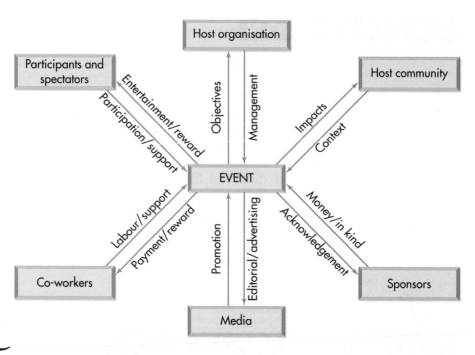

HE HOST ORGANISATION

Events have become so much a part of our cultural milieu that they can be generated by almost any part of the government, corporate and community sectors (see table 3.1).

Governments create events for a range of reasons, including the social, cultural, tourism and economic benefits generated by events. Some government departments have an events brief as part of their delivery of services, for example, State events corporations, ministries of Arts, Sport and Recreation and ministries of Racing. Other departments generate events as a means to achieve related objectives — Tourism to increase and extend tourist visits, Ethnic Affairs to preserve cultures and encourage tolerance and diversity, and Economic Development to assist industry and generate jobs. Many other departments are involved in one-off events to promote specific goods and services such as health promotions, Seniors Week, and Heritage Week. Such events may celebrate special days such as Australia Day, Anzac Day or World Environment Day. They are often characterised by free entry and wide accessibility, and form part of the public culture.

The corporate sector is involved in events at a number of levels. Companies and corporations may sponsor events in order to promote their goods and services in the marketplace. They may partner government departments in the presentation of events that serve common or multiple agendas. Companies may also create their own events in order to launch new products, increase sales or enhance corporate image. These events, although they may still offer free entry, can be targeted at specific market segments rather than at the general public.

EVENT GENERATORS	TYPES OF EVENT
GOVERNMENT SECTOR Central government	Civic celebrations and commemorations e.g. Australia Day, Centenary of Federation
Event corporations	Major events — focus on sporting and cultural events
Public space authorities	Public entertainment, leisure and recreation events
Tourism	Festivals, special interest and lifestyle events, destinational promotions
Convention bureaus	Meetings, incentives, conventions, exhibitions
Arts	Arts festivals, cultural events, touring programs, themed art exhibitions
Ethnic affairs	Ethnic and multicultural events
Sport and recreation	Sporting events, hosting of State, national and international events
Gaming and racing	Race meetings and carnivals
Economic development	Focus on events with industry development and job creation benefits
Local government	Community events, local festivals and fairs
CORPORATE SECTOR Companies and corporations	Promotions, product launches and image building sponsorships
Industry associations	Industry promotions, trade fairs, conferences
Entrepreneurs	Ticketed sporting events, concerts and exhibitions
Media	Media promotions, e.g. concerts, fun runs, appeals
COMMUNITY SECTOR Clubs and societies	Special interest group events
Charities	Charity events and fundraisers
Sports organisations	Local sporting events

Within the corporate sector there are also entrepreneurs whose business is the staging or selling of events. These include sports or concert promoters who present ticketed events for profit, and conference organisers or industry associations who mount conferences or exhibitions for the trade or public, for example, wine shows, equipment exhibitions or medical conferences. Media organisations often become partners in events organised by other groups, but also stage events for their own promotional purposes or to create program content. Examples are radio stations promoting their identity through concerts, newspapers promoting fun runs, or television networks presenting Christmas carol programs live to air.

Still other events emanate from the community sector, serving a wide variety of needs and interests. These may include service club fundraisers, car club gatherings, local art and craft shows — the spectrum is as wide as the field of human interest and endeavour. All of these sources combine to create the wonderful tapestry of events that fill our leisure time and enrich our lives.

Whether events emanate from the corporate, government or community sectors will determine the nature of the host organisation. If the host is from the corporate sector, it is likely to be a company, corporation or industry association. The event manager may be employed directly by the host organisation, or on a contract basis with the organisation as the client. If the host is from the government sector, the host organisation is likely to be a government or council department. Again the event manager may be a direct employee, or a contractor if the event is out-sourced. If the host is from the community sector, the host organisation is more likely to be a club, society or committee, with a higher volunteer component in the organisation.

Whatever the host organisation, it is a key stakeholder in the event, and the event manager should seek to clarify its goals in staging the event. These will often be presented in a written brief as part of the event manager's job description or contract. Where they are not, it will be worthwhile spending some time to clarify these goals and put them in a written form as a reference point for the organisation of the event, and a guideline for the evaluation of its eventual success.

THE HOST COMMUNITY

Event managers need to have a good grasp and understanding of the broad trends and forces acting on the wider community, as these will determine the operating environment of their events. The mood, needs and desires of the community will determine its receptiveness to event styles and fashions. Actively gauging and interpreting these are basic factors in the conceptualising of successful events.

Among the current significant forces acting on the community are globalisation and technology, which are combining to make the world seem both smaller and more complex. These forces are impacting on almost every aspect of our lives, including events. Giddens (1990) defines globalisation as 'the intensification of worldwide social relations which link distinct localities in such a way that local happenings are shaped by events occurring many miles away and vice versa'.

This process is speeded up by technology and the media, which have the power to bring significant local events to a worldwide audience, overcoming the barriers of national boundaries and cultural differences. This is exemplified by the global television coverage of major sporting events. World championships and mega-events such as the Olympics and World Cup Soccer are beamed instantly to live audiences throughout the world, giving them previously unimagined coverage and immediacy.

As global networks increasingly bring the world into our lounge rooms, the question arises of how local cultures can maintain their own uniqueness and identity in the face of global homogenisation. International arts festivals increasingly draw from the same pool of touring companies to produce similar programs. Local festivals and celebrations must increasingly compete with international products, and the raised expectations of audiences accustomed to streamlined television production. The challenge for many events is how to function in this increasingly global environment, while expressing the uniqueness of local communities and addressing their specific interests and concerns.

Globalisation is also impacting on corporate events as companies increasingly plan their marketing strategies, including their event components, on a global level. This has resulted in some local Australian event companies being bought out by overseas companies in an attempt to create networks that can serve the international needs of their clients. This approach sometimes comes unstuck as different markets in, say, New York, Sydney and Hong Kong reflect different event needs and audience responses. However, the forces of globalisation are likely to lead to an increasing standardisation of the corporate event product and market.

Simultaneously, the all-pervasive Internet and advances in information technology are increasing the availability and technological sophistication of events. Basing his forecast on projections by leading futurists and trends in the event management industry, Goldblatt (2000) predicts '24 hour, seven day per week event opportunities for guests who desire to forecast, attend, and review their participation in an event'. He also predicts that events will eventually become 'totally automated enabling event professionals to significantly expand the number of simultaneous events being produced using fewer human staff'. As a counter trend, Goldblatt also points out that 'with the advance of technology individuals are seeking more high touch experiences to balance the high tech influences in their lives. Events remain the single most effective means of providing a high touch experience'.

Event managers must be aware of these trends, and learn to operate in the new global environment. Paradoxically, live events may increasingly become the means by which communities confirm their own sense of place, individuality and cultural uniqueness.

■ Working with *the host community*

It is important to recognise the impact of the event on the host community, and for it to own and participate in the event. The host community may include residents, traders, lobby groups and public authorities such as council, transport, police, fire and ambulance brigades. The event manager should aim to identify and involve community leaders and to consult them in the planning of the event.

Councils may have certain requirements, such as parade and catering permits. Often police and councils will combine to form a 'one stop shop' for such matters as street closures, special access and parking arrangements.

If the event is large enough to impact significantly beyond the boundaries of the venue, a public authorities' briefing may identify innovative ways to minimise the impact and manage the situation. For example, the Australia Day fireworks spectacular at Sydney's Darling Harbour regularly attracts 300 000 spectators, most of whom used to depart immediately after the end of the fireworks, causing an hour-long traffic jam on the surrounding freeways. By stepping down the entertainment in stages, working with point duty police and implementing one-way traffic in some areas, the delay was reduced to less than half that time.

Host communities have past experience of different events, and event managers can draw on this knowledge to ensure an event's success. In Sydney, public authorities consciously used major occasions such as Australia Day and New Year's Eve as practice runs for the Olympics, with event organisers, public transport and public authorities working together to trial operations and refine solutions.

In addition to formal contact with authorities, the event manager should be aware of the all-important local rumour mill that can often make or break the host community's attitude to the event. In the early 1970s, the Aquarius Festival was staged by the Australian Union of Students at Nimbin in northern New South Wales. Part of the philosophy of the festival was to avoid all paid advertising, on the grounds that advertising would create a consumer mentality with people expecting the festival to be done for them. 'You are the program — the festival is what you make it' was the message to participants. The belief was that word of the festival would spread 'on the lips of the counter culture' — that a good idea would have the power to sell itself.

Twenty thousand people from all over Australia, as well as from some odd corners of the globe, eventually made the journey to Nimbin. But there were some fascinating rumours and counter rumours spread by its supporters and detractors along the way. At times the rumours promised a spectacular festival, and then just as suddenly they would reverse, giving the impression that the festival would be a disaster. Tracking, containing and managing these rumours became a core task in organising the festival, and provided a good object lesson in the best publicity of all — word of mouth.

Fifteen years after the Aquarius Festival, Stephen Hall, who was Director of Special Events for New South Wales' massive celebrations of Australia's Bicentenary, was asked how the events program was going. He replied that the Sydney public had become so satiated with events that normal publicity had become completely ineffective, and that only one thing mattered — word of mouth.

South Bank in Brisbane

South Bank in Brisbane is an example of urban renewal arising from a major event, and of an ongoing host organisation staging public events for their cultural, tourism and economic benefits to a city.

South Bank was a run-down, semi-industrial precinct across the river from the Brisbane city centre when it was chosen as the location for a world exposition to coincide with the celebrations of Australia's Bicentenary in 1988. Staged on the theme 'leisure in the age of technology', Expo 88 was a popular success, resulting in an additional 11.8 million visitor nights in Queensland with a total expenditure of $555 million (National Centre for Studies in Travel and Tourism 1998, cited in Mules 1998). It was equally popular with local residents, who averaged 7.8 visits each over the six months of the event (Craik 1992, cited in Mules 1998).

Following the success of Expo, the South Bank Corporation (SBC) was formed in 1989 to develop the 16 hectare area of the Expo site into the South Bank Parklands, and to plan for the remainder of the 42 hectare precinct under its jurisdiction. Its stated mission is 'to plan and facilitate the development and operation of a successful, world class leisure, business and residential Precinct for the enjoyment of South Bank visitors and the economic benefit of Brisbane's community and investors' (South Bank Parklands Corporation 2000).

Under the administration of the SBC, South Bank has been developed to include the Brisbane Convention and Exhibition Centre, an Imax Theatre and Hoyts Cinema complex, hotels, commercial buildings and apartments. Cultural facilities in addition to the original Queensland Art Gallery now include the Queensland Performing Arts Complex, the Queensland Theatre Company, Opera Queensland, Queensland Museum, the State Library of Queensland and the Queensland Conservatorium. South Bank Parklands has become a major celebration space for the city on occasions such as Christmas, New Year's Eve and Australia Day, and entertains Brisbane residents and visitors throughout the year. Having been christened by Expo 88, South Bank has become a dynamic contributor to the contemporary life and image of Brisbane.

SPONSORS

Recent decades have seen enormous increases in sponsorship, and a corresponding change in how events are perceived by sponsors. There has been a shift by many large companies from seeing sponsorship as primarily a public relations tool generating community goodwill, to regarding it as an important part of the marketing mix. Successful major events are now perceived as desirable properties, capable of increasing brand awareness and driving sales. They also provide important opportunities for relationship building through hosting partners and clients. Corporations invest large amounts in event sponsorship, and devote additional resources to supporting their sponsorships in order to achieve corporate objectives and sales goals.

Sweaney (1997) defines commercial sponsorship as 'a high profile form of collaborative marketing between organisations which usually involves an investment in an event, facility, individual, team or competition, in return for access to an exploitable commercial potential'.

In order to attract sponsorships, event managers must offer tangible benefits to sponsors, and effective programs to deliver them. Large corporations such as Coca-Cola and Telstra receive hundreds of sponsorship applications each week, and only those events which have a close fit with corporate objectives and a demonstrable ability to deliver benefits will be considered.

■ Sponsors as *partners in events*

It is important for event managers to identify exactly what sponsors want from an event, and what the event can deliver for them. Their needs may be different from those of the host organisation or the event manager. Attendance numbers at the event, for example, may not be as important to them as the media coverage that it generates. It may be important for their chief executive to officiate, or to gain access to public officials in a relaxed atmosphere. They may be seeking mechanisms to drive sales, or want to strengthen client relationships through hosting activities. The event manager should take the opportunity to go beyond the formal sponsorship agreement, and to treat the sponsors as partners in the event. Some of the best ideas for events can arise from such partnerships. Common agendas may be identified which support the sponsorship and deliver additional benefits to the event.

Toyota was a major sponsor of the Grand Australian Sumo Tournament held in Sydney and Melbourne in June 1997. Toyota supported its sponsorship with a Sumo Sale national advertising campaign in television and print media, which contributed to the Sumo visit being seen as a major cultural event celebrating the centenary of Australia/Japan relations. The sponsorship helped to promote sales for Toyota, as well as increasing the profile of the event. Likewise in 1992, State Bank supported its sponsorship of Sydney's Sesquicentenary celebrations with a campaign through its branches, and an enormous birthday cake in its colours, which was cut and distributed at Darling Harbour. The sponsorship identified State Bank with the celebrations, and provided the event with an additional promotional outlet through the bank's customers.

As part of their sponsorship of the Sydney Olympic Torch Relay, AMP created the 'Ignite the Dream' tour which travelled the entire Australian route of the relay, creating local celebrations in each town and city. AMP presented replicas of the Olympic cauldron to participating towns and used the Torch Relay to help reposition itself as a contemporary organisation with close community ties.

MEDIA

The expansion of the media, and the proliferation of delivery systems such as cable and satellite television and the Internet, have created a hunger for media product as never before. The global networking of media organisations, and the instant electronic transmission of media images and data, have made the global village a media reality. When television was introduced to Australia in time to cover the Melbourne Olympic Games in 1956, the world still relied largely on the physical transfer of film footage to disseminate the images of the Games interstate and overseas. Australia's Bicentennial celebrations in 1988 featured an Australia-wide multi-directional television link-up which enabled Australians to experience the celebrations simultaneously from a diverse range of locations and perspectives, seeing themselves as a nation through the media as never before. The opening ceremony of the Winter Olympic Games in Nagano in 1998 featured a thousand member world choir singing together from five different locations on five continents, including the forecourt of the Sydney Opera House. Global television networks followed New Year's Eve of the new millennium around the world, making the world seem smaller and more immediate. When the 2000 Olympics began, a simultaneous global audience estimated at two and a half billion people were able to watch the event tailored to their own national perspectives, with a variety of cameras covering every possible angle. Events such as the funeral of Diana, Princess of Wales, have become media experiences shared by millions as they are beamed instantly to a global audience. In Britain alone, the Princess's death attracted record media coverage.

This revolution in the media has in turn revolutionised events. Events now have a virtual existence in the media at least as powerful, sometimes more so, than in reality. The live audience for a sports event or concert may be dwarfed by the television audience. Indeed, the event may be created primarily for the consumption of the television audience. Events have much to gain from this development, including media sponsorships and the payment of media rights. Their value to commercial sponsors is greatly increased by their media coverage and profile. However, the media often directly affect the way events are conceptualised and presented, as in the case of One Day Cricket or Super League, and can have a profound effect on the relationship of the event with its live audience. So far sports events have been the main winners (and losers!) from this increased media attention. The range of sports covered by television has increased dramatically and some sports, such as basketball, have been able to rise from relative obscurity in Australia to assume a high media profile, largely because of their suitability for television production and programming.

The available media technology influences the way that live spectators experience an event. Sweaney (1997) reported on the Seven Network's construction of a state-of-the-art digital broadcasting centre adjacent to the Melbourne Docklands Stadium, which is the new home for Seven in Melbourne. The wiring of the stadium allows for digital television and enables every spectator to have a unique seat with personalised communication services. Increasingly, spectators' viewing capabilities are technologically enhanced to parallel those of people watching at home.

Media interest in events is likely to continue to grow as their ability to provide community credibility and to attract commercial sponsors is realised. Parades, spectacles, concerts and major public celebrations are areas of potential interest to the media, where the need to make good television is likely to influence the direction and marketing of events. The role of the media can vary from that of media sponsors to becoming full partners — or even producers — of the event.

Whatever the role of the media, it is important for the event manager to consider the needs of different media groups, and to consult them as important stakeholders in the event. Once the media are treated as potential partners, they have much to offer the event. The good media representative, like the event manager, is in search of the good idea or unusual angle. Together they might just dream up the unique approach that increases the profile of the event and provides value in turn to the media organisation. The print media might agree to publish the event program as editorial or as a special insert, or might run a series of lead-in stories, competitions or special promotions in tandem with sponsors. Radio or television stations might provide an outside broadcast, or might involve their on-air presenters as comperes or special participants in the event. This integration of the event with the media provides greater reach and exposure to the event, and in turn gives the media organisation a branded association with the event.

CO-WORKERS

The event team that is assembled to implement the event represents another of the key stakeholders. For any event to be truly effective, the vision and philosophy of the event must be shared by all of the team, from key managers, talent and publicist, right through to the stage manager, crew, gatekeepers and cleaners. No matter how big or small, the event team is the face of the event, and each is a contributor to its success or failure.

Most people have experienced events which went well overall, but were marred by some annoying detail. There are different ways of addressing such problems, but team selection and management are always crucial. The Disney organisation has a system where the roles of performer, cleaner, security and the like are merged in the concept of a team looking after the space. The roles tend to ride with the needs of the moment — when the parade comes through, it is all hands on deck! The daily bulletin issued to all staff members reminds them that customers may visit Disneyland only once in their lives, and their impressions will depend forever on what they experience that day. This is a very positive philosophy that can be applied to all events.

PARTICIPANTS AND SPECTATORS

Last but not least are the 'punters' on the day — the participants and spectators for whom the event is intended and who ultimately vote with their feet for the success or failure of the event. The event manager must be mindful of the needs of the audience. These include their physical needs, as well as their needs for comfort, safety and security. Over and above these basic requirements is the need to make the event special — to connect with the emotions. A skilled event manager strives to make events meaningful, magical and memorable. Hemmerling (1997) describes the criteria by which spectators judge an event:

■ Their main focus is on the content, location, substance and operation of the event itself. For them the ease with which they can see the event activities, the program content, their access to food and drinks, amenities, access and egress etc., are the keys to their enjoyment. Simple factors such as whether or not their team won or lost, or whether they had a good experience at the event will sometimes influence their success measures. Secondary issues, such as mixing with the stars of the show, social opportunities, corporate hospitality and capacity to move up the seating chain from general admission to premium seating are all part of the evaluation of spectator success. ■

DEVELOPING THE EVENT CONCEPT

Goldblatt (1997) suggests the 'Five Ws' as important questions to ask in developing the event concept. These are:
- *Why* is the event being held? There must be compelling reasons that confirm the importance and viability of holding the event.
- *Who* will be the stakeholders in the event? These include internal stakeholders, such as the board of directors, committee, staff and audience or guests, and external stakeholders such as media and politicians.
- *When* will the event be held? Is there sufficient time to research and plan the event? Does the timing suit the needs of the audience, and if the event is outdoors, does it take the likely climatic conditions into account?

- *Where* will the event be staged? The choice of venue must represent the best compromise between the organisational needs of the event, audience comfort, accessibility and cost.
- *What* is the event content or product? This must match the needs, wants, desires and expectations of the audience, and must synergise with the why, who, when and where of the event.

An important part of developing the event will be identifying unique elements and resources which can make the event special, and contribute to its imagery and branding. Australia Day at Darling Harbour in 1993 had to be special, as an important International Olympic Committee delegation was scheduled to attend. It was the largest single delegation to visit Sydney, and its purpose was to conduct a final inspection of the city before the vote to decide the host city for the 2000 Olympics was held. The organisers identified Sydney Tower as having the potential to be transformed by pyrotechnics into a giant Olympic Torch. The idea was workshopped and incorporated into the event, creating a memorable image, which made the cover of *Time* magazine and played a part in convincing the delegation that Sydney was capable of staging a major celebration if awarded the Olympic Games.

■ Brainstorming

Once the parameters of the event have been set, it is desirable to *brainstorm* the concept of the event, letting the imagination soar and consulting as many stakeholders as possible. A good way to do this is to meet with them individually at first, establishing relationships and allowing each stakeholder to become comfortable with their role in the event. In these discussions ideas will arise, but the process should be acknowledged as exploratory, not yet seeking to reach fixed conclusions.

Once the diverse stakeholders are brought to the meeting table, the ideas will start to flow. This is a time to ignore restraints of practicality — of cost, scale or viability. That time will come. The task is to create and to dream, and no idea should be dismissed as too wild to consider. The goal is to discover the right idea, the one that resonates so that everyone recognises it and is inspired by the challenge and the potential that it offers. This is where the skills of an event director come to the fore — the ability to draw out ideas, to synthesise content and eventually to engineer compromise. No matter how good an idea or how strong its support, eventually it must serve the objectives of the event, and be deliverable within the available resources. With some good fortune, this idea may be identified in a single meeting, but most often the process will take several meetings and weeks or months of patience and hard work. But the results will be worthwhile if a strong vision for the event emerges, one that is shared and supported by all stakeholders, and which inspires confidence and commitment. This process is at the very heart of creative event planning, and when it works well it is one of the joys of being in the business.

■ The synergy *of ideas*

Most good events emerge from a synergistic group process. Such a process was illustrated in 1993, when the New South Wales Australia Day Council brought together a group of people to devise a program of celebrations for the Sydney Olympic bid announcement.

The brief had some unusual features. The announcement of the successful bid to stage the 2000 Olympic Games was to be made by IOC President Juan Antonio Samaranch in Monte Carlo at 4.27 a.m. Sydney time.

The event organisers faced a challenging dilemma. If Sydney was successful, it created an opportunity for a memorable celebration, and for images of the winning city to be beamed around the world by the media. If Sydney lost, its inhabitants were unlikely to be impressed by being woken up before dawn.

With a collective brains trust of some of Sydney's top event directors and media strategists, the organisers set about the challenge of answering the brief. The selection of a venue presented a difficult choice. As Homebush Bay had been selected as the Olympic site, it made sense to reveal it to the world. On the other hand, the Sydney Opera House is undoubtedly the symbol of Sydney, instantly recognised around the world.

In the end, as is often the case with difficult choices, it was decided to include both. A party would be staged for the site workers and school children at Homebush Bay, and an official reception and public celebration would be held several kilometres away on the west side of Circular Quay, with the Opera House in the background. If Sydney was successful, the two parties would be connected by a series of pyrotechnic rockets which would be fired up into the air at intervals along the harbour foreshore. Thus the approach of A and B (win or lose) scenarios started to emerge. Media strategists began work on the images that would feature in the television transmission that was planned for the winning city. A live cross of one minute provided a unique window of opportunity to showcase Sydney to the world. The organisers favoured the image of fireworks exploding over the Opera House, but how to dress the Opera House in celebratory mode?

The answer came from one of those marvellous synergistic processes, with one person building on the idea of another until the solution was revealed. It started with the idea of laser image projections beamed on the Opera House shells. The obvious content was the ribbon device that was the logo for the bid. Finally the idea emerged: why not place the ribbon on the outline of the shells, which were the original inspiration for the logo? It was one of those ideas which everyone instantly recognised as the right idea, but for which no single individual could totally claim credit.

Good ideas have a habit of winning support, and the concept was rapidly adopted by a cooperative Opera House management and the lighting sponsor Philips, who had the technical expertise and commitment to carry it through. When Samaranch uttered the words, 'And the winner is... Sydney!', they were ready with the switch, to reveal the idea to the world.

With the increased involvement of governments and the corporate sector, events are required to serve a multitude of agendas. The successful event manager must be able to identify and manage a diverse range of stakeholder expectations. Major stakeholders are the host organisation staging a particular event, and the host community, including the various public authorities whose support will be needed. Both sponsors and media are important partners, and can make important contributions to an event in support and resources beyond their formal sponsorship and media coverage. The vision and philosophy of the event should be shared by co-workers in the event team, and the contribution of each should be recognised and treated as important. Ultimately it is the spectators and participants who decide the success or failure of an event, and it is crucial to engage their emotions.

Once the objectives of the event and the unique resources available to it have been identified, the next priority is to brainstorm ideas with stakeholders so that a shared vision for the event can be shaped and communicated. No event is created by one person, and success will depend on a collective team effort.

Questions

1 Who are the most important stakeholders in an event, and why?

2 Give examples of different events staged by government, corporate and community groups in your region and discuss their reasons for putting on these events.

3 Focusing on an event that you have experienced first-hand, list the benefits that the event could offer a sponsor or partner.

4 Using the same event example that you discussed in the last question, identify suitable media partners and outline how you would approach them to participate in the event.

5 What are the means by which an event creates an emotional relationship with its participants and spectators?

6 What events can you think of that demonstrate a unique vision or idea? What techniques have been used to express that vision or idea, and why do you consider them to be unique?

7 Imagine you are planning an event in the area where you live. What are its unique characteristics, and how might these be expressed in the event?

8 Name a major event that you have attended or in which you have been involved, and identify the prime stakeholders and their objectives.

The Birdsville Races,
Queensland

Birdsville is an outback town in far western Queensland. It sits on the edge of the Simpson Desert, 1585 km west of Brisbane. The isolated town of Birdsville is just a dot on the map near where the Queensland, New South Wales and South Australia borders meet. The Birdsville Track is best known as the loneliest road in Australia.

The small depot which emerged as a customs point for stock and supplies entering South Australia gradually grew through cattle droving, with supplies being transported on camels, and later through access to railways and pastoral activity. Before Federation, Birdsville was a thriving community of 270 residents, three hotels, two general stores, and other businesses. Today, this solitary community boasts a hotel, an inland mission hospital, a caravan park, an airport, a police station, a sports centre, residences and a store.

The town's annual Picnic Race Meeting, which is held over the first weekend in September, has captured the imagination of the city-bred Australian. In recent years annual pilgrimages to the Birdsville Races have become popular for seekers of iconic, authentic tourism experiences. The town's present population of around 100 people comes to life during the four days of the Birdsville Picnic Race Carnival with between 5000 and 8000 recorded as attending the event to celebrate life in the outback.

The Birdsville Races began in 1882. The facilities at the outback racetrack consist of an old tin shed, sandhills and dusty tracks; but top-class horses travel from the coast to compete. The Birdsville Hotel becomes the focus of legendary alcohol consumption. The pub, built two years after the races began, is a storehouse of over 50 years' worth of stockmen's memorabilia, hats, photographs and souvenirs of the Birdsville Races.

The race weekend is about more than just two days of horseflesh and a racetrack. The festivities of the event commence on Friday night with the Ringers Dance, a casual affair with other social events continuing on Saturday night with the Birdsville Races Grand Ball demanding smart casual attire. Fred Brophy's Boxing Troupe provides evening entertainment from Wednesday through to Sunday nights. Other aspects of the experience include side-shows, stalls, bull-riding, people-watching and a great deal of alcohol consumption.

Local mayor David Brooks has indicated that the Birdsville Races are valuable to the host community because they provide locals with a chance to experience a difference in their usual lives; they allow locals to briefly mix with an unfamiliar society and create a clear sense of belonging, identity and community involvement. Event attendees need to come fully equipped for a camping experience, together with a sense of humour and a sense of adventure.

The event generates money for the local economy. There are no supermarkets or convenience stores. There is a small general store designed to service the permanent residents. Any revenue not leaked sustains local businesses, charitable organisations, schools and medical staff for a considerable time. Profit from the staging of the event is given to the Royal Flying Doctor Service, the local hospital and the resident nurse. The amount raised in 1998 was between $40 000 and $60 000. Employees from these services manned the entry gates in order to receive the entrance fee directly. Frontier Services received a similar amount in 1998, while the revenue raised from the recycling of beer cans is donated every year to the local school. Prize money offered at the races ranges between $6000 and $17 000.

The event has dramatically increased the amount of tourism to the region. Moneys raised have improved the amenities available to residents and visitors. There is now a tourism information centre and a library, and track facilities have been improved. The event provides sharp contrast for visitors with their (usually) mundane daily lives. It is the catalyst for visitors to explore a distinctive, desolate landscape. The international media's increasing interest in the races and their globally beamed images attract more visitors, especially at race time, but also throughout the season when it is comfortable to drive there. Distinctive markets like the 'grey nomad' touring-by-car market, young backpackers and workers in regional Australia look for a relaxed recreational experience. Celebrities attending now get coverage in the national press. Websites are promoting opportunities to share the landscape and the event.

There are several ways of getting to Birdsville. One is to self-drive, preferably in a four-wheel-drive vehicle; another is to fly. For the race weekend, over 350 aircraft are attracted to the township. Another option is a six-day coach package which includes camp accommodation and some meals. Available accommodation consists of 18 units at the pub which is booked out years in advance. People bring swags and tents and camp out on the banks of the Diamantina River.

Aspects of planning and management are handled in an informal manner in Birdsville. Organisers are obliged to bring the resources required for the event in from outside. They have a mental plan for the effective conduct of an event which has distinctive impacts on the town and its infrastructure. Experience has lead community leaders to make specific management choices. Care is required to deal with the more than 350 aircraft which fly in to deposit their passengers. Twenty-four bar attendants are recruited from within the community. Environmental concerns for waste management are dealt with by contract cleaners, Pink Bins. This Brisbane-based company has a five-year contract for the removal of rubbish from the site and for the provision of portable toilets and showers. Racing officials and stewards come from established racing institutions while the rules and regulations of the Australian Jockey Club are adhered to, ensuring the smooth running of the races.

The Royal Flying Doctor Service and Frontier Service staff provide volunteers to collect entrance fees at the gates to the races; and 17 stallholders provide food services, each responsible for their own staff needs. Extra nursing staff and doctors are recruited from outside the region, while 15–20 police are recruited from regional stations. Volunteers at the event are rewarded with a free Birdsville Races badge which provides them with free access to the races and both the Friday and Saturday night balls.

A unique method of crowd control has been developed. When an incident occurs within the crowd, the troublemakers are encouraged to visit the 'boxing tent' as a means of venting their anger or frustrations. The erection of the boxing tent is the responsibility of Fred Brophy and his boxing troupe. Repeat visitors demonstrate their own code of ethics which is used as an alternative means of crowd control.

McCafferty's Coachlines supply coaches and drivers to ferry visitors to the race track which is five kilometres from the township. Earnings from these trips are donated to the Royal Flying Doctor Service. The preparation of the race track is undertaken by five members of the Birdsville racing committee who also play an important role in constructing the outside barrier of the racetrack. Ron Goodall, an independent operator, is responsible for the mechanical bull-riding activities.

Bookmakers are required to accept bets from visitors. The absence of totalisator facilities means that security staff are relieved of the extra pressure of securing cash from the races. Bookmakers are responsible for the security of their own money. Stringent licensing by the AJC minimises unscrupulous activity.

Horse racing is a popular recreational pursuit of Australians. The Birdsville Races are hosted by a unique community. They provide distinctive entertainment for the growing number of domestic and overseas visitors. The event is unlike any other on the nation's annual racing calendar.

Ros Derrett
adapted from Stickens, Howle & Lucock (1998)

Questions

1 How does the community deal with the human resource management issues of the Birdsville Races?

2 What is the potential impact on Birdsville of global media coverage of the races?

3 How must the small community deal with the possible environmental concerns from hosting the races?

REFERENCES

Giddens, Anthony 1990, *The Consequences of Modernity*, Polity Press, Cambridge.

Goldblatt, Dr Joe Jeff 1997, *Special Events — Best Practices in Modern Event Management*, Van Nostrand Reinhold, New York.

Goldblatt, Dr Joe Jeff 2000, 'A future for event management: the analysis of major trends impacting the emerging profession', in *Events Beyond 2000: Setting the Agenda — Event Evaluation, Research and Education Conference Proceedings*, eds J. Allen, R. Harris, L. K. Jago & A. J. Veal, Australian Centre for Event Management, University of Technology, Sydney.

Hemmerling, Mal 1997, 'What makes an event a success for a host city, sponsors and others?', paper presented to The Big Event New South Wales Tourism Conference, Wollongong, NSW.

Mules, Trevor 1998, 'Events tourism and economic development in Australia', in *Managing Tourism in Cities*, eds D. Tyler, Y. Guerrier & M. Robertson, John Wiley & Sons, New York.

South Bank Parklands Corporation 2000, www.south-bank.net.au (accessed 21 September 2000)

Stickens, A., Howle, L. & Lucock, A. 1998, *Birdsville Races*, Southern Cross University, www.tq.com.au (unpublished student paper).

Sweaney, Karen 1997, 'Sponsorship trends', and 'Developing the Docklands', *Australian Leisure Management*, vol. 1, no. 3, pp. 18–19, and vol. 1, no. 5, p. 16, respectively.

4

Economic analysis
of events

LEARNING OBJECTIVES

After studying this chapter, you should be able to:

- describe the reasons why governments become involved in events
- understand the importance of the point of view from which economic impact studies are undertaken
- describe and compare the different models available to measure the impacts of events
- identify and discuss issues in identifying event expenditure
- discuss the wider impacts that need to be taken into account in evaluating events
- demonstrate an awareness of the strategies employed by governments in promoting the business opportunities provided by events
- discuss the impacts of the Sydney Olympic Games
- understand the use of predictive models in forecasting the impacts of events.

INTRODUCTION

The recent explosion of events, and the parallel increase in the involvement of governments and corporations, has led to an increasing emphasis on their economic analysis and benefits. Understandably, governments considering the investment of substantial taxpayers funds in events want to know what they are getting for their investment, and to compare this with other options. Sponsors and corporate partners investing what are often now considerable sums in events want to compare this with other potential uses of their marketing budgets. This climate has given rise to the detailed study of events by economists, and the development and application of increasingly sophisticated techniques to their economic analysis and evaluation. The economic analysis of events is still a young discipline, and differing methodologies and approaches often give rise to a healthy debate on their relative merits and accuracy. Unfortunately, the debate among professionals and the desire by host organisations to present their events in the best possible light can sometimes give rise to suspicion of the process and its findings. The development of a rigorous, highly regarded and generally accepted economic evaluation discipline is an important step towards a respected and professional event industry.

GOVERNMENT INVOLVEMENT IN EVENTS

Traditionally, events have been staged by communities or governments because of their perceived social, cultural or sporting benefits and value. This situation began to change dramatically in the early 1980s when major events began to be regarded as desirable commodities in many parts of the world because of their perceived ability to deliver economic benefits through the promotion of tourism, increased visitor expenditure and job creation.

Mules (1998) dates this change in attitude in Australia to around 1982–86, with the staging of the Commonwealth Games in Brisbane (1982), the Formula One Grand Prix in Adelaide (1985), and the America's Cup Defence in Perth (1986–87). He notes that around this time state governments began to be aware of the economic significance of events, aided by studies such as that of the Formula One Grand Prix (Burns, Hatch & Mules, cited in Mules 1998) which established that the income generated by the event exceeded the cost to the South Australian Government of its staging.

As outlined in chapter 1, various state governments in Australia have pursued vigorous event strategies from the 1980s up to the present, building strong portfolios of annual events and aggressively bidding for the right for their State to host major one-off events. In unveiling his Government's new major events strategy in August 2000, Victorian Premier Steve Bracks announced expenditure on major events in his state with an annual cap of $40 million. He detailed a portfolio of ongoing events with a total economic impact of $277.3 million, and one-off events between 2000 and 2002 with a total economic impact of $99.8 million (Bracks 2000).

Apart from interstate rivalry and political kudos, what motivates and justifies this level of government involvement in what might otherwise be seen as a largely commercial enterprise? The answer, according to Mules (1998), lies in what he terms the spillover effects of events. While many major events might make an operational loss from the point of view of the event, they produce benefits for related industry sectors such as travel, accommodation, restaurants, hirers and suppliers of equipment, and so on. They may also produce long-term benefits such as destination promotion resulting in increased tourism spending. However, it is not possible for this wide range of benefits to be captured by a single organisation. Hence, governments sometimes play a role in funding or underwriting events in order that these generalised benefits might be obtained.

However, in considering the appropriate levels of financial support for events, it is necessary for governments to develop a full picture of their costs and benefits, and of their likely impacts on the wider economy.

THE IMPORTANCE OF THE POINT OF VIEW

The first issue to consider in assessing the economic impacts of events is the point of view of the study (Faulkner 1993; Mules 1999). For example, a commercial organisation or entrepreneur will be concerned primarily with the financial income and expenditure of the event, and whether or not at the end of the day the event is likely to make a profit. Governments, however, will need to look further at the wider economic impacts of the event on the host community.

A national government will be concerned with the impact on the gross domestic product, or GDP. From this viewpoint, only income attracted from outside the country will be regarded as significant. For example, income from overseas visitors to the Sydney Olympic Games constitutes 'new' money into the economy and will be counted, whereas income from visitors travelling from Melbourne to Sydney simply constitutes a transfer of spending from one part of the country to another, and will be ignored. By the same token, the proceeds from overseas sponsorships and the sale of international media rights will be counted as income, but not those from Australian sponsorships or sale of media rights.

From the state viewpoint, only event-generated expenditure sourced from outside the State will impact on the gross State product, or GSP. Thus grants from a national government for an event will be treated as injected expenditure, provided that they do not displace or interfere with existing grant allocations. For example, in a study of the 1985 Adelaide Grand Prix (Burns & Mules 1989), a special grant of $5 million by the Commonwealth Government was counted as income from the perspective of the South Australian economy. On the other hand, a $1 million grant from the South Australian Jubilee 150 Board was treated as a cost to the State economy, since it represented an internal item of funding with no new injection of funds into the State economy.

Similarly, a study from the regional viewpoint will consider the impact on the gross regional product, or GRP, the regional equivalent of the GDP. Visitors to the Tamworth Country Music Festival are likely to have a large effect on the GRP, but a lesser effect on the GSP and a still smaller effect on the GDP. In general, the more narrowly the host community is defined, the larger the injected expenditure and the larger is the resulting economic impact, provided that there is not too great a leakage from goods and services procured from outside the host community.

The viewpoint of an economic impact study is most likely to be that of the underwriting or funding body, whose major concern will be to determine the impact of the event on its own level of the economy.

EVENT PROFILE

EventsCorp Western Australia

EventsCorp rose out of the hosting of the America's Cup by Fremantle in 1986–87, and the desire of the Western Australian Government to realise the potential tourism benefits that could be leveraged from this and other major international events. In doing so, it pioneered government involvement in events in Australia, and established a model that has since been emulated by other Australian states and attracted international attention.

In selecting events to support, EventsCorp researches their potential using criteria such as economic and media impacts, event frequency, private sector investment, tourism activity and potential for development. It then establishes partnerships with sporting bodies, government authorities, corporations or individuals to bid for, stage and market these events.

EventsCorp has developed several initiatives in the marketing of events including:
- 'picture postcards' — 15-second snapshots of Western Australian tourism icons incorporated in international television coverage of events
- the *Best on Earth in Perth* calendar of events, which provides a catalyst to develop travel packages in conjunction with the tourism industry
- state-of-the-art Web sites such as that for the Qantas 2000 ITU Triathlon World Championships that allowed international competitors to register and receive detailed competition information online, and fans to witness the event action and obtain up-to-the-minute results for individual events.

Through the efforts of EventsCorp, Western Australia has hosted a number of major events including the FINA World Swimming Championships (twice), the ITU World Triathlon Championships (twice), the UCI World Track Cycling Championships and the Telstra Rally Australia annual round of the World Rally Championships. From its commencement in 1997 to June 2000, the Best on Earth in Perth calendar of events has contributed over $190 million to the State's economy.

Conducting an economic impact study (EIS) will involve collecting all of the relevant data relating to the expenditure for the event. However, this expenditure has flow-on effects that need to be taken into account in calculating the economic impact of the event (Faulkner 1993). For example, money spent on a meal purchased by the visitor to an event will flow on to firms that supply the restaurant with food and beverage items. The money spent on the meal is referred to as direct expenditure, and the flow-on effect to suppliers as indirect expenditure. The event may also stimulate additional activity in the economy, resulting in increased wages and consumer spending. This is referred to as induced expenditure. A number of models (Hunn & Mangan 1999; Mules 1999) are available to the researcher to capture and measure these different levels of expenditure (see figure 4.1).

■ **Figure 4.1**
The process of establishing the economic impact of an event

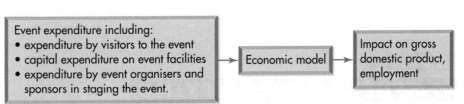

■ Input–output *analysis*

The most commonly used model is input–output analysis, which uses a series of input–output tables to aggregate the total impact of the expenditure on the economy, expressed as a multiplier ratio. Multipliers reflect the impact of the event expenditure as it ripples through the economy, and vary according to the particular mix of industries in a given geographical location. It should be noted that the use of multipliers is controversial, and some studies prefer to concentrate on the direct expenditure of the event as being more reliable, although this does not give a true picture of the complex impact of the event expenditure on the economy.

■ Computable general *equilibrium models*

Computable general equilibrium models aim to quantify the direct effect or shock to the economy as the result of expenditure generated by the event, and to model this shock by the use of a system of equations that are solved simultaneously to return the economy to equilibrium. They are able to include a variety of variables in the macroeconomic environment, and provide a more sophisticated and complete representation of the economy. However, their level of difficulty and expense tends to restrict their use to the evaluation of large scale events.

■ Benefit–cost *analysis*

Benefit–cost analysis is used by governments in order to quantify the opportunity cost of allocating resources to an area compared with the alternative use of these resources. It reflects the view that the true cost of an event to the community is the diversion of resources from other purposes. It takes a 'big picture' view, and is useful in ranking net social costs and benefits against agreed goals. However, a weakness is that there may not be common agreement with regard to the social value of an event; for example, different sections of the community may place different values on events such as the Australian Grand Prix or the Sydney Olympics.

It should be noted that these models are not necessarily mutually exclusive, and can sometimes be used in combination; for example, the ground-breaking study of the Adelaide Grand Prix (Burns, Mules & Hatch, cited in Mules 1998) used a combination of the input–output model and benefit–cost analysis to evaluate its impacts on the South Australian economy. Some researchers have also noted that the use of different models often achieves similar results (Burgan & Mules 2000; NSW Treasury and the Centre for Regional Economic Analysis, University of Tasmania 1997).

*I*SSUES IN IDENTIFYING EVENT EXPENDITURE

Regardless of the model that is used, success in identifying the economic impact of an event will depend on accurately identifying the expenditure of the event from the perspective of the study. According to Faulkner (1993), the impacts of the event derive from three sources:
- expenditure by visitors from outside the region
- capital expenditure on facilities required for the conduct of the event
- expenditure incurred by event organisers and sponsors associated with the staging of the event.

However, there are several issues, it is argued (Faulkner 1993; Burns & Mules 1989), that need to be taken into account in order to form a true picture of the economic impact of an event.

■ Switching

The visitor expenditure that can legitimately be attributed to an event is based on the increase in the number of visitors over those who would have visited the region in any case. Those who would have visited at another time, but have changed the timing of their visit to coincide with the event, are said to have 'switched' the timing of their visit, and their expenditure should not be counted. On the other hand, locals who are influenced by the event to spend their holidays at home rather that travel outside the region represent expenditure that would otherwise have been lost to the region, and should be counted. In a survey of the Adelaide Festival of Arts, 10.3 per cent of Adelaide residents surveyed indicated that they were 'vacationing at home' due to the festival, and a further 7000 residents indicated that they would travel out of town more often for cultural experiences if not for the festival. The incremental expenditure by these two groups was estimated at $3.4 million (Centre for South Australian Economic Studies, cited in Crompton & McKay 1994).

Switching can also occur in a geographical sense; for example, people visiting Sydney for the Olympics who would otherwise have visited other holiday destinations can be said to have 'switched' their expenditure to Sydney. This process can occur in reverse, with Sydneysiders choosing to leave the city during the Olympics because of perceived overcrowding and disruption to normal activities. This reaction, known as the repulsion effect, was widely observed at the Atlanta Olympics and many celebrations of the new millennium. Potential visitors may also be deterred by expectations of exorbitant prices and congestion. Known as displacement costs, this was estimated in a study of the 1984 Los Angeles Olympics at US$163 million (Economics Research Association, cited in Crompton & McKay 1994).

■ Leakages

Expenditure on an event has an impact on the host community only if it is spent in that community. Goods or services required to be purchased outside the community represent 'leakages' in expenditure, and should not be counted in the calculation of economic impacts from this perspective. Thus payments outside of Australia to the international copyright owner of an event would have a negative effect on the GDP, as would the importation of goods or services from a capital city for a regional event on the GRP.

■ Relevance *of infrastructure*

New infrastructure required to stage an event can provide a lasting legacy to the community of improved transport, communications, sporting or cultural facilities. The capital costs of this infrastructure are regarded as a cost to the event if provided by the host community. However, they may simply involve the bringing forward of building or construction projects that were already planned, thus involving the time switching of already committed expenditure. The long-term value of new event facilities will be decided by their ongoing relevance to community needs. The building of new venues at Homebush Bay for the Sydney Olympics resulted in competition by Stadium Australia with the existing Sydney Football Stadium, and by the SuperDome with the existing Sydney Entertainment Centre. This duplication of venues may undermine their long-term value as a legacy of the Games. In some cases it may be more economical to stage events that can be accommodated by existing event infrastructure, or the cost-effective upgrading of existing facilities.

■ Hidden *costs*

Expenditure on building facilities and on staging the event is regarded as a cost if it is borne by the host community, or as a benefit if it is funded from external sources. However, many events fail to identify all of the costs in staging the event. For example, services provided by government departments (such as police, transport, road and traffic authorities) may represent opportunity costs to the community, but may not show up on the balance sheet of the event. Care must be taken to identify all of the costs of the event so that the total (net) impact of the event can be accurately assessed. For example, costs borne by arms of government other than the South Bank Authority in staging Expo 88 in Brisbane were estimated at between $400 million and $600 million (Donohue, cited in Mules 1998).

*W*IDER IMPACTS OF EVENTS ·····························

As discussed earlier, the expenditure generated by events forms only a part of the complex set of factors that governments need to take into account in evaluating their impacts. There are a number of wider effects that need to be taken into account, both in the short and the long term, including tourism promotion, business opportunities, commercial activity and employment creation.

■ Tourism *promotion*

Tourism is an important factor in the economic impact of events because, as discussed earlier, the spending of visitors from outside the host community provides an injection of 'new money' into the economy — the equivalent of export earnings. Events can increase the number of tourists and extend their length of stay and expenditure. Tracking the number of tourists and their expenditure patterns is vital in assessing the economic impacts of events.

However, events have other tourism impacts that may be more long term and intangible. The media exposure and awareness of the event may result in an increased profile of the host city as a tourism destination. Visitors may be impressed by the destination, and may decide to make a return visit at a later time. The long-term value of these impacts may be considerable, but may be difficult to document and evaluate in the short term.

In a study of the 1989 Australian Motorcycle Grand Prix in Victoria (National Institute of Economic and Industry Research 1989), 57 per cent of non-Victorian visitors reported that it was likely they would return to Victoria for a holiday within two years. In many cases, this was qualified by the comment, 'only if there is a Grand Prix'.

The Wales Tourist Board undertook a major marketing and promotional campaign in relation to the Rugby World Cup in Wales in 1999. Its overall aim was to use the tournament as an opportunity to attract additional visitors in order to raise the profile of the host nation and to secure lasting tourism benefits. Over 330 000 people were estimated to have visited Wales as a result of the event. In a survey of international Rugby fans conducted before and after the Rugby World Cup, fewer than 20 per cent had visited Wales during the event. Of those who had, almost 70 per cent thought it likely that they would return on holiday. Among those who had seen coverage of the event on television, 25 per cent thought that they would be much more likely to visit Wales on holiday as a result. Research indicated that around 135 000 trips may be generated from the UK over the next five years, potentially worth around 15 million pounds (Anon. 2000).

■ Business *opportunities*

Events can provide their host communities with a strong platform to show-case their expertise, host potential investors and promote new business opportunities. The media exposure generated by the success of an event can dramatically illustrate the capacity, innovation and achievements of event participants or the host community:

> ■ World attention on Australia's technological capabilities followed the victory of Australia II in the 1983 America's Cup Challenge race off Newport, Rhode Island. The twelve metre yacht was a veritable floating advertisement of the nation's development of modern computer systems, advanced metals technology and synthetic fabrics. The win meant a boost for Australia's fledgling high technology industries (Anon., cited in Newman 1989). ■

Burns and Mules (1989) described the potential business opportunities provided to South Australia by the successful staging of the Grand Prix:

> ■ Special events, such as the Grand Prix, can attract the interest of entrepreneurs to this state, increase the state's bargaining position, enable the state to market its products relatively cheaply, affect the attitude of residents towards local products, promote investment, encourage exports and favourably affect the terms of trade.
> Significant long term benefits would flow to this state if ability to stage the Grand Prix were to be seen by others as ability to handle large and complex installations. ■

They also pointed out that these benefits would accrue only if deliberate strategies were put in place to harness these opportunities:

> ■ Special events are enabling mechanisms. They represent opportunities. Unless the community is willing and able to capitalise on these opportunities, nothing need necessarily result. ■

Governments are increasingly aware of the potential of major events to create business opportunities, and of the importance of implementing appropriate strategies to maximise these opportunities. During the Sydney Olympics, the New South Wales Government spent $3.6 million on a trade and investment drive coinciding with the Games (Humphries 2000). There

ASKHAM BRYAN

LEARNING RESOURCES

were more than 60 business related events, board meetings of international companies, briefings and trade presentations. Forty-six international chambers of commerce were briefed on business opportunities, and more than 500 world business leaders, Olympic sponsors and NSW corporate executives attended four promotional events. NSW Treasurer Michael Egan was quoted in the report as saying 'We'll be benefiting from the Games well after we think the benefits have worn off and in ways that will never show up in statistics'.

Little research has been done on analysing business development strategies in relation to events, and on quantifying the amount of business generated by these strategies. More work needs to be done so that event enhancement frameworks are better understood and their outcomes assessed.

■ Commercial *activity*

Whatever the generation of new business at the macro level, undoubtedly the suppliers of infrastructure, goods and services profit from the staging of major events. But do these benefits trickle down to traders and small business operators?

A survey of 1000 tourism-related businesses was conducted in relation to the Rugby World Cup in Wales in 1999 (Anon. 2000). The accommodation sector fared best, with two-thirds of accommodation providers experiencing improvements in business performance, and a 7.5 per cent increase in room rates by operators in Cardiff and the south-east of Wales. Around half of the food and drink outlets reported increased performance. This sector also reported making considerable investment in promotional activities and small-scale product development. In the retail sector, over half of those who responded thought that, despite improvements in average spend, the event had impacted negatively on their overall performance.

A study by Muthaly, Ratnatunga, Roberts and Roberts (2000) used a case study approach to examine the impact of the Atlanta Olympics on seven small businesses in Atlanta. The case study included:

- a wholesale restaurant equipment dealer, which expanded its existing business and current line of equipment resulting in a 70–80 per cent increase in revenue as a result of the Games
- a one-person home rental business specifically started to provide bed and breakfast type housing for Olympic visitors that lost US$23 000 due to lack of any significant Games business
- a frozen lemonade stand franchise that employed up to 50 people at four fixed and three roving locations — the business failed due to problems with inventory, staffing, unanticipated and unregulated competition, and lower than expected attendance at the Games
- an established beverage distributor, who became an approved Games vendor and reported increased profits through additional sales by his usual customers and a firm policy of not extending credit to new customers

- a craft retail location at Stone Mountain Park, a major tourist attraction for Atlanta and the south-east where some Olympic events were located. The owner lost about US$10 000 on a special line of Olympic theme dolls, sculptures and so on due to added costs and lack of customers
- a United Kingdom based currency service and foreign exchange business that established two locations downtown near the Olympic Park, and two uptown near the retail and residential heart of the city — the principal felt that it was not a very successful business project due to the changing nature of the market (people using credit or debit cards in place of currency) and lack of communication with Olympic organisers
- an established sporting goods retail store that reported increased sales of established lines and regular merchandise, but not of Olympic merchandise stocked to sell in front of the store. The owner reported considerable staffing difficulties due to poor transport planning and absenteeism as a result of the Games.

The authors of the study concluded that:

> ■ Many businesses made money during the Atlanta Olympics, both large and small. Delta Airlines did very well; some local law firms associated with the Games did extremely well; local construction firms had great years leading up to the Games. Niche players who carefully watched their risk faired very well. The more established the business, the higher was the probability of success. ■

However, they also stated that for many entrepreneurs:

> ■ dreams of big profits melted into heartache. One of the main reasons was that, to the surprise of all, the masses never came. Further, those that did come did not spend the amount of money expected. The tour buses sat empty, the area's attractions remained relatively unseen by fresh eyes and few rental homes hosted vacationing visitors. The simplest explanation for this reversal of expectations was the important finding that the Olympic consumer proved to be a very different creature from the ordinary tourist or business traveller: an unpredictable hybrid — sports-mad, tight-fisted and uninterested in traditional tourist attractions. ■

From these and other studies, it would appear that the anticipated benefits of major events to traders and small business operators are sometimes exaggerated, and that the results are often sporadic and uneven. It would also seem that benefits are more likely to accrue to those businesses that are properly prepared, and that manage and invest wisely in the opportunities provided by events. More research needs to be done in this field to identify appropriate strategies to enhance the benefits of events to small business.

■ Employment *creation*

By stimulating activity in the economy, expenditure on events can have a positive effect on employment. Employment multipliers measure how many full-time-equivalent job opportunities are supported in the community as a result of visitor expenditure. However, as Faulkner (1993) and others point out, it is easy to overestimate the number of jobs created by major events in the short term. Because the demand for additional services is short lived, employers tend to meet this demand by greater utilisation of their existing staff rather than by employing new staff members. Existing employees may be released from other duties to accommodate the temporary demand, or may be requested to work overtime.

Studies by Arnold and Bishop and Hatch (cited in Crompton & McKay 1994), examined employment adjustments as a result of the Adelaide Grand Prix by interviewing transportation and restaurant managers. They found that companies in both types of businesses met the demand for increased labour by increasing the hours of existing employees. There were virtually no new permanent jobs generated in the transport area as a result of the Grand Prix, and some restaurants reported that they hired casual workers to meet requirements.

A study of the 1989 Australian Motorcycle Grand Prix in Victoria (National Institute of Economic and Industry Research 1989) estimated the total Victorian employment increase attributable to the Grand Prix to be 50 positions in annual equivalent terms. This would translate to several hundred over the short duration of the event, allowing for increased overtime.

A survey of business generated by the Rugby World Cup in Wales in 1999 estimated that around 2000 people were employed on a temporary or part-time basis during the event, and that the tournament generated increased working hours for 4000 positions (Anon. 2000).

THE ECONOMIC IMPACTS OF THE SYDNEY OLYMPIC GAMES

A study of the Sydney Olympic Games for the New South Wales Government (New South Wales Treasury and the Centre for Regional Economic Analysis at the University of Tasmania 1997) looked at their predicted impacts in terms of annual impacts during each of the three phases of the Games:

- the pre-Games (preparation/construction) phase, 1994–95 to 1999–2000
- the Games year, 2000–01
- the post-Games phase, 2001–02 to 2005–06.

Acknowledging a degree of uncertainty surrounding the estimation of direct impacts, a range of scenarios was presented. The central scenario projected an average annual impact on the New South Wales gross State product (GSP) of more than $0.75 billion (or more than half a percentage point) in the construction phase, $1.7 billion in the Games year, and almost 100 000 full-time-equivalent annual jobs over the 12-year period (see table 4.1 on the opposite page).

■ Table 4.1 *Economy-wide impact of the Sydney Olympics — central scenario,*
annual average by period

		GROSS DOMESTIC PRODUCT (1995–96 $ MILLION)	REAL HOUSEHOLD CONSUMPTION (1995–96 $ MILLION)	EMPLOYMENT ('000 ANNUAL JOBS)
Pre-Games, 1994–95/99–00	New South Wales	750	350	10.1
	Australia	775	275	11.1
Games year, 2000–01	New South Wales	1700	350	24.0
	Australia	1550	525	29.4
Post-Games, 01–02/05–06	New South Wales	400	375	3.0
	Australia	425	650	0.4

All values have been rounded to the nearest $25 million.

(**Source:** *NSW Treasury and the Centre for Regional Economic Analysis,*
University of Tasmania 1997)

The Games were expected to increase inbound tourism to Australia, with the number of extra international tourists expected to reach a peak of almost 340 000 in 2001 before gradually returning to the non-Olympic underlying trend. The study assumed a small increase in labour productivity as a consequence of the experience gained from running the Games, and some increase in Australian exports as a consequence of the Olympics exposure. However, the study concluded that, while the size of the direct impacts of the Games would be of some significance, they would be of less importance than the macroeconomic environment in which the Games took place.

During the Games, commentators resorted to graphic devices to illustrate the sheer magnitude of their impact. A Channel 7 news broadcast on the opening day of the Games (Channel 7 2000) compared it to the impact of staging 35 Grand Prix's simultaneously on each of the 16 days of the Games. Jamal (2000) described the area in and around the central business district being cleared of rubbish as part of a round-the-clock clean-up operation as the equivalent of 600 football fields. Sheehan (2000) described the size of the International Broadcast Centre and the spaces set aside for the media at the competition venues (around 120 000 square metres) as the equivalent of the Empire State Building full of media personnel — about 21 000 of them — writing and broadcasting about the Olympics and Australia.

The scale and profile of the summer Olympic Games provide a unique opportunity to study and assess the impacts of a mega-event. The evaluation of the Sydney Olympics is likely to have far reaching effects on future government strategies for the use of events as catalysts for economic development. A range of studies were conducted on the Games, including a

Sydney 2000 Olympic Impacts Study by the Cooperative Research Centre for Sustainable Tourism (Faulkner, Spurr, Chalip & Brown 2000). This study aimed to examine the impact of the Games on Australia's international tourism market performance, and the range and effectiveness of leveraging strategies employed to influence the competitiveness of Australian destinations. The results of this and other studies of the Games should improve our understanding of the impacts of major events, and how best to leverage them to maximise their tourism and economic benefits.

As this book went to press, final reports on the economic impacts of the Games were not yet available. However, the general consensus of preliminary reports and media coverage was not only that the Games had paid their way and would reap considerable tourism and trade benefits into the future, but that they had also had a considerable effect on the pride and psyche of the nation. New South Wales Premier Bob Carr probably summed up the popular opinion when he said (Carr 2000):

■ It's happened in a way I couldn't have expected. I thought: yes, challenging sporting festival with great indications for tourism. It's proved much more than that . . . This has been something larger and more profound. I'm not sure precisely what. ■

PREDICTIVE MODELS FOR FORECASTING THE IMPACTS OF EVENTS

It is expensive and time consuming for governments to conduct detailed economic impact studies of all events. For this reason, various researchers have attempted to construct predictive models based on comparisons with accumulated data from previous similar events, in order to provide simpler means of forecasting event impacts.

This task was first attempted in Australia in a study undertaken for the Commonwealth Government (Mules et al., cited in Mules & McDonald 1994) that attempted to establish predictive equations that could forecast the number of international spectators at future sporting events. Although difficulties were experienced in obtaining sufficient data, the study found a relationship between the number of participants from a particular country and the number of spectators from that country, thus concluding that the nature of the event and the number of participating competitors are important factors in forecasting. For larger events, the study concluded that there were too many variables to permit any general principles, and that such events therefore need to be analysed on their own merits.

In 1998, Tourism New South Wales commissioned the development of a framework for assessing the economic impact of events that would enable it to discern trends and project the likely impacts of events by type and by location (Dwyer, Mellor, Mistilis & Mules 2000). The framework traces the inscope expenditure (i.e. 'new money' attracted from outside the event area) by visitors, accompanying persons, organisers, participants, sponsors and media. It also includes a system of weightings for benefits such as

- community development
- civic pride
- long-term promotion

and for negative impacts such as

- disruption of resident lifestyles
- traffic congestion
- noise
- vandalism
- resident exodus
- the interruption of normal business.

Raw data for events are entered into the framework using a template fact sheet under the direction of the program. A computerised forecasting model, based on the framework, facilitates the generation of fact sheets and forecasting reports. Although currently at a basic stage, the designers of the framework believe that it will increase effectiveness as more data are gathered and fed into the system.

To increase the effectiveness of the framework as an instrument of forecasting event impacts, the authors collated data from a wide range of published event impact studies in Australia (see table 4.2 on the following page). They conclude from the examination of this data that:

> ■ Overall it appears that car/motor and sporting events are more uniform in injected expenditure and degree of economic impact and are more likely to have greater economic impacts than arts/cultural events. In contrast, arts/cultural events range in degree of economic impacts, from minimal to large. The same range of economic impact was seen in both city and regional located events.
>
> Whilst the data were incomplete and inconsistent and cannot be relied on absolutely, some trends are apparent. For example, both city and regional events range in degree of economic impact. Therefore the choice of one or another type of locality will not in itself predict the size of economic impact. On the other hand, it appears that type of event is a greater predictor of large economic impact, namely in the car/motor and sport categories. ■

Given the range and complexity of factors, it seems that predicting the economic impacts of events is at best an imperfect science. Even more so is the development of effective strategies for improving event outcomes. However, as the number of studies grows and the available bank of data increases, so does our understanding of the discipline and our confidence in its ability to predict and influence event outcomes.

Table 4.2 Estimates of numbers and expenditure associated with selected events in Australia (1998 values)

EVENT	NUMBER OF INSCOPE VISITORS			EXPENDITURE PER DAY		AVERAGE LENGTH OF STAY IN STATE		INSCOPE EXP. VISITORS	INSCOPE EXP. SPONSORS	TOTAL INSCOPE EXP.	ECONOMIC IMPACTS ON STATE		
	I'STATE	O'SEAS	TOTAL	I'STATE	O'SEAS	I'STATE	O'SEAS				OUTPUT	VALUE ADDED	EMPLOY-MENT
CAR/MOTOR													
Formula One													
1985	17 920	1 600	19 520	90	127	5	9.9	10.1	19.7	29.8	81.5	28.60	
1988	22 280	3 400	25 680	98	66	5.7	11.7	15.1	17.26	32.4		31.6	
1992	16 082	2 695	18 777	159	160	5.6	10.6	18.89	14.50	33.4		42.5	
1996	11 738	5 176	16 916	242	379	4.8	5.6	24.61	9.3	33.9		98.6	96
Average	17 005	3 218	20 223	147	183	5.3	9.5	18.85	15.20	34.00		50.3	2270
Motorcycle Grand Prix													
1989	38 000	2 505	40 500	110	208	6.2	11.1	31.7	7.9	39.6			
1991	16 720	1 520	18 240	134	193	6.8	10.8	18.4	9.7	28.1		54.2	
Average	27 360	2 010	29 370	122	201	6.5	11.0	25.8	8.4	34.2			
Indycars													
1994	12 939	4 838	17 777	204	185	5.4	15.9	28.5	15.8	44.3			
1995	9 727	4 086	13 813	185	201	6.5	11.4	21.1	10.4	31.5			
1991	16 720	1 520	18 240	134	193	6.8	10.8	18.4	9.7	28.1			
Average	12 266	4 430	16 696	145	185	6.5	13.8	22.9	11.4	34.3			
Drag racing													
1998	3 151	498	3 649	N/A	N/A	N/A	N/A	0.943	0.69	1.633	N/A	1.4 (local)	43 jobs (local)
OTHER SPORT (OTHER THAN CAR/MOTOR)													
World Cup Athletics													
	5005	1088	6093	189	119	4.9	8.0	4.6	8.5	14.2	N/A	39.6	332
World Masters Games													
	11 361	3476	14 837	100	282	12.7	14.9	41.6	2.4	44.0	N/A	54.8	580
Australian Masters Games													
1987	1 385	317	1 702	104									
1989	2 828	199	3 027										
1993	970	1 074	2 044										
1995	4 169	901	5 070										

ART/MUSIC/CULTURE/LIFESTYLE

EVENT	NUMBER OF INSCOPE VISITORS			EXPENDITURE PER DAY		AVERAGE LENGTH OF STAY IN STATE		INSCOPE EXP. VISITORS	INSCOPE EXP. SPONSORS	TOTAL INSCOPE EXP.	ECONOMIC IMPACTS ON STATE		
	I'STATE	O'SEAS	TOTAL	I'STATE	O'SEAS	I'STATE	O'SEAS				OUTPUT	VALUE ADDED	EMPLOYMENT
Gay & Lesbian Mardi Gras													
1993	3 511	1 810	5 321	150	307	5.6	11.8	9.55	N/A	9.6		21.3	730
1998	4 845	3 633	8 478	435	347	4.7	12.1	25.2	N/A	25.2		41.1	N/A
Average	4 178	2 722	6 900	293	327	5.0	12.0	18.9	N/A	18.9			
Expo													
1998	894 000	170 000	1 064 000	168	141	10.1	14.1	1858	N/A	1858	2006	560	19 308
Adelaide Festival													
1990		N/A	N/A	N/A	N/A	N/A	N/A	N/A	N/A	N/A	N/A	11.0	N/A
1996	4 730	450	5 180	160	140	7.0	10.8	6.0	3.4	9.4		132	270

(**Source:** *Dwyer, Mellor, Mistilis & Mules 2000*)

Since the 1980s, governments in Australia have become increasingly aware of the potential tourism and economic benefits of events, and bid competitively for the right to host and stage them. The cost of events and the level of competitiveness between rival governments have placed great importance on the accurate assessment of their economic impacts. All governments need to be aware of the impacts of events, whether their perspective be the local, state or national economy.

Assessment of the economic impact of events is based on identifying their expenditure and measuring its impact on the economy using one of a number of economic models. These models vary in their levels of cost and complexity, but all depend on the accurate assessment of the event expenditure. Issues such as switching, leakage and hidden costs must be taken into account so that an accurate picture of event expenditure is formed. Governments must consider the opportunity costs of supporting events as opposed to other avenues of investment. They must also consider the wider impacts of events, such as the image enhancement of tourism destinations, the promotion of business opportunities, and the generation of employment. The Sydney Olympic Games provide an opportunity to examine the economic benefits of this mega-event on the Australian economy. Due to the cost of undertaking individual economic impact studies, researchers have attempted to devise predictive models based on the accumulated data of previous events. One such model developed for Tourism New South Wales is designed to discern trends and predict the likely impacts of events by type and by location. As the amount of data on events expand, such models are likely to become increasingly effective, and our confidence in predicting and influencing the outcomes of events is likely to improve.

Questions

1. List and describe what you consider to be the main reasons why governments support events.

2. Briefly describe the benefits that tourism and businesses derive from events.

3. Is there a government organisation that bids for and assists events in your state or region? If so, what criteria does it use to fund events, and how does it measure event outcomes/benefits?

4. Identify three major events that have been staged in your area or state that have been subjected to economic impact assessments. Compare the methodologies and findings of these assessments, and contrast the economic outcomes of the events.

5 Choose one of the events identified in question 4, and see if you can answer the following questions by a careful study of the economic impact assessment of the event:

- What was the point of view of the assessment (local, regional, State or national)?
- What switching of visits/expenditure can you identify in relation to the event?
- What additional employment was generated by the event?
- What are some of the strategies that were used to enhance the outcomes of the event?
- Can you suggest additional strategies that might have been used, or that might be used in the future, to improve the outcomes of the event?

Wagner's Ring Cycle:
an insight into an international high quality special event

The internationally acknowledged major work of the full cycle of Wagner's four operas *Der Ring des Nibelungen* (also called the 'Ring Cycle') was staged in Adelaide in late 1998. There were three complete cycles performed and each cycle was completed in a seven- or eight-day period. It was the first complete performance of this opera series in Australia.

A notable characteristic of this event, and one which makes it considerably significant as a case study of the economic importance of special events, is that the *expressed* strategy in staging the event was to attract as large an audience as possible from interstate and overseas. Members of this audience were also expected to be generally higher spenders than normal visitors. For most events, local attendees make up most of an audience and are the basis for the overall financial success of the event.

Because of this strategy the event was:
• staged very much as an economic event
• very entrepreneurial; that is, there was a higher risk attached to its success than most special events. Although international experience suggested a fairly strong market, it was untested in the Australian context.

The detailed pre-event economic impact study which was prepared to aid the final decision about staging the event was evidence of this strategy. The pre-event analysis provided three economic impact scenarios. Scenario 1, or the base scenario, was based on visitor spending equivalent to the average tourist expenditure in South Australia and was seen by the arts industry to be somewhat conservative, while Scenario 2 (based on average expenditure by visitors to the Adelaide Festival of Arts) and possibly Scenario 3 (based on an even higher average level of expenditure) were viewed as more likely.

	VISITOR EXPENDITURE	TOTAL VALUE ADDED IMPACT
Scenario 1	$4.6 million	$6.9 million
Scenario 2	$6.9 million	$9.1 million
Scenario 3	$12.4 million	$13.7 million

An audience survey, plus surveys of visiting performers and support staff, together with the financial operating detail, provided data to measure the economic impact in an ex-post study. The audience survey also included a range of questions designed to obtain information to assist planning for future events. There were 985 audience survey responses which represented an overall response rate of 60 per cent with the out-of-state response rate being 65 per cent.

The event attracted almost 3600 event-specific visitors to South Australia, including about 100 performers and support staff.

The event itself was an enormous undertaking on a relatively shoe-string budget. To minimise both costs and risks it was based on a minimalist production staged previously in Paris and used the same sets, costumes and French production team. The aim had been to trial this production and, if a success, it would lead to a more ambitious production in the future. In fact, the audience surveys indicated that the minimalist production format was a major area of criticism while acclaim for the mainly Australian performers, including orchestra, was very strong.

The target audience was considerably narrower than a normal special event, not only because its appeal was to a small section of the global population, but also because the cost of participation was quite high. Tickets for attendance at the full cycle ranged from $450 to $950 with the majority of the seats being in the more expensive category. Most of the audience attended a complete cycle. Added to the ticket cost was the expenditure on food, drink and accommodation for periods which averaged 8.6 days in South Australia for interstate visitors and 10.7 days for international visitors plus the cost of transport to Adelaide (mainly by air).

Most of the interstate audience came from Sydney (42 per cent) and Melbourne (23 per cent) while the main country of origin of international visitors was New Zealand (51 per cent), USA (22 per cent) and UK (15 per cent). Over 80 per cent of all visitors were aged 50 or more.

Because of the targeted audience, there was avid interest in all things Wagnerian and, specifically, the Ring Cycle. Consequently, a number of ancillary events were presented in Adelaide during the opera season. This was part of the economic strategy to increase the visitor expenditure. Prices for these ancillary events were generally not cheap. Among the lower cost options for example, the cost of the series of pre-performance lectures was $60. However, some exhibitions were free.

The ancillary events included:
- pre-performance lectures
- an exhibition of set designs, costumes, lithographs and photographs
- 'The Ring Around the World in Posters'
- 'King Ludwig and Wagner' (photographic exhibition)
- classic Wagner on screen (rare screening of three movies related to The Ring)
- 'Sunday Afternoon with Richard Wagner' (a one-act play)
- a three-day international symposium on a variety of topics related to Wagner
- various other exhibitions and events, including Wagner Parties, Friends of the Opera Luncheon, and tours.

Almost three-quarters of the visitors attended an ancillary event, compared to less than half of the local audience. The estimated expenditure of these event specific visitors on the ancillary events was almost $0.5 million, which indicates their importance in the total experience of the main event. By comparison, the same group spent just over $0.2 million on tours and day trips while in South Australia.

Two-thirds of the overseas visitors participated in an organised day or half-day tour, compared to 26 per cent of interstate residents.

Of the visitors, 80 per cent visited some region of South Australia during their stay (not necessarily on organised trips), although only 20 per cent actually stayed overnight outside of Adelaide.

Expenditure on Ring Cycle tickets by out-of-State visitors was $2.55 million. In addition there was ticket expenditure of $0.25 million from local residents who said they would have travelled outside the State to holiday had 'The Ring' not been performed in Adelaide. Given the significant expenditure involved in attending the performance and the high level of satisfaction placed on actually attending such a production, it is quite valid to allow that the attendance of these people was a substitute for a trip outside the State and hence their related expenditure was retained in, rather than lost to, the State.

The total non-ticket expenditure of event specific visitors and performers amounted to $6.6 million in South Australia. Total operating or staging expenditure was $7.8 million (with about half being spent within the State) and approximately 43 per cent of the total was financed from external sources such as visitor ticket revenue and sponsorships and grants from interstate or overseas. Expenditure supported by funds provided from State Government grants, local ticket expenditure and local sponsors is not 'new' expenditure within the State but merely 'switched' from other options.

Standard input–output methodology was used to estimate the economic impact of staging the event, with an indication of a net addition to GSP of around $10 million and the creation of the equivalent of 200 full-time jobs sustained over one year.

Successful events may well lead to longer term benefits, especially if the event is closely allied with tourism marketing. However, the value of these longer-term benefits are difficult to quantify and, while important, were not assessed in this study.

Other recent cultural and special events in South Australia have resulted in estimated average per-visitor contributions to GSP ranging from $1470 to $1650. By contrast the higher per-visitor contribution of $2780 by 'The Ring' visitors reflects the nature of the event.

The high return achieved by 'The Ring', which was underwritten by the State Government only to the extent of $2.7 million, reflects several factors, namely the high ticket prices which attracted a generally high spending audience, the high percentage of the audience who visited from outside the State, the length of each cycle which saw patrons spend longer in South Australia and undertake more activities than is the norm for many other special events and the larger than average length of stay by these visitors, and the fact that their level of spending was higher than that of the average visitor.

The interstate and overseas visitors constituted approximately 59 per cent of ticket sales, which is a much higher percentage than that achieved by other special events.

The estimated actual economic impact of 'The Ring' is most closely consistent with the pre-event Scenario 2 outcome, but the estimated average length of stay by interstate and overseas visitors was somewhat shorter than the pre-event estimate. That is, they stayed for shorter periods but spent more per day during that period.

Important lessons can be learned from a comparison of the assumptions underlying the pre-event evaluation and the actual outcome — lessons which will be valuable in planning future events. Two main reasons can be identified as to why the high Scenario 3 economic impact was not achieved.

First, interstate and international visitors for 'The Ring' did not, on average, stay as long in the State as the more optimistic pre-event scenario assumed. The results of the audience survey indicates that the average length of stay for international visitors was 10.3 nights while for the most optimistic scenario it was 15. For interstate visitors it was 8.5 nights compared to the pre-event estimate of 10.

Clearly, if a bigger economic impact is sought from similar future productions, then appropriate efforts will need to be made to encourage interstate and overseas visitors to spend longer in South Australia. Such efforts would not be futile because many respondents to the survey indicated dissatisfaction with the inflexibility of the travel packages offered for 'The Ring'. It is also not clear that the packages included adequate opportunities to incorporate visits to other regions of the State, or that such options were adequately promoted. Some reported that they had only been able to purchase tickets as part of a complete package including travel, which limited their scope to make their own arrangements. The very small number of international and interstate visitors who spent overnight stays in regions of South Australia, other than Adelaide, during their visit tends to further indicate that these opportunities were not adequately canvassed.

The second reason why the high economic impact scenario was not achieved was because the average spending of visitors was less than assumed for that scenario. Actual average daily non-ticket expenditure was $183 for international visitors where the high scenario estimate was $333, and $165 for interstate visitors compared with the scenario estimate of $183. Although this world-class event was expensive in terms of ticket prices and the cost of getting to Adelaide, many visitors were still budget conscious and chose cheaper accommodation and tried to limit their daily expenditure.

However, the event was still extremely successful, both artistically and from an economic viewpoint. The pre-event analysis assumed 2000 interstate visitors and 840 overseas visitors but the event analysis indicated 2760 interstate visitors and 730 overseas visitors — well above total expectations.

The economic potential of high quality events such as 'The Ring' cannot be ignored. Opportunities to increase the potential appeal of such events might include:
- better links between attending the event and opportunities to enjoy South Australia, especially its wine and food and the State's regions — better, more flexible packages would assist

- expanding the opportunity to participate in high quality ancillary events
- improved marketing of the event with readily available information sources for the event and about South Australia — package providers need to be well informed on touring opportunities.

Janine Molloy
Research Economist
South Australian Centre for Economic Studies, Adelaide University

This case study is based on research undertaken for the South Australian Tourism Commission and Arts SA by the South Australian Centre for Economic Studies in association with Richard Trembath Research and Robyn Kunko Market Research: *Wagner's Ring Cycle, Adelaide, 1998: A Study of the Economic Impact of the Event and Associated Issues* (May 1999).

Questions

1 How could a change in the mix of interstate and international visitors improve the economic outcomes of an event such as this? Discuss options and their implications.

2 What specific strategies could be implemented to encourage out of state visitors to spend more during their stay? List a range of options and discuss which strategies would be best in terms of ease of implementation and likelihood of success.

3 How important is adequate information in terms of marketing such an event on the international market?

4 How important is flexibility within the packages provided in terms of increasing average length of stay and hence the economic impact? Discuss the various ways such flexibility could be incorporated into packages.

REFERENCES

Anon. 2000, *Rugby World Cup 1999 Economic Impact Evaluation: Summary Report*, Segal Qunice Wicksteed Limited and System Three, Edinburgh.

Bracks, S. 2000, *Government Unveils New Major Events Strategy*, http// www.dpc.vic.gov.au (accessed 11 September 2000).

Burgan, B. & Mules, T. 2000, 'Event analysis — understanding the divide between cost benefit and economic impact assessment', in *Events Beyond 2000: Setting the Agenda — Event Evaluation, Research and Education Conference Proceedings*, eds J. Allen, R. Harris, L. K. Jago & A. J. Veal, Australian Centre for Event Management, University of Technology, Sydney.

Burns, J. P. A. & Mules, T. J. 1989, 'An economic evaluation of the Adelaide Grand Prix', in *The Planning and Evaluation of Hallmark Events*, eds G. J. Syme, B. J. Shaw, M. D. Fenton & W. S. Mueller, Avebury, Aldershot, England.

Carr, R. 2000, 'This is history, it's profound, says Premier', *Sydney Morning Herald*, 2 October 2000, p. 13.

Channel 7, 2000, News Broadcast, 16 September 2000.

Crompton, J. L. & McKay, S. L. 1994, 'Measuring the impact of festivals and events: some myths, misapplications and ethical dilemmas', *Festival Management and Event Tourism*, vol. 2, no. 1, pp. 33–43.

Dwyer, L., Mellor, R. Mistilis, N. & Mules, T. 2000, 'A framework for evaluating and forecasting the impacts of special events', in *Events Beyond 2000: Setting the Agenda — Event Evaluation, Research and Education Conference Proceedings*, eds J. Allen, R. Harris, L. K. Jago & A. J. Veal, Australian Centre for Event Management, University of Technology, Sydney.

EventsCorp Western Australia 2000, www.events.tourism.wa.gov.au (accessed 21 September 2000).

Faulkner, B. 1993, *Evaluating the Tourism Impact of Hallmark Events*, Occasional Paper No. 16, Bureau of Tourism Research, Canberra.

Faulkner, B., Chalip, L., Spurr, R. & Brown, G. 2000, 'Sydney 2000 Olympics tourism impacts study', in *Events Beyond 2000: Setting the Agenda — Event Evaluation, Research and Education Conference Proceedings*, eds J. Allen, R. Harris, L. K. Jago & A. J. Veal, Australian Centre for Event Management, University of Technology, Sydney.

Humphries, D. 2000, 'Benefit to economy is unseen', *Sydney Morning Herald*, 23 August 2000, p. 8.

Hunn, C. & Mangan, J. 1999, 'Estimating the economic impact of tourism at the local, regional, State or Territorial level, including consideration of the multiplier effect', in *Valuing Tourism: Methods and Techniques*, eds K. Corcoran, A. Allcock, T. Frost & L. Johnson, Bureau of Tourism Research, Canberra.

Jamal, N. 2000, 'Cleaners sweep 600 footy fields of rubbish a day', *Sydney Morning Herald*, 21 September 2000.

Marsh, I. & Levy, S. 1998, *Sydney Gay and Lesbian Mardi Gras: Economic Impact Statement 1998*, Sydney Gay and Lesbian Mardi Gras Ltd, Sydney.

Mules, T. 1998, 'Events tourism and economic development in Australia', in *Managing Tourism in Cities*, eds D. Tyler, Y. Guerrier & M. Robertson, John Wiley & Sons, New York.

Mules, T. 1999, 'Estimating the economic impact of an event on a local government area, region, State or Territory', in *Valuing Tourism: Methods and Techniques*, eds K. Corcoran, A.Allcock, T. Frost & L. Johnson, Bureau of Tourism Research, Canberra.

Mules, T. & McDonald, S. 1994, 'The economic impact of special events: the use of forecasts', *Festival Management and Event Tourism*, vol. 2, no. 1, pp. 45–53.

Muthaly, S. K., Ratnatunga, J. Roberts, G. B. & Roberts, C. D. 2000, 'An event-based entrepreneurship case study of futuristic strategies for Sydney 2000 Olympics', in eds J. Allen, R. Harris, L. K. Jago & A. J. Veal, *Events Beyond 2000: Setting the Agenda — Event Evaluation, Research and Education Conference Proceedings*, Australian Centre for Event Management, University of Technology, Sydney.

National Institute of Economic and Industry Research 1989, *The Economic Impact and Tourism Value of the 1989 Australian Motorcycle Grand Prix on Phillip Island*, a report for the Department of Sport and Recreation and the Victorian Tourism Commission prepared by the National Institute of Economic and Industry Research, Melbourne.

Newman, P. W. G. 1989, 'The impact of the America's Cup on Fremantle — an insider's view', in *The Planning and Evaluation of Hallmark Events*, eds G. J. Syme, B. J. Shaw, D. M. Fenton & W. S. Mueller, Avebury, Aldershot, England.

NSW Treasury and the Centre for Regional Economic Analysis, University of Tasmania 1997, *The Economic Impact of the Sydney Olympic Games*, NSW Treasury, Sydney.

Sheehan, P. 2000, 'Dining out on a feast of flattery', *Sydney Morning Herald*, 18 September 2000, p. 23.

PART 2 EVENT STRATEGY

Detailed planning, inspirational leadership, sound human resource management and dynamic marketing are all key elements of successful event management. This part of the book examines the planning function in some detail, and looks at the formation, leadership and training of event teams. This section looks also at the event marketing process, and details strategic methods that event managers can employ to market their events competitively.

The planning
function

LEARNING OBJECTIVES

After studying this chapter, you should be able to:

- discuss the significance of the planning process in achieving desired event outcomes
- discuss the strategic planning process as it applies to events
- describe selected organisational structures evident in the events area.

$\mathcal{I}$NTRODUCTION

This chapter overviews the concept of planning as it applies to the conduct of events. It begins by discussing the centrality of planning to the overall success of an event and then moves on to describe the strategic event planning process. This process is identified as comprising a number of sequential and inter-related steps, each of which is briefly described here. Additionally, this chapter examines the range of organisational structures from which an event manager must select in order to support and implement their planning efforts.

$\mathcal{W}$HAT IS PLANNING?

In its simplest form, the planning process consists of establishing where an organisation is at present, where it is best advised to go in the future, and the strategies or tactics needed to achieve that position. In other words, the planning process is concerned with ends and the means to achieve those ends.

Perhaps the value of planning is best summed up by the words of the famous American General, Douglas MacArthur, who observed that: 'Without a plan you're just a tourist'. MacArthur's comments allude to the value of planning in focusing an organisation (such as an event organising committee) on particular objectives and in the creation of defined pathways by which these objectives can be achieved. Central to the establishment of such pathways is an understanding of internal (e.g. available resources) and external (e.g. current economic conditions) factors that will condition any decisions that are made. For example, it would probably be unrealistic to set an objective of increasing attendance at an international conference for executives from the pharmaceutical industry, if that industry was experiencing a severe global downturn in the demand for its products.

To engage productively in the planning process an event manager needs to keep in mind a range of matters. Central amongst these are the need to monitor and evaluate progress; coordinate decisions in all areas so that event objectives are progressed; and communicate with, inspire and motivate those responsible for carrying out the various elements of the plan. These matters are taken up in later chapters.

While acknowledging the power of planning as a management tool it should also be noted that actually engaging in it involves some measure of discipline on behalf of the event manager. As Sir John Harvey-Jones, a past chairman of ICI in the United Kingdom, notes:

> ■ Planning is an unnatural process: it is much more fun to do nothing. The nicest thing about not planning is that failure comes as a complete surprise, rather than being preceded by a period of worry and depression. ■

Event managers also need to keep in mind that plans, as Hannagan (1998) and Thompson (1997) note, need to be adapted to changing circumstances. Additionally they need to be conscious of not falling foul of planning 'pitfalls'.

These include overplanning and becoming obsessed with detail as opposed to overall strategic considerations; viewing plans as one-off exercises rather then active documents to be regularly consulted and adapted; and seeing plans as conclusive rather than directional in nature (Johnson & Scholes 1999).

PLANNING FOR EVENTS

Where does the event planning process begin? The answer to this question depends on whether the event is being conducted for the first time or if it is a pre-existing event. In the case of a new event, the event manager may be required to first work through the broad concept of the event with key stakeholders and then undertake a feasibility study. If this study deems that the event is likely to meet certain key criteria (such as profitability), they would then move to develop plans for its creation and delivery. In instances where an event is pre-existing and open to the bidding process (e.g. a conference or sporting event), a decision needs to be made initially as to whether or not (after a preliminary investigation) the event might be actively sought via the preparation of a bid document. If the answer is 'yes', a more detailed feasibility study might be conducted to identify such things as the costs and benefits associated with hosting it before preparing a formal bid. If a bid is prepared and it is successful, then detailed event planning would commence. The process associated with event planning in the context of new events and those attracted through the bidding process is shown in figure 5.1.

■ **Figure 5.1**
The event planning process

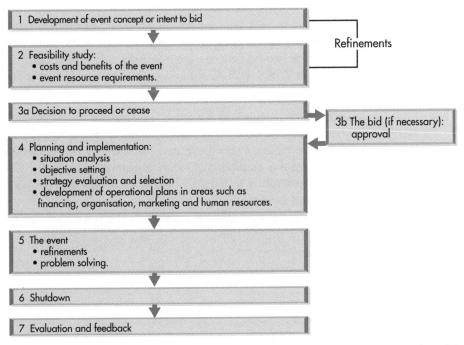

*(**Source:** after Getz 1997, p. 76)*

It should also be noted that event managers often find themselves in situations where they are planning for recurring events such as annual festivals. In this situation steps 1 to 4 in figure 5.1 are not relevant. The process in this instance begins with an appraisal of the current situation faced by the event and its past plans. This process is likely to result in changes to existing objectives and/or strategies, and the development of revised/new plans in areas such as marketing, human resources and finance.

EVENT PROFILE
The New South Wales Centenary of Federation Committee

To celebrate the centenary of Federation, the Federal Government formed a national council. Every state and territory established a centenary of Federation committee to coordinate planning for a year-long, nationwide program of celebrations and commemorations.

Research and proposal
In February 1996, the Australia Day Council of New South Wales (ADCNSW) wrote to the Premier offering its expertise to the New South Wales Government in developing and implementing a program of activities to mark the centenary of Federation in 2001. The government responded by asking the ADCNSW to develop a full proposal and provided a grant for the necessary research required.

Over four months, the ADCNSW undertook 50 interviews with leaders in the community to seek their advice on the most appropriate way to celebrate the anniversary of the creation of the Commonwealth. In addition, research was conducted into the Federation events held in 1901 through the State Library of New South Wales, Film Australia and the National Film and Sound Archive.

Committee structure
The ADCNSW proposal to the State Government recommended that a state committee be created to oversee planning and the formation of advisory committees to focus on specific areas of operation. This model was based on the success of the existing ADCNSW structure. Importantly, it was to be a separate organisation to the ADCNSW. All appointees would be voluntary and approved by the Premier.

The seven advisory committees established covered
• finance and sponsorship
• education, history and civics
• arts and events
• parade
• marketing and communications
• ceremonies
• community relations.

These advisory committees were made up of leaders in a broad range of related fields, who came together in a voluntary capacity to ensure that the New South Wales Centenary of Federation Committee (NSWCOFC) had appropriate knowledge and experience to call on when planning the event.

Determination of mission, aims and objectives
The proposal to the government included the suggested aims and objectives of the NSWCOFC. One of the clearest outcomes of the research and interview process was that the program for the centenary of Federation needed to be both a celebration of success and a commemoration of past challenges and mistakes. The aims and objectives were discussed and ratified by the NSWCOFC at its second meeting. The key aims were:
- provide genuine and extensive opportunities for the involvement of all the people of New South Wales, and in particular, for regional communities
- create inclusive, visionary and community driven celebrations that are of lasting significance for future generations
- encourage interest in the community in the processes that led to the creation of the Commonwealth and what it has meant to the Australian nation
- implement programs, events, celebrations, legacies and educational initiatives for the community that have enduring and worthwhile results and benefits
- work together with indigenous and ethnic community and other community organisations and networks throughout New South Wales.

Each advisory committee also used these goals as a basis for establishing their own goals, programs and activities.

Federation Day
A clear example of how the structure of the organisation was critical to the success of one of the many events it conducted was Federation Day, 1 January 2001.

The three events on this day — the commemoration, parade and centennial ceremony — were all produced by the NSWCOFC. They attracted crowds of more than 580 000 people in Sydney, as well as a national television audience of over one million viewers.

While all parts of the organisation were involved in one way or another with these events, four advisory committees had the most significant roles. They were the ceremonies, parade, marketing and communications, and finance and sponsorship committees. These advisory committees determined strategies, made event programming decisions, were responsible for ongoing monitoring of activities against objectives, and provided feedback and advice to their relevant staff teams. Major decisions and recommendations were carried forward by the chair-people of these committees to the NSWCOFC for approval.

Given the large scale of events on this day, the NSWCOFC had to monitor logistics and bring together teams on issues related to event development, such as traffic management plans and the preparation of various council approval applications. Representatives from all teams met monthly to discuss key issues, document overall strategies and ensure that team meetings with outside agencies, such as the New South Wales Police and the Roads and Traffic Authority, were coordinated across the organisation. In addition, the NSWCOFC actively participated in the ongoing government coordination process for all agencies involved in major events.

Cross-project teams were established to manage the planning of common activities, such as uniforms, accreditation, volunteers, and two-way communication systems and protocols. As part of the risk management strategy, all managers held meetings dedicated solely to Federation Day during the six weeks prior to 1 January 2001.

Source: *Michelle Morgan, Marketing and Communications Manager, ADCNSW.*

ELEMENTS OF THE EVENT PLANNING PROCESS

■ Concept or *intent to bid*

In the context of new events this stage involves making decisions concerning such matters as the type/form of the event (e.g. festival, parade), duration, location/venue, timing, and key program elements that will serve to make the event unique or special. Once the event concept is sufficiently developed it can then be subjected to more detailed analysis. (*Note*: Detailed discussion of developing event concepts can be found in chapter 3.) In instances where bidding is involved, events for which bids can be made need first to be identified. Once this is done a preliminary assessment can be made as to their 'fit' with the capabilities of the event organising body and the hosting destination. Events deemed as worth further investigation will then be the subject of more detailed scrutiny via a feasibility study.

■ Feasibility *study*

The event planner needs to establish the ability of the organisation they represent, and perhaps also the host area, to conduct the event, along with its costs and benefits, before deciding to proceed. The considerations that may be taken into account in conducting a feasibility study are many. These may include (depending on the event) likely budget requirements; managerial skill needs; venue capacities; host community and destination area impacts; availability of volunteers, sponsors and supporting services (e.g. equipment hire firms); projected visitation/attendance; infrastructure requirements; availability of public/private sector financial support; level of political support for the event; and the track record of the event in terms of matters such as profit. It should be noted that the level of detail and complexity associated with these studies will vary. An event such as the Olympic Games, for example, is likely to involve a more lengthy and detailed process than, say, a state sporting championship or an association conference.

■ Bid preparation: *approval*

This step is required in instances where it is decided to bid for an existing event based on the outcomes of a feasibility study. The bidding process involves a number of steps, specifically:
- identifying resources that can be employed to support the event (e.g. venues, government grants)
- developing a critical path for the preparation and presentation of a bid document to the 'owners' of the event
- development of an understanding of the organisation conducting the event and the exact nature of the event itself
- identifying the key elements of past successful bids
- preparation of a bid document.
  Only if a bid is successful is the next stage in the event planning process progressed to.

■ Decision to *proceed or cease*

In the case of new events the outcomes of the feasibility study will directly determine if and when the event will proceed.

■ Planning and *implementation*

The next part of this chapter examines this step in detail, and proposes a strategic event-planning process. This process is designed to deliver the event on time and in a way that meets predetermined objectives by way of the creation of an appropriate strategy and supporting operational plans. This aspect of the planning process also creates the need for monitoring and evaluation systems to ensure progress towards the event's objectives (see chapters 10 and 15). Additionally an appropriate organisational structure through which the event can be conducted is determined at this stage. Choices regarding these structures are discussed in the latter part of this chapter. A significant contextual element associated with this stage is the event budget, which, although discussed briefly later in this chapter, is examined in detail in chapter 10.

■ The *event*

Once an event is under way the monitoring and evaluation systems developed in the previous stage should provide feedback that can be used to refine/change aspects of the event as appropriate.

■ Event *shutdown*

As part of the planning process it is necessary to develop a plan to close the event down. This plan will involve the development of a time line and the allocation of responsibilities for such tasks as the breakdown and removal of site structures and the collection of equipment. This aspect of event planning is discussed in chapter 13.

■ Evaluation *and feedback*

As was noted previously, built into the various operational plans should be evaluation processes, the outcomes of which should find their way into a final report (see chapter 15). This report will generally deal with the various areas for which operational plans have been developed, and discuss these in the light of the objectives that were set for them. Additionally, this document should indicate the extent to which the event was successful in achieving its broader objectives. Problems and issues that arose should also be identified and, if the event is to be repeated, suggestions made as to how these might be addressed in the future. This information should then be incorporated into the planning process for the next event.

*E*VENTS AND THE STRATEGIC MANAGEMENT PROCESS

In the previous section planning was discussed from the perspective of a series of general steps through which the event manager progresses. This section expands on the planning and implementation component of this process from a strategic perspective.

The strategy process is about determining the current situation faced by an event (strategic awareness), the strategic options available to an event manager (strategic choices) and mechanisms for implementing and evaluating/monitoring chosen strategies (strategic implementation) (Thompson 1997, p. 51). The context in which this process takes place is that of the purpose/vision/mission of the event. In figure 5.2 the strategic planning process associated with events is outlined. Each of the elements of this process is discussed in turn in this section.

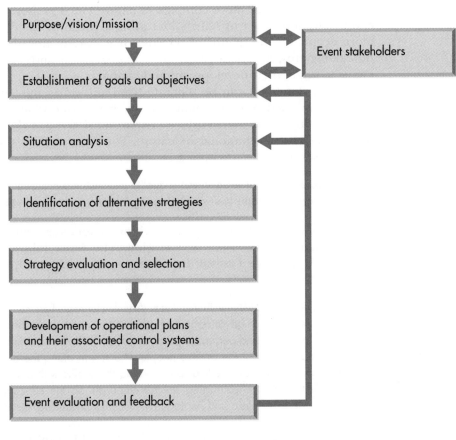

■ **Figure 5.2**
Strategic planning process for events

Purpose/vision/mission

Event stakeholders

Establishment of goals and objectives

Situation analysis

Identification of alternative strategies

Strategy evaluation and selection

Development of operational plans and their associated control systems

Event evaluation and feedback

*E*LEMENTS OF THE STRATEGIC EVENT PLANNING PROCESS

■ **Purpose, vision** *and mission statements*

At minimum a clear statement as to its purpose should underpin every event. This statement in turn will be conditioned by the needs of the various stakeholder groups with an interest in the event. Such groups may include client organisations, the local community, government at various levels, potential attendees and participants, sponsors and volunteers.

In the case of many events, particularly those of a corporate or public relations nature, a considered statement as to its purpose is all that is really required to provide sufficient direction and focus. An example of such a statement is that developed for Tourism Awareness Week 2000, conducted by Tourism Tasmania, which states that it is concerned with:

■ educating Tasmanians about the benefits of the tourism industry for their state economically and socially (www.tourismtasmania.com.au/org/community_aware/taw2000/openingdisplay.htm). ■

For events that are more complex in nature (such as most public events) and involve a number of stakeholder groups, it can be beneficial to reflect more deeply on the matter of purpose. It is evident that many events are now doing this, and as a result are creating vision and/or mission statements to guide their development and conduct.

A vision statement can be separate from an event's mission, or the two may be combined. Vision statements usually describe what the event seeks to become in the long-term future (Thompson 1997, p. 141). They are also often brief and motivational in nature. For example, the Oregon Shakespeare Festival's states its vision as:

■ to create theatre of extraordinary quality in which we proceed with daring to fulfil our artistic dreams (www.orshakes.org/about/mission.html). ■

Some events use more expansive vision statements, which are really a combination of both vision and mission. The Bunk Johnson/New Iberia Jazz, Arts & Heritage Festival, Louisiana, is one such example. Its vision is stated as:

■ The Bunk Johnson/New Iberia Jazz, Arts & Heritage Festival Inc. is a non-profit corporation for advancement of scholarly research, collection and preservation of the visual and performing arts, crafts, oral traditions, culinary practices, history and cultures of the diverse people who reside along the Bayou Teche in south Louisiana. We are dedicated to sharing these gifts with others through an annual festival and encouraging special emphasis on the education of young people in the arts, music and heritage (www.bunkjohnson.org/festival). ■

It should be noted that vision statements need not necessarily be written down, providing they are shared and understood by those involved with the event. It would be fair to say, for example, that while no formal vision statement existed at the time the Sydney Gay and Lesbian Mardi Gras began, those involved with it understood clearly that its long-term goal was about achieving equality and social acceptance.

A mission statement describes in the broadest terms the task that the event organisation has set for itself. If the event has also established a vision statement, then the mission needs to be viewed in terms of fulfilling this vision. Such statements, at their most advanced, seek to define an event's purpose, identify major beneficiaries and customer groups, indicate the broad nature of the event and state the overall philosophy of the organisation conducting it (including an intent to be partially or fully self-funding). Several event mission statements that, to varying degrees, fulfil these criteria have been provided in table 5.1. In reviewing these you should note that it is the mission statement for the Greek Orthodox Folk Dance Festival that perhaps best meets most of these criteria. Once established, a mission statement acts as the basis upon which goals and objectives can be set and strategies established. They also serve to provide a shorthand means of conveying to staff (either paid or voluntary) an understanding of the event and what it is trying to achieve.

■ Table 5.1 *Sample event mission statements*

EVENT	MISSION STATEMENT
Cherry Creek Arts Festival, Colorado	The mission of the Cherry Creek Arts Festival organization is to create access to a broad array of arts experiences, nurture the development and understanding of diverse art forms and cultures, and encourage the expanding depth and breadth of cultural life in Colorado (www.cherryarts.org/cherry/Cherry/index.htm).
Greek Orthodox Folk Dance Festival, San Francisco	The Greek Orthodox Folk Dance Festival Ministry is dedicated, through Orthodox Christian Fellowship and committed leadership, to promoting, encouraging and perpetuating Greek heritage and culture among individuals, families and communities expressed in folk dance, folk art, music and language (www.greece.org/FDF/mission.html).
Northern Lights Festival Boreal, Ontario	The mission of Northern Lights Festival Boreal is to facilitate the development of, participation in, and appreciation of, the arts in our community (www.nlfb.on.ca).
Vision Festival, South Carolina	The Vision Festival presents art on the terms that uphold and expand the concepts of each musician, dancer, painter, and poet — those who have died and laid down the tracks, and those who are still creating. A masterpiece is an ongoing project that lasts a lifetime. Art must be presented, it must be seen and heard. It is for the enrichment of all those who attend and those who do not. It is about lights shining and not being buried. It is ultimately about the greatest art, that is, living (www.geocities.com/SoHo/Lofts/2553/vision-fest.html).

■ Goals *and objectives*

Once an event's mission has been decided, the event manager must then move on to establish the event's goals and/or objectives. Goals are broad statements that seek to provide direction to those engaged in the organisation of the event, as can be seen from table 5.2. Objectives in turn are used to quantify progress towards an event's goals and as such set performance benchmarks and allow event organisations to assess what aspects of their planning have succeeded or failed. It should be noted that the terms 'goals' and 'objectives' are often used interchangeably but they are really distinct concepts. It should also be noted that for some forms of event (particularly those of a corporate nature) the step of creating goals prior to establishing objectives often is not necessary. The establishment of goals is useful when the event is complex in nature and involves a number of stakeholder groups. In such instances they serve a useful role in building on the event's mission statement to provide direction and focus to the event organisers activities.

Useful criteria that can be applied to the establishment of objectives are summed up by the acronym SMART, which refers to the fact that they should be:

Specific: focused on achieving an event goal (or, if no goals have been developed, its purpose)

Measurable: expressed in a way that is quantifiable

Agreeable: those responsible for their achievement need to have agreed to them

Realistic: the event organisation must have the human, financial and physical resources to achieve them

Time specific: to be achieved by a particular time.

Each event will obviously vary in terms of the objectives it establishes. Examples of such objectives follow:

- *Economic objectives*
  - percentage return on monies invested or overall gross/net profit sought
  - dollar value of sponsorship attracted
  - percentage of income to be raised from fundraising activities
  - percentage increase in market share (if the event is competing directly with other similar events)
- *Attendance/participation*
  - total attendance/attendance by specific groups (e.g. people from outside the area, members of a company's distribution network)
  - size of event in terms of stallholders/exhibitors/performers/attendees
  - number of local versus outside artists
  - percentage of an area's cultural groups represented in a program
  - number of community groups involved with the event
- *Quality*
  - percentage level of attendee/exhibitor/stallholder/sponsor/volunteer satisfaction
  - number of participants/speakers/performers who have international reputations
  - number of complaints from attendees/exhibitors/stallholders/volunteers
- *Awareness/knowledge/attitudes*
  - percentage of attendees or others exposed to the event that have changed levels of awareness/knowledge as a result of the event
  - percentage of attendees or others exposed to the event who have altered their attitudes as a result of it.
- *Human resources*
  - percentage of staff/volunteer turnover
  - percentage of volunteers retained from previous year.

■ **Table 5.2** *Sample event goals*

EVENT	GOALS
Northern Lights Festival Boreal (NLFB), South Carolina	NLFB is committed to operating in a professional, fiscally responsible manner with the goal of financial self-sufficiency.
	NLFB is committed to reflecting the cultural diversity of Northern Ontario in its operations and programming.
	NLFB is committed to treating all performers and artists and their work professionally, with dignity, respect and fairness.
	NLFB is committed to developing, promoting and advocating for local artists and performers.
	NLFB is committed to developing, supporting and honouring the work of its volunteers, Board and staff.
	NLFB is committed to the accountability of the Board of Directors.
	NLFB is committed to developing, supporting and acknowledging the interests of its audiences.
	NLFB is committed to cultivating relationships with the community, other arts and cultural organizations, umbrella groups, sponsors and other community groups.
	(www.nlfb.on.ca)

EVENT	GOALS
Greek Orthodox Folk Dance Festival, San Francisco	To establish and maintain an administrative body to achieve the purposes outlined in the mission statement.
	To provide leadership skills to perpetuate the Ministry through the practice of acquired leadership skills in the administation of this organization.
	To bring people together in Orthodox Christian Fellowship and love, creating greater communion and stronger ties through interaction with fellow Orthodox Christians and promoting ethical and moral standards befitting the life of an Orthodox Christian.
	To promote, encourage and perpetuate Greek heritage and culture through outreach activities that inform others of the Ministry's events, opportunities and commitment to its purposes and goals. (www.greece.org/FDF/mission.html)

■ Situation *analysis*

A useful process that can be employed to gain a detailed understanding of an event's internal and external environment (or surroundings) is a strengths, weaknesses, opportunities and threats (SWOT) analysis. This process may involve referring to a range of existing information sources, including data collected previously on the event, census data and general reports on relevant matters such as trends in leisure behaviour. Additionally it may be necessary to commission studies to fill information gaps, or to update the event on particular matters. For example, a deeper understanding of the needs, wants, motives and perceptions of current or potential customer groups may be deemed necessary before acting to change an event in an effort to increase attendance.

The external environment consists of all those factors that surround the event and which can impact on its success. A thorough scanning of the full range of factors that make up the external environment should aid the event manager in his or her decisions regarding such matters as target market(s) selection, programming, promotional messages, ticket pricing, and when to conduct the event. Threats to the event (e.g. proposed changes to legislation regarding outdoor consumption of alcohol) or the emergence of new competing events can also be identified through this process.

The main components of the external environment of concern to event managers are examined in this section, along with some selected matters associated with each that have the potential to impact upon events.

- *Political/legal:* The deliberations of all levels of government become laws or regulations which affect the way in which people live in a society. For example, the laws regulating the consumption of food and alcoholic beverages have changed radically in Australia since the 1950s, making outdoor food and wine festivals possible.
- *Economic:* Economic factors such as unemployment, inflation, interest rates, distribution of wealth, and levels of wages and salaries can impact on the demand for events. For example, declining living standards in a particular region may require an event to have reduced ticket prices, or if the situation is bad enough, to be cancelled.

- *Social/cultural:* Changes in a population's ethnic/religious make-up or leisure behaviour can act to influence demand for events. These changes can provide opportunities (e.g. a demand for multicultural events) or pose threats (e.g. an increased tendency to engage in home-based leisure activities). Existing attitudes among a population towards particular matters can also be a factor of interest to event managers. For example, the love of sport possessed by many Sydneysiders was 'tapped' by the organisers of the Sydney 2000 Olympics, both to generate demand and to create a climate of tolerance for the various disruptions associated with this event. The culture of a particular place can also provide a rich resource on which event managers can draw. For example, the architecture, traditions, beliefs, food and artistic skills associated with a particular area can be embraced, selectively or collectively, by events.

- *Technological:* Changes in equipment and machines have revolutionised the way people undertake tasks, including aspects of event management (see chapter 13). One example of this is the use of the Internet to promote festivals, exhibitions and events. Entering the word 'festival' into an Internet search engine will produce links to a multitude of events in all parts of the globe. Another example is the use of the Internet as a vehicle for the conduct of events such as conferences. Internet sites are now also appearing that serve to support event professionals, students and educators by providing information, directories, and resources. EPMS.net (www.epms.net), developed by an author of this text, is one example.

- *Demographic:* The composition of society in terms of age, gender, education and occupation changes over time. A striking example is the entry of the baby boomers' generation (people born between 1945 and 1960) into middle age. The generation that gave the world rock'n'roll, blue jeans and relaxed sexual mores is, and will continue to be, a large market for event managers, and will always have very different needs to the preceding and succeeding generations.

- *Physical:* Concern over such matters as pollution and waste generation within the broader community is finding its way into the way events are conducted. Many councils and waste boards actively encourage event organisers to 'green' their events (see www.wastewiseevents.waste boards.nsw.gov.au). Another consideration of note for event managers regarding the environment is changing weather patterns brought about by the impact of greenhouse gases. Such changes have the potential to impact on outdoor events, particularly regarding when they are conducted.

- *Competitive:* Other events that seek to attract a similar audience need to be monitored. In this regard, comparisons relating to such matters as programs and pricing are useful. Such events need not necessarily be similar in nature, and as such they are sometimes difficult to identify. For example, a consumer exhibition organiser recently suffered a significant decline in demand for an event as it was scheduled to occur at the same time as a visiting US aircraft carrier decided to conduct a public open day.

When the analysis of the external environment is complete, the next step in the strategic planning process is to undertake an internal analysis of the event organisation's physical, financial, informational and human resources in order to establish its strengths and weaknesses. Areas of strength or weakness associated with an event include level of management or creative expertise; quality of supplier relationships; ownership or access to appropriate physical plant such as stages, and sound systems; quality of event program elements; access to appropriate technology such as ticketing systems; level of sophistication of event management software systems; access to financial resources; event reputation; size of volunteer base; quality of relationships with government; strength of linkages with potential sponsors.

■ Identification *of strategy options*

The environmental scanning process gathers crucial information that can be used by the event manager in selecting strategies to achieve the event's mission and objectives. Strategies must utilise strengths, minimise weaknesses, avoid threats and take advantage of opportunities that have been identified. A SWOT analysis is a wasted effort if the material gathered by this analytic process is not used in strategy formulation.

Several generic strategies, which can be adopted by festival and event managers, are summarised below.

Growth strategy

Late twentieth century human endeavour appears to be characterised by an obsession with size. In events, this is expressed in a desire to be bigger than last year; than other events; than other communities' events. Bigger is often thought to be better, particularly by ambitious event managers. Growth can be expressed as more revenue, more event components, more participants or consumers, or a bigger share of the event market. It is worth pointing out that bigger is not necessarily better, as some event managers have discovered. An example of this is the Sydney Festival (a cultural festival that takes place in Sydney each January). It adopted a growth strategy by absorbing other events taking place in Sydney in January and calling them 'umbrella' events. Some critics observed that by doing this the festival lost focus. A subsequent festival director responded by concentrating the festival on Sydney Harbour foreshores and decreasing the number of event components but increasing their quality.

It is important to recognise that an event does not necessarily have to grow in size for its participants to feel that it is better than its predecessors — this can be achieved by dedicating attention to quality activities, careful positioning and improved planning. However, a growth strategy may be appropriate if historical data suggest that there is a growing demand for the type of event planned, or a financial imperative necessitates increasing revenues. The annual Woodford Folk Festival in Queensland, for example, expanded the focus of its program by including contemporary rock acts in an attempt to appeal to a market segment with a strong propensity to attend music events. Increased revenue gained in this way was directed at repaying the festival's debt.

Consolidation or stability strategy

In certain circumstances it may be appropriate to adopt a consolidation strategy — that is, maintaining attendance at a given level by limiting ticket sales. The effectiveness of this strategy is based on the fact that supply is fixed while demand grows; eventually ticket prices will be increased, allowing the quality of inputs into the event to be improved. Strong demand for tickets to the Port Fairy Folk Festival, for example, has allowed this event to sell tickets well in advance, cap attendance numbers and further enhance the quality of its program.

Retrenchment strategy

An environmental scan may suggest that an appropriate strategy is to reduce the scale of an event but add value to its existing components. This strategy can be applicable when the operating environment of an event changes. Retrenchment can seem a defeatist or negative strategy, particularly to longstanding members of an event committee, but it can be a necessary response to an unfavourable economic environment or major change in the sociocultural environment. For example, the management of a community festival may decide to delete those festival elements that were poorly patronised and focus on only those that have proven to be popular with its target market. Likewise, exhibitions may delete an accompanying seminar program and focus on the core purpose of the exhibition.

Combination strategy

As the name suggests, a combination strategy includes elements from more than one of these generic strategies. An event manager could, for example, decide to cut back or even delete some aspects of an event that no longer appeals to the targeted market for the event, while concurrently growing other aspects.

■ Strategy evaluation *and selection*

Most management writers such as Thompson (1997) and Johnson and Scholes (1999) believe that strategic alternatives can be evaluated by using three main criteria:

1. *Appropriateness/suitability*: Strategies and their component parts should be consistent. That is, strategies selected should complement each other and be consistent with the environment, resources, and values of the event organisation.
2. *Acceptability/desirability*: Strategies should be capable of achieving the event's objectives. They should focus on what the environmental scan has identified as important and disregard the unimportant. Event companies should, however, be careful not to overlook potential risks involved in the strategy, for example, financial or environmental risk, or the risk of the required skills not being available in the organisation.

3. *Feasibility*: The proposed strategy should be feasible. It should work in practice, considering the resources available (e.g. finance, human resource, time). The strategy should also meet key success factors (e.g. quality, price, level of service).

Once again it is important to stress that the strategies chosen must be congruent with the findings of the SWOT analysis, or the environmental scan becomes a waste of time and intellectual energy, and results in inappropriate strategy selection.

■ Operational *plans*

Once the strategic thrust of the event has been agreed the implementation of the plan can commence. This process can be carried out by means of a series of operational plans.

Operational plans will be needed for all areas central to the achievement of an event's objectives and the implementation of its strategy. Areas for operational planning will therefore be likely to vary with events; however, it would be common for such plans to be developed in areas such as marketing, finance, human resources, administration, operations, and research and evaluation. Event managers may choose to break these areas up further, and create plans in areas such as risk management, sponsorship, environmental management, communication, programming, transportation, merchandising, media coverage and relations, community and police, volunteers, and visitor services.

Each area for which operational plans are developed will require a set of objectives that in turn progress the overall event strategy; action plans and schedules; details of individuals responsible for carrying out the various aspects of the plan; monitoring and control systems, including a budget; and an allocation of resources (financial, human and supporting equipment/services).

As many festivals, exhibitions and events are not one-off events, but occur at regular intervals — yearly, biennially or, in the case of some major sporting events, every four years, standing plans can be used in a number of operational areas. Standing plans are made up of policies, rules and standard procedures and serve to reduce decision-making time by ensuring similar situations are handled in a predetermined and consistent way.

Policies can be thought of as guidelines for decision making. An event may, for example, have a policy of only engaging caterers that meet particular criteria. These criteria might be based on licensing and insurance. Policies in turn are implemented by way of following established detailed instructions known as procedures. In the case of the previous example, procedures may require the person responsible for hiring caterers to inspect their licence and insurance certificates, check that they are current, and obtain copies for the event's records. Rules are statements governing conduct or action in a particular situation. For example, an event may establish rules regarding what caterers can and cannot do with the waste they generate on site, or on what they can sell or cannot sell.

■ Control *systems*

Once operational plans are implemented mechanisms are required to ensure that actions conform to plans. These mechanisms take the form of systems that allow performance to constantly be compared to objectives. Performance benchmarks (such as ticket sales over a given period) are particularly useful in this regard. Meetings and reports are generally central to the control process, as are budgets. Budgets allow actual costs and expenditure to be compared with those projected for the various operational areas. A detailed discussion of the control and budgeting processes appears in chapter 10.

■ Event evaluation *and feedback*

Evaluation is a neglected area of event planning, frequently with few resources and little thought being directed to it. Yet it is only through evaluation that event managers can determine how successful or otherwise their efforts have been in achieving whatever objectives were set for the event. It is also through this means that feedback can be provided to stakeholders, problems and shortcomings of the planning process can be identified and improvements suggested if the event is to be repeated. Key considerations regarding evaluation from an event manager's perspective include when to evaluate, how to evaluate, and what to evaluate. The answers to these questions are provided in chapter 15.

*O*RGANISATIONAL STRUCTURE

During the planning process, the organisational structure of the body responsible for the event must also be decided. In the same way that a house takes its shape from its structural framework, an event organisation's strategies and objectives are the products of its structure.

Given the range of events as well as differences in their scale and level of access to event management expertise, it is not surprising that a range of organisational structures can be found in use in the area. In this section the most common of these are identified and discussed.

■ Simple *structures*

As the name suggests, a simple structure has a low level of complexity. As figure 5.3 illustrates, all decision making is centralised with the event manager, who has total control over all the activities of staff. This is the most common structure in small event management businesses as it is flexible, adaptable to changing circumstances, easy to understand, and has clear accountability — the manager is accountable for all the activities associated with the event. The flexibility of this structure commonly means staff are expected to be multi-skilled and perform various functions. This can mean individual jobs are more satisfying, and produce higher levels of staff morale. However, this structure has some potential limitations. As staff do not have the opportunity to specialise they may not achieve a high level of expertise in any one area. Additionally, once an event organisation grows beyond a certain size decision making can become very slow — or even non-existent — as a single executive has to make all decisions and carry out all the management functions. Also, if the manager has an autocratic style, staff can become demoralised when their expertise is not fully utilised. There is also an inherent risk in concentrating all information about the management of an event in one person — obviously, sickness at an inappropriate time could prove disastrous.

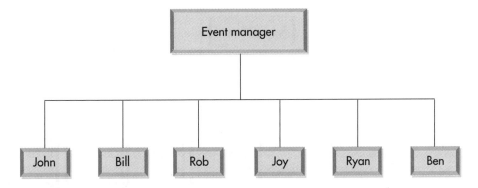

■ **Figure 5.3**
Simple organisational structure

■ **Functional** *structures*

As the name suggests, a functional structure departmentalises (i.e. groups related tasks) in a way that encourages the specialisation of labour (paid and/ or voluntary). Benefits of this form of structure are that individuals or groups (such as committees) can be given specific task areas, thus avoiding any overlap of responsibilities. Additionally it is possible using this form of structure to easily add additional functions as the needs of the event require. In figure 5.4 an example of such a structure is given in the form of the Australian Open Tennis Championships. Potential limitations of this approach include problems of coordination due partly to a lack of understanding of other tasks and conflict between functional areas as those doing the tasks attempt to defend what they see as their interests. Various approaches can be used to prevent these problems arising. These include employing multi-skilling strategies that require the rotation of staff through different functional areas; regular meetings between the managers/chairs of all functional areas; general staff meetings and communications (such as newsletters) that aim to keep those engaged on the event aware of matters associated with its current status (e.g. budgetary situation, the passing of milestones). All these activities are essential elements of the leadership function of the event manager, and are discussed in more detail in chapter 6.

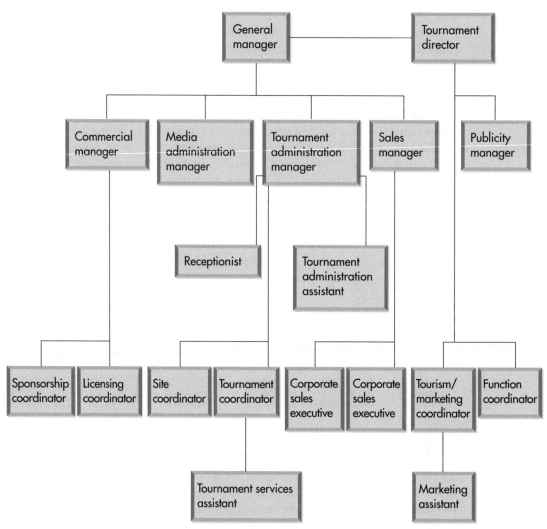

■ **Figure 5.4** *Tennis Australia: Australian Open organisational structure*

■ **Program-based** *matrix structures*

Another way of organising committees or groups into an organisational structure is treating the various aspects of an event program as separate (but related) entities. For example, organisers of a multi-venue sporting event may choose to have separate committees with responsibility for all tasks associated with event delivery at each location (see figure 5.5). In order to do this each committee/group leader would be required to manage a team of people with a comprehensive range of event-related skills. If this structure is employed, it is sound practice, as Getz (1997) notes, to have some tasks, such as security, communications and technical support, cut across all program areas to prevent duplication and enhance coordination.

	Event manager		
	Venues		
Support systems	Showground team	Soccer field (Killarney Heights) team	Soccer field (Forestville) team
Communications			
Transport			
Security			

A project-based matrix structure has several inherent advantages including allowing groups/individuals to engage directly with the task at hand (producing and delivering an event) and facilitating intergroup communication and cooperation. In using this structure a high value must be placed on coordination so that the event is presented as a unified whole.

■ **Multi-organisational** *or network structures*

Most event management companies are relatively small in size (fewer than 20 people), yet many conduct quite large and complex events. This is possible because these organisations enlist the services of a variety of other firms and organisations. In effect they create 'virtual organisations' in order to conduct the event, which disappear immediately after it has finished. This process is represented in figure 5.6 which shows various suppliers being enlisted by an event management firm to create a structure capable of creating and delivering an event. It should be noted that this process of growing an organisational structure quickly by contracting outside firms to perform specific functions is common in many forms of events, including public events such as festivals. Such an approach makes sense in situations where it is impractical to maintain a large standing staff when they can be used only for a limited period each year. Other advantages include usage of specialist firms with current expertise and experience contracted on a needs basis, with no 'down time'. Budgeting can also be much more exact as most costs are contracted and therefore known beforehand. This structure also allows for quick decisions in instances where the core management group is made up of only a few people or one individual.

As with the other structures previously discussed, there are also possible disadvantages to be considered. These include issues associated with quality control and reliability of supply as contractors are involved in performing many tasks; and coordinating employees, from various other organisations, who lack a detailed understanding of the event. Nevertheless, the concept of the network structure is supported by contemporary management thinking on downsizing, sticking to core activities and outsourcing, and can be very effective for certain kinds of events.

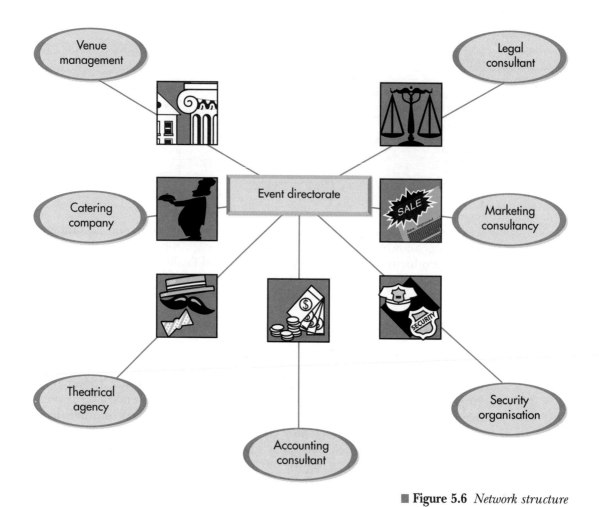

■ **Figure 5.6** *Network structure*

UMMARY

Planning is the basis for all successful events. To be successful, an event manager must gain a clear understanding of why the event exists (its vision/ mission), what it is trying to do for whom (its goals and/or objectives), and decide the strategies needed to achieve these objectives. These strategies in turn need to be implemented through a range of operational plans developed within the context of an overall event budget. These plans need to be monitored and adjusted as appropriate in the light of changing circumstances, and evaluated against the objectives set for them, and the overall objectives of the event. Additionally an appropriate organisational structure is needed to 'steer' these processes. In this regard the event manager can select from a number of options, depending on their assessment of the advantages and disadvantages of each.

Questions

1   Explain the key difference between a vision and mission statement.

2   Undertake an Internet search of a particular event type (e.g. festivals), identify four events that have established mission statements and compare these to the criteria given in this chapter.

3   Conduct an interview with the manager of a particular event with a view to identifying the key external environmental factors that are impacting upon their event.

4   Construct a general check list that can be used to assess the strengths and weaknesses of a particular type of event (e.g. festival, conference). This task will probably require interviews to be conducted with several event managers.

5   Identify several events, determine if they have established objectives, and assess these against the SMART criteria discussed in this chapter.

6   Categorise the organisational structures of three events with which you are familiar, or about which you can obtain this information.

7   Explain the difference between a strategic plan and an operational plan.

8   Briefly discuss the difference between a policy and a procedure.

9   Explain why stakeholders are significant from the perspective of establishing vision and mission statements.

10   Critically examine the strategic planning process of a particular event in the light of the processes discussed in this chapter.

Sydney Theatre Company
Foundation Fundraising Party

Purpose of the event

The Sydney Theatre Company (STC) held its first fundraising party in 1995. The theme of that party was a (K)night of Medieval Mayhem. This first fundraising party attracted 1100 guests and became a landmark annual event for the STC. The success of the first event prompted the establishment of the STC Foundation, with the purpose of raising money specifically for the company and its research and development program. Since then, the STC has hosted various themed parties each year, except for 2000 because of the Olympics.

The producers aim to take the guests out of the everyday and into a theatrical interpretation of another time and place. The format of the night consists of drinks preceding a three-course dinner. Three major production numbers featuring choreographed song and dance surround the central fundraising activity of the night, the auction. The latter part of the evening is either live or club music depending on the party's theme. Shows are spectacular, with large numbers of performers (for Trocadero there were over 500) and many surprise elements. All STC Foundation events have been hailed as parties of the year with Trocadero named by the *Sydney Morning Herald* as one of the best parties of the decade.

Reason for fundraising

Research and development ensure the future of any theatre company. Without the ability to experiment and develop new projects, theatres are restricted to staging existing works or those developed by companies that are more affluent. Before the establishment of the STC Foundation, all research and development were funded by box office receipts. This resulted in the company's director having either to program a subscription series of safe choices to guarantee sufficient revenue, or limit research and development to an affordable minimum. Without guaranteed funding, development of long-term projects was not possible.

Organisation

As an established theatre company, STC is in a unique position, having considerable resources in personnel skilled in every area of production, plus substantial staging materials, props and wardrobe. It also has the advantage of being able to broker deals with suppliers based on an ongoing connection with the Company.

However, the party must be scheduled into STC's busy year to ensure staff availability and avoid clashes with main stage productions. So that STC's resources are not overloaded, freelance personnel are brought in to manage key areas. The final party production team is structured as follows:

Producers: STC
Director: STC

Technical director: STC
Box office and marketing: STC
Production manager: freelance
Design and choreography: freelance
Stage management: freelance
Sound, lighting, staging and catering: contract
Public relations: freelance
Security: contract

All other crew and staff are drawn from the STC on either a paid or volunteer basis.

There are two producers for STC events: Wayne Harrison, who directs the show, and Camilla Rountree, who manages the other organisational aspects and coordinates the entertainment and sponsorship.

Planning the time line

February:
- The theme for the party is chosen by the producers and presented to the Foundation for a date to be chosen.
- Once the theme is adopted, creating the image for the party commences. This image must convey the mood of the event as well as lending itself to an invitation, poster and program. It is therefore an important marketing tool.
- The producers engage the designer and choreographer and find a suitable venue. Once these three elements are in place, the entertainment can be planned.

April:
The main organisation of the event begins.
- A meeting of the creative team is called, involving the choreographer, the designer and the producers. The director outlines his or her ideas and the first of many discussions takes place. Over the following months the content of the show will change several times within the overall concept. This may be due to availability of artists, complications with staging, budget constraints or the advent of that most wonderful of things, 'a great idea'.
- A budget is drawn up, taking into account all projected costs at commercial rates, plus a contingency. As there is never sufficient money, sponsorships and deals are always necessary.
- The designer is given a broad outline of what will be needed to stage the event: the nature of the show; the number of guests; the number of corporate tables; whether a buffet or sit down dinner is planned and any other specific requirements. The designer then draws up a floor plan to scale. This is the blueprint for the night and is used by every department. It will show seating arrangements, placement of performance areas and their dimensions, entrances, exits, catering and bar areas, and facilities such as toilets, taps, fire equipment and lighting grids. Without this plan, the party cannot progress to the next stage.

May:
- Work has commenced on sponsorships.
- Caterers have been contracted and briefed.
- Hiring companies have been given the dates.
- Details of the party are placed in EXSTCE, the STC magazine that is sent to the subscriber base of 20 000. This promotes advance bookings so the STC Box Office is briefed.

June:
- Regular planning meetings commence, involving the creative team and the technical director. By this stage the producers are sourcing and booking artists for the show.

July:
- All the printed material for the party has now been approved and is sent to the printers.
- Advertisements are placed in STC subscription series programs.

August:
- Invitations are posted.
- The box office appoints an extra person to be responsible for processing bookings for the party.
- The publicists commence the job of creating media awareness of the party by sending out press releases.

September:
- The production manager joins the team. From this point on he or she takes over the detail of staging, lighting, sound and catering needs. The production manager works closely with the STC technical director and the producers to coordinate work being carried out in-house with that being done by external contractors. Regular trips to the location are required to make sure every department is familiar with the venue.
- The designer finalises details for staging and building of props, table lighting and the dressing of the room.

October:
- The costume designer joins the team. Where original costumes are required, fabrics are bought and made up in the STC workrooms. Other clothes are sourced from various hiring and theatre companies. Costumes for waiters and ushers are organised. Artists are called in for fittings.
- A catering coordinator ensures that all glassware, cutlery and crockery are suitable, that the quantities are correct and that everything is delivered on time, collected after the event and returned to its source.
- Music tracks are prepared by a musical director. If a live band or orchestra is performing for a production number, music charts will have to be prepared for the musicians.
- The production manager prepares a preliminary running order for the show. This schedules every aspect of the night from the arrival of the guests to the last dance track. Sometimes at this point problems arise with timing and logistics and the running order has to change.

Three weeks prior:
- Seating is finalised and tickets are posted to guests.
- All artists' contracts are finalised.
- A production assistant commences. It is the production assistant's job to send out delivery details for everything required for the event, to coordinate artists and prepare cell sheets for rehearsals and wardrobe checks.

Two weeks prior:
- Rehearsals commence.
- Program for the night is finalised and printed.

Production week
Monday:
- The riggers commence. Once they have finished, construction of the staging starts. Depending on the scale, this can take a day or more. Lighting and sound usually take about two days. Security guard at night.

Thursday:
- The room is ready for a rough rehearsal.
- Plotting of the sound and lighting begins.
- Wardrobe is set up at the venue and fittings for extras held.
- Cold rooms arrive and are switched on ready for food and beverage delivery.

Friday:
- Tables and chairs are set up.
- All catering requirements are delivered.
- Generators and 'porta-loos' are delivered as needed.
- Rehearsals take place with sound and lighting checks.

Saturday:
- Tables are set.
- Dressing of the venue is completed.
- The caterers begin the on-site preparation of the food.
- Rehearsals all day, so lunch is provided for the cast and crew.

On the night:
- Everyone on standby from one hour before the guests arrive.
- Last minute checks take place, and then it us up to the professionalism of everyone involved to make sure the night runs smoothly.

Sunday:
- Clean up begins as soon as the last guest leaves.
- Staging, lighting and sound equipment is struck.
- Catering equipment is packed ready for collection.
- Tablecloths bundled. Tables and chairs stacked.
- Props and wardrobe packed.

Monday:
Everything is collected and the venue cleaned.

Outcomes

The STC Foundation parties have been particularly successful both artistically and as fundraisers, bringing in over $200 000 per event.

Summary

To run a successful event there are five golden rules:
1. Plan well in advance.
2. Once you have chosen your theme stick to it, but remain flexible enough to allow ideas to develop.
3. Employ people who are expert in their fields.
4. Learn what elements to prioritise; some things are more difficult to organise than you think.
5. For a fundraiser, remember your objective and be constantly on the alert for ways of doing things inexpensively but with style.

If you have a clear vision of what you want to achieve, are working with skilled people and have enough time, you can overcome many difficulties, even budget overruns. Budgets usually blow out in the last few days when problems that have not been foreseen must be solved with money. With careful planning and enough time, most problems can be avoided. The last ingredient is always luck; added to a professional approach to event planning, things are usually right on the night.

The 1998 Sydney Theatre Company Foundation Party was produced by the then STC Executive Producer Wayne Harrison and Camilla Rountree, Producer, Foundation Events.

By Camilla Rountree, former Producer, Foundation Events and Wayne Harrison, former Executive Producer, Sydney Theatre Company

Questions

1 Write a purpose statement for the STC Foundation events.

2 Describe two key objectives for the event. In what ways do these correspond to the SMART principle?

3 Describe the strategies that the STC Foundation party uses to achieve its objectives.

4 Construct an organisational chart for the event.
   (a) What type of organisational structure does it demonstrate?
   (b) Suggest reasons why this structure would suit the requirements of this event.

5 Write a position description for the position of Producer, Foundation Events in the event organisation.

6 Construct a policy document for the event that lists appropriate policies and procedures for producing the event.

7 Would you classify the process described in the case study as a single-use plan or a standing plan? Explain your answer.

REFERENCES

Beardwell, I. & Holden, L. 2001, *Human Resource Management: A Contemporary Perspective*, 3rd edn, Pearson Education, London.

Catherwood, D. & Van Kirk, R. 1992, *The Complete Guide to Special Event Management*, John Wiley & Sons, New York.

Cole, G. A. 1996, *Management: Theory and Practice*, 5th edn, Letts, London.

Cole, G. A. 1997, *Strategic Management*, Letts, London.

Getz, D. 1997, *Event Management and Event Tourism*, Cognizant Communications, New York.

Hanlon, C. & Jago, L. 2000, 'Pulsating Sporting Events', in *Events Beyond 2000 — Setting the Agenda, Proceedings of the Conference on Evaluation, Research and Education*, eds J. Allen, R. Harris, L. K. Jago & A. J. Veal, 13–14 July, Sydney, Australian Centre for Event Management, University of Technology, pp. 93–104.

Hannagan, T. 1998, *Management Concepts & Practices*, 2nd edn, Financial Times/Pitman Publishing, London.

Heskett, J., Sasser, W. & Schelesinger, L., 1997, *The Service Profit Chain*, The Free Press, New York.

Johnson, G. & Scholes, K. 1999, *Exploring Corporate Strategy*, 5th edn, Prentice Hall Europe, Hemel Hempstead.

Keung, D. 1998, *Management: A Contemporary Approach*, Pitman Publishing, London.

Mullins, L. J. 1999, *Management and Organisational Behaviour*, 5th edn, Financial Times/Pitman Publishing, London.

Stoner, J. A. F., Freeman, R. E. & Gilbert Jr., D. R. 1995, *Management*, 6th edn,, Prentice Hall, Englewood Cliffs, New Jersey.

Thompson, J. L. 1997, *Strategic Management: Awareness and Change*, 3rd edn, International Thompson Business Press, London.

Websites

www.tourismtasmania.com.au/org/community_aware/taw2000/openingdisplay.htm

www.orshakes.org/about/mission.html

www.bunkjohnson.org/festival

www.cherryarts.org/cherry/Cherry/index.htm

www.greece.org/FDF/mission.html

www.nlfb.on.ca

www.geocities.com/SoHo/Lofts/2553/vision-fest.html

www.wastewiseevents.wasteboards.nsw.gov.au

www.epms.net

6

Human resource
management and
events

LEARNING OBJECTIVES

After studying this chapter, you should be able to:

- describe the human resource management challenges posed by events
- list and describe the key steps in the human resource planning process for events
- describe approaches to determining human resource needs for events
- list areas, in the context of events, where human resource policies and procedures might be required
- describe event staff and volunteer recruitment and selection processes
- describe approaches to training and professional development relevant in an event context
- discuss staff supervision and evaluation practices that an event manager might engage in
- describe practices associated with the termination, outplacement and re-enlistment of event staff and volunteers
- describe approaches that can be employed to motivate event staff and volunteers
- describe techniques that can be used for event staff and volunteer team-building
- describe general legal considerations associated with human resource management in an event context.

INTRODUCTION

Effective planning and management of human resources is at the core of any successful event. Ensuring that an event is adequately staffed with the right people, who are appropriately trained and motivated to meet its objectives, is fundamental to the event management process. This chapter seeks to overview the key aspects of human resource planning and management with which an event manager should be familiar. It begins by examining considerations associated with human resource management in the context of events. It then moves on to propose a model of the human resource management process for events and to discuss each of the major steps in this model. Selected theories associated with employee/volunteer motivation are then described, followed by a brief examination of techniques for staff and volunteer team building. The final part of this chapter deals with legal considerations associated with human resource management. It should be noted that issues associated with volunteer management receive significant coverage in this chapter because of the role volunteers play in the conduct of many types of events.

CONSIDERATIONS ASSOCIATED WITH HUMAN RESOURCE PLANNING FOR EVENTS

The context in which human resource planning takes place for events can be said to be unique for two major reasons. First, and perhaps most significantly, many events have a 'pulsating' organisational structure (Hanlon & Jago 2000). What this means is that they grow in terms of personnel as the event approaches, but quickly contract when it ends. From a human resource perspective, this creates a number of challenges including obtaining paid staff given the short-term nature of the employment offered; short time lines for hiring and selection of staff, and for developing and implementing staff training; and the need to shed staff quickly. Secondly, volunteers, as opposed to paid staff, often make up the bulk of people involved in delivering an event. Indeed, in some instances events are run entirely by volunteers. The challenges presented by this situation are many, and relate to such matters as sourcing volunteers, quality control, supervision, training and motivation. Later parts of this chapter suggest responses to these challenges.

THE HUMAN RESOURCE PLANNING PROCESS FOR EVENTS

Human resource planning for events should not be viewed simply in terms of a number of isolated tasks, but as a series of sequential interrelated processes and practices that take their lead from an event's vision/mission, objectives and strategy. For example, if an event seeks to grow in size and attendance, it will need a human resource strategy to support this growth through such means as increased staff recruitment (paid and/or volunteer) and expanded (and perhaps more sophisticated) training programs. If these supporting human resource management actions are not in place, problems such as high staff/volunteer turnover due to overwork, poor quality delivery and an associated declining market place image may result, jeopardising the event's growth strategy.

Events will obviously differ in terms of the level of sophistication they display in the human resources area due to such factors as the resources they have available to them in terms of money and expertise. Contrast, for example, a local community festival that struggles to put together an organising committee and attract sufficient volunteers with a mega-event such as the Olympic Games. Nonetheless, it is appropriate that the 'ideal' situation is examined here — the complete series of steps that an event manager should proceed through regarding human resource planning. This is so because, by understanding these steps and their relationships to one another, event managers will give themselves the best chance of managing human resources in a way that will achieve their event's goals and objectives. As a way of introducing you to how this process can be applied to events, a case study dealing with the successful volunteer program at the Sydney Olympic Games has been included in this chapter.

While a number of general models of the human resource management process can be identified, the one chosen to serve as the basis of discussion in this chapter is that proposed by Getz (1997). This model, displayed in figure 6.1, was chosen as it represents an attempt to display how this process works within an event context.

■ **Figure 6.1**
The human resource planning process for events

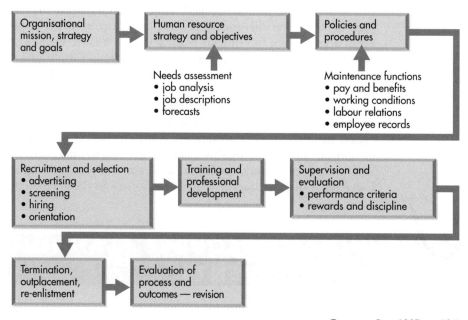

(**Source:** *Getz 1997, p. 184*)

■ Human resource strategy *and* *objectives*

This stage in the human resource management process for events involves a variety of activities, including establishing guiding strategies and objectives; determining staffing needs; and undertaking a job analysis and producing job descriptions and specifications. Each of these tasks is discussed in turn in this section.

Strategy

An event's human resource (HR) strategy seeks to support its overall mission and objectives. This linkage can be demonstrated by reference to the following examples that identify a few selected areas in which an organisation might set objectives and the subsequent focus on supporting human resource management objectives and activities:

- cost containment — improved staff/volunteer productivity, reduced absenteeism, decreased staff numbers
- improved quality — better recruitment and selection, expanded employee and volunteer training, increased staff and volunteer numbers and improved financial rewards and volunteer benefits
- improved organisational effectiveness — better job design, changes to organisational structure, and improved relations with employees and volunteers
- enhanced performance regarding social and legal responsibilities — improved compliance with relevant legislation such as that relating to occupational health and safety, antidiscrimination and equal employment opportunity.

Whatever human resource management objectives are set for an event, they need to meet the SMART criteria discussed in chapter 5.

Staffing

The main strategic decision area for event managers regarding human resources is that of staffing, as without a staff there is nothing really to 'strategise' about! Event managers need to make decisions about how many staff/volunteers are needed to deliver the event; what mix of skills/qualifications/experience is required; and when in the event planning process these staff/volunteers will be needed (e.g. event shutdown stage only). One way of undertaking this task in the context of events has been suggested by Getz (1997, p. 186), and involves a three-stage process:

1. Identify all tasks associated with event creation, delivery and shutdown. For example, site-related tasks might include site design and layout, setting up fencing, erecting tents and stages, positioning/building toilets, and placing signs and waste containers.
2. Determine how many people are needed to complete the range of tasks associated with the conduct of the event. For example, do all the tasks have to be done in order, by the same work crew, or all at once by a larger crew? What level of supervision will be required? What tasks can

be outsourced and what must be done by the event itself? Will more staff than normal be required to perform tasks (e.g. security) because of some specific circumstance (e.g. a visit by a celebrity to the event)?

3. Make a list of the numbers of staff/volunteers, supervisors and the skills/ experience/qualifications needed to form the 'ideal' work force for the event.

The most difficult task in this process is step 2, particularly if the event is new. Armstrong (1999) claims that by far the most common approach used in business to answering this question is managerial judgement. Such an observation is also likely to apply to the world of events. That is, the event manager, or various functional managers if the event is large enough, calculate how many, and what type, of human resources are needed to meet their objectives. In doing so they are likely to take into account such factors as their prior experience; demand forecasts for the event; the number of venues/ sites involved; skill/expertise requirements; previous instances of similar (or the same) events; degree of outsourcing possible; availability of volunteers; and strategies adopted by the event.

In the case of some tasks associated with the conduct of events, it is possible to estimate staffing needs by engaging in some basic arithmetic. For example, the number of people who can pass through a turnstile per hour can be easily calculated by dividing the processing time for an individual into 60 minutes. Let us assume the figure generated in this way is 240 (i.e. 240 people can be processed in an hour through one turnstile). Next, an estimate of event attendance (including peaks and troughs in arrivals) is required. Let us now assume that total attendance for the event has been fairly consistent at 5000 over the past three years, with 80 per cent (4000) of people arriving between 9 a.m. and 11 a.m. If this number of people are to be processed over a two-hour period, about eight turnstiles would need to be open (i.e. 240 transactions per hour × 2 hours, divided by the number of attendees over this time, i.e. 4000). Based on these calculations eight turnstile operators would be required for the first two hours. After this time the number of operators could be dramatically decreased.

Job analysis

Job analysis is an important aspect of this stage of the human resource planning process. It involves defining a job in terms of specific tasks and responsibilities and identifying the abilities, skills and qualifications needed to perform it successfully. According to Stone (1998), questions answered by this process include:

- What tasks should be grouped together to create a job or position?
- What should be looked for in individuals applying for identified jobs?
- What should an organisational structure look like and what inter-relationships should exists between jobs?
- What tasks should form the basis of performance appraisal for an individual in a specific job?
- What training and development programs are required to ensure staff/ volunteers possess the needed skills/knowledge?

The level of sophistication evident in the application of the job analysis process will obviously differ between events. Some small-scale events, for example, that depend exclusively, or almost exclusively, on volunteers may simply attempt to match people to the tasks in which they have expressed an interest. Under such circumstances, it is still nonetheless likely that some consideration would need to be given to factors such as experience, skills and physical abilities.

Job descriptions

Job descriptions are another outcome of the job analysis process with which event managers need some measure of familiarity if they are to effectively match people (both employees and volunteers) to jobs. Specifically, a job description is a statement identifying why a job has come into existence, what the holder of the job will do, and under what conditions the job is to be conducted (Stone 1998).

Job descriptions commonly include the following information.

- *Job title and commitment required* — locates the paid or voluntary position within the organisation, indicates the functional area where the job is to be based (e.g. marketing coordinator, assistants to the parking supervisor), and states the job duration/time commitment (e.g. one year part-time contract involving two days a week).
- *Salary/rewards/incentives* associated with position. For paid positions a salary, wage, or hourly rate will need to be stated, along with any other rewards such as bonuses. In the case of voluntary positions, consideration should be given to identifying benefits such as free merchandise (e.g. T-shirts, limited edition souvenir programs), free/discounted meals, free tickets and end of event parties, all of which can serve to increase interest in working at an event.
- *Job summary* — a brief statement describing the primary purpose of the job. For example, the job summary for an event operations manager may read: 'Under the direction of the event director, prepare and implement detailed operational plans in all areas associated with the successful delivery of the event'.
- *Duties and responsibilities* — a list of major tasks and responsibilities associated with the job. This list should not be overly detailed, identifying only those duties/responsibilities that are central to the performance of the job. Additionally it is useful to express these in terms of the most important outcomes of the work. For example, for an event operations manager, one key responsibility expressed in outcome terms would be the preparation of plans encompassing all operational dimensions of the event, such as site set-up and breakdown, security, parking, waste management, staging and risk management.
- *Relationships* with other positions within and outside the event organisation. Questions that need to be answered in this regard include: What positions report to the job? (For example, an event operations manager may have all site staff/volunteers associated with security, parking, staging, waste management, utilities and so on reporting to him/her). To what position(s) does the job report? (For example, an event operations manager may report only to the event director/manager.) What outside organisations will the position

need to liaise with in order to satisfactorily perform the job? (For example, an event operations manager may need to liaise with local councils, police, roads and traffic authorities, and local emergency service providers.)

- *Skills/knowledge/experience/qualifications/personal attributes* required by the position. In some instances, particularly with basic jobs, most deficiencies in these areas may be overcome quickly with training. However, for more complex jobs (voluntary or paid), such as those of a managerial or supervisory nature, individuals may need to possess experience, skills or knowledge before applying. Often a distinction is drawn between these elements, with some seen as essential while others are noted as desirable. Specific qualifications may also be required. Increasingly, for example, job advertisements for event managers are listing as desirable formal qualifications in event management. Personal attributes, such as the ability to work as part of a team, to be creative, to work to deadlines and to positively represent the event to stakeholder groups, may also be relevant considerations.
- *Authority* vested in position. What decisions can be made by the position without reference to a superior? What expenditure limits are there on decision making?
- *Performance standards* associated with the position. Criteria will be required by which performance in the position will be assessed. While these apply more to paid staff than to voluntary positions, they should still be considered for the latter. This is particularly the case if the volunteers hold significant management or supervisory positions where substandard performance could jeopardise one or more aspects of the event. If duties and responsibilities have been written in output terms, as discussed previously, these can be used as the basis of evaluation.

While job descriptions for paid positions often involve most, if not all, the information noted previously, voluntary positions are often described in far more general terms. This is so because they often (but not always) involve fairly basic tasks. This is evident from figure 6.2, where job descriptions are given for several voluntary positions associated with the National Folk Festival.

■ **Figure 6.2**
National Folk Festival— selected volunteer job descriptions

Festival information office
Where do you find the disabled toilets? Who do you let know that none of the lights in the camping ground are on? Have you found... a child, bracelet, my car keys?... These are the types of questions and problems faced every few minutes in the festival office. With the help of 'The Manual' and experienced volunteers you'll work out the answers. It's a great place for people who have good customer service skills and are good problem solvers. It's fast, furious, and very rewarding. If you like to be in the thick of things this is the place for you.

Ticket office
Is the busiest area to volunteer for the festival. You sell entry to the festival, and exchange tickets for wristbands for people who've already paid for entry. If you want to learn how to use cash registers and EFTPOS then this is one place where you get lots of experience really quickly. Because it is so busy time passes quickly here, and it is one of the most popular areas for groups of friends to volunteer together.

(**Source:** *National Folk Festival 2001*)

Job specification

A job specification is derived from the job description and seeks to identify the experience, qualifications, skills, abilities, knowledge and personal characteristics needed to perform a given job. In essence it identifies the types of people that should be recruited and how they should be appraised. The essential and desirable criteria shown in figure 6.3 provide an example of how job specifications are used in the recruitment process.

■ Figure 6.3
Job
advertisement
for an event
manager

EVENTS MANAGER, Clerk. Grade 7/8, Sydney Botanic Gardens. Pos. no. R8G 9716. Total remuneration package valued to $51 005 p.a. (salary $43 328–$47 960). Responsible for managing community and commercial use of Gardens' lands, including special events and venue hire. **Essential:** Demonstrated extensive experience in events management or related industry. Excellent oral and written communication skills. Demonstrated customer service, negotiation, team and interpersonal skills. Well-developed administrative, planning, staff and financial management skills. Ability to manage competing demands for land use. Computer skills in word processing, spreadsheets and venue booking systems. Current driver's licence. Ability to implement EEO, OH & S policies and practices. **Desirable:** Database skills. An understanding of the role of a botanic garden. Tertiary qualifications in events management or a related field. Membership of ISES. Inquiries: Andrew Mitchell (02) 9231 8119.

■ Policies *and procedures*

Policies and procedures are needed to provide the framework in which the remaining tasks in the human resource planning process take place — recruitment and selection; training and professional development; supervision and evaluation; termination, outplacement, reemployment; and evaluation. According to Stone (1998), policies and practices serve to:

- reassure all staff that they will be treated fairly (e.g. seniority will be the determining factor in requests by volunteers to fill job vacancies)
- help managers make quick and consistent decisions (e.g. rather than a manager having to think about the process of terminating the employment of a staff member or volunteer they can simply follow the process already prescribed)
- give managers the confidence to resolve problems and defend their positions (e.g. an event manager who declines to consider an application from a brother of an existing employee may point to a policy regarding employing relatives of existing personnel if there is a dispute).

Human resource practices and procedures for events are often conditioned, or determined by, those public or private sector organisations with ultimate authority for them. For example, a local council responsible for conducting an annual festival would probably already have in place a range of policies and procedures regarding the use of volunteers. These would then be applied to the event. Additionally, a range of laws will influence the degree of freedom management of an event has in the human resource area. For example, laws regarding occupational health and safety, holiday and long service leave, discrimination, dismissal and compensation will all need to become integrated into the practices and policies an event adopts.

If an event manager goes to the time and effort to develop policies and procedures, he or she will also need to ensure these are communicated to all staff, and applied. Additionally, resources will need to be allocated to this area so that the 'paperwork' generated by those policies and procedures can be stored, accessed and updated/modified as required. Such paperwork may include various policy/procedure manuals and staff records such as performance evaluations and employment contracts.

Again, the larger (in terms of number of staff and volunteers) and more sophisticated (in terms of management) the event, the more likely it is that it would have thought more deeply about policy and procedure concerns. Nonetheless, even smaller events would benefit in terms of the quality of their overall human resources management if some attempt were made to set basic policies and procedures to guide their actions.

■ Recruitment *and selection*

The recruitment of paid and volunteer employees is essentially about attracting the 'right' potential candidates to the 'right' job openings. Successful recruitment is based on how well previous stages in the human resource planning process have been conducted, and involves determining where qualified applicants can be found and how they can be attracted to the event organisation. It is a two-way process, in that the event is looking to meet its human resource needs at the same time as potential applicants are trying to assess whether they meet the job requirements, wish to apply for the position and see value in joining the organisation. A diagrammatic representation of the recruitment process is given in figure 6.4.

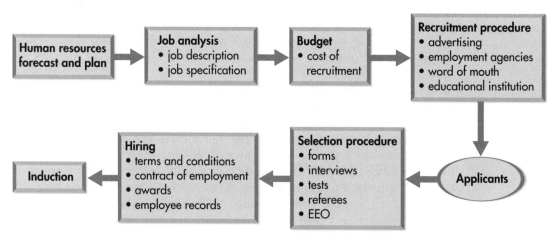

■ **Figure 6.4** *The recruitment and selection process for paid and voluntary employees*

(**Source:** *adapted from Clark 1992*)

How event managers approach the recruitment process will depend very much on the financial resources they have available to them. With large events there is likely to be a budget set aside for this purpose, designed to cover costs such as recruitment agency fees, advertising, travel expenses of non-local applicants and search fees for executive placement firms. The reality for most events, however — particularly those relying heavily of volunteers — is that they will have few resources to allocate to the recruitment process. Nonetheless, through a variety of means, they can still successfully engage in this process by:

- using stakeholders (e.g. local councils, community groups, sponsors and event suppliers) to communicate the event's staffing needs (volunteer and paid) through to their respective networks. McCurley and Lynch (1998), in the context of volunteers, call this approach 'concentric circle recruitment' as it involves starting with the groups of people who are already connected to the event or company and working outwards. It is based on the premise that volunteers are recruited by someone they know, for example friends or family, clients or colleagues, staff, employers, neighbours or acquaintances such as members from the same clubs and societies.
- writing sponsorship agreements in a way that requires the sponsor, as part of their agreement with the event, to provide temporary workers with particular skills, e.g. marketing
- identifying and liaising with potential sources of volunteers/casual staff, including universities and TAFE colleges (projects and work placements may be specially created for these groups, particularly if they are studying festival, exhibition and event management), job centres, religious groups, service clubs (such as Lions and Rotary), community service programs, senior citizen centres and retirement homes, chambers of commerce, and community centres
- determining the make-up (e.g. age, sex, occupations) and motivations of existing volunteers, and using this information as the basis of further targeted recruitment
- gaining the assistance of local and specialist media (e.g radio, TV, newspapers, specialist magazines) in communicating the event's human resource needs — this process will be greatly assisted if one or more media organisations are in some way (such as through sponsorship) associated with the event
- targeting specific individuals within a community with specialist skills to sit on boards or undertake specific tasks, such as those associated with the legal and accounting aspects of conducting an event
- registering with volunteer agencies such as Volunteering NSW/ACT/NT/SA/QLD/Tasmania
- conducting social functions at which, for example, existing volunteers or staff might be encouraged to bring potential candidates, or to which particular groups/targeted individuals are invited.

Once an appropriate pool of applicants has been identified, the next step is to select from among them those that best fit the identified available positions. It is important to approach this process systematically, employing appropriate tools, to avoid the costs (financial and otherwise) that come from poor selection (increased training time, high turnover of staff/volunteers, absenteeism, job dissatisfaction and poor performance).

A useful starting point in the selection process is the selection policy. This should have been developed earlier in the policy and procedures stage of the human resource planning process. In constructing such a policy thought needs to be given to:

- outlining how the event organisation intends to comply with equal employment opportunity legislation
- approaches to measuring the suitability of candidates (e.g. simple rating scales based on set criteria)
- the source of people (e.g. will the event organisation promote from within where possible?)
- the decision makers (i.e. who will have the final decision on who to engage?)
- selection techniques (e.g. will tests be employed? Will decisions be made after one interview or several?)
- the organisation's business objectives (e.g. do the candidates selected have the qualities and qualifications to progress the event's objectives?)

The application process will vary based on the needs of the position, the number of applications anticipated and the resources of the event organisation. In cases where a large number of applications are anticipated, it may be appropriate to consider screening applicants by telephone by asking a few key questions central to the position's requirements (e.g. do you have a qualification in event management?). Those individuals who answer these questions appropriately can then be sent an application. In the case of volunteers, applicants for positions in small-scale events may be asked to simply send in a brief note indicating what skills/qualifications they have, any prior relevant experience and the tasks they would be interested in doing. In larger events, volunteers may be asked to complete a registration form such as that developed by the National Folk Festival (see figure 6.5).

However basic, application forms for paid employees generally seek information regarding educational qualifications, previous employment, and other information deemed relevant to the position by the applicant. The names and contact details of referees who can supply written and/or verbal references are also normally required. Additionally a curriculum vitae (CV) is generally appended to these forms. Once received, applications allow unsuitable applicants to be culled, and those thought suitable to be short-listed and invited to attend an interview. In the case of volunteers, they may simply be notified that they have been accepted and asked to attend a briefing session.

When selecting among applicants, Robertson and Makin (1986) (cited in Beardwell & Holden 2001) suggest taking into account:

- *past behaviour:* The use of past behaviour can be employed to predict future behaviour. That is, the manner in which a person completed a task in the past is the best predictor of the way that person will complete a task in the future. Biographical data (obtained from the curriculum vitae or application form), references and supervisor/peer group ratings are commonly the major sources of such information.

VOLUNTEER
REGISTRATION 2001

Mail to: National Folk Festival, PO Box 156, CIVIC SQUARE, ACT 2608
Fax: (02) 6247 0906 email: volunteer@folkfestival.asn.au

Office Use Only

Master/Vol ID No:_____

1st Pref:_____

National Folk Festival

TELL US ABOUT YOU: (in confidence)

Surname: _____

First Name: _____ Title:_____

Are you over 18? ❑ Yes ❑ No (If under 18 please give date of birth: ____/____/____

Address: _____

Suburb/Town: _____ State: _____ Postcode: _____

Phone: (h) _____(w) _____ (m) _____

Email: _____

Emergency Contact: _____ Phone: _____

Special Requirements (eg. wheelchair access): _____

Have you volunteered with the Festival before? ❑ Yes ❑ No

If yes, which years? ❑ 1993 ❑ 1994 ❑ 1995 ❑ 1996 ❑ 1997 ❑ 1998 ❑ 1999 ❑ 2000

Area(s) previously worked: _____

SKILLS:
Do you have any of the following skills/experience/qualifications you would like to make use of?

❑ Current First Aid Certificate

❑ Childcare

❑ Cash Handling

❑ Customer Service

❑ Basic Admin

❑ Telephone Skills

❑ Marketing

❑ Management & Team Supervision Skills
    Computing:
    ❑   - Database
    ❑   - Web page
    ❑   - Desktop Publishing

❑ Art/Craft Skills

❑ SecurityTraining/Experience

❑ Other (please specify)

Trade Qualifications:
    ❑   - Carpenter
    ❑   - Joiner
    ❑   - Electrician
    ❑   - Welder
    ❑   - Plumber

❑ Handyman Skills

❑ Ticketed Plant Operator

❑ Bus/Truck/Forklift Licence

❑ Sound Systems

❑ Training

❑ Massage/Reiki etc

❑ Languages (please specify)

_____

■ **Figure 6.5** *National Folk Festival volunteer registration form*   (**Source:** *National Folk Festival 2001*)

- *present behaviour:* A range of techniques can be used to assess current behaviour, including:
  - tests — these may be designed to measure aptitude, intelligence, personality and basic core skill levels (e.g. typing speeds)
  - interviews (see later discussion)
  - assessment centres — these organisations conduct a series of tests, exercises and feedback sessions over a one- to five-day period to assess individual strengths and weakness
  - portfolios/examples of work — these are used to indicate the quality/type of recent job-related outputs. For example, an applicant for the position of a set designer for a theatrical event may be asked to supply photographs of his or her previous work.
- *future behaviour:* If appropriate, interview information can be supplemented with observations from simulations. For example, if the position is for a sponsorship manager, applicants can be asked to develop a sponsorship proposal, and demonstrate how they would present this proposal to a potential sponsor.

As interviews are likely to be the most common means of selection used by event organisations it is worthwhile spending some time looking at how best to employ this approach.

■ Interviews

Research, according to Stone (1998), clearly indicates that the interviewing process should be undertaken using a structured approach so that all relevant information can be covered and direct comparisons made between candidates. In this regard Mullins (1999) suggests the use of a check list on which key matters to be covered in the interview are listed. A sample check list for a paid position associated with an event is shown in figure 6.6. Checklists should also be used if interviews are to be conducted for volunteers. In such instances answers might be sought to questions regarding the relationship between the volunteer's background/experience and the position(s) sought; reasons for seeking to become involved with the event; level of understanding about the demands/requirements of the position(s) (e.g. time and training); and whether they have a physical or medical condition that may impact on the types of positions for which they can be considered (keeping in mind EEO legislation).

Applicant responses flowing from the interview process need to be assessed in some way against the key criteria for the position. One common means of doing this is a rating scale (e.g. 1 to 5). When viewed collectively, the ratings given to individual items lead to an overall assessment of the applicant in terms of how they fit with the job, the event organisation and its future directions.

Interviews may be conducted on a one-on-one basis, or via a panel of two or more interviewers. The latter has some advantages in that it assists in overcoming any idiosyncratic biases that individual interviewers might have, allows all interviewers to evaluate the applicant at the same time and on the same questions and answers, and facilitates the discussion of the pros and cons of individual applicants.

INTERVIEWER'S CHECKLIST

Name of applicant: _____ Date: _____

Position sought: _____

Understanding of responsibilities and requirements of the position (e.g. number of staff responsible for, working hours, reporting structure/requirements):

_____

_____

_____

Knowledge of event organisation/event vision, mission, goals, industry standing:

_____

_____

_____

Main qualifications for position: _____

Relationship of position to personal career goals: _____

Salary requirements: _____

Last organisation worked for: length of employment, responsibilities, career progress made, reasons for leaving, compatibility with supervisor(s), problems with supervisors and approach to dealing with them, what was liked/disliked about the job:

_____

_____

_____

_____

Applicant notified of outcome _____ Date/time: _____

Once the preferred applicant has been identified, the next step is to make a formal offer of appointment, by mail or otherwise. In the case of paid event staff, the short-time nature of many events means that any offer of employment will be for a specific contracted period. The employment contract generally states what activities are to be performed, salary/wage levels, and the rights and obligations of the employer and employee (see figure 6.7). In the case of volunteers, a simple letter of appointment, accompanied by details regarding the position may be all that is necessary. It is also appropriate to consider supplying volunteers with a statement about their rights and those of the event organisation regarding their involvement in the event (see figure 6.8). Once an offer has been made and accepted, unsuccessful applicants should be informed as soon as possible.

■ **Figure 6.7**
*General
components
of an
employment
contract*

GENERAL COMPONENTS OF AN EMPLOYMENT CONTRACT

- A statement of job titles and duties
- The date of employment commencement
- Rate of pay, allowances, overtime, method and timing of payment
- Hours of work including breaks
- Holiday arrangements/entitlement
- Sickness procedure (including sick pay, notification of illness)
- Length of notice due to and from the employee
- Grievance procedure
- Disciplinary procedure
- Work rules
- Arrangements for terminating employment
- Arrangements for union membership (if applicable)
- Special terms relating to confidentiality, rights to patents and designs, exclusivity of service, and restrictions on trade after termination of employment (e.g. cannot work for a direct competitor within six months)
- Employer's right to vary terms and conditions subject to proper notification

■ **Figure 6.8**
*Rights and
responsibilities
of volunteers
and voluntary
organisations*

RIGHTS AND RESPONSIBILITIES OF VOLUNTEERS AND VOLUNTARY ORGANISATIONS

Both the volunteer and the organisation have responsibilities to each other. The volunteer contracts to perform a specific job and the organisation contracts to provide the volunteer with a worthwhile and rewarding experience. In return, each has the right to some basic expectations of the other.

Volunteers have the right to:

- Be treated as co-workers. This includes job descriptions, EEO, OH&S, anti-discrimination legislation and organisational grievance processes
- Be asked for their permission before any job-related reference, police or prohibited person checks are conducted
- A task or job worthwhile to them, for no more than 16 hours a week on a regular basis
- Know the purpose and 'ground rules' of the organisation
- Appropriate orientation and training for the job
- Be kept informed of organisation changes and the reasons
- A place to work and suitable tools
- Reimbursement of agreed expenses
- Be heard and make suggestions
- Personal accident insurance in place of workers' compensation insurance
- A verbal reference or statement of service, if appropriate.

Organisations have the right to:

- Receive as much effort and service from a volunteer worker as a paid worker, even on a short-term basis
- To select the best volunteer for the job by interviewing and screening all applicants. This might include reference and police checks and, where appropriate, prohibited person checks for roles which involve working directly with children
- Expect volunteers to adhere to their job descriptions/outlines and the organisation's code of practice
- Expect volunteers to undertake training provided for them and observe safety rules
- Make the decision regarding the best placement of a volunteer
- Express opinions about poor volunteer effort in a diplomatic way
- Expect loyalty to the organisation and only constructive criticism
- Expect clear and open communication from the volunteer
- Negotiate work assignments
- Release volunteers under certain circumstances.

(**Source:** *School of Volunteer Management 2001*)

■ Induction

Once appointees (paid or voluntary) commence with an event organisation, a structured induction program designed to begin the process of 'bonding' the individual to the event organisation needs to be conducted. Getz (1997, p. 189) suggests a range of actions be taken as part of an effective induction program:

- provide basic information about the event (mission, objectives, stake-holders, budget, locations, program details)
- conduct tours of venues, suppliers, and offices and any other relevant locations
- make introductions to other staff and volunteers
- give an introduction about organisational culture, history and working arrangements
- overview training programs.

In addition to these actions, it is sound practice to discuss the job description with the individual to ensure they have a clear understanding of such matters as responsibilities, performance expectations, approaches to performance evaluation, and reporting relationships. At this time other matters associated with the terms and conditions of employment should also be discussed/reiterated, including probationary periods, grievance procedures, absenteeism, sickness, dress code, security, holiday/leave benefits, superannuation, salary and overtime rates, and other benefits such as car parking and meals. One means of ensuring mutual understanding of these matters is to have the staff member/volunteer read and sign their position description. An example of a position description that could be used for this purpose for volunteers is given in figure 6.9.

■ **Figure 6.9**
Example of a job description and contract for a volunteer

VOLUNTEER JOB DESCRIPTION AND CONTRACT
Job Title: _____
Supervisor: _____
Location: _____
Objective (Why is this job necessary? What will it accomplish?): _____
Responsibilities (What specifically will the volunteer do?): _____
Qualifications (What special skills, education, or age group is necessary to do this job?): _____
Training provided: _____
Benefits (parking, transportation, uniforms, food and beverage, expenses): _____
Trial period (probation, if required): _____
References required (yes or no): _____
Any other information: _____
Date: _____
Signature of volunteer (Signatures to be added at time of mutual agreement): _____
Signature of supervisor: _____

(**Source:** *Bradner 1997, p. 75*)

The induction process can also be facilitated by the development of an induction kit for distribution to each new staff member or volunteer. Bradner (1997) suggests that this kit should contain items such as:

- an annual report
- message from the organising committee chairperson/CEO welcoming staff and volunteers
- name badge
- staff list
- uniform (whether it be a T-shirt or something more formal)
- list of sponsors
- list of stakeholders
- any other appropriate items, e.g. occupational, health and safety information and newsletters.

A central outcome of the induction process should be a group of volunteers and staff who are committed to the event, enthusiastic and knowledgeable about their role in it and aware of what part their job plays in the totality of the event.

■ Training *and professional development*

Training and professional development are both, according to Stone (1998), concerned with changing the behaviour and job performance of staff and volunteers. Training is focused on providing specific job skills/ knowledge that will allow people to perform a job or to improve their performance in it. Professional development, on the other hand, is concerned with the acquisition of new skills, knowledge and attitudes that will prepare individuals for future job responsibilities.

Both training and professional development are significant in driving the success of an event, acting to underpin its effective delivery. For small and mid-sized events much training is on-the-job with existing staff and experienced volunteers acting as advice givers. This approach, while cheap and largely effective, does have limitations. The major one is that it is not often preceded by an assessment of the event's precise training needs, and how best to meet them within resource limitations.

A formal approach to training needs assessment will serve to determine if training that is currently taking place is adequate and if there are training needs that are not being met. Additionally such an assessment would generate suggestions about how to improve training provided by the event. These suggestions might include:

- sending, or requesting stakeholder/government support to send, staff/ volunteers on training programs dealing with specific areas or identified training need (e.g. risk management, event marketing, and sponsorship)
- identifying individuals associated with the event who would be willing to volunteer to conduct training sessions
- commissioning consultants/outside bodies such as TAFE, to undertake specific training

- encouraging staff/volunteers to undertake event-specific training programs, now provided by some TAFE systems, universities and event industry associations, in return for certain benefits (e.g. higher salaries, appointment to positions of greater responsibility/satisfaction).

When trying to identify what training is required to facilitate the effective delivery of an event, the central consideration is to determine the gap between the current performance of staff and volunteers and their desired performance. This can be achieved by:

- performance appraisals of existing staff/volunteers (what training do staff identify as being required to make them more effective)
- analysis of job requirements (what skills are identified in the job description)
- survey of personnel (what skills staff state they need).

■ Supervision *and evaluation*

As a general rule the bigger and more complex the event, the greater the need for staff/volunteers to perform a supervisory function. This function may be exercised through a variety of means including having would-be supervisors understudy an existing supervisor, developing a mentoring system, or encouraging staff to undertake appropriate professional development programs.

One of the key tasks of supervisors and managers is that of performance appraisal. This task involves evaluating performance, communicating that evaluation and establishing a plan for improvement. The ultimate outcomes of this process are a better event and more competent staff and volunteers. Stone (1998) proposes a dynamic performance appraisal program (see figure 6.10) based on goal establishment, performance feedback and performance improvement.

■ **Figure 6.10**
Dynamic performance appraisal program

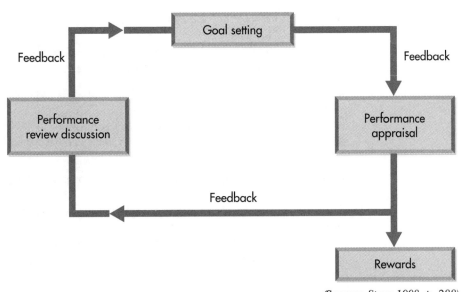

(**Source:** *Stone 1998, p. 288*)

Goals, according to Stone (1998), should be mutually arrived at between a supervisor and a volunteer or staff member. These goals, while they will be specific to the particular job, are likely to relate to matters such as technical skills and knowledge; problem solving/creativity, planning and organising, interpersonal skills, decision making, commitment to quality and safety, achievement of designated results, attitudes and personality traits, reliability/punctuality, and professional development. It is important that measurements associated with determining progress towards goals are established, otherwise there is little point in setting goals in the first place. For example, a person charged with overseeing waste management for an event may be assessed in terms of the percentage of material recycled from the event, levels of contamination in waste, percentage of attendees (as determined by survey) that understood directions regarding the placement of waste in containers, and the level of complaints regarding such matters as full bins. Other areas for assessment might include those associated with personal development (enrolment and completion of a specific course), interpersonal relationships (opinions of supervisors/co-workers) and problem solving/creativity (approaches employed to respond to the unexpected).

Performance, in terms of progress towards the established goals, can be assessed in a variety of ways, including staff and volunteers being ranked relative to one another from 'best' to 'worst' and grading on-the-job performance in terms of descriptors such as superior, good, acceptable, marginal, unsatisfactory. Getz (1997) provides a listing of useful scaling techniques which have been reproduced in figure 6.11.

■ **Figure 6.11**
Types of measurement for performance appraisals

TYPES OF MEASUREMENT FOR PERFORMANCE APPRAISALS

(a) Checklist of tasks:
- ■ satisfactorily completed
- ■ not satisfactorily completed.

(b) Subjective grading of the quality of work:

1	2	3
High quality	Medium	Low quality

(c) Objective measurement in key result areas, such as:
- ■ cash handling (e.g. amount of losses)
- ■ food preparation (e.g. measure wastage, violations of health regulations, orders taken accurately)
- ■ information (e.g. all questions answered accurately)
- ■ security (e.g. no site intrusions; incidents dealt with according to policy and law)

(d) Customer satisfaction (e.g. number and types of complaint; compliments received)

(e) Customer satisfaction scales (e.g. How satisfied are you with the service provided by . . .?):

1 2 3 4 5 6 7 8 9 10
Not at all   Completely

(Source: *Getz, 1997, p. 194)*

Once an appraisal has been conducted there should be a follow-up review discussion in which the supervisor/manager and the staff member/volunteer mutually review job responsibilities, examine how these responsibilities have been performed, explore how performance can be improved, and review and revise the staff members/volunteers short-term and long-term goals. The interview process should be a positive experience for both parties. To this end it is worthwhile considering providing training to the managers/supervisors involved in this process so that they adhere to certain basic practices such as preparing for the interview by reviewing job descriptions, reviewing previous assessments, being constructive not destructive, and encouraging discussion.

Integral to the appraisal system are rewards which in the case of paid staff come in the form of salaries, bonuses, profit sharing, promotion to other jobs or other events, and benefits such as cars and equipment usage (e.g. laptop computers). A range of options also exist to reward volunteers for their efforts. These include:

- training in new skills
- free merchandise (e.g. clothing, badges, event posters)
- hospitality in the form of opening and closing parties, free meals/drinks
- certificates of appreciation
- opportunities to meet with celebrities, sporting stars and other VIPs
- promotion to more interesting volunteer positions
- public acknowledgement through the media and at the event
- free tickets to the event.

The 'flip side' to rewards — that is, discipline — also requires managerial consideration. To this end it is useful to have in place specific policies and practices that reflect the seriousness of different behaviour/actions, and these should be communicated to all staff (paid and voluntary). These are likely to begin with some form of admonishment and end with dismissal. It should be noted that many of the approaches to disciplining paid employees (e.g. removing access to overtime) are not applicable to volunteers. Approaches that may be applied to this group include reassignment, withholding rewards/benefits, and simple admonition by a supervisor.

■ Termination, outplacement *and* *reenlistment*

Whether employing staff on contract or as permanent employees, event managers will occasionally be faced with the need to terminate the services of an individual. This action may be necessary in instances where an employee breaches the employment contract (e.g. repeatedly arrives at the workplace intoxicated) or continually exhibits unsatisfactory performance. This need may also arise when economic or commercial circumstances of the organisation conducting the event are such that it needs to shed staff (e.g. insufficient revenue due to poor ticket sales).

Various legal issues surrounding termination need to be understood by those involved in event management. These issues relate to unfair or unlawful dismissal, and are spelt out in the *Commonwealth Workplace Relations Act (1996)*. Essentially employers are required to give employees an opportunity to defend themselves against allegations associated with their conduct or capacity, and in cases of unsatisfactory performance, warn and counsel the employee before terminating his or her service. These requirements, it should be noted, do not apply to contracted or casual employees, or to staff on probation. A need can also arise from time to time to dismiss volunteers. Getz (1997) suggests a variety of approaches that can be employed for this purpose. These include making all volunteer appointments for fixed terms, with a need to reapply and be subjected to screening each time the event is conducted, and the use of job descriptions and performance appraisals to provide evidence for taking appropriate action.

Outplacement is the process of assisting terminated employees (or indeed volunteers), or even those who choose to leave the event organisation voluntarily, to find other employment. By performing this function the event organisation is providing a benefit to employees for past service, as well as maintaining and enhancing its image as a responsible employer. In the case of an event organising firm that decides to downsize, as indeed many did after the Sydney Olympic Games, this process could lead to staff being aided to take up positions in, for example, corporations operating their own event divisions or large events that maintain a full-time staff year round. Even volunteers who are no longer needed because, for example, the event for which they worked is not continuing can be helped into other positions by being put into contact with volunteer agencies or other events.

With recurring events, such as annual festivals, opportunities often exist to reenlist for paid or voluntary positions. For example, many staff from the Sydney Olympic Games have taken up positions within the organisation responsible for the Athens Olympics. To maintain contact with potential volunteers and past staff between events a variety of approaches can be employed, including newsletters (see the National Folk Festival Web site, http://www.folkfestival.asn.au/Pages/volunteers.html for an example), social events, offering benefits to reenlist, and making personal contact by phone between events.

■ Evaluation of process *and outcomes*

As with all management processes, a periodic review is necessary to determine how well, or otherwise, the process is working. To conduct such a review it is necessary to obtain feedback from relevant supervisory/management staff, and/or from organising committee members in the case of a voluntary event. A specific time should then be set aside, perhaps as part of a larger review of the event, to examine the extent to which the process as a whole, and the various elements of it, achieved the objectives that were originally set for it. Once the review is complete, revisions can then be made to the process for subsequent events.

MOTIVATING STAFF AND VOLUNTEERS

Motivation is a key, if implicit, component of the human resource management process. It is what commits people to a course of action, enthuses and energises them and enables them to achieve goals, whether the goals are their own or their organisation's. The ability to motivate other staff members is a fundamental component of the event manager's repertoire of skills. Without appropriate motivation, paid employees and volunteers can lack enthusiasm for achieving the event's corporate goals, for delivering quality service, or can show a lack of concern for the welfare of their co-workers or event participants.

In the context of volunteers, it may be thought that pure altruism (an unselfish regard for, or devotion to, the welfare of others) is an important motive for seeking to assist in the delivery of events. Although this proposition is supported by Flashman and Quick (1985), the great bulk of work done on motivation stresses that, although people may assert they are acting for altruistic reasons, they are actually motivated by a combination of external and internal factors, most of which have little to do with altruism. As Moore (1985, p. 1) points out, 'volunteers clearly expect to obtain some reward for their participation and performance'.

Much work has been done over many years by researchers from a variety of disciplines on what motivates people, particularly in the work place. Perhaps the most relevant and useful of these within the context of festivals and events are content theories and process theories.

■ **Content** *theories*

Content theories concentrate on what things initially motivate people to act in a certain way or, as Mullins (1999, p. 415) points out, 'are concerned with identifying people's needs and their relative strengths, and the goals they pursue in order to satisfy these needs'. Figure 6.12 represents the essential nature of theories of this type.

■ **Figure 6.12**
Basis of content theories of motivation

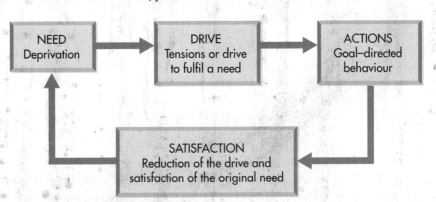

(**Source:** *Peach & Murrell 1995*)

Content theories assert that a person has a need — a feeling of deprivation — which then drives the person towards an action, which can satisfy that need. Abraham Maslow's (1954) hierarchy of needs, illustrated in figure 6.13, popularised the idea that needs are the basis of motivation.

■ **Figure 6.13**
Maslow's hierarchy of needs

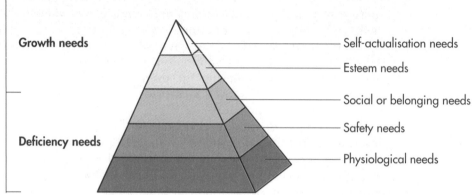

(**Source:** *Maslow 1954*)

In essence, Maslow's theory proposes that lower order needs must be satisfied before people are motivated to satisfy the next, higher need. That is, people who are trying to satisfy physiological needs of hunger and thirst have no interest in satisfying the need for safety until their physiological needs are satisfied. The first three needs are perceived as deficiencies; they must be satisfied in order to fulfil a lack of something. In contrast, satisfaction of the two higher needs is necessary for an individual to grow emotionally and psychologically.

Although little empirical evidence exists to support Maslow's theory, it can give insights into the reasons why people volunteer. People who feel a need for social interaction, making new friends or belonging to an organisation may be acting to satisfy social needs. Those who are motivated by the need for gaining the esteem of friends and family by performing a particular task that is prestigious in some way might be seeking to satisfy esteem-related needs. Finally, people may volunteer in order to undertake a task that they believe will help them achieve their potential as a person and thereby be self-fulfilled.

Another researcher who falls within the ambit of content theory is Herzberg (1968). He argued that some elements, which he called hygiene factors, did not of themselves motivate or satisfy people. Among these factors were pay levels, policies and procedures, working conditions and job security. However, the absence or perceived reduction in these items can stimulate hostility or dissatisfaction towards an organisation. He further argued that other factors, which he called motivators, did of themselves lead to goal-directed behaviour. These elements include achievement, recognition and interesting work. Herzberg's theory is illustrated in figure 6.14.

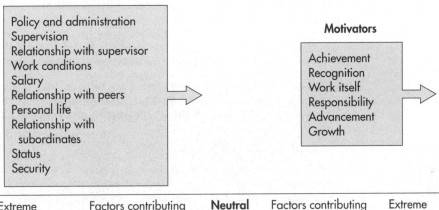

■ **Figure 6.14**
Herzberg's two-factor theory of motivation

Hygiene factors

Policy and administration
Supervision
Relationship with supervisor
Work conditions
Salary
Relationship with peers
Personal life
Relationship with
  subordinates
Status
Security

Motivators

Achievement
Recognition
Work itself
Responsibility
Advancement
Growth

| Extreme Dissatisfaction | Factors contributing to job dissatisfaction | **Neutral** | Factors contributing to job satisfaction | Extreme Satisfaction |

(**Source:** *adapted from Herzberg 1968*)

Herzberg's theory suggests that event managers can motivate staff and volunteers by:

• instituting processes of recognising achievement
• empowering staff so they can take responsibility for the outcomes of their part of the event
• providing opportunities for them to grow in skills, experience and expertise.

At the same time, event managers need to be conscious of certain hygiene factors that can act as demotivators. These might include attitudes of supervisors; working conditions such as the length of meal/coffee breaks and hours of work; the status of one job compared with another (e.g. waste management officer versus publicity coordinator), and policies such as the type/quality of uniforms given to volunteers.

Content theories, such as those of Herzberg and Maslow, provide managers with an understanding of work-related factors that initiate motivation, and focus attention on the importance of employee needs and their satisfaction. They do not, however, explain particularly well why a person chooses certain types of behaviour to satisfy their needs (Peach & Murrell 1995). Process theories, the subject of the next section, take up this challenge.

■ Process *theories*

Representative of process theories of motivation are Adams's (1965) equity theory and Vroom's (1964) expectancy theory.

Equity theory

Equity theory, as the name suggests, is based on the reasonable premise that all employees (or for that matter volunteers) expect to be treated fairly. This being the case, if one employee or volunteer perceives a discrepancy in the outcomes he or she receives (e.g. pay, type of work allocated) compared to those of other employees or volunteers, that employee or volunteer will be motivated to do more (or less) work. This situation is represented in the equation below:

$$\frac{\text{My rewards (outcomes)}}{\text{My contributions (inputs)}} = \frac{\text{Your rewards (outcomes)}}{\text{Your contributions (outcomes)}}$$

What an employee or volunteer sees as fair in terms of compensation (monetary or non-monetary) will obviously be subjective. The best way of maintaining an awareness of what an individual is thinking in this regard is to ensure open lines of communication are developed and maintained. If inequity is perceived and goes unnoticed, a number of outcomes are possible, including:

• a reduction in effort
• pressure to increase remuneration
• exit from the organisation.

Expectancy theory

Expectancy theory holds that the motivation to act in a particular way comes from a belief that by doing something a particular outcome will result (expectancy). This outcome will result in a reward (instrumentality). The rewards for accomplishing this outcome are sufficient to justify the effort put into doing it (valence). Motivation, under this theory, can therefore be expressed as:

$$\text{Motivation} = \text{Expectancy} \times \text{Instrumentality} \times \text{Valence}$$

This being the case, whenever one of the elements in this equation approaches zero the motivational value of a particular decision is dramatically reduced. Event managers need to be aware of this and therefore try to maximise all three motivational components. In other words, there must be a clear payoff if employees and volunteers are to perform at a high level. To understand what this payoff needs to be for each staff member and volunteer is difficult; however the chances of doing so are greatly increased if lines of communication are kept open, and a genuine effort is made to understand each individual.

As an example of how expectancy theory works, take the situation of a person who decides to work on their local community festival. They may have certain expectations:

• an *expectancy* that by working on the event they will gain certain new skills
• that these new skills in turn will enhance their future employability, thus creating an *instrumentality*
• that the jobs for which they will be able to apply with these new skills are ones that they believe they would find extremely rewarding, adding a strong degree of *value* to the circumstances.

If all three factors are strongly positive then motivation will be high.

It is from this theoretical framework that Peach and Murrell (1995, pp. 238–9) derive their reward and recognition techniques, which are shown in table 6.1.

REWARD SYSTEMS THAT WORK	RECOGNITION TECHNIQUES
Rewards that integrate the needs of the individual and the organisation in a win–win understanding	Carefully constructed systems that are built on the motives and needs of volunteers — individualised need recognition for each person
Rewards based on deep appreciation of the individual as a unique person	Recognition integrated into task performance, where clear performance objectives are established
Rewards based on job content, not conditions — rewards intrinsic to the job work best	Corporate growth and development objectives also become opportunities for recognition
Assignment of tasks that can be performed effectively, leading to intrinsic need satisfaction	Longevity and special contributions recognised frequently, not just every 10 years
Consistent reward policies that build a sense of trust that effort will receive the proper reward	Recognition grounded deeply on the core values of the organisation; what is recognised helps as a role model
Rewards that can be shared by teams so that winning is a collective and collaborative experience	

(**Source:** *Peach & Murrell 1995*)

TECHNIQUES FOR EFFECTIVE STAFF AND VOLUNTEER TEAM BUILDING

As was noted at the outset of the chapter, event organisations often come together quickly and exist for short periods of times. This being the case, one of the greatest challenges faced by an event manager is creating a sense of 'team' with a strong desire to progress the event's objectives. In the context of volunteers Nancy McDuff (1995, pp. 208–10), an internationally recognised authority on volunteer programs, has proposed a fourteen-element formula for effective team building and maintenance. These points are outlined below:

- *Teams are a manageable size.* Most effective teams are between two and 25 people, with the majority fewer than 10.
- *People are appropriately selected to serve on a team.* Care and attention should be paid to selecting people with the right combination of skills, personality, communication styles and ability to perform, thereby improving the chances of the team being successful.
- *Team leaders are trained.* Leaders who find it difficult to delegate and want to do everything themselves make poor leaders. Try to ensure team leaders have training in supervision skills.
- *Teams are trained to execute their tasks.* It is unrealistic to expect teams to perform effectively without appropriate training. The training should include the team's role in the activity and how that role contributes to its overall success.

- *Volunteers and staff are supported by the organisation.* Teams must feel that the administration is there to support their endeavours, not to hinder them.
- *Teams have objectives.* The purpose of the team is spelt out in measurable objectives. Having a plan to achieve those objectives helps build trust.
- *Volunteers and staff trust and support one another.* People trust each other when they share positive experiences. As each team is aware of the organisation's objectives and how their role helps to achieve those objectives, they trust their co-workers and support their efforts.
- *Communication between volunteers and the event organisation is both vertical and horizontal.* Communication, which means sending 'meanings' and understandings between people, is a process involving an active and continuous use of active listening, the use of feedback to clarify meaning, reading body language, and the use of symbols that communicate meaning. Communication travels in all directions — up and down the reporting line and between teams and work groups. Working together is facilitated by good communication.
- *The organisational structure promotes communication between volunteers and staff.* The organisation's structure, policies and operating programs permit and encourage all members of the organisation to communicate with their co-workers, their managers and members of other departments. This help builds an atmosphere of cooperation and harmony in the pursuit of common objectives.
- *Volunteers and staff have real responsibility.* A currently fashionable concept of management is 'empowerment'. This means giving staff authority to make decisions about their work and its outcomes. Let us look at the example of, say, a group of volunteers having the somewhat mundane task of making sandwiches. If they are empowered with the authority to decide what sandwiches to make, how to make them, and where to sell them, their enthusiasm for the task will probably be enhanced and there will be a corresponding improvement in outcomes.
- *Volunteers and staff have fun while accomplishing tasks.* Managers should strive to engender an atmosphere of humour, fun and affection between co-workers within the culture of the organisation. Such actions as ceremonies to acknowledge exemplary contributions to the event, wrap-up parties, and load-in celebrations can facilitate this.
- *There is recognition for the contributions of volunteers and staff.* Paid staff should express formal and informal appreciation of the work of volunteers, and the work of the paid staff should be publicly recognised and appreciated by volunteers. This mutual appreciation should be consistent, public and visible.
- *Volunteers and staff celebrate their success.* Spontaneous celebrations with food, drink, friendship and frivolity should be encouraged by management of the event to celebrate achievement of objectives. The event manager should allocate a budgeted amount for these occasions.
- *The entire organisation promotes and encourages the wellbeing of volunteer teams.* Everyone in the organisation sees him- or herself as part of a partnership and actively promotes such relationships.

Once teams are in place and operating effectively, the event manager should monitor their performance and productivity by observing their activities and maintaining appropriate communication with team leaders and members. If deficiencies are noticed during the monitoring procedure, appropriate action can be taken in terms of training, team structure or refinement of operating procedures in a climate of mutual trust.

LEGAL OBLIGATIONS

Event managers need to be mindful of laws and statutes that impact upon the employee and employer relationship, some of which have previously been noted in this chapter. Areas covered by these laws and statutes include occupational health and safety (OH&S), discrimination, employee dismissal, salaries/wages, and working conditions (e.g. holiday and long service leave, superannuation and workers' compensation). To obtain current information on these matters event managers should consider contacting the following organisations:

- Worksafe Australia (OH&S)
- Human Rights and Equal Opportunity Commission (discrimination)
- Australian Industrial Relations Commission (dismissal)
- State/Territory Department of Industrial Relations (wages and working conditions).

Event managers should also remember that there are common law requirements regarding the duties of parties to an employment relationship. In the context of volunteers, common law precedents provide rights to damages if negligence can be shown on behalf of an event organiser.

SUMMARY

Event managers should approach the task of human resource management not as a series of separate activities but as an integrated process involving a number of steps, taking as their starting point the event organisations mission, strategy and goals. These steps have been identified in this chapter as human resources strategy and objectives; policies and procedures; recruitment; training and professional development; supervision and evaluation; termination, outplacement and reenlistment; and evaluation and feedback. It has been shown here that these steps have application to the employment of both paid and volunteer staff, as well as to events of varying size and type. This chapter has also dealt with the issue of motivation, examining two broad theoretical perspectives on the matter, process and content theories. The final sections of this chapter dealt with mechanisms for developing task teams to conduct events and the legal considerations associated with human resource management.

Questions

1. Interview the organiser of an event of your choice and ask him or her what legal/statutory requirements impact upon human resource management processes and practices.

2. In the context of a specific event, identify the policies and procedures regarding human resource management. Collect examples of forms and other material that support them.

3. Develop a job specification for the position of event manager for a special event of your choice.

4. List the questions that you would ask a candidate during an interview for the position given in question 3.

5. In the context of a small community festival, undertake a job analysis.

6. Identify all voluntary positions involved in the event examined in question 5, and write brief job descriptions for each position.

7. Propose an induction and training program for the event identified in question 5.

8. Critically review the human resource management process employed by an event of your choice. Use the steps identified in this chapter as the framework for your analysis.

9. Discuss general approaches that you might employ to motivate the volunteer staff associated with an event. Which of these approaches would be most appropriate for an event such as the one you examined in question 8?

10. Discuss in general terms how you would go about evaluating the performance of event volunteers or paid staff.

··

Secrets to the success of the
volunteer program at the Sydney 2000 Olympic and Paralympic Games

Volunteers — never underestimate them. Always respect them and their 'power', always adopt the shared responsibility focus, always prepare them well, always expect the best from them, always give back to them as much as you expect from them, and always share ownership with them. Oh, and never ever take them for granted.

Volunteers are the backbone of many events, as well as being central to our society's service provision in areas such as welfare, recreation, the environment, the arts, and emergency services. Their 'visibility' and profile hit its peak in Australia in 2000 when the largest of all events was conducted in Sydney — the Olympic and Paralympic Games.

Remember them? Sixty-two thousand volunteers doing all sorts of specialist and non-specialist roles — who performed so magnificently that the President of the IOC declared them (at the Closing Ceremony of the Olympic Games) 'the most wonderful and dedicated volunteers ever'. The ultimate wrap, and so thoroughly deserved — not just for their five million hours of time but more importantly the quality of their efforts and the lasting images they created with visitors.

Positioning volunteers as an integral part of the Games workforce was critical to the success of the Games. Whether paid or unpaid, all staff of the organising committee were part of one team — all dedicated to the same result of a fabulous and memorable Games and one where people left our shores with great impressions of our country, city and people.

We embraced our volunteers, we trusted them, and we empowered them. But, with those rights came responsibilities — we had high expectations of them and there was never any shirking from that message. The volunteers wanted to be 'close' to the Games, they wanted to later 'brag' about their role in making the Games successful, they wanted to be busy and expected us to keep them busy, and importantly they expected to be judged on their performance. Exactly what we also wanted.

The single most important reason for the success of the volunteer program at the Games was the sense of ownership that volunteers were encouraged to take over the event. A little esoteric you might say but that single message drove their attitudes and their performance. Responsibility also accompanied that ownership. 'We may not represent our country again in so visible a way' was uppermost in their minds. Equally was their attitude that they had to 'hang in there' with us even during the tougher times — they did.

What else made it work? A number of things — securing the right people (no, not every applicant got a job nor should that ever be the case); making sure each job was clearly defined and understood (yes, there were job descriptions and required skill sets in great volume); matching the volunteers to those jobs; intensive training (induction, job-specific, and venue training) that promoted the need for high performance and customer service; good Aussie hospitality and having a sense of fun; detailed operational policies and procedures; and a comprehensive recognition and appreciation strategy. And finally, training of our paid staff in the management of volunteers was absolutely vital to effective management and job satisfaction for our volunteers (high retention rates were experienced at both events).

Sound easy? It wasn't. But gratifying and satisfying it surely was. Certainly, the program was not perfect, but the overall approach to volunteer management (as outlined here) was well conceived, and the fundamentals sound, leaving a lasting positive impression with our visitors and the Australian community as a whole.

David Brettell
Program Manager Venue Staffing and Volunteers
Sydney Olympic & Paralympic Games 2000

Managing staff
at the Australian Open

The Australian Open comes from a long tradition of tennis championships. The Australasian Tennis Championships began in 1905. It became the Australian Championships in 1927, then the Australian Open in 1969. These championships have been staged at six different venues within Australia and New Zealand, but since 1988 the Australian Open has been located at Melbourne Park. The championship is part of the Grand Slam Tournament which includes the French Open (Stade Roland Garros, Paris), Wimbledon (Wimbledon, London) and the US Open (Flushing Meadows, New York). The event is growing in popularity each year. In 1999, the economic impact of the Australian Open was calculated as A$114.2 million, with nearly 40 000 interstate and overseas visitors coming to Melbourne.

The Australian Open employs more than 2000 staff across different areas of the tournament, including 200 courtesy car drivers, 206 ball persons, 312 umpires, 68 court servicers and 60 scoreboard operators. Added to this number are the staff employed by outsourced companies that supply, for example, catering and equipment. With more than half a million people attending the 2000 Australian Open, managing this number of paid staff makes the Australian Open one of the most complex and intense hallmark events during the year. The Australian Open is unique in that no other event in Australia runs for 14 consecutive days. This case study explores the human resource issues that confront management at the event.

There are a number of different types of employee at the Australian Open, but the common theme is the development of an organisational culture of professional staff in a relaxed and friendly environment. Management work hard to develop, as much as possible, a sense of teamwork and common goals for employees. Volunteers who were given gratuities once occupied many of the positions that are now paid positions. The need for greater professionalism and consistent quality service has paved the way for these jobs becoming paid positions. Rewards for these staff include pay, as well as access to available seats at the various courts, free meals, uniforms and some free transport.

The success and status of the event has made it a very attractive event to potential employees. Unlike most other events, the Australian Open does not need to advertise its positions. Each year thousands of applications for jobs, particularly ball persons, are received by the Australian Open. Applications can now be made on the Web site www.ausopen.org. Applications for ball persons are taken immediately following the championship, with the selection of the successful candidates occurring in May. Training ensures that the Australian Open has a high level of professionalism. Other priorities for training employees focus on customer awareness and the policies and procedures for an effective and safe environment.

The role of the courtesy car drivers has grown over the years. There are more than 200 drivers and seven supervisors to coordinate them. It is important for these drivers to observe protocol and the privacy of the players and celebrity guests. However, in return for these services the drivers, who were originally volunteers, are paid and are also provided with the 'fringe benefits' mentioned earlier. Their role is a particularly important one: they get players and celebrities to the courts safely and punctually. The careful selection of these drivers is one of the keys to the success of this increasingly important service at the Australian Open.

The Australian Open is an extremely successful event and this is due, in part, to the activities associated with watching and playing tennis. Providing the right facilities is a high priority for Melbourne Park, as is the provision of a wide range of quality food outlets for the thousands of spectators who attend each day. To fulfil this priority requires hiring a large, but temporary, work force. Delaware North (Australia) Pty Ltd caters for the Australian Open. The company hires an extra 1500 staff for various catering outlets. These outlets cover corporate, public and vending catering services. Each area requires specific skills and training. With eight main corporate areas, 28 public food outlets, more than 130 vendors and over 180 kitchen staff, Delaware North requires 'fail-safe' recruitment and selection methods. Attracting the right staff is one of the keys to the success of catering for such large crowds.

Delaware North uses the major Australian newspapers to place its advertisements. Headlines such as 'It's not Rafter we're after, it's you!' convey the sense of enjoyment that Delaware North wants its staff to gain. More importantly, however, the catering company demands a high level of expertise and professionalism from its temporary work force. The key attributes that the company is keen to obtain are those of experience and skill in food and beverage, the ability to work under pressure, and excellent customer service skills. All of these skills are tested in various ways during the selection processes. The company also uses students and graduates from hospitality and tourism courses that are offered at local TAFE and universities.

Hiring staff for the Australian Open, which is held in late January each year, begins in the September of the previous year, although many of the staff are retained from year to year. In order to hire such large numbers of appropriate staff, Delaware North runs group interviews that explore the candidates' previous work experience, their customer service skills and attitudes and why the candidates would wish to work at the Australian Open. These interviews run for approximately two hours and also include briefings on the company, the Australian Open, standards required for uniforms and grooming as well as the expectations of training and induction sessions.

The induction sessions need to be very well planned and executed. While operational issues such as timesheets, security, dress codes and disciplinary issues are important, it is the customer service skills and attitudes that are the priority and these sessions are scrutinised and improved each year. Another key issue is that of protocol. For example, a staff member who attempted to take a photo of the women's tennis champion, Martina Hingis, was immediately disciplined and the issue required delicate handling from senior staff. Other misconduct, such as intoxication, use of abusive language to either customers or other employees and the failure to observe safety measures, warrants instant dismissal. All staff are provided with a staff handbook that outlines these categories. Induction also covers occupational health and safety, legal issues and media protocol.

Catering staff hired for the 14 days of the Australian Open require accreditation. This involves having the appropriate identification paperwork as well as training in food hygiene and responsible service of alcohol.

The Victorian Catering Award covers all staff hired by Delaware North and the compulsory training is provided free by the company. Accredited staff have access to free transport on certain public transport and staff dining facilities are available at discounted prices. These rewards are tangible and consistent across the board for those hired by Delaware North. Staff have a clear understanding of what is required and what they will receive in return for their services.

The key issue for the Australian Open, and for companies such as Delaware North, is to provide a consistent standard of quality service using committed staff. To gain commitment from staff, these organisations must provide an event that staff are proud to be associated with, and a clear understanding of the role that they have in making the event a success. The importance of the recruitment, selection, induction and training processes cannot be underestimated. Even more important is that the staff return, year after year, to make the event the success that it is. Managing the staff well means that the spectators and players will enjoy the event and begin a cycle of success for all concerned.

Marg Deery
Victoria University, Melbourne

Questions

1 What are some of the key attributes, skills and attitudes that the Australian Open would desire of (a) a ball person and (b) a courtesy car driver? How would you assess these attributes?

2 The Australian Open, in the past, 'employed' a large number of volunteers. Why have these volunteer positions become paid positions for the 14-day event?

3 List and explain the ways in which the Australian Open and companies such as Delaware North can improve the recruitment, selection and training of the staff they employ for the event. What ways are there to reward and motivate the staff other than those mentioned in the case study?

4 The Australian Open is an extremely successful major event in Australia. What are the threats to the success of this event, referring particularly to the management of the human resources?

REFERENCES

Adams, J. S. 1965, 'Inequity in social exchange', in *Advances in Experimental Social Psychology*, ed. L. Berkowitz, Academic Press, New York.

Armstrong, M. 1999, *A Handbook of Human Resource Management Practice*, 7th edn, Kogan Page, London.

Beardwell, I. & Holden, L. 2001, *Human Resource Management: A Contemporary Perspective*, 3rd edn, Pearson Education, London.

Bradner, J. 1997, 'Recruitment, orientation, retention', in *The Volunteer Management Handbook*, ed. T. Connors, John Wiley & Sons, New York.

Clark, R. 1992, *Australian Human Resources Management*, McGraw Hill, Sydney.

Flashman R. & Quick, S. 1985, 'Altruism is not dead: a specific analysis of volunteer motivation', in *Motivating Volunteers*, ed. L. Moore, Vancouver Volunteer Centre, Vancouver.

Getz, D. 1997, *Event Management and Event Tourism*, Cognizant Communication Corporation, New York.

Hanlon, C. & Jago, L. 2000, 'Pulsating sporting events', *Events Beyond 2000 — Setting the Agenda*, eds J. Allen, R. Harris, L. K. Jago & A. J. Veal, Proceedings of the Conference on Evaluation, Research and Education, 13–14 July, Sydney, Australian Centre for Event Management, University of Technology, pp. 93–104.

Hertzberg, F. 1968, 'One more time: how do you motivate employees?', *Harvard Business Review*, 46, no. 1 (January–February).

Maslow, A., 1954, *Motivation and Personality*, Harper & Row, New York.

McCurley, S. & Lynch, R. 1998, *Essential Volunteer Management*, 2nd edn, Directory of Social Change, London.

McDuff, N. 1995, 'Episodic volunteering', in ed. T. Connors, *The Volunteer Management Handbook*, John Wiley & Sons, New York.

Moore, L. 1985, *Motivating Volunteers*, Vancouver Volunteer Centre, Vancouver.

Mullins, L. J. 1999, *Management and Organisational Behaviour*, 5th edn, Financial Times/Pitman Publishing, London.

National Folk Festival 2001, available from http://www.folkfestival.asn.au/Pages/volunteers.html (accessed 5 May 2001).

Peach, E. & Murrell, K., 1995 'Reward and recognition systems for volunteers', in *The Volunteer Management Handbook*, ed. T. Connors, John Wiley & Sons, New York.

School of Volunteer Management 2001, *Rights and Responsibilities of Volunteers and Voluntary Organisations* (pamphlet), Sydney.

Stone, R. 1998, *Human Resource Management*, 3rd edn, John Wiley & Sons, Brisbane.

Vroom, V. 1964, *Work and Motivation*, John Wiley & Sons, New York.

The marketing
of events

LEARNING OBJECTIVES

After studying this chapter, you should be able to:

- describe how the marketing concept can be applied to festivals and special events

- understand the needs and motivations of festival and event customers

- conduct a market segmentation analysis to establish appropriate target markets for an event

- forecast the probable demand for an event

- construct a marketing plan for an event that contains appropriate pricing, promotion, place and product strategies.

The parent of modern marketing and the originator of the marketing concept of the four Ps (product, price, place, promotion), E. Jerome McCarthy, defines the marketing concept as 'the idea that an organization should aim all its efforts at satisfying its customers — at a profit' (McCarthy & Perreault 1987, p. 7). The entire focus of an organisation should be on satisfying the wants and needs of an identified group of people with some homogeneous characteristic — the target market. This is in contrast to the popular view of marketing that assumes it is concerned only with selling or advertising. Marketing does not encompass only these activities, but much more. In 1960, Theodore Levitt, the Harvard University marketing authority, said '[m]arketing...views the entire business process as consisting of a tightly integrated effort to discover, create, arouse, and satisfy customer needs' (Levitt 1980, p. 16). This chapter describes the marketing process.

Following is a definition of marketing in the context of events:

■ Marketing is that function of event management that can keep in touch with the event's participants and visitors (consumers), read their needs and motivations, develop products that meet these needs, and build a communication program which expresses the event's purpose and objectives (Hall 1997, p. 136). ■

To illustrate these concepts, the following list shows the marketing activities that an event manager undertakes to produce a successful festival or special event:
• analyses the needs of the target market to establish appropriate event components, or 'products'
• establishes what other competitive events could satisfy similar needs to ensure their event has a unique selling proposition
• predicts how many people will attend the event
• predicts at what times people will come to the event
• estimates what price they will be willing to pay to attend
• decides on the type and quantity of promotional activities telling the target market about the event
• decides on how tickets to the event can reach the target market
• establishes the degree of success for the marketing activities.

All of these activities, essential for a successful event, are part of the marketing function. This chapter explores how the event manager carries out these functions to achieve the objectives set out in the event strategic plan discussed in chapter 5.

These marketing concepts are then further expanded in chapter 8, which discusses the marketing of events in a strategic fashion.

■ The need *for marketing*

Some critics of the marketing concept argue that some cultural festivals and events should not be concerned with the target market's needs, but with innovation, creativity and the dissemination of new art forms. The argument goes that consumers' needs are based on what they know or have experienced and therefore consumers will not accept innovative or avant-garde cultural experiences. Thus, if the marketing concept of focusing on customer needs is used, nothing new will ever be produced. As Dickman states, 'administrators were reluctant to even use the word [marketing], believing that it suggested 'selling out' artistic principles in favour of finding the lowest common denominator' (1997, p. 685).

This attitude, while perhaps understandable, is based on a misunderstanding of marketing principles and techniques and can be self-defeating for the following reasons.

- The use of marketing principles gives event managers a framework for decision making that should result in successful events that still allow for innovation and creativity, but cater for a target market segment that has a need for novelty and the excitement of the new.
- Sponsoring bodies require some certainty that their sponsorship will be received by the target market they seek. Sound marketing practices will help convince them that a festival or event is an appropriate medium for them to communicate to their target market.
- All three levels of government financially assist many festivals and events. They usually fund only those events whose management can demonstrate some expertise in marketing planning and management.
- Consumers, particularly those resident in major cities, have an enormous range of leisure activities from which to choose to spend their disposable income. This means that a festival or special event, which, by definition, can be categorised as a leisure activity, will attract only those who expect to satisfy one of their perceived needs. Therefore, any festival or event needs to be designed to satisfy the identified needs of its target market. Failure to do this usually results in an event that is irrelevant to the needs of its target market and does not meet its objectives.

■ Consumer *expectations*

The marketing concept is just as applicable to a leisure service such as an event as it is to any other product. In fact, it could be even more so, as a leisure service, like other services, is intangible, variable, perishable and inseparable.

For example, consider a customer attending an outdoor jazz and blues festival. Unlike the purchase of goods, there is nothing tangible the customer can pick up, touch, feel or try before purchase. They merely decide to attend the festival based on expectations that a particular need (for entertainment, social interaction, a novel experience, self-education and so on) will be met.

Consumer expectations come from a combination of marketing communications from the festival organiser, word-of-mouth recommendations from friends and family, previous experience with this or similar events, and the brand image of the event. The service the customer receives — being entertained — is inseparable from the consumption of the service. In other words, instead of purchasing a good in a shop and then consuming that good somewhere else, production and consumption of the service are simultaneous or inseparable. Customers do not purchase by chance, but have to make a conscious decision to travel to the event site.

Even when markets are tightly segmented into a group of people with a common characteristic, members of the group may have differing perceptions of the benefits they have received from the event experience. This comes about because people are slightly different in their perceptions and attitudes, and therefore their perception of the service they receive and the people they receive it from may be variable. For example, two close friends may attend the jazz and blues festival. One may perceive all the services provided as terrific, yet the other may not be as enthusiastic, despite having experienced the same service.

If the weather is poor on the day of the festival and attendance is affected, unsold tickets for that day cannot be stored and sold when the weather improves. In other words, leisure services are extremely perishable.

It is these characteristics of leisure experiences such as festivals and events that makes careful, structured thinking and planning of the marketing function integral to the success of any event.

MARKETING MIX

Getz proposes this definition of marketing for events:

> ■ Marketing events is the process of employing the marketing mix to attain organizational goals through creating value for clients and customers. The organization must adopt a marketing orientation that stresses the building of mutually beneficial relationships and the maintenance of competitive advantages (Getz 1997, p. 250). ■

This definition introduces the concept of the marketing mix which McCarthy and Perreault (1987, p. 5) define as 'the controllable variables that the company puts together to satisfy a target group'. McCarthy and Perreault identified these variables as product, price, promotion and place, and each of these variables is discussed in depth in this chapter. 'Controllable' means that the event manager can manipulate or alter these variables in order to achieve an event's marketing objectives.

'Product' encompasses all of the elements that make up the festival or event. This includes such things as the entertainment offered, standard of service, food and beverage facilities, opportunities for social interaction, consumer participation in the event, merchandising, staff interaction with customers and the 'brand' image the festival or event enjoys among the target market.

'Price' means the value consumers place on the event experience and are prepared to pay. This value is determined by the strength of the need the leisure experience satisfies and alternative leisure experiences offered by other events and other leisure service providers. The price of an event experience can be varied according to the type of customer (e.g. pensioner concessions) or the time of consumption (e.g. discounted price for previews).

Promotion is, as Middleton (1995) points out, the most visible of the four Ps of the marketing mix. It includes all of the marketing communication techniques of advertising, personal selling, sales promotion, some merchandising (T-shirt sales featuring the event, for example), publicity and public relations, and direct mail. Potential consumers are motivated to purchase the leisure experience offered by the event by the design of these messages.

'Place' has two meanings in event marketing. As well as signifying the geographical location of the event, it also means the purchase point(s) for tickets to the event. For example, the place for a jazz and blues festival not only means the venue (e.g. Byron Bay Showground), but also the method of distribution of tickets to the event (e.g. are they sold only at the gate, or can they be pre-purchased and, if so, where?)

Some marketing writers have developed variations on the original four Ps. For example, Cowell (1984) proposes a seven-P marketing mix of:
• product
• price
• promotion
• place
• people
• physical evidence (layout, furnishing of venue, sound quality)
• process (customer involvement in the leisure service).
However, the last three Ps are just part of the product element of the marketing mix.

Getz goes one P further and proposes an eight-P mix of:
• product (the service offered)
• place (the location)
• programming (elements and quality of style)
• people (cast, audience, hosts and guests)
• partnerships (stakeholders in producing the event)
• promotion (marketing communications)
• packaging and distribution of tickets
• price (1997, p. 251).
It is Middleton's view that 'it helps the understanding of a central marketing concept to focus on an unambiguous, easy to understand four Ps' (1995, p. 66). The product consists of elements that vary according to the target market, the venue, and other stakeholders. While splitting product into various other 'P' elements may cause muddled marketing thinking and action, it can also assist event marketers to think strategically. These concepts are further pursued in chapter 8.

Table 7.1 summarises the four Ps of the marketing mix and considers the variable elements of each.

FOUR Ps	ELEMENTS
Product:	
• design characteristics/packaging	Location, staging, entertainment mix, food and beverage provision, seating, queuing, decoration, theme, lighting
• service component	Number of service staff, degree of training, uniforms, standard of service quality
• branding	Prominence given to name of event and what that name means to consumers
• reputation/positioning	Where event is to be positioned in terms of consumer demand — up-market to mass market
Price:	
• time of consumption	Discounted prices at times of low demand
• promotional price	Concessional prices for certain target markets
Promotion:	
• advertising — television, radio, newspaper, magazine, outdoor	The promotional mix
• sales promotion — merchandising, public relations	
• flyers and brochures	
• personal selling via a sales force	
Place:	
• channels of distribution	Tickets available through an agency such as Ticketek or sold by mail from a mailing list

The term 'promotional mix' refers to the many components that can constitute marketing communications between an event and its potential audience (or consumers). It is these variables that the event manager can manipulate to achieve an event's objectives. However, it must be noted that the product, the promotion and the place (if a ticketing agency or direct mail is to be used) require a commitment to upfront expenditure before any revenue is obtained from ticket sales. It is therefore important that the marketing planning processes are thorough, thoughtful and realistic in their forecast of both revenue and expenditure. Any muddle in the marketing process can have disastrous consequences for the viability and longevity of any event.

Figure 7.1 shows how the marketing mix fits in the context of the event organisation and its environments. Chapter 5 discussed how the strategic planning process went about choosing appropriate strategies that can achieve the event's objectives. Some of those strategies are concerned with marketing and will result from a marketing planning process that is embedded in the strategic planning process. These concepts of strategic marketing are further elucidated in chapter 8.

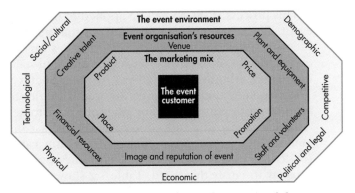

Figure 7.1 *How the marketing mix fits in the context of the event organisation*

(**Source:** *adapted from Middleton 1995*)

The core of the planning process, as the marketing concept suggests, is the consumer. The event's features should satisfy the needs of a carefully chosen consumer segment. All marketing efforts focus on these needs and how they can be satisfied, either profitably or in a way that achieves the objectives of the event.

The inner ring contains the marketing variables of the four Ps that the event director (or its marketing manager in a large event) can manipulate. A realistic estimate of the revenue and sponsorship that an event or festival can generate, however, determines the funds that can be spent on product enhancement, promotion and ticket distribution.

■ The marketing *environment*

The marketing efforts of an event do not occur in isolation. They are obviously constrained by the resources of the event organisation. For example, if an event has very few volunteers to assist with all aspects of customer interaction, it would be unrealistic to embark on a process of increasing the quality of customer service. In other words, the marketing effort is constrained by the use of available resources.

The main elements of this environment — socio/cultural, technological, physical, economic, political and legal, and competitive and demographic, were discussed in detail in the planning chapter on pages 109–111. They should be revisited and explored when analysing the marketing environment.

*T*HE EVENT CUSTOMER

The following acronym helps explain the customer decision-making process (Morgan 1996, p. 80):

Problem recognition
Information search
Evaluation of alternatives
Choice of purchase
Evaluation of post-purchase experience.

This process (PIECE) can be applied to the decision to attend a festival or event. The consumer identifies a need that may be satisfied by attending an event or other leisure experience, searches for information about such an experience in different media (entertainment section of newspapers, radio, magazines, friends and relatives), then evaluates the alternatives available. The customer then compares the needs the leisure experience can satisfy against a list of attributes. For example, a customer seeks an opportunity to enhance family ties and chooses to attend a community festival that contains elements that all members of the family can enjoy. After experiencing (or 'consuming') the event, the customer evaluates the experience for its capacity to satisfy that need. Table 7.2 shows the implications for event marketers of this process.

■ Table 7.2 *The event consumer decision process and the implications for marketing*	STAGE IN THE CONSUMER DECISION-MAKING PROCESS	IMPLICATIONS FOR MARKETING STRATEGIES	MARKETING DECISIONS
	Recognition of the need	Selection of appropriate target market(s)	Which market — mass or focused?
	Search for information	Promotional mix variables	Direct mail, publicity, paid advertising, or other types of advertising?
	Evaluation of the alternatives	Event elements design Promotional message	Change the product? Change the promotional mix?
	Choice at point-of-sale	Ease of purchase	What are the incentives for sellers?
	Evaluation of leisure experience	Service quality	What type of post-event research will be undertaken? How will consumer satisfaction be monitored?

The starting point for this marketing process is the needs of the customer that may be satisfied by attending a festival or event. Little empirical research on needs and motivations for event customers has been published in Australia. However, academic research carried out in North America in recent years gives insights into this issue (Roslow, Nicholls & Laskey 1992; Mohr et al. 1993; Saleh & Ryan 1993; Uysal, Gahan & Martin 1993; Getz 1991).

Based on their research of customers of a jazz festival and a handcraft festival in Saskatchewan, Canada, Saleh and Ryan (1993) tentatively suggest a sequential decision-making process for festival attendance that supports Morgan's PIECE model. Figure 7.2 illustrates this process. The missing element of evaluation (E) occurs after the leisure experience has occurred.

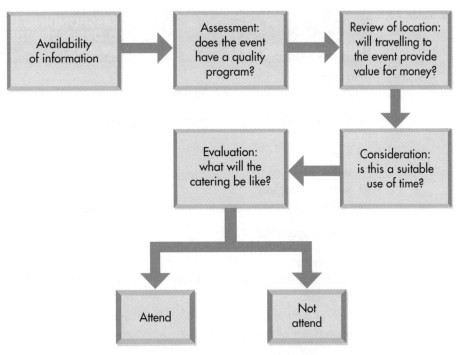

Figure 7.2
A sequential decision-making model for attending a festival or special event

(**Source:** *adapted from Saleh & Ryan 1993*)

A study of customers at a community festival in South Carolina by Uysal, Gahan and Martin (1993) and a study of attendees of a North American hot air balloon festival by Mohr et al. (1993) reported that the five principal motivations (or need satisfiers) for attending festivals are:

- *socialisation*: being with friends, people who are enjoying themselves and people who enjoy the same things
- *family togetherness*: seeking the opportunity so the family can do something together and to bring the family together
- *excitement/thrills*: doing something because it is stimulating and exciting
- *escape*: getting away from the usual demands of life and having a change from daily routine
- *event novelty*: experiencing new and different things and/or attending a festival that is unique.

Although the motivations for visiting both festivals were the same, the order was slightly different. Visitors to the community festival placed 'escape' at the top of their motivations, whereas visitors to the hot air balloon festival considered 'socialisation' the most important motivator. This suggests that visitors to specialised festivals are highly motivated by a desire to socialise with people who share their interests, while visitors to community festivals are more motivated by 'escape' from the ordinariness of day-to-day life.

Getz (1991) adapts Maslow's theory of people having a needs hierarchy. Maslow proposed that needs are satisfied in the following order: physiological, safety, social, self-esteem, self-development. Getz adapted this to propose a three generic needs model. Table 7.3 is an adaptation of Getz's theory.

■ Table 7.3
*Needs,
motives and
benefits
offered by
events*

NEEDS AND MOTIVES	CORRESPONDING BENEFITS AND OPPORTUNITIES OFFERED BY EVENTS
Physical Physiological needs motivate the need to:	
• eat and drink	Eat and drink new, different food and drink.
• exercise	Participate in sporting activities.
• relax	Relaxing entertainment
• search for security	Recreation in a secure environment.
• find sexual gratification.	Meet people.
Social/interpersonal The need for belonging, friendship and love motivate:	
• socialising with family and friends	Share a new and different environment.
• romance	Meet new people.
• links to cultural and ethnic roots	Renew ties to ethnic and cultural groups.
• expressions of community and nationalism	Share in the use of appropriate symbols and rituals.
• pursuit of recognition for accomplishments.	Gather prestige from attending an event.
Personal The need for understanding, aesthetic appreciation, growth and self-development motivates:	
• a quest for knowledge	Formal/informal learning
• seeking new experiences	Unique programs
• creativity	Participate in artistic endeavours.
• fulfilment of ambitions.	Participate in something unique and special.

(**Source:** *adapted from Getz 1991*)

Morgan (1996) identified five other social factors that can influence consumers' leisure behaviour. These can be described in the context of event participation as follows:

1. *Family influences*: the desires of children will often influence the leisure behaviour of their parents. The need for family cohesion and the enhancement of familial ties is a strong motivator for many people. This explains the enormous numbers of children accompanied by exhausted parents that can be found at the show bag pavilion of agricultural shows around Australia. Many festivals include entertainment for children for this reason.

2. *Reference groups*: groups who influence the behaviour of those with whom they come into close contact (such as peers, family, colleagues and

neighbours) are called 'primary reference groups'. Those who have less frequent contact are called 'secondary reference groups'. Most people tend to seek the approval of members of their reference groups. If it is generally accepted in a particular reference group that attendance at a particular festival is appropriate behaviour, then members of that group are likely to attend. If not, then attendance is very unlikely. Showing examples of a typical reference group (e.g. a nuclear family group) enjoying themselves at a festival can send a message to a target market that may well respond favourably.

3. *Opinion formers*: within any group, some people will be opinion leaders. That is, their opinions on new leisure experiences are sought by the group and generally accepted. These opinion leaders are often media or sporting personalities, which is the reason many of them make a very substantial living endorsing new products and leisure services. The adoption of new leisure services follows a normal distribution curve. Innovators (generally opinion leaders within a group) are the first to try the experience. Early adopters who are a little more careful about adopting the innovation follow them. However, they still act as opinion leaders for the great majority. Laggards are the last to try something new. Therefore, the promotional messages for any new festival or event should be directed at those who have been identified as opinion formers or innovators.

4. *Personality*: Stanton, Miller and Layton define personality as 'an individual's pattern of traits that influence behavioural responses' (1994, p. 138). People can be introverted/extroverted, shy/self-confident, aggressive/retiring, dynamic/sluggish. It is well known that personality affects consumer behaviour. Unfortunately, as personality is difficult to measure in terms of consumer behaviour, it is a marketing tool that is difficult to use. However, festivals that celebrate adventure or sporting prowess would be unlikely to appeal to shy, retiring personalities.

5. *Culture*: Australia is an example of a culturally diverse country. Within Australia live diverse groups who have different designs for living. Each of these cultural groups has different buying habits, leisure wants and needs, and attitudes and values. If a particular cultural group is a desired market segment, the four Ps of the marketing mix can be manipulated in order to appeal to that group.

TARGET MARKET SEGMENTATION

Most events do not appeal to everybody. As Hall (1997) observes, the marketing planning activities of event managers must include an understanding of the behaviour of visitors to an event. This includes identifying those market segments that are likely to have their needs satisfied by the event activities or, alternatively, to ensure the event contains those elements which can satisfy an identified target market's needs. The process of identifying appropriate target markets is known as market segmentation. Segmentation can occur by geography, demography or lifestyle (psychography).

Geographic segmentation is concerned with the place of residence of event visitors. A community festival, for example, would probably decide to focus on local residents as the first step in their segmentation exercise. However, if the festival is thought to be of broader interest because of its potential product content, the marketing net could be spread wider. The potential geographic spread could be:

• local residents of the area
• day visitors from outside the immediate area
• intrastate domestic tourists
• interstate domestic tourists
• international inbound tourists
• school excursions.

The chosen geographic segmentation depends on the leisure experience provided by the festival or event. For example, an event such as a capital city agricultural show (e.g. the Royal Easter Show in Sydney) would have a state-wide geographic segmentation and probably an interstate market segment for its more specialised event experiences.

Demographic segmentation concerns the measurable characteristics of people, such as age, gender, occupation, income, education and cultural group. A demographic segmentation tool often used by marketers is a socio-economic scale based on occupation (usually the major income generator in family units). Table 7.4 details the scale in an event context.

■ **Table 7.4** *A classification of socioeconomic market segments for events*

GROUP	SOCIO-ECONOMIC GROUP	OCCUPATIONAL EXAMPLES	TYPES OF EVENTS GROUP IS LIKELY TO ATTEND	APPROXIMATE % OF POPULATION
A	Upper middle class	Higher managerial or administrative, professional: lawyers, doctors, dentists, captains of industry, senior public servants, senior military officers, professors	Cultural events such as fundraisers for the opera, classical music festivals	3
B	Middle class	Intermediate managerial, administrative or professional: university lecturers, head teachers, pharmacists, middle managers, journalists, architects	Cultural events (but purchasing cheaper seats), food and beverage festivals, historical festivals, arts and crafts festivals, community festivals	15

GROUP	SOCIO-ECONOMIC GROUP	OCCUPATIONAL EXAMPLES	TYPES OF EVENTS GROUP IS LIKELY TO ATTEND	APPROXIMATE % OF POPULATION
C	Lower middle class	Supervisory, clerical, junior managerial or administrative: clerks, sales representatives, nurses, teachers, shop managers	Most popular cultural events, some sporting events, community festivals	24
D	Skilled working class	Skilled blue collar workers: builders, fitters, waterside workers, police constables, self-employed tradespersons	Motor vehicle festivals, sporting events, community festivals	28
E	Working class	Semiskilled and unskilled workers: builder's labourers, factory workers, cleaners, delivery drivers	Some sporting festivals, ethnic festivals	17
F	Social security	Those at the lowest level of subsistence: pensioners, casual and part-time workers	Very little, except occasionally free community events	13

(**Source:** *adapted from Morgan 1996*)

Although the data in table 7.4 originated in Britain, they are relevant to all developed countries. Media buyers in advertising agencies first used these classifications, as the system is a very good predictor of reading and viewing habits. For example, in general, As and Bs read broadsheet newspapers, such as the *Sydney Morning Herald* and the *Age* in Melbourne, whereas Cs, Ds, and Es read the tabloid press, such as the *Daily Telegraph* and the *Herald Sun*.

However, these classifications are not always an accurate guide to income. For example, many Cs earn considerable incomes. The essential difference between As, Bs, Cs and the other categories is in the level of education. The higher the level of education, the higher the propensity a person has to participate in cultural activities, including arts and community festivals (Torkildsen 1983). Morgan observes that the age at which individuals terminate their formal education (16 years, 18 years, or after higher education, at 21 years) can indicate their ambition, intelligence and, importantly for event managers, their curiosity about the world in which they live (1996, p. 103). For directors of festivals and events that include cultural elements, their target market is an educated one.

Other demographic variables are gender and age. Women and men occasionally have different needs and some events cater for these different needs. The years in which people are born can affect their outlook on life, their attitudes and values, and their interests. Depending on the event, one or several of these generations can be targeted. Table 7.5 shows the different generations born in the twentieth century.

■ **Table 7.5**
The generations born in the twentieth century

GENERATION	BORN	AGE IN 2000	FORMATIVE YEARS
World War I	Pre-1924	77+	Pre-1936
Depression	1924–34	66–76	1936–46
World War II	1935–45	55–65	1947–57
Early boomers	1946–54	46–54	1958–66
Late boomers	1955–64	36–45	1967–76
Generation X	1965–76	24–35	1977–88
Echo boom	1977–94	7–23	1989–2000

(**Source:** *Getz 1997*)

Another method of age segmentation is by life cycle, as shown in figure 7.3. This relies on the proposition that people's leisure habits vary according to their position in the life cycle. For example, full nesters are the target market for events that feature elements for both children and adults, whereas AB empty nesters are the perfect market for a cultural festival featuring quality food and drink and arias from well-loved operas.

■ **Figure 7.3**
The family life cycle

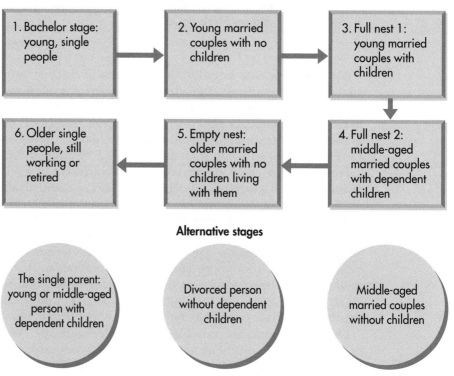

(**Source:** *Stanton, Miller & Layton 1994, p. 97*)

However, care should be taken not to resort to age stereotypes. Many baby boomers, in or approaching their 50s, are fit, active and interested in all types of culture, popular and contemporary, as well as high culture festivals such as classical music or theatre. It could be argued that the most successful community festivals are those which are inclusive of all age groups, rather than focusing on just one age group.

The Australian Bureau of Statistics (ABS) publishes a great deal of data taken from each census that categorises residential areas according to the demographics of the residents of that area, for example *Sydney, a Social Atlas: 1996 Census of Population and Housing*. A separate edition is published for every Australian capital city after each census and is a valuable store of demographic information categorised by geographic area (i.e. geodemographic). Cities are broken down into small areas called census collection districts of 200–300 households. The demographic variables of age, ethnicity, education, income, family type, membership of the paid labour force and dwelling type are shown for these districts. Directors of community festivals should find these data very useful for product planning.

Psychographics — segmenting a market according to its lifestyle and values — is another segmentation technique that could be a useful planning tool for event directors. The Roy Morgan Research Centre conducted a study of Australian values and lifestyles, then segmented consumers into these market segments with shared values and attitudes:
- visible achievement
- something better
- socially aware
- young optimists
- a fairer deal
- look at me
- basic needs
- real conservatism
- traditional family life
- conventional family life (Stanton, Miller & Layton 1994, p. 103).

The names of these groups are somewhat self-explanatory. For example, the socially aware group (seven per cent of all people) see themselves as community-minded and socially responsible. They are 'progressive' in their opinions and are likely to be involved in conservation and environmental matters. They are likely to be found on the committees of community festivals.

However, like personality segmentation, psychographic segmentation of a market has some serious limitations for an event marketeer. It is very difficult to accurately measure the size of the lifestyle segments in a quantitative manner. Another problem is that a given lifestyle segment simply might not be accessible... through a firm's [event organisation's] usual distribution system or promotional program (Stanton, Miller & Layton 1994, p. 104).

What this type of segmentation can do for an event marketeer is to provide another technique for clear and focused thinking about the characteristics of the target market sought, and the benefits that these groups seek in a leisure experience.

To be effective, market segments must be:

- measurable; that is, the characteristics of the segment (socioeconomic status, gender age, etc.) must be accessible to the event marketeer
- substantial enough to be worth the effort of targeting
- accessible by normal promotional channels
- actionable by the event organisation in terms of the marketing budget and other resources (Morgan 1996).

PRODUCT PLANNING

The product of an event is a leisure experience that has been carefully produced to satisfy a target market's identified needs. The word 'product' is used, as marketing theory applies to the production of both tangible goods and intangible services. (Chapter 3, 'Conceptualising the event', explores this process.) Figure 7.4 shows this process diagrammatically.

■ **Figure 7.4**
The process of creating an event product

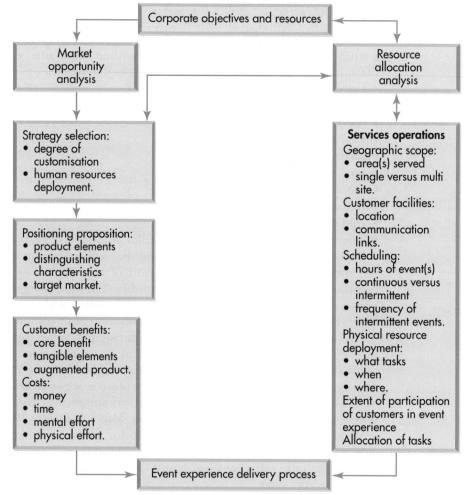

The new concepts introduced in figure 7.4 are customer benefits and costs. The section on pricing further explores the concept of costs (see page 180). Morgan states that a leisure service (or product) contains three elements:

- the core benefit that the customer experiences — an enjoyable leisure experience that satisfies some need(s)
- the tangible benefit that helps deliver the core benefit — the venue, the seating, decoration and so on
- the augmented product; that is, the additional features that differentiate this event from its competitors — artists, service quality, type of people attracted to the event, parking or transportation facilities, ease of access and exit and so on.

The event planner needs to be aware of all three elements (Morgan 1996, p. 136).

This introduces an important characteristic of the marketing of leisure services — people are part of the product. In other words, much of the event consumer satisfaction comes from interactions with the other people attending the event. This means that the event manager needs to ensure that the audience is compatible, and has some homogenous characteristic to facilitate social interaction.

■ Product *development*

This section discusses some product development issues that will help in understanding what constitutes a leisure product, how it evolves and how it can be analysed.

Branding gives an event an easily recognisable identity. One of the best-known brands in the world is the five interlocking rings of the Olympics — a special event. Because leisure experiences are intangible, branding is particularly important as it reassures potential consumers that the service will deliver the benefits promised. Clever use of the brand helps the event manager make an intangible phenomenon more tangible for the event consumer.

The product life cycle (shown in figure 7.5) illustrates that all events follow a similar pattern of participation as they go through the stages of introduction, growth, maturity and eventual decline. Australian event history is littered with examples of festivals or special events that were once very popular and now no longer exist. For example, the Sydney Waratah and Folkloric festivals and the State Bank Multicultural Carnival no longer exist, yet thousands of people once attended these events. Attendance at Australia Day festivals has waxed and waned as the 'product' has been changed to reflect changing community needs. Once, only hundreds attended the celebrations staged for this day. Now, because of a rejuvenation of the Australia Day celebration 'product', attendances are again healthy. To avoid the decline, event managers need to closely monitor public acceptance of the content of their event product to ensure that it is still congruent with the leisure needs of contemporary society.

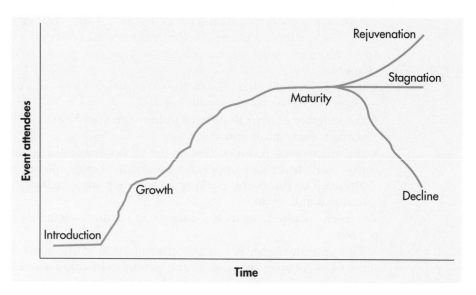

A simple yet highly useful tool for clear and effective thinking about product strategies is Ansoff's matrix (1957), shown in figure 7.6. An event that considers its product is appropriate yet is not drawing large numbers may consider a market penetration strategy — that is, using advertising or other forms of promotion to attract more of the same target market. If it is thought that the event leisure experience can reach a different target market without changing the product, a market development strategy can be used. It may be that monitoring consumer satisfaction shows that the current product is not satisfying consumer needs. It would then be necessary to develop new and different products that can. If the event adopted a corporate strategy of growth, it may be appropriate to develop new products for a new market. For example, consumer monitoring might show that the AB section of the population is not attending an event. A product strategy of diversification would result in an event product that would satisfy this target group's needs.

■ **Figure 7.6**
*Ansoff's
product/
market
matrix*

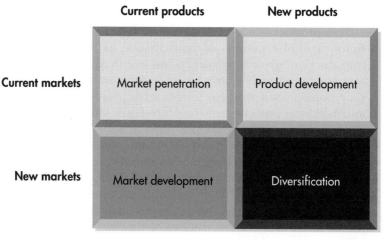

(**Source:** *Ansoff 1957*)

■ Consumer *satisfaction*

Because leisure services are intangible, inseparable and variable, defining service quality is difficult. A definition that examines quality service from the viewpoint of the consumer is 'quality service occurs when the consumers' expectations of the leisure service match their perceptions of the service received'. Quality service is based on perceptions rather than something tangible. Not every customer will be satisfied all the time. However, one of the corporate objectives set out in an event's strategic plan should be a measurement of consumer satisfaction; for example, 95 per cent of event participants will give a satisfied or higher rating of the event. Figure 7.7 shows how consumer dissatisfaction can occur.

■ **Figure 7.7**
Quality: the fit between customer expectations and perceptions

(**Source:** *Morgan 1996, p. 159*)

The consumer's perceptions of the leisure experience are formed from the technical and functional qualities of the experience, external factors such as wet weather, and personal factors such as an argument with a partner occurring at the event. The consumer's expectations of the event are determined by:

• marketing communications — advertising, publicity, brochures, signs and price that are used to promote the event

- word-of-mouth recommendations from friends and relatives who describe their experiences of this or similar events
- personal experience of this or similar events.

When the consumer's perceptions of the leisure experience match or exceed their expectations, a quality experience has been delivered and the outcome is a satisfied consumer.

Zeithaml, Parasuraman and Berry (1990) are the world's leading researchers on quality customer service and consumer satisfaction with a service. They have reduced their original 10 determinants of service quality to a top five:

- *assurance* — because staff give the appearance of being knowledgeable, helpful and courteous, event consumers are assured of their wellbeing
- *empathy* — the event staff seem to understand the consumers' needs and deliver caring attention
- *responsiveness* — the staff are responsive to the needs of the consumer
- *reliability* — everything happens at the event in the way marketing communications promised
- *tangibles* — the physical appearance of the event equipment, artists and staff meet expectations.

Concentrating on these aspects of service will result in outcomes that meet corporate service objectives.

PRICING

Festivals and events are leisure activities. Most Australians live in areas that offer many leisure options. This means that price can have a major effect on demand for an event and is an important aspect of an event's marketing mix. Some events charge no entrance fee to consumers, but there are still costs to the consumer of attending, as well as costs for the producer. This section discusses the non-cash costs of price, how price is used in event marketing, the concept of value for consumers, different types of costs, appropriate pricing strategies and issues involved in pricing.

Price has many uses. In a market economy like Australia's, the more highly sought a particular good or service is, the higher the price, so fewer people can purchase it. For an event, price can determine the number of consumers who attend the event. For example, a mass-market event such as an agricultural show must keep its price at a level of affordability to its customers — middle income, middle Australia. On the other hand, an event such as a fund raiser for the Sydney Theatre Company (STC) can ask a much higher price as its target market is much smaller (socioeconomic group AB who are subscribers to the STC), but wealthier and therefore willing to pay for a perceived quality experience. However, the high price can represent quality (or 'value for money') to the potential consumer and influence the decision to purchase.

The three foundations of pricing strategies are:
1. costs
2. competition — the market
3. value to the customer.

Value is the sum of all the perceived benefits (gross value) minus the sum of the perceived costs. Therefore, the greater the positive difference between perceived benefits and costs, the greater the net value to the potential consumer. In the STC fund-raiser example, potential consumers compare the perceived benefits — dinner, drinks, entertainment, parking, opportunities to socialise, prestige, novelty of an unusual night out — with the perceived costs — money and non-cash costs. If the STC have adequately communicated these benefits, consumers will perceive that the event offers value and purchase tickets.

Not all costs to the event consumer are cash. Other costs incurred are:
- time — the opportunity cost of the time spent consuming the event experience compared with using that time to enjoy another leisure experience
- the physical efforts required to consume the leisure experience — travel, energy expended
- psychic costs — mental effort to engage in the social interaction required, feeling uncomfortable in certain social settings
- sensory costs — unpleasant climate, uncomfortable seating, unattractive physical environment and unlikeable companions.

Event managers must consider these elements of consumer costs and attempt either to alleviate any difficulties, or to promote them in such a way that they become part of the event. In most events, the people who attend the event become part of the event product. For example, part of the product of the STC fund-raiser is rubbing shoulders with the 'glitterati' who attend. Alternatively, a middle-aged non-drinker will probably not feel comfortable at an event that is largely attended by young men in their twenties who are enjoying many alcoholic beverages.

Types of event costs are:
- fixed — costs that do not vary according to the number of event consumers, for example venue rent, interest, light, heat and power, volunteer uniforms, artist fees
- variable — costs that vary according to the number of consumers, for example, number of paper plates used at a food festival, catering at a product launch, extra staff required to serve additional customers.

Analysis of costs is the first step in calculating an appropriate price for the event. The next element to consider is the price of competitive leisure experiences. If a similar leisure experience has a price of x, the choices are to (1) match and charge price x, (2) adopt a cost leadership strategy and charge $x - 25$ per cent, or (3) adopt a differentiation strategy and use a price of $x + 50$ per cent and use marketing communications to promote the value of the event.

Three generic pricing strategies can be used to achieve event objectives. A revenue-oriented strategy seeks to set a price that will maximise revenue by charging the highest price that the target market will possibly pay. The Sydney Theatre Company's fund-raiser is an example of a revenue-oriented pricing strategy. An operations-oriented pricing strategy seeks to balance supply and demand by introducing cheaper prices for times of low demand and higher prices at times of higher demand. Agricultural shows are examples of events that use an operations-oriented pricing strategy. Finally, a target market strategy uses different prices for different target markets. For example, a three-day music festival could have one price for those who want to participate for all three days (the fanatic market), a day price for the not-so-keen, and another price to see a headline act.

Figure 7.8 shows the thought processes necessary to construct a coherent pricing strategy. It is also necessary to understand if the event price is elastic or inelastic. If lowering the price can increase demand, the event price is elastic. If the demand for the event will not change, regardless of price reductions, the price is inelastic. These events are usually specialised. Obviously, it would be foolish to attempt to increase revenue by lowering the price of an inelastic event. Figure 7.9 summarises all event pricing issues.

■ **Figure 7.8**
Selecting price strategies for events

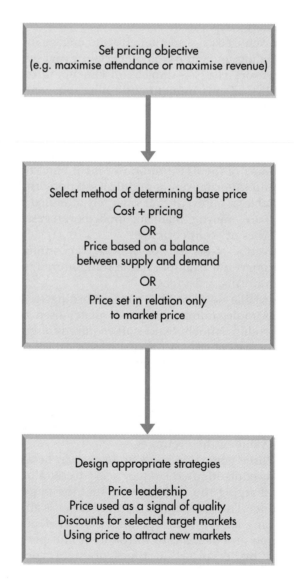

Set pricing objective
(e.g. maximise attendance or maximise revenue)

Select method of determining base price
Cost + pricing
OR
Price based on a balance
between supply and demand
OR
Price set in relation only
to market price

Design appropriate strategies

Price leadership
Price used as a signal of quality
Discounts for selected target markets
Using price to attract new markets

How much should be charged?
■ What costs must be covered?

■ How sensitive are customers to different prices?

■ What are leisure competitors' prices?

■ What levels of discounts to selected target markets are appropriate?

■ Should psychological pricing ($10.95 instead of $11) be used?

What should be the basis of pricing?
■ Should each element be billed separately?

■ Should one admission fee be charged?

■ Should consumers be charged for resources consumed?

■ Should a single price for a bundled package be charged?

Who shall collect payment:
■ the event organisation or

■ a ticketing intermediary?

Where should payment be made:
■ at the event,

■ at a ticketing organisation, or

■ at the customer's home using the Internet or telephone?

When should payment be made:
■ when tickets are given out or

■ on the day of the event?

How should payment be made:
■ cash — exact change,

■ credit card,

■ EFTPOS, or

■ token?

(**Source:** *adapted from Lovelock et al. 2001*)

PROMOTION

Promotion literally means to move forward or to advance. In the marketing context, promotion refers to all of the communication activities that an event director can use to tell the target market about the benefits of the event and consequently advance its sales. These activities are sometimes referred to as the promotional mix or the communications mix of the event. This mix is an integral part of an event's marketing strategy, as figure 7.10 illustrates. The target market, the positioning of the event and its competitive strategy all play a role in deciding the marketing objectives of an event. Decisions about the make-up of the event product, the pricing strategy to be adopted, how tickets to the event are to reach the target market, and by what means prospective customers are to be informed of the event benefits are then made.

Advertising is any form of non-personal promotion paid for by the event organisation. Radio, television, newspapers, magazines, the Internet, billboards or mobile platforms such as buses or taxis can be used for advertising. The mainstream media such as capital city television, newspapers and radio can be very expensive to use. The creative process of producing the messages can also be expensive, especially if it is done by an advertising agency.

■ **Figure 7.10**
The relationship between marketing and promotional strategy

(**Source:** *adapted from Morgan 1996*)

Publicity includes all those activities not directly paid for that communicate with the event's target market. An advantage that event directors have is that people generally enjoy reading about the leisure experiences of sport, the arts and entertainment that an event produces. It is therefore somewhat easier to get publicity for an event than for a more mundane activity. However, the event director must be aware that for a story to be used by the media, it must have some news value (that is, it must be new and of interest to the reader, viewer or listener), be well-written and come from a reliable source. It is therefore important that all such publicity has the imprimatur of the event director.

Sales promotion, sometimes called below-the-line promotion by advertising agencies because they do not receive commission on these activities, comprises those activities that use incentives or discounts to increase sales. Examples of sales promotion are family days at an event where families receive a group discount or a free bottle of fizzy drink when they buy a ticket. Sales promotions can generate extra sales in particular target market sub-segments.

Direct selling is communicating directly with potential customers in the target market group by the use of a mailing list, the telephone or the Internet. An existing event should have a list of people who have previously attended the event. These data can be gathered quite simply by, for example, conducting a free raffle that requires attendees to supply their name and address. Other events may also sell their mailing lists. This may well be the most cost-effective form of promotion for an ongoing event that appeals to a tightly defined target market.

As Getz (1997, p. 305) points out, the role of the promotional mix is to:
• create or increase awareness of the event
• create or enhance a positive image
• position the event relative to its competition
• inform target markets of pertinent details of the event
• generate demand for the event
• remind target markets of the event's details.

Decisions on promotional strategy must focus on the target market. For example, an event with a large, mass market such as an agricultural show (e.g. the Sydney Royal Easter Show) can use television advertising as a promotional device, whereas a small community festival's promotional mix is limited to publicity and advertising in the local paper. Each of the promotional techniques and their advantages and disadvantages are shown in table 7.6.

■ Table 7.6 *The advantages and disadvantages of different types of promotion*

PROMOTIONAL TYPE	MEDIUM	ADVANTAGES	DISADVANTAGES	USE FOR
Advertising	Television	Wide reach, conveys excitement and colour, can lend credibility	Expensive to produce and transmit	Large, mass market events
	Radio	Can be targeted by music tastes, quick to produce, cheaper	Difficult to cut through the clutter of other radio advertisements and programs	Musical events
	Newspapers	Wide reach, short lead time; suburban newspapers tightly target a community	Can be expensive; widely distributed papers may not tightly target the audience	Community festivals
	Magazines or newsletters	Tightly targeted	Long lead times for events	Special interest events
	Posters/outdoor	Cheap, can be displayed where target market congregates	Can deface buildings, can be ripped down	Youth, community, special interest events
	Flyers	Cheap, effective if well designed, tightly targeted	Need volunteers to distribute	Youth, special interest
Sales promotion	Price discounts for particular types of customers	Generates revenue	Can dilute revenue if groups not carefully chosen	Large, mass market events
	Cross-promotion with a sponsor	Generates sales for the sponsor, can result in additional sales	Sponsor's image may overtake the event's	Most events
Publicity	Television	Adds credibility, large audience	Must have a televisual angle	All events
	Press	Gives credibility; can be a large or targeted audience	Must be of interest to the general reader	All events

(continued)

PROMOTIONAL TYPE	MEDIUM	ADVANTAGES	DISADVANTAGES	USE FOR
Publicity (*cont.*)	Speciality magazine or paper	Audience is tightly targeted	Has a long lead time	Special interest events
Direct to target market	Mail, phone or e-mail	Little waste, can be very cost effective	Results depend on quality of mailing list	Special interest events
	Internet	Cheap to produce as can usually be done by a volunteer, easy to change messages, can be used to sell tickets direct	Penetration is currently quite small, many people wary of giving credit card information through the Internet	A target market that is technologically advanced

When the appropriate type of promotion and medium has been chosen, the next step is to decide on the message(s). George and Berry (1981) have some cogent advice on services promotion that has been adapted for event directors:

- advertisements should feature the event's artists and staff, rather than models
- provide tangible clues to counteract the intangible nature of the event by showing physical facilities at the event site
- seek continuity over time by use of recognisable symbols, spokespersons, trademarks or music
- promise what is possible to foster realistic expectations.

Other guidelines worthy of consideration are:

- make the service more tangible and recognisable by using representatives of the target market enjoying the event product to illustrate the benefits of the event
- ensure all promotion is integrated with all other aspects of the marketing mix. Use one consistent image or message so that the target market is not confused.

A question that many event directors find difficult to resolve is the amount to be spent on promotion — the budget. Ray's (1982) advice on three methods of deciding the budget is a useful framework for thinking through this question.

Judgemental approaches can be either arbitrary or a percentage of sales. An arbitrary decision may be based on what was spent last year or for a similar type of event. Alternatively, the amount can be decided as a percentage of sales — either last year's or the anticipated sales. As Ray points out, this is analogous to putting the cart before the horse because the promotional strategy is to produce sales, not to control the amount spent on promotion. What these budgeting methods can do is to give the event director a comfort zone in which to work. That is, they are less open to criticism because that was the amount spent last year.

The competitive parity approach consists of budgeting at least the same, if not more, than the competition is spending. The competition for an event is all other leisure activities, so this may prove very difficult to establish. It is important to have sufficient voice not to get lost in the 'clutter', but matching the budgets of other leisure activities is certainly not recommended as:

- the leisure market is complex and it is probably impossible to establish what all possible competitors are spending
- it is doubtful if many events have the revenue potential to support such a costly exercise.

The objectives and strategy approach comes from the marketing process of setting marketing objectives, then communication objectives, then deciding what strategies are needed to achieve these objectives. For example, a marketing objective of selling 10 000 tickets flows to a communication objective of telling a potential market of 100 000 people of the benefits of the event. The strategies to be decided are the creative, the make-up of the promotional mix and the medium (or media) to be used. From this process comes a cost that must be realistic. It would be very foolish to spend $5000 on promotion for an event that has a forecast revenue of $7000.

PLACE

'Place' refers to both the site where the event takes place (the venue, which was dealt with earlier) and the place at which consumers can purchase their tickets. For most events, this means deciding whether to use a ticketing agency. Ticketing agencies widen the distribution network, make it easier for customers to purchase tickets, speed up the entry of customers at the venue, and provide a credit card acceptance service and a telephone booking service. However, they charge both the event organisation and the customer. Their use depends on the type of event, any other purchase facility that can be used, the willingness of the target market to pay for a ticketing service and its relative affordability.

Selling tickets via a ticketing agency, or some other distribution network such as the Internet, does have distinct advantages for the event producer. Ticket sales can be monitored and decisions made regarding the amount of promotion necessary to achieve marketing objectives based on hard information. The security problems inherent in accepting cash at the door are alleviated. Because customers pay in advance, the cash flow to the event producer occurs weeks or even months before production, with obvious advantages for the financial health of the event organisation.

The use of the World Wide Web (WWW) or Internet as a distribution medium for events is rapidly gaining in popularity as event directors realise its advantages, which can be summarised as:

- *speed* — consumers can purchase tickets without leaving their desk or home, without queuing or waiting for a phone operator to become available
- *consumer ease* — consumers can view at their leisure the different products of a festival, and select the shows that best suit their pocket and program, without slowing queues or feeling pressured from a box office sales person
- *revenue* — ticket revenue comes from the buyer's credit card, which facilitates security and ease of collection
- *modernity* — more and more consumers expect services such as events to be available for purchase on the WWW. Without this facility, the event may have an image of being dated.

An interesting example of the use of the WWW for distribution of tickets is the Melbourne International Comedy Festival (http://www.comedyfestival.com.au/tickets/), a multi-venue, multi-show festival. The festival uses a ticketing agency — Ticketmaster 7.com — that has both physical box offices throughout Melbourne and an online booking facility. Consumers have a choice of booking online, by phone, or from a box office. However, the ticketing charge of $6.88 remains, even if the consumer chooses the online medium.

The East Coast Blues and Roots Festival, held at Byron Bay each Easter, uses a different WWW distribution tactic. Its site, http://www.bluesfest.com.au/2001/tickets01.html, offers four channels: phone, mail order, the Ticketek web site for online ticket purchase, or a Ticketek box office. If the first two are used, a charge of $3.50 is added to the ticket price for the registered mail used to send the tickets to the consumer.

Neither of these festivals, nor any others found in an extensive search of Australian festival web sites, has their own online booking system that can accept bookings and credit card details electronically at no charge to the consumer. However, due to the burgeoning of e-commerce and its rapid acceptance by Australian consumers, and the ease with which a web site can be constructed and modified, it seems likely that before too long most major events will have their own online booking facility, and perhaps rely on that and venue door sales for distribution.

*M*ARKET RESEARCH

The need for market research in event organisations is based on one simple premise: the lower the quality (or, indeed, the complete absence) of data used for marketing decisions, the higher the risk of marketing failure. The data collected are usually organised into a marketing information system that Stanton, Miller and Layton define as 'an ongoing, organised set of procedures and methods designed to generate, analyse, disseminate, store and later retrieve information for use in making marketing decisions' (1994, p. 48).

The type of information required by event managers varies according to the type of event. Table 7.7 shows some useful categories of marketing research. The table, however, looks a little more complex than it really is, as most, if not all, of the information requirements shown in table 7.7 can be collected from a simple survey of a random sample of event customers as they leave the event. (For those interested in learning more about this topic, an excellent book on research methods is A. Veal (1997), *Research Methods for Leisure and Tourism.*)

■ **Table 7.7**
Categories of event marketing research

RESEARCH CATEGORY	USES	TYPICAL MARKETING USE
Market analysis	Marketing planning	Measurement and projections of market volume and target market size
Consumer research	Segmentation and positioning	Quantitative measurement of customer attitudes, profiles and awareness; qualitative assessment of consumer needs and perceptions
Promotion studies	Effectiveness of marketing communication	Measurement of consumer reaction to all types of promotion
Performance evaluation	Control device	Measurement of customer satisfaction with event

Figure 7.11 on the following page shows a simple survey that can be used or modified by event managers to collect market research data. A randomly selected sample of about 100 attendees should be sufficient to obtain useable data that can be processed into meaningful marketing information. In this context, 'random' means that all event customers have an equal chance of being selected for the survey. For example, as customers exit the event, every tenth customer is asked to participate, rather than selecting those thought most likely to respond favourably to the request. The information obtained from the survey can be analysed using a computer software package such as Statistical Package for the Social Sciences (SPSS), or simply by using a pocket calculator and a piece of paper.

One final caveat: creativity, good judgement and courage to make decisions are important qualities for the event manager. Do not succumb to paralysis through analysis. Market research aids competent event management, but does not replace it.

■ **Figure 7.11**
*Sample
customer
details and
satisfaction
survey. This
survey would
be completed
by the
interviewer.*

SAMPLE CUSTOMER DETAILS AND SATISFACTION SURVEY

Introductory remarks: 'Excuse me, we are carrying out a survey to establish how satisfied our customers are with the festival/event. Could you spare a few minutes to answer a few questions?'

1. On a scale of one to five where one is completely dissatisfied and five is very satisfied, could you tell me how you rate

the venue	1	2	3	4	5
entertainment	1	2	3	4	5
food and drink	1	2	3	4	5
toilet facilities	1	2	3	4	5
access/parking	1	2	3	4	5
ticketing arrangements	1	2	3	4	5
cost	1	2	3	4	5
helpfulness of staff	1	2	3	4	5

2. How did you hear about the festival/event?

   advertisement ☐ friends told me ☐ went last year ☐ mail ☐

   saw a poster ☐ other ☐

3. Will you come next year?

   Yes ☐ No ☐

4. Do you have any other comments about the event? ....

   ....

5. What is your postcode?

6. What educational level have you achieved?

   year 10 ☐ year 12 ☐ TAFE qualification ☐ bachelor's degree ☐

   post graduate ☐

7. What is your occupation?

8. Gender   Male ☐ Female ☐

9. Age group   15–19 ☐

   20–29 ☐

   30–59 ☐

   60+ ☐

THE MARKETING PLAN

The next and final step in the marketing planning process is to incorporate marketing objectives and strategies into the strategic plan for the event. Figure 7.12 illustrates this process. The marketing plan is not separate from the strategic plan, but part of it. Figure 7.10 also shows that a sound understanding of marketing principles is essential knowledge for an event manager.

■ **Figure 7.12**
Incorporating marketing into the strategic plan

(**Source:** *adapted from Morgan 1996)*

A common misconception held by many in the festival and event area is that marketing means nothing more than advertising. As this chapter has shown, marketing is a structured and coherent way of thinking about managing an event or festival to achieve the objectives of customer satisfaction and either profit or increased awareness of a cause or movement.

The core of the marketing concept is a focus on the customer, in this case the event attendee. This implies that good marketing flows from a complete understanding of the customers — who they are, where they live and what their needs are. This comes from good research and event managers communicating with and observing their customers. From this knowledge come appropriate marketing strategies that can achieve an event's objectives. Given this understanding of the customer and the external environments in which the event operates, appropriate product, price, promotion and distribution strategies can be implemented.

Questions

1. Why should event managers focus on the needs of their customers, rather than the needs of the event organisers?

2. What are the advantages of market segmentation to an event manager?

3. Name five needs that can be satisfied by attending a community festival.

4. What essential ingredients must a publicity campaign contain to be effective?

5. What considerations other than costs must be considered when deciding on price for an event?

6. What factors must be considered when deciding place (distribution) strategies for an event?

7. What are the advantages of conducting consumer research?

8. What elements constitute an effective marketing communication?

9. Why is it important to show representatives of the target market in marketing communications messages?

....

The McLaren Vale
Sea and Vines Festival

South Australia is widely acknowledged as Australia's 'Festival State' — an image it proudly adopts as a result of many festival theme events being hosted there almost all year round, notably in the areas of food, wine and the performing arts. The small town of McLaren Vale is situated only 35 kilometres due south on the A13 highway from the centre of Adelaide, the State capital and focal point. Adelaide has a total population of about 1.1 million people.

Like many similar communities, McLaren Vale would probably have remained a small and relatively unknown place if it were not for two things: first, the unprecedented growth and 'hype' experienced in the Australian wine industry during the late 1980s and throughout the 1990s and, second, the birth of a festival event moulded around the wine product, an event that subsequently became known as the Sea and Vines Festival. McLaren Vale has furthermore been repeatedly judged by winemakers as the source of the best shiraz grapes in Australia. Stunning rich fruit driven red and crisp flavoursome white wines are being produced. McLaren Vale is situated about five kilometres due east from the waters of Gulf St Vincent on the Fleurieu Peninsula and its proximity to the source of various seafood varieties is an important reason for the origin of the Sea and Vines Festival.

The first McLaren Vale Sea and Vines Festival was held in May 1992 and featured 12 of its finest wineries serving fresh South Australian oysters with a variety of delicate sauces. For the first two years it was offered as a one-day event, but since 1995 the format changed to a two-day event held on the Sunday and Monday of the long weekend in July. At the time of its inception the organisers felt that, in the absence of any significant scheduled activity in the region during this long weekend, positioning the event in the long weekend would enable them to claim 'ownership' of the weekend, which fell during the school and university winter semester break. In the initial years of the event, the festival was established as a platform from which to launch a limited number of single seafood varieties in conjunction with the regional seafood industry. At the time it was felt that, given the location, the event could be more expansive in terms of the variety of seafoods. With the exception of Port Lincoln, McLaren Vale is the only region near the capital city of Adelaide with close links to the Fleurieu Peninsula coast and, not surprisingly, the branding term adopted was 'proximity to the coast'.

The hosting of the festival event has raised the awareness profile of McLaren Vale tremendously. From its humble beginnings, the festival has grown into a prestigious gourmet weekend. The event has given McLaren Vale a regional brand image: close to a main population centre, near the sea, really good wines, and reflecting the relaxed lifestyles enjoyed by its local community. Originally the Southern Development Board, Adelaide (now Onkaparinga City Council) was involved and the name 'From the Sea and Vines' was adopted, but in 1996 the McLaren Vale Winemakers Inc. took up the total management and ownership of the event. Soon afterwards in 1997, a state-of-the-art McLaren Vale and Fleurieu wine and food visitor centre building was completed. This building also contained the offices of the winemakers and gave both the town and festival a definite physical focus.

David Dean, general manager of McLaren Vale Winemakers, emphasises that the overriding goal was to create a strong regional brand identity for McLaren Vale by combining good wine, good food and good service with the natural physical attractions and attributes the area has to offer. At present the overall objective is to continue building 'brand McLaren Vale' as a premium wine tourism destination and to reinforce its connection with the lifestyle industry. Secondary objectives vary and include selling pallets of wine, building 'brand McLaren Vale' as a food and wine destination, and using its proximity to Adelaide to create awareness of McLaren Vale as a single-day destination.

The format of the Sea and Vines Festival is a somewhat novel one. The wineries prepared to host the event were grouped into four geographical clusters/routes (described as 'loops') in relation to their proximity to one another. The loops were colour-coded for identification purposes into pink, blue, purple and orange, with each loop containing four wineries, directly involving a total of 16 wineries in this manner. At each winery a three-course lunch in the form of a seafood main dish with one of the wines of the winery as accompaniment was served and a band provided live music entertainment at no extra charge for the entire day, which started at 11.00 a.m. and ended about 5.30 p.m. All this sold for a blanket price of $9 per head, with tickets obtainable at the visitor centre. Each winery offered a different seafood dish, its own wine, and a specific type of live music. For example, one winery would have calamari as the main dish, with a brass band playing jazz while the winery 'next door' offered oysters to the tune of 1970s Rolling Stones pop music. All this information, together with a map portraying the loops and the wineries' locations, was contained in the festival fold-up brochure.

At most wineries marquee tents were erected outside the winery buildings to house the band, wine tasting, tables and seating for lunch. A number of portable toilets were placed outside. A courtesy shuttle service ran continuously between wineries, dropping people off and picking others up who wished to move on to the next winery. There was also a premium bus ticket service between Adelaide and McLaren Vale for the event, providing attendees with an affordable and safe transport option. The shuttle service between wineries was free and entirely staffed by volunteers. The McLaren Vale Sea and Vines Festival is the only event in South Australia to offer patron transport services. In the planning of the event it was intended that a bus would complete its loop in about 30 minutes. Each loop had its own bus that originated from the visitor centre, which was the central point where festival attendees gathered. Here they also bought lunch tickets and wine-tasting glasses. It was not possible to switch loops without first returning to the visitor centre.

The 2000 Sea and Vines Festival was held on Sunday and Monday, 12–13 July in perfect sunny weather. For the previous two years the weather had been particularly bad and in 1999 many attendees complained profusely about the muddy conditions. In spite of this, at least 15 000 people ('paying customers') attended, on the basis of a figure compiled on the number of plates of food and wine glasses sold. As mentioned, a plate cost $9 while commemorative wine-tasting glasses were sold for $3 each. At times, there were long queues at the visitor centre for the purchasing of tickets and wine glasses. The wine glass stocks ran out towards the latter half of the second day. In addition to wine supplied by each winery with lunch, wine could be bought by the glass and cost $3 per glass throughout. Festival attendees could also buy wine per bottle or case to take home through winery cellar-door sales.

The advertising and promotion leading up to the event was quite extensive; for example it included a television advertisement from a Channel 10 sponsorship that consisted of 66 spots to the value of about $31 000 over a 28-day promotional period prior to the event. Channel 10, which specifically targets the 18–35-year age bracket as its prime audience, has been a sponsor of the event since 1995. Radio gave support to the promotion of the event only in the form of a SAFM community announcement. The main thrust of the campaign consisted of 65 000 fold-up colour brochures that were distributed to various points and were available during the event at participating wineries as well as at the visitor centre. Some were also mailed out to all addresses on the mailing list two months before the event. At the festival it soon became evident that people used these brochures mainly as pocket maps and to obtain information about the types of food and music available at the individual wineries. A major focus of the 2000 festival was to attract an increased number of interstate and overseas visitors. While recognition is growing, the McLaren Vale Wine region is still not widely recognised by the consuming Australian public, and is virtually unknown in many international markets.

For a couple of weeks immediately after the festival, wine sales at the wineries that were not included in the loops picked up through cellar-door sales as a result of people's exposure to the wineries on the loops during the festival. A bit of a 'honeymoon' period followed after the festival for the McLaren Vale region in general.

Based on the experience of previous years, the organisers were aware that the two festival days served to segment attendees into two distinct groups — on Sunday, younger, professional, singles and couples (under 35 years); on Monday, older, more conservative, settled families with children (adults over 35 years).

Mindful of the fact that the success of wine tourism rests heavily upon the entire experience that the visitor has, the organisers decided to conduct a satisfaction survey on festival attendees on both days, by means of a random sampling technique and intercept personal interviewing of 141 attendees using a structured questionnaire and conducted at the wineries and information centre. This included obtaining attendee demographics, wine consumption and event satisfaction information. The survey covered all the loops. In brief descriptive format, the main findings are described on the following pages.

- Demographics: female (54%); male (46%); 18–35 years old (44%); 35+ years old (56%), with largest age segments 22–28 years old (24%) and 46–60 years old (30%);
- Education level: post-Year 12 education (69%); university bachelor degree and higher (43%);
- South Australian residents (89%); interstate (8%); overseas (3%).
- Attendees who are normally wine drinkers (94%);
- Attendees who bought wine at cellar doors for home consumption (22%);
- Average number of Sea and Vines Festival attendances (including 2000) (2.23);
- Method by which attendees heard about the 2000 Sea and Vines Festival (more than one method/choice was possible): friends or colleagues told me (41%); advertisement in newspaper/magazine (26%); went last year (22%); festival brochure (14%); television (11%); living in McLaren Vale (11%); radio (7%); all other methods (4%).

A five-point satisfaction scale was used to measure the satisfaction of attendees with the following aspects of the event: festival's theme; brochure and poster; music (bands at wineries); entertainment (excluding music); lunch (seafood dish); wine served with lunch; seating arrangements at lunch; toilet facilities; access/ parking arrangements; ticketing arrangements; cost aspect overall; courtesy bus service; ease of moving around; composition of the loops; helpfulness of the staff; and McLaren Vale as centre-point.

Whereas the responses of attendees generally reflected a high level of satisfaction and enjoyment, the strongest indications of dissatisfaction (up to 25% of attendees expressed dissatisfaction on some aspects) were encountered in the areas of:
- food — ran out as early as 1 p.m. with complaints also about high cost, not value for money and the quantity (portion size) of food served;
- seating at lunch — generally experienced as inadequate, and sharing tables with strangers was a problem;
- music — high volume level and the music type played;
- bus transport — traffic congestion resulted in some attendees waiting for over an hour to be picked up; as a result these visited only one or very few
- wineries. Forty per cent of attendees used their own transport, compounding the traffic congestion problem;
- access and parking — access was generally difficult and parking was not clearly signposted;
- overcrowding — some had to queue for longer than one hour to get lunch, and for tickets.

As is the case with most events of a commercial nature, the bottom line regarding the event's future and success is whether people would attend it again:
- Attendee will revisit the festival next year (2001): 88%;
- Attendee's first attendance of the festival: 48%.

Food and wine festivals have become quite popular in Australia and competition for the wine tourists' dollar, both intra- and interstate, is increasing. It is also true that, despite planning the growth of such events, there are problems and

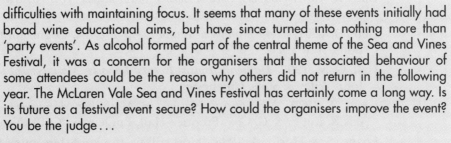

difficulties with maintaining focus. It seems that many of these events initially had broad wine educational aims, but have since turned into nothing more than 'party events'. As alcohol formed part of the central theme of the Sea and Vines Festival, it was a concern for the organisers that the associated behaviour of some attendees could be the reason why others did not return in the following year. The McLaren Vale Sea and Vines Festival has certainly come a long way. Is its future as a festival event secure? How could the organisers improve the event? You be the judge . . .

Johan Bruwer
Senior Lecturer: Wine Marketing
Adelaide University, Australia
(with thanks to McLaren Vale Winemakers Inc.)

Questions

1 What 'business' is the McLaren Vale Sea and Vines Festival organising committee operating?

2 What is the nature of the Sea and Vines Festival event's brand image?

3 Describe the Sea and Vines Festival's product, promotional, pricing and distribution strategies in a paragraph each.

4 Describe the Sea and Vines Festival's target markets and competitive strategy.

5 In terms of the results obtained from the consumer satisfaction survey conducted at the 2000 festival, explain the nature of the 'quality gap' that apparently exists in detail and suggest remedial actions that should be taken.

6 How should the apparent discrepancy between the percentage of first attendees of the festival and those who indicate that they will re-attend next year be interpreted? If you were the organisers, how would you address this issue?

REFERENCES

Ansoff, I. 1957, 'Strategies for diversification', *Harvard Business Review*, September–October, pp. 113–124.

Cowell, D. 1984, *The Marketing of Services*, Heinemann, London.

Dickman, S. 1997, 'Issues in arts marketing', in *Making It Happen: The Cultural and Entertainment Industries Handbook*, ed. R. Rentschler, Centre for Professional Development, Kew, Victoria.

George, W. & Berry, L. 1981, 'Guidelines for the advertising of services', *Business Horizons*, July–August, pp. 52–56.

Getz, D. 1991, *Festivals, Special Events and Tourism*, Von Nostrand Reinhold, New York.

Getz, D. 1997, *Event Management and Event Tourism*, Cognizant Communications, New York.

Hall, C. M. 1997, *Hallmark Tourist Events: Impacts, Management and Planning*, John Wiley & Sons, Chichester.

Levitt, T. 1980, 'Marketing myopia', in *Marketing Management and Strategy*, eds K. Kotler & C. Cox, Prentice Hall, Englewood Cliffs, New Jersey.

Loane, S. & Horin, A. 1998, 'Most still tie the knot, but much later', *Sydney Morning Herald*, 20 April, p. 4.

Lovelock, C., Patterson, P. & Walker, R. 2001, *Services Marketing*, 2nd edn, Pearson Australia Education, Sydney.

McCarthy, E. & Perreault, W. 1987, *Basic Marketing*, Irwin, Homewood, Illinois.

Middleton, V. T. C. 1995, *Marketing in Travel and Tourism*, Butterworth-Heinemann, Oxford.

Mohr, K., Backman, K., Gahan, L. & Backman, S. 1993, 'An investigation of festival motivations and event satisfaction by visitor type', *Festival Management and Event Tourism*, vol. 1, pp. 89–97.

Morgan, M. 1996, *Marketing for Leisure and Tourism*, Prentice Hall, London.

Ray, M. 1982, *Advertising and Communication Management*, Prentice Hall, Englewood Cliffs, New Jersey.

Roslow, S., Nicholls, J. & Laskey, H. 1992, 'Hallmark events and measures of reach and audience characteristics', *Journal of Advertising Research*, July/August, pp. 53–59.

Saleh, F. & Ryan, C. 1993, 'Jazz and knitwear: factors that attract tourists to festivals', *Tourism Management*, August, pp. 289–297.

Stanton, W., Miller, K. & Layton, R. 1994, *Fundamentals of Marketing*, 3rd edn, McGraw Hill, Sydney.

Torkildsen, G. 1983, *Leisure and Recreation Management*, Spon, London.

Uysal, M., Gahan, L. & Martin, B. 1993, 'An examination of event motivations', *Festival Management and Event Tourism*, vol. 1, pp. 5–10.

Veal, A. 1997, *Research Methods for Leisure and Tourism*, Pitman, London.

Zeithaml, V., Parasuraman, A. & Berry, L. 1990, *Delivering Quality Service: Balancing Customer Perceptions and Expectations*, The Free Press, New York.

8

Strategic marketing
of events

LEARNING OBJECTIVES

After studying this chapter, you should be able to:

■ define strategic marketing in the event context

■ construct a C-PEST analysis for an event

■ construct appropriate marketing objectives for an event

■ summarise the C-PEST analysis and an analysis of the event organisation's resources and weaknesses into a marketing SWOT analysis

■ from this, devise relevant strategies that can achieve marketing objectives

■ construct a strategic marketing plan.

INTRODUCTION

E. Jerome McCarthy's four Ps (product, price, place, promotion) of marketing, which are the foundation of modern marketing techniques, are discussed in the previous chapter. That framework gives event managers and marketers an ability to think coherently about their event product and its ability to satisfy its consumers' needs, how it is priced, how it is to be promoted, and where and how tickets to the event can be purchased or obtained.

In this chapter, this framework for thinking about marketing an event is expanded to introduce the techniques of strategic marketing. This gives event marketers another framework in which to think in a logical and coherent fashion about their event product, who it appeals to, what are its features, and how it can be priced and distributed (or placed) and promoted. It introduces that much-overworked word of the twenty-first century, strategy.

WHAT IS STRATEGIC MARKETING?

As Fifield (1992) points out, the overuse of this word simply causes confusion among marketing practitioners, managers of all types, and festival and special event managers. It is worthwhile, therefore, to spend a little time discussing the origins of the word, and its meaning in the context of event management and its concomitant marketing.

The word is derived from the Greek *strategia*, meaning the art of a general of an army, and was originally used by the military to describe actions taken to achieve military objectives or — as the chapter on planning defines objectives — desired future ends.

In the last decades of the twentieth century, the word entered the lexicon of business management to mean how an organisation marshals and utilises its resources to achieve its business objectives, within an ever-changing political, economic, sociocultural and technological environment. The chapter on event planning describes this process. In this chapter the process is linked to the marketing function to provide a coherent framework in which event managers can produce outcomes that satisfy an event's marketing objectives and, concurrently, the event's overall objectives.

Strategy is:
- longer term, rather than short term. Once a marketing strategy is decided, it can be wasteful of resources, not to mention the disruption to the event production, to change to another. Therefore careful thought is required before deciding on what strategies to use to achieve objectives.
- not another word for tactics. Strategy is the broad overall direction that an event takes in order to achieve its objectives, and tactics are the detailed manoeuvres or programs that carry out the strategy. Tactics can be changed as market conditions change, but the overall direction — the strategy — remains constant.

- based on careful analysis of internal resources and external environments — not a hasty reaction to changes in the market
- essential to survival. As Fifield (1992, p. 9) rather nicely points out, 'if you don't know where you are going, any road will get you there'. Well-thought-out marketing strategies enable event managers to achieve the objectives of their event.

This chapter explores this link between the overall objectives of the event and how its marketing strategies are developed to help achieve these objectives by describing each step in the process. However, it is helpful to aid understanding of the concept to end this section with a definition of strategic event marketing. It is certainly not the only one, as a perusal of any book with strategic marketing in its title can attest. Fifield (1992) identifies nine different definitions, all slightly different, from nine prominent marketing authors. Nevertheless, this definition encapsulates the essence of the concept for event managers:

■ *Strategic event marketing* is the process by which an event organisation aligns business and marketing objectives and the environments in which they occur, into market activity. ■

ꝒTEP 1: THE MISSION AND OBJECTIVES

Figure 8.1 shows diagrammatically the forces that influence an event organisation's mission, the start point for any strategic plan.

■ **Figure 8.1**
Constructing the mission

This can be illustrated by the example of the 25th Sydney Festival 2001. The key implementers are probably Mr Leo Schofield, the festival director, Mr Bob Carr, the premier of the State of New South Wales, and its minister for the arts, a major sponsor of the festival, and the chair of the board of the Sydney Festival, Sydney's lord mayor, Councillor Frank Sartor. It is their values that give the event its vision for the future and the broad direction it takes to get there. The long-term objective is to continue to hold the festival on a yearly basis. The needs of the stakeholders are summarised in table 8.1.

STAKEHOLDER	REQUIREMENTS
Staff of festival	To be part of a successful and recognised cultural event that is career enhancing
Sponsors	To be associated in a positive manner with an event that appeals to the target market of the sponsor
State government	To be associated with an arts festival that is entertaining, artistically progressive, critically acclaimed and does not need extra finance from the government of NSW
City council	That the public facilities of the city are used in a manner that enhances their worth and does them no physical damage, while encouraging visitation and spending in the CBD
Police and ambulance service	To be appreciated and included in the planning of major events that attract large numbers of people
Providers of food and beverages in the city	Consumers are to be attracted in large numbers
Consumers	To be entertained and stimulated by the best that Australian and overseas artists can provide

From this analysis a mission statement can be constructed that is a concise and precise statement of the direction and purpose of an organisation. The mission of the 25th Sydney Festival 2001 is encapsulated in these words:

■ This 25th Sydney Festival again celebrates our best and their best, a unique assembly of talent for a unique city. Enjoy our birthday with us in January (http://www.sydneyfestival.org.au/). ■

From this statement comes what Ferrell, Lucas and Luck (1994) refer to as what the organisation represents and the groups it serves. It can be seen from this mission that the 25th Sydney Festival offers the best of both Australian and foreign artistic talent to the people of Sydney, in a way that is not replicated anywhere else. This statement sets the foundation for the strategic marketing of the festival, which is designed to achieve its marketing objectives.

Strategic marketing is a planning tool that emphasises thorough analyses. Rao and Steckel (1998) believe that good judgement is not enough to make good strategic decisions. These can come only from a thorough analysis of competitor activities, the political, economic, sociocultural and technological environments in which the event occurs, and of the event organisation's internal resources.

Figure 8.2 shows the elements that make up this analysis, and each is discussed in turn. The international artistic environment is included, as changes occurring in the world of artistic endeavour need careful monitoring and analysis by event and festival managers. It must be stressed that these analyses are done for a very good reason — to establish opportunities and threats for the festival or event and its management. From this, strategies are formulated to take advantage of the opportunities and to neutralise threats identified from the analysis.

■ **Figure 8.2**
Elements of the environment analysis

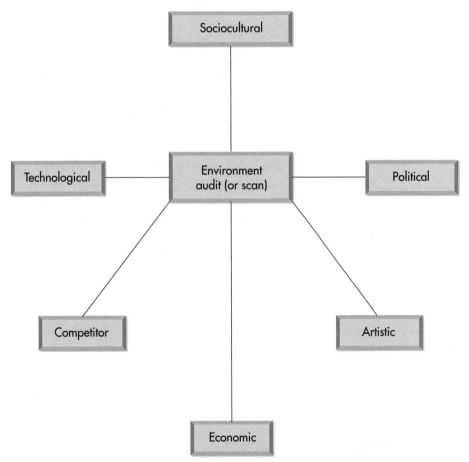

The Re-branding of Sydney's Royal Easter Show

The Royal Agricultural Society of New South Wales has produced Sydney's Royal Easter Show for over 120 years. In 1998 it moved from its traditional venue at the Sydney Showgrounds at Moore Park, an inner city suburb of Sydney, to a custom-built site at Homebush in the geographical centre of Sydney, where it attracted a record crowd of 1.26 million, higher than the previous record crowd of 1.23 million set in 1947. The Moore park site became the site of Fox studios and its associated leisure precinct.

What is of interest is that it took more than 50 years, and a move to a site that was to become a venue for the Sydney Olympics 2000, for the attendance record to be broken. This is an obvious symptom of an event product not adapting to sociocultural and demographic environmental changes. The rural population of New South Wales has been in relative decline since the 1940s, with a concurrent increase in the urban population, which led to a decline in interest in the traditional show activities of displays of agricultural produce and the sale of show bags.

To counter this the show was re-branded in 2000 as the 'Great Australian Muster', 'to give the Show a fresh identity and enforce it as a uniquely Australian event' (http://www.greataustralianmuster.com/aboutus.htm).

The elements that now make up the show now include: *Celebrate Australia* — a celebration of Australia's bush heritage featuring bush skills put to the test in a Stockmen's Challenge; an International Rodeo Challenge; a production entitled *The Man from Snowy River*, which is an action packed reenactment of the famous poem by Banjo Patterson; a show entitled *Hell West and Crooked Outback Stunt Show* which is a high-energy action-packed 30-minute show of stunts featuring fights, falls, fire, music and explosions; and International Test Wood Chopping.

These elements convey to the ever-growing urban population of Sydney their image of an idealised rural life where the pioneers of Australia do battle with the physical environment to produce the rugged Australian of myth and legend.

Event marketing is concerned with identifying consumer needs and then satisfying them within the boundaries of the organisation's mission. The marketers of the Royal Easter Show have realised that the sociocultural and demographic environments of Australia have changed, and have altered their product (a leisure experience) to reflect these changes.

■ Competitor *analysis*

Michael Porter (1990), the seminal writer on competitor analysis and strategy, identified four elements that impact on an industry's competitors, which are shown in figure 8.3. Though Porter was describing generic industry and its potential for profit, this analytical tool is just as valid for the festival and event manager and is a very useful framework to analyse the forces that impact on competitor activity. As an example, each element is discussed in the context of the Sydney Festival 2001.

■ **Figure 8.3**
The four competitive forces

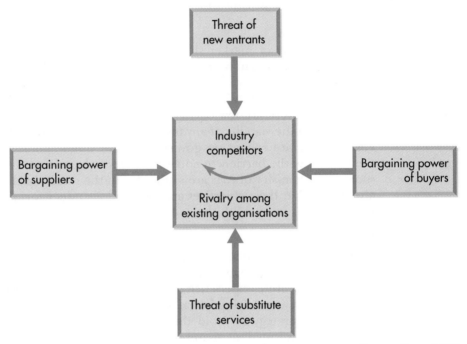

(**Source:** *Porter 1990*)

Suppliers

Suppliers to a festival such as this are venues, artists and physical resources needed to produce shows such as lighting and staging. Generally, unless there are other artistic festivals occurring simultaneously in other parts of the world, no difficulties should exist. However, as the mission of the Sydney Festival 2001 is to provide the best of Australian and world talent to its consumers, it may find that some suppliers of highly valued artists have great power to increase the cost of the talent, or the conditions under which they perform. From this analysis could evolve a product strategy of building long-term relationships with agents and other festivals to ensure continuity of supply at a reasonable prices. This strategy of building long-term relationships could also be applied to the management of venues such as the Sydney Opera House, which would ensure appropriate venues are available when required for the festival at an affordable price. It can therefore be seen that under some circumstances suppliers have considerable power, and strategies need to be developed to counteract this power.

Buyers

As the buyers of the Sydney Festival 2001 experiences are large in number, little power is concentrated in their hands. The only power they have is their price sensitivity to the festival's offerings. That is, as its mission is to provide the best, and the best can be expensive, resulting in higher ticket prices, consumers may decide that a particular offering does not give value for money, and stay away in droves, much to the embarrassment of the festival organisers and the sponsors. The art of the marketer is to know, intuitively perhaps but better based on experience and market research, at what price level this sensitivity arises.

New entrants

This is a threat of market share lost to another festival offering similar experiences. Australian history is littered with festivals that are no more. For example, Sydney's Waratah festival was once the festival highlight for Australia's biggest city. Now it is just a fading memory of middle-aged Sydney residents. If there are few barriers to entry for new entrants, this can be a real threat to the viability of any festival. However, as festivals like the Sydney Festival 2001 are reliant on government and other sponsors for much of their funding, the barriers to entry are quite high, as long as major sponsors such as the Ministry of Arts are satisfied with the results of the festival. This also means that their objectives are met, and a strategy for maintaining this sponsorship is to establish their objectives, and then ensure they are met.

Substitutes

This is based on the marketing premise that consumers are not purchasing a service, but a package of benefits — in this case stimulating entertainment. If a substitute experience can offer an entertainment that is more satisfying, or just as satisfying but at a cheaper price, then substitutes can be a threat. One strategy to avoid this is to offer a unique experience, which cannot be substituted, to an appropriate market segment.

■ Environment *analysis*

Once this analysis is done, the analysis turns to the environments in which the festival or event operates. Again each are discussed in turn, and the Sydney Festival 2001 used as the example. However, a caveat is necessary. As Aaker (1995, p. 27) opines, 'it is important to limit environmental analysis to the manageable and relevant, because it is easy to get bogged down by excessive volume and scope'. In other words, stick to what is significant to the organisation for strategy development in that environment. And remember, the purpose of the analysis is to identify opportunities and threats in order to develop strategies that can take advantage of the opportunities and negate threats, in order to achieve the event's marketing objectives.

Political environment

All three levels of government can be active players in either producing or sponsoring events. In the case of the Sydney Festival, both the New South

Wales government and Sydney City Council play an active role in sponsorship and the supply of venues. This suggests that strategies to maintain this involvement are necessary, especially if a change of government occurs.

Economic environment

Factors that can impact on strategic choice for events are the future direction of the economy; foreign exchange rates; interest rates; employment rates; growth in household income; and government fiscal policy. For example, because of a fall in the value of the Australian dollar compared to United States dollars, the cost of bringing foreign artists to Sydney for the festival increases dramatically. Product strategies need to be developed to maintain the event's mission of bringing the best of talent, within a shrinking US dollar budget to pay for it.

Sociocultural environment

Factors that can impact on marketing strategies are the size and variety of cultural/sub-cultural groups in the target market; changes in lifestyle; changes in work patterns; changes in the demographic make-up of a community; changes in types of entertainment demand; changes in education levels; and changes in household make-up. Organisers of the Sydney Festival might observe, for example, that women are having children at a later age than previous generations. This means that a target market of women aged 18–30 is not as occupied with child rearing as previously, and could have more time and income to attend festival events.

Technological environment

Changes in this environment could prove very challenging to event organisations. For example, the introduction of large screen DVD television to affluent Australian homes (a target market of the Sydney Festival) may mean that this group may decide to stay at home for their entertainment. While this is unlikely, event managers must be alert to technological innovation that could impact on their event.

Artistic environment

The arts of all types are characterised by constant change, as new ways of expression are developed. An event manager's or festival director's product strategies generally include offering new artistic experiences to the consumers. To do this, relevant aspects of the artistic environment need be closely monitored, and appropriate innovations included in the event's product range. This generally means travel to centres of artistic innovation around the world, a chore that most festival directors stoically accept.

It must be stressed that this analysis is not something that is done yearly for the construction of the annual marketing plan, but is an ongoing process, conducted by a thorough reading of professional and popular journals, networking with industry colleagues, and travelling to trade fairs or other events. As well, it must always be understood that the purpose of the analysis is to identify opportunities and threats and then develop marketing strategies to align opportunities and strengths and to negate threats and weaknesses.

■ Internal *resources*

This brings us to the next step in the analysis — internal resources. Classic economists categorise the resources available to an entrepreneur as land, labour and capital. In event or festival organisations these resources are human resources, physical resources and financial resources.

Human resources (labour)

This audit analyses the number and type of staff and volunteers available, their skills and how these match the skills required to produce the event, the costs of employing them, and what strengths they may have that can be utilised in innovative ways. For example, an analysis of the Sydney Festival 2001 would show that the festival's director is very well known and is held in great respect by the media. A promotion strategy therefore could be to use the director as the public face of the festival, and to promote the festival by media release and media interview, rather than more expensive paid advertising.

Physical resources (land)

For an event organisation this category includes computer hardware and software, offices, desktop publishing equipment, access to venues at competitive rates and the use of conference rooms in buildings of some significance. For example a strength could be a sophisticated computer program that is capable of supplying timely management information on all aspects of the festival. Physical resources can also include such intangibles as the public perception of the event and its branding and logo.

Financial resources (capital)

Without the availability of suitable finance, no strategy can be put into place. Availability of, or access to, funds is an obvious strength for any event organisation. This includes the ongoing involvement of government and corporate sponsorship funds. Without it, a serious weakness is identified that must be corrected if marketing objectives are to be met.

■ SWOT *analysis*

Once this analysis, or resource audit as some marketing writers refer to it, is completed, a strengths, weaknesses, opportunities, threats (SWOT) analysis can be developed. This is, as Tribe (1997) describes it, a summary of relevant aspects of the C-PEST and internal resources analyses, which enables the event marketer to develop marketing strategies that marry opportunities and strengths, improve weaknesses and negate threats — and, just as importantly, develop strategies that will achieve marketing objectives and the business objective of the event organisation. This task is made easier if all the data collected are summarised into no more than 10 bullet points for each section of the SWOT.

$\mathcal{S}$TEP 3: THE TARGET MARKET

This step in the strategic marketing process uses again the concept of the buyer decision-making process, discussed in chapter 7 by the use of the PIECE acronym. Figure 8.4 offers another perspective on the consumer decision-making process, which shows the complex number of variables that influence consumer choice of event attendance.

■ **Figure 8.4**
The complex pattern of buying influences

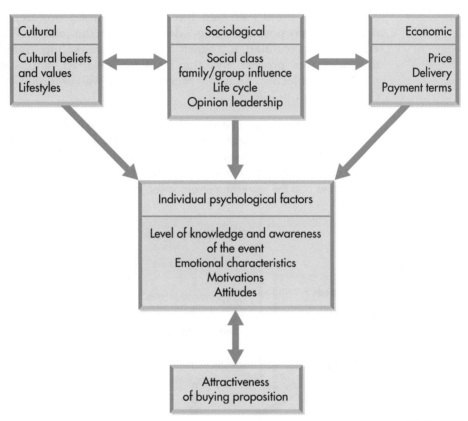

(**Source:** *Fifield 1992*)

This schema gives event marketers a framework in which to think about the characteristics of the customers that they wish to attract and a method of segmenting them demographically, geographically, psychologically and attitudinally. Though chapter 7 discussed this in some detail, figure 8.4 gives another perspective on target market segmentation. For example, the Sydney Festival 2001 has an extensive product range — categorised into music, dance, visual arts, family, theatre and cinema, free outdoor and opera/music theatre. Each of these categories has different offerings, appealing to different sub-markets. For example, the visual art category has 12 different offerings. Using figure 8.4 as the framework, a mental snapshot can be developed of the target market for the visual arts category of the festival, and then this market segment can be further broken down into the market for each offering.

Of course, something must be done with this information, or why bother? The characteristics of the target market influence the marketing strategies and tactics employed to achieve marketing objectives and are the subject of step four.

STEP 4: MARKETING STRATEGY

Now that an event's mission has been set, broad overarching objectives decided, a corporate strategy decided and the external and internal environments scanned, it is timely to consider marketing strategy. Figure 8.5 illustrates this process and the elements involved, and starts with the marketing objective. Cravens, Merriless and Walker (2000, p. 272) make this important point:

■ For marketing to be a beneficial business discipline its expected results must be defined and measurable. A marketer (including an event marketer) must be adept at formulating . . . objectives that are suitable and appropriate to the nature, needs and circumstances of the enterprise, achievable within the constraints of available resources and the marketing environment, and be measurable. ■

■ **Figure 8.5**
Marketing strategy development

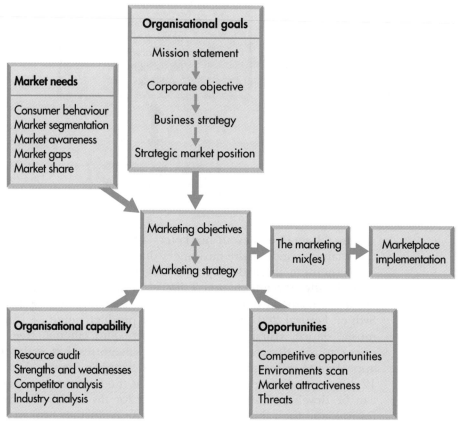

(**Source:** *adapted from Fifield 1992*)

Examples of marketing objectives for a festival such as the Sydney Festival 2001 are to:

- increase box office receipts by 10 per cent over 2000
- increase percentage of seats sold in all ticketed events from 72 per cent to 75 per cent
- decrease loss-making events from five to two
- retain 90 per cent of sponsors for 2002
- increase publicity generated in print and electronic media by 15 per cent from 2000.

It is important to stress again how marketing objectives, like all objectives, must be measurable, and not expressed in vague terms that make measurement impossible. While it is tempting to do this, as it makes it difficult for the marketer to be held accountable, this temptation must be resisted. Clearly defined and measurable objectives give the marketer the ends, and then strategies and their concomitant tactics can be formulated to provide the means. As figure 8.5 implies, there is a reciprocal relationship between the objectives and the strategies designed to achieve them.

This obviously means that the dimensions of the objective impacts on what strategies are used. For example, consider a possible objective of the Sydney Festival 2001 of increasing box office receipts by 10 per cent over the previous year. This is a substantial amount, much higher than the inflation rate of three per cent This implies that a business objective of the festival is to grow substantially each year, in order to satisfy the entertainment and cultural demands of a more diverse audience base. The objective, and the strategies to achieve it, are chosen after careful analysis of the market needs, organisational capability and opportunities, illustrated in figure 8.5.

The analysis of the market and its entertainment and cultural needs shows that several significant groups that make up the diverse Sydney population are not being satisfied with appropriate product offerings. This is what is meant by a market gap, which can be closed by strategic marketing. Analysis of the festival organisation's resources shows that it can produce product offerings that fill that gap. This is confirmed when an analysis is made of the sociocultural environment, which establishes that an opportunity exists for growing the festival by providing cultural experiences for market segments previously ignored.

Another example of how the framework can assist in strategic thinking (to introduce another over-used phrase of the business lexicon) is from the resource audit. It is established that a strength of the festival organisation is that the director is very well known in Sydney and is an authority on all things artistic and cultural. From this strength comes the objective of increasing publicity generated in the print and electronic media by 15 per cent over the previous year. The strategy to achieve this is to use the director as the face of the festival, and to use the director, rather than a public relations person, as the spokesperson. From these two examples, it can be seen that a rigorous and thorough review of all the elements shown in figure 8.5 is most useful in formulating marketing objectives and the strategies employed to achieve them.

Now that the marketing objectives for the event are set, and strategies decided, it is time to implement them. This is done by means of the marketing mix, introduced in the previous chapter on event marketing. As the great majority of festivals and special events operate in one marketplace, this a relatively straightforward activity. Once all the elements shown in figure 8.5 are identified, it then becomes the job of the event marketer to create a marketing mix consisting of products that meet consumer needs that are priced at an appropriate level, promoted so that potential consumers are aware of the product, are motivated to purchase, and can easily access purchase of tickets. Bordon (in Ferrell, Lucas & Luck 1994) identified 12 elements and first used the term 'marketing mix' in 1965 to describe the range of marketing activities used by marketers. These 12 were pared down to four by McCarthy (1975) into the now familiar four Ps. Table 7.1 in chapter 7 shows the marketing mix for events, using the four P concept.

However, it may be useful to consider a seven P marketing mix for services first put forward by Booms and Bitner (1981), which introduces the Ps of People, Process and Physical Evidence. Figure 8.6 shows their concept in the context of event marketing. Though in the chapter on the marketing of events it is stated that a four P mix is superior as splitting the product P into three other Ps may cause muddled thinking, it may be worthwhile in some circumstances to use this marketing mix model, as it may be helpful to clarify thinking on the various aspects of the event's product.

■ **Figure 8.6**
The event 7P marketing mix

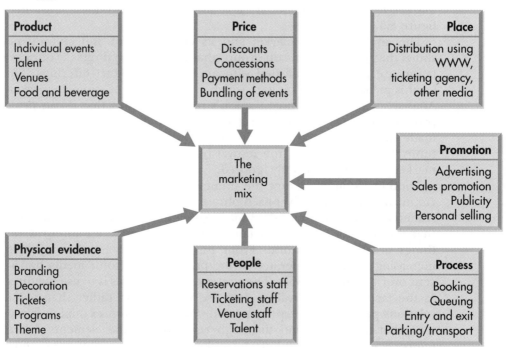

Product
Individual events
Talent
Venues
Food and beverage

Price
Discounts
Concessions
Payment methods
Bundling of events

Place
Distribution using WWW, ticketing agency, other media

The marketing mix

Promotion
Advertising
Sales promotion
Publicity
Personal selling

Physical evidence
Branding
Decoration
Tickets
Programs
Theme

People
Reservations staff
Ticketing staff
Venue staff
Talent

Process
Booking
Queuing
Entry and exit
Parking/transport

(**Source:** *adapted from Booms & Bitner 1981*)

For example, the People P can concentrate the mind of the event marketer on the people services needed by event consumers, and the personal characteristics and skills of staff needed to successfully do the tasks required, and thereby deliver an appropriate level of customer service. By thinking about the Physical Evidence P, the event marketer can ensure that all the tangible aspects of an event such as programs, tickets, the event logo and venue decoration have a congruent theme that synergistically adds to the event experience. The Process P enables thought to be given to those ancillary activities of the event that, if done poorly, can give an event a poor reputation. The Sydney 2000 Olympic Games is a recent example of where the Process P was given much commendation by the public and media critics, because of the excellence of the transport links to the Games' venues and the high standard of spectator services at the venues. This did not just happen, but was a result of careful analytical thinking about the event processes.

A new phrase has now been introduced — marketing tactics. If marketing strategy gives the broad general direction to go to achieve an objective, tactics provide the detailed map. In other words, the tactics are the detail of how the strategy is carried out. For example, suppose a strategy for the 2001 Sydney Festival is to use the director as the festival's spokesperson, and this is to be the main promotional tool. The tactics of this are the style of media releases, where and when they would be done, on what topic, and the ways and means of keeping the media conferences fresh and original. It was stressed at the beginning of the chapter that strategies are longer term, and should not be changed without very good reason.

■ **Figure 8.7**
From strategy to tactics

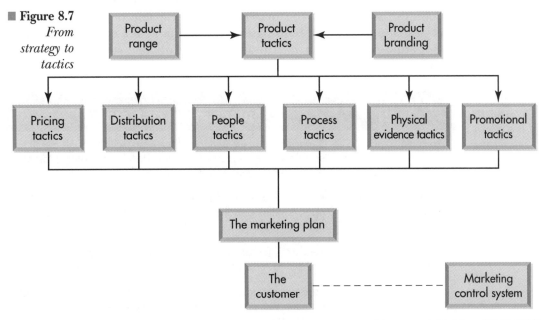

(**Source:** *adapted from Fifield 1992*)

Tactics, however, can and should be changed as market conditions change. For example, if it is discovered that the tactic of holding media events for the Sydney Festival in the board room of the Opera House is not achieving the required amount of print and electronic coverage, the venue could be shifted to a less formal environment that better reflects the essence of the festival and its events.

The marketing chapter discusses event marketing tactics in some detail, so it is redundant to do so again here. However, it is timely to emphasise that appropriate tactics are the product of the analytical thought process described in this chapter. Sound strategic analysis should result in sound tactics.

STEP 6: THE MARKETING PLAN

It is of no value for event marketers, except if they are a sole practitioner, to undertake this analytical strategic marketing thought process, if they do not share it with anybody. As was discussed in the chapter on planning, most events have a governing body that approves major expenditure. So the first role of the written marketing plan is usually to get approval for the recommended marketing expenditure that quantifies the marketing plan. A second and just as important reason is that it communicates to all relevant staff members the event's marketing objectives, strategies and tactics, the reasons why they are chosen, and who is responsible for tactical action. Figure 7.12 (on page 191) outlines one possible structure of a strategic marketing plan.

Another structure is shown in table 8.2. This is not prescriptive. Every organisation faces different circumstances, so it is not sensible to prescribe a definitive structure of the marketing plan, capable of being applied to every situation. However both figure 7.12 and table 8.2 can serve as check lists for the construction of a practical and workable strategic marketing plan.

■ **Table 8.2**
A structure of a strategic marketing plan

ELEMENT OF PLAN	DESCRIPTION OF ELEMENT
Executive summary	Synopsis of major aspects of the plan, with enough detail to enable senior executives to understand the strategic thrust without being bogged down in detail
Situation analysis	Relevant variables of strengths and weaknesses; relevant opportunities and threats, current objectives and strategy (if appropriate)
Strengths and weaknesses	Relevant internal concerns; strengths recognised by customers; abilities to form a sustainable competitive advantage
Opportunities and threats	Relevant changes in the PEST environments that may either threaten the event organisation or provide marketing opportunities

ELEMENT OF PLAN	DESCRIPTION OF ELEMENT
Desired outcomes of the plan	Quantified marketing objectives of the event
Marketing strategies	Description of strategies designed to meet objectives
Tactics	Details of how, when and by whom strategies are to be implemented
Product/market match	Description of target market, benefits as perceived by target market
Budgets	Costs and timings allocated to each element of the marketing mix; projected revenues
Control mechanisms	Measures of performance; monitoring methods

(**Source:** *adapted from Ferrell, Lucas & Luck 1994*)

UMMARY

Good marketing does not happen through serendipity, but is the result of rigorous analytical thought, structured in such a way as to identify sustainable competitive advantage for the event organisation. The result of this thinking and research is a marketing plan that can attain an event's objectives in a cost-effective manner. And, of course, that can satisfy the first requirement of any successful marketer — satisfying customers' needs.

Questions

1. In your own words, define a marketing strategy and a tactic. Give an example of both in the context of an event with which you are familiar.

2. Why is a stakeholder analysis necessary for the construction of a meaningful mission statement? Give an example of an event's mission, and its stakeholders.

3. Who are the major suppliers of artistic talent to arts festivals? Give two examples of these sorts of organisations and their role, and a summary of their power.

4. What is the result of a change of government for publicly funded arts organisations? How can this affect community festivals?

5. What is meant by a market gap? Give an example of one, and what an event marketer could do to fill that gap.

Cyber-dancing into the new *millennium: the marketing of* Interdance

'Just log on to party, party, party' was the message that went out to all young Queenslanders to participate in a unique, State-wide cyber-dance event called *Interdance* on New Year's Eve, 1999. The brainchild of Millennium Events organisers within Centenary of Federation (Qld), *Interdance* was the final event in a series of millennium celebrations sponsored by the Premier's Department to reflect the needs and interests of 12–17-year-old Queenslanders. This concept of one State-wide, interactive event meant that young people could dance in the new millennium with friends, hook up on the Web or do both via seven dance parties staged in different towns and cities, all linked by an Internet Webcast and a big screen videocast of parties around the State. With over 11 000 hits on Backchat (the chat room) on New Year's Eve, it would have been tempting for organisers to see this result and other Web statistics as the primary measure of success. Yet, more complex marketing objectives underpinned *Interdance* as the capstone event within the Millennium Celebrations Program (MCP). Other key events in the program included Gig2K (a four day, youth cultural festival culminating on New Year's Eve), the Rainbow Serpent Parade (an indigenous New Year's Eve celebration), Vision Millennium (State-wide youth public art awards held in 1999) and Xit 99 (artists in residence working with regional youth to express visions of the future).

The objectives, strategy and marketing mix for the Millennium Celebrations Program (in which *Interdance* featured as one component of the event product mix) were devised to carefully reflect a well-researched theme of 'renewal and inclusion'. A strategic emphasis on youth, the environment, multiculturalism and indigenous Australians was planned to combine traditional festivities with future visions and provide a legacy for *all* future Australians. Under this thematic umbrella, the overall goals of the MCP were to:
• provide meaningful millennium celebrations that had a lasting legacy for Queensland
• to be as inclusive of as many Queenslanders as possible
• to build awareness of the Centenary of Federation as we went into the official first day of the new millennium, 1 January 2001.

In this context, the operational objectives for the *Interdance* event were (1) to facilitate safe, alcohol and drug free, youth cultural events targeted at under-18s in regional areas on New Year's Eve, and (2) use the Internet to link these events together, thereby creating an interactive and holistic event for Queensland youth.

However, the statements of the targeted outcomes for the *Interdance* event were much more indicative of the results sought within the target market. In this regard, the organisers sought to:

- create a unique, innovative event that, by using emerging technology, united the State on the eve of the new millennium
- overcome the perception of isolation and heighten inclusion for regional youth
- provide an opportunity to create a broader understanding of the diversity of youth issues within the State.

While maximising the tangible participation of youth in the event was pivotal to achieving these outcomes, much of the success of *Interdance* depended on an acute awareness of environmental issues and the stakeholders involved in the delivery of the event experience. During the Xit 99 project conducted over the previous summer, consultations with young people and youth officers in the regions explored the issues impacting upon the artistic direction of the projects. Based on evidence of disaffected youth in Queensland, including statistics on youth suicide, crime and unemployment, a number of regions (in addition to Brisbane city) were selected for Xit 99, many of which became locations for *Interdance* on New Year's Eve. Seven venues for *Interdance* were ultimately chosen — Brisbane, Nerang (Gold Coast), Ipswich and Deception Bay, and the more dispersed locations of Maryborough, Emerald and Thuringowah/Townsville.

Apart from risk management factors associated with ensuring a safe and alcohol-free environment, major challenges were presented by the innovative nature and scope of the event. There were the complex logistics of delivering a live Internet broadcast which was also broadcast live at each venue and on television via Briz 31. In addition, organisers needed to manage the videoconference linkup of all venues and the hosting of six live chat rooms, each themed on a different music style (e.g. Rock Room and Grunge Room). Because it was the 'turn of the century' New Year's Eve, organisers battled to find technicians who were prepared to work and travel to some of the remote locations involved in *Interdance*. Few people wanted to work on the 'night of nights' and securing equipment was very expensive, so cooperation depended on 'selling' the *Interdance* concept to these stakeholders.

In effect, the technological environment of *Interdance* was intense and complicated by the overwhelming public issue and potential threat of the Y2K bug. Each township or city venue also presented a different sociocultural and geographic setting that impacted upon the nature and scope of competing youth entertainment and the propensity for event participation. Strategic alliances were formed with diverse stakeholders including regional councils, corporate organisations, community groups and media in order to deliver dance parties with multimedia presentations in each town or city.

Due to the nature of the project, partnerships with supply-side stakeholders providing technological support were among the most critical to the event's success. From an operational perspective, each dance party location required ISDN line installation, training of venue staff with view station units, organisation of Internet accounts for each venue and management of acceptable levels of broadcast quality. Market satisfaction with the *Interdance* experience hinged on party-goers and people at home being able to preview and switch between live footage from different dance party venues. In this regard, the partnership between *Interdance* organisers and the multimedia provider (QANTM) became crucial in shaping a successful event product.

The media was also a key stakeholder in ensuring that a very high number of young people throughout Queensland were aware of the event and stimulated to get involved. Commencing with a media launch that involved the Premier engaging in an 'online chat' with young Queenslanders, the promotional mix for *Interdance* included the integrated use of State-wide publicity; the Millennium Celebrations Web site and information line, a 30-second radio commercial aired in all regions and *Interdance* posters, postcards, T-shirts and hats. Several activities such as a schools' competition and radio-sponsored prize packs containing event merchandise were designed to jointly promote the Gig2K youth festival and *Interdance*.

Media releases and media interviews with Millennium Celebrations organisers were 'pumped out' throughout December to all corners of the State. All media including regional and metropolitan television, radio and newspapers climbed aboard to offer strong support for the *Interdance* concept. Headlines alluding to a 'cyber celebration', a 'pulsating New Year' and 'New Year casts out the party net' reinforced messages about *Interdance* in both coastal and remote locations. The Briz 31 telecast for five hours of the Webcast on New Year's Eve capped off a very intensive promotional campaign.

The marketing element of 'place' or distribution became intrinsic to both the event product design and the way in which *Interdance* was promoted. From the outset, the need for widespread 'inclusion' of youth from different geographic areas meant that an online distribution of the dance party experience offered the best solution. This was the first occasion in Queensland when the diverse technical mediums of the Internet, television and videoconferencing had worked together to deliver an online entertainment event of this nature. The 'free' description of the event was strongly emphasised both in terms of the zero price tag and the alcohol- and drug-free nature of the staged dance parties. However, as with all not-for-profit community events, the 'free to consumer' benefit was achieved through dollar contributions and in-kind support from participating stakeholders — in this case, the Queensland Government, the media, local government authorities and many others in the communities involved.

In terms of the reach and appeal of *Interdance* within the Queensland youth market, Web statistics and survey research indicated strong awareness levels and usage patterns for the *Interdance* site across the State. Backchat was highly successful and 7500 postings occurred under more than 1000 individual log-on names. While the home page was accessed about 600 times, a lot of those hits were generated by people from areas not in the vicinity of a dance party venue. As the *Interdance* site was open on most computers at dance venues throughout the night, multiple uses of the one 'hit' meant that the extent of home page access was far higher than Web statistics indicated. However, the actual numbers of young people who went to the dance venues varied greatly throughout the State.

In Brisbane, the Y2K factor appeared to impact on attendance figures, with only one-third of the anticipated audience turning out on the night. By contrast, young people in the Central Queensland town of Emerald really turned on to *Interdance* with an attendance number that exceeded all expectations. Overall, research suggested that the multimedia concept, the notion of cyber-events and the supporting promotions were enthusiastically embraced by the market.

Interdance was rated as the most successful event in the Millennium Celebrations Program in terms of delivering on the theme of 'inclusion'. Event research provided strong evidence of youth participation from a number of rural and isolated areas as well as positive attitudes about the online dance party. By utilising innovative technology, *Interdance* effectively decentralised the State's millennium celebrations and joined together young people, many of whom might otherwise have been disenfranchised from a major celebration of the new century.

Ms Robyn Stokes
Lecturer, Queensland University of Technology
with Mr Lenny Vance
Managing Director, Buzz Events (formerly Manager of Queensland Government's Millennium Celebrations Program)

Questions

1 Based on available information, produce a brief C-PEST analysis for *Interdance*.

2 Critically evaluate the objectives of the cyber-dance concept, nominating how you would improve on their formulation.

3 Prepare a 50-word statement of the overall marketing strategy for *Interdance*, drawing together key information offered within the case.

4 In your view, is there greater evidence of strategic or tactical success in this case? Why?

5 Discuss any other research or evidence that you feel might have provided a more comprehensive measurement of the marketing success of the *Interdance* event.

REFERENCES

Aaker, D., 1995, *Strategic Market Management*, John Wiley & Sons, New York.

Booms, B. & Bitner, M. 1981, 'Marketing strategy and organization structures for service firms', in *Marketing of Services*, eds J. Donnely & W. George, American Marketing Association.

Cravens, D. Merriless, B. & Walker, R. 2000, *Strategic Marketing Management for the Pacific Region*, McGraw Hill, Sydney.

Ferrell, O., Lucas, G. & Luck, D. 1994, *Strategic Marketing Management: Texts and Cases*, South Western Publishing, Cincinnati.

Fifield, P. 1992, *Marketing Strategy*, Butterworth Heinemann, Oxford.

McCarthy, E. J. 1971, *Basic Marketing: A Managerial Approach*, R. D. Irwin, Homewood, Ill.

Porter, M., 1990, *Competitive Advantage of Nations*, Free Press, New York.

Rao, V. & Steckel, J. 1998, *Analysis for Strategic Marketing*, Addison-Wesley, Reading, Mass.

Tribe, J. 1997, *Corporate Strategy for Tourism*, International Thompson Business Press, London.

3

EVENT
ADMINISTRATION

This part of the book looks at the systems that event managers can use to put the event plan into action. The chapter on sponsorship looks at how to identify, obtain and manage sponsorships. The following chapter looks at budgeting for events, and how the budget process can be used as a controlling mechanism in the implementation of an event. The chapter on legal and risk management describes the legal factors that event managers need to be aware of, and how to identify, minimise and manage the risks inherent in an event. This section looks also at how information technology is changing the landscape of events, and how event managers can use it to strengthen their systems and transform their events.

9
Sponsorship
of events

LEARNING OBJECTIVES

After studying this chapter, you should be able to:

■ discuss the use of sponsorship in the context of festivals and events

■ discuss those forces acting to drive the expanded use of sponsorship as a promotional medium by private and public sector organisations

■ describe the key benefits sought by organisations through their use of sponsorship

■ describe the approaches organisations employ when screening sponsorship proposals

■ list the key elements of an event's sponsorship policy

■ discuss major factors influencing an event manager's decision to seek or not to seek sponsorship

■ describe approaches an event manager might use to identify suitable sponsors for an event

■ describe key considerations in the development of effective sponsorship proposals and business plans

■ describe the approaches event managers can employ to maintain positive and enduring relationships with sponsors.

INTRODUCTION

Sponsorship is central to the revenue stream of many new and continuing events. Event managers, therefore, commonly find themselves in the situation of being actively engaged in such tasks as identifying sponsors, preparing sponsorship proposals and servicing sponsors. This chapter addresses these matters, as well as trying to develop in readers an understanding of why sponsorship has increased in popularity as a promotional medium and the nature of the benefits organisations (both public and private) seek through its use.

WHAT IS SPONSORSHIP?

Sponsorship, once a grey area of marketing, is now an accepted part of the promotional mix (see chapter 7) of many organisations. As with other parts of this mix (advertising, personal selling, sales promotions and public relations) it is used to communicate with a particular target group or groups in order to achieve specific objectives. There are many definitions of sponsorship, but the core elements of such definitions are very similar, as can be seen from the following three examples:

> ■ Sponsorship — an investment in sport, community or government activities, the arts, a cause, individual, or broadcast which yields a commercial return for the sponsor. The investment can be made in financial, material, or human terms (Smart Marketing Street Wise Workshops 2001).
>
> A cash and/or in-kind fee paid to a property (such as an event) in return for the exploitable commercial potential associated with that property (International Events Group 1995, cited in Getz 1997, p. 216).
>
> The purchase of the, usually intangible, exploitable potential rights and benefits associated with an entrant, event or organisation which results in tangible benefits for the sponsoring company (image/profit enhancement) (Geldard & Sinclair, 1996, p. 6). ■

Taken collectively, these definitions indicate a number of key dimensions of sponsorship. First, it is a commercial transaction/investment and not a donation, a view some seekers of sponsorship sometimes take. Second, sponsorship may take the form of either a direct payment or the provision of in-kind services/products. Third, the return sought from sponsorship is one that will ultimately positively affect either the profitability of a business or, as is the case with public sector sponsors, provide some other benefit (e.g. generating awareness of the health problems associated with smoking).

While not explicit in the definitions provided, it should be stressed that sponsorship involves the development of a reciprocal relationship between the organisation providing the sponsorship and the organisation receiving it, in this case in the form of the event. This reciprocity element of the sponsorship process is illustrated in figure 9.1.

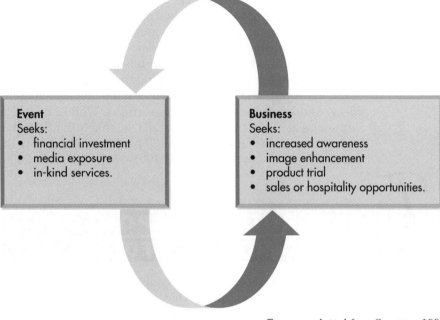

Figure 9.1
Exchange relationship in event sponsorship

Event
Seeks:
- financial investment
- media exposure
- in-kind services.

Business
Seeks:
- increased awareness
- image enhancement
- product trial
- sales or hospitality opportunities.

(**Source:** *adapted from Crompton 1994*)

*E*NVIRONMENTAL FACTORS INFLUENCING SPONSORSHIP USE

Sponsorship, as noted earlier, has become an accepted part of most marketer's promotional 'tool kits'. Along with the more traditional components of this 'kit' (e.g. advertising, sales promotions), sponsorship is increasingly being incorporated into promotional campaigns aimed at achieving specific organisational goals. The reasons for this can be found, in part, in a variety of changes that have occurred in the business environment. According to Crompton (1994), these changes have included:

- increases in the cost of television advertising
- loss in the effectiveness of television advertising due to the introduction of the remote control, allowing viewers to change channels whenever an advertisement appears
- growth in the number of media outlets (including pay TV channels, radio stations and specialist magazines), making it difficult for promotional messages to 'cut through the clutter'
- expansion in the number of pay TV channels (satellite and cable) and their subsequent need for program material. This has provided many more opportunities for events, especially sports events, to be televised, thus enhancing the potential exposure available to the sponsors of events.
- growth in the commercialisation of sport, both amateur and professional, providing expanded opportunities for organisations to engage in sponsorship

- increases in the number of products/services on the market, accompanied by a drop in the number of companies (by merger and take-over) producing them. This has increased the need for producers to enhance their relationships with the retailers of their products/services through such means as entertainment and hospitality.

Sponsorship has been able to exploit these environmental changes because of the many potential benefits it offers as a promotional medium (these benefits are addressed in the following section). While exact figures for sponsorship spend are hard to find in Australia, it is likely that a similar situation exists here to that in the UK where research has identified a more than 100 per cent increase in its use over the period 1991–98 (IPSOS RSL 2000).

THE ATTRIBUTES OF SPONSORSHIP AS A PROMOTIONAL MEDIUM

Sponsorships are taken up by organisations on the basis of their assessment of the benefits they offer. What individual organisations see as benefits depend on the strategic objectives they are pursuing at any one time. An event manager therefore needs an understanding of the full suite of potential benefits associated with sponsorship so that they can customise their sponsorship offerings. From a corporate perspective, various writers (e.g. Sunshine, Backman & Backman 1995; Geldard & Sinclair 1996) have attempted to identify benefits that can be delivered through sponsorship. These include:

- access to specific target markets

  Example: A conference of medical specialists in a particular field might provide a significant opportunity for the manufacturers of particular drugs/medical equipment to gain access to a large number of potential buyers/decision makers at one time and in one place.

- corporate/brand image creation/enhancement

  Example: Banks are viewed poorly by many country residents because of the number of branch closures that have occurred in recent years. Sponsorship of rural shows, festivals and other events might offer a means of addressing this situation.

- awareness of an organisation and/or its services/products

  Example: A manufacturer of sporting goods wishing to break into a new geographic market might seek to sponsor a number of televised sporting events as part of their overall promotional strategy.

- product identification with a particular lifestyle

  Example: A maker of a new alcoholic beverage might sponsor youth-oriented events, such as rock music festivals, as they wish to develop an association between their product and a demographic that is young, fun seeking and keen to experiment with new things.

- relationship building with distribution channel members

  Example: A corporation may be seeking to develop stronger relationships with the firms that distribute or purchase its products. To do this they may agree to sponsor an event if as part of the sponsorship package they receive such benefits as complimentary tickets, permission to erect their own hospitality tent on site, and invitations to special functions. These benefits in turn would be used as part of their efforts to build these relationships.

- merchandising opportunities

  Example: A benefit that a brewery might be seeking through a sponsorship is exclusive rights to the sale of its beverages at the event.

- demonstration of product attributes

  Example: Agricultural field days provide opportunities for products to be demonstrated to potential buyers. Producers of farming equipment may therefore be seeking, through the sponsorship of such events, opportunities to gain direct access to farmers in a way that will allow them to either conclude sales during the event, or soon after it.

- sales generation

  Example: As part of a sponsorship a firm may be granted the opportunity to directly sell their products/services to attendees at an event.

- component of employee reward and recognition systems

  Example: An organisation might see the sponsorship of a sporting event that allows them access to a corporate box and/or an allocation of tickets as a means of rewarding or motivating staff.

- maintenance of a climate of consent for an organisation's activities

  Example: An organisation might support a number of charity events in order to create an image in the community that it is a good corporate citizen.

It should also be kept in mind that public sector organisations (e.g. local councils and government departments/authorities/commissions/agencies) engage in sponsorship. A number of the benefits noted previously in the context of corporations are equally applicable to them. For example, many of these organisations need to communicate with particular groups to generate awareness of their products/services, or an issue (e.g. road safety). Additionally, as was noted in chapters 2 and 4, local, State or federal governments may be willing to support events through sponsorships, grants or contributions towards infrastructure construction, because of the broader-based community benefits they bring with them. For example, some events (e.g. festivals, sporting events) may act to stimulate economic development in an area, create a greater sense of identity within a community, or enhance a community's infrastructure base.

In order to attract sponsorship, event organisers need therefore to think in terms of how they can provide benefits such as those previously listed. In other words, what specifically do they have to 'sell' that sponsors will see these benefits in? Each event will obviously vary in this regard, but common items include the agreement to purchase product from a sponsor, e.g. alcohol, transport, food; event naming rights; exclusivity (capacity to lock out competition); networking opportunities; merchandising rights; media exposure; signage; advertising in media with sponsor to reinforce the association of the sponsor with the event; the capacity to demonstrate product; hospitality services; and tickets (full price/discounted).

THE SPONSORSHIP SCREENING PROCESS

Commonly organisations apply a screening process to sponsorship proposals as they seek to determine the extent to which the benefits that are of specific relevance to them are present. An understanding of this screening process is useful to the event manager as it assists in crafting their sponsorship proposals. Crompton (1993) uses the acronym CEDAR EEE to identify what he considers to be the major elements of the sponsorship screening process employed by corporations. The acronym is derived from:

Customer audience
Exposure potential
Distribution channel audience
Advantage over competitors
Resource investment involvement required
Event's characteristics
Event organisation's reputation
Entertainment and hospitality opportunities.

These criteria are expanded in figure 9.2.

■ **Figure 9.2**
Screening criteria used by businesses to determine sponsorship

1. Customer audience
Is the demographic, attitude and lifestyle profile of the target audience congruent with the product's target market?
What is the on-site audience?
Is sponsorship of this event the best way to communicate about the product/service to this target audience?

2. Exposure potential
What is the inherent news value of the event?
What extended print and broadcast coverage of the sponsorship is likely?
Will the extended coverage be local, regional or national? Is the geographical scope of this media audience consistent with the product's sales area?
Can the event be tied into other media advertising?
Can the company's products/services be sold at the event?
What is the life of the event?
Are banners and signage included in the sponsorship? How many and what size? Will they be visible during television broadcasts?
Will the product's name and logo be identified on promotional material for the activity?
Event posters — how many?
Press releases — how many?
Point-of-sale displays — how many?
Television advertisements — how many and on what station(s)?

Radio advertisements — how many and on what station(s)?

Print advertisements — how many and in what print media?

Internet advertisements (on the event Web site, banner advertisements) — how many and on what site(s)?

Where will the product name appear in the event program? Front or back cover? Number and site of program advertisements? How many programs?

Will the product's name be mentioned on the public address system? How many times?

Can the sponsor have display booths? Where will they be located? Will they be visible during television broadcasts?

3. Distribution channel audience

Are the sponsorship's advantages apparent to wholesalers, retailers or franchisers? Will they participate in promotions associated with the sponsorship?

4. Advantages over competitors

Is the event unique or otherwise distinctive?

Has the event previously had sponsors? If so, how successful has it been in delivering the desired benefits to them? Is it strongly associated with other sponsors? Will clutter be a problem?

Does the event need co-sponsors? Are other sponsors of the event compatible with the company's product? Does the company want to be associated with them? Will the product stand out and be recognised among them?

If there is co-sponsorship, will the product have category and advertising exclusivity?

Will competitors have access to signage, hospitality or event advertising? Will competition be allowed to sell product on site?

If the company does not sponsor it, will the competitor? Is that a concern?

5. Resource investment involvement required

How much is the total sponsorship cost, including such items as related promotional investment, staff time and administrative and implementation effort?

Will the sponsorship investment be unwieldy and difficult to manage?

What are the levels of barter, in-kind and cash investment?

Does the event guarantee a minimum level of benefits to the company?

6. Event's characteristics

What is the perceived stature of the event? Is it the best of its kind? Will involvement with it enhance the product's image?

Does it have a 'clean' image? Is there any chance that it will be controversial?

Does it have continuity or is it a one-off?

7. Event organisation's reputation

Does the organisation have a proven track record in staging this or other events?

Does it have the expertise to help the product achieve its sponsorship goals?

Does the organisation have a reputation and an image with which the company desires to be associated?

Does it have a history of honouring its obligations?

Has the company worked with this organisation before? Was it a positive experience?

Does it have undisputed control and authority over the activities it sanctions?

How close to its forecasts has the organisation been in delivering benefits to its sponsors?

How responsive is the organisation's staff to sponsors' requests? Are they readily accessible?

Is there insurance and what are the company's potential liabilities?

8. Entertainment and hospitality opportunities

Are there opportunities for direct sales of product and related merchandise, or for inducing product trial?

Will celebrities be available to serve as spokespeople for the product? Will they make personal appearances on its behalf at the event, in other markers, or in the media? At what cost?

Are tickets to the event included in the sponsorship? How many? Which sessions? Where are the seats located?

Will there be access to VIP hospitality areas for the company's guests? How many will be authorised? Will celebrities appear?

Will there be clinics, parties, or playing opportunities at which the company's guests will be able to interact with the celebrities?

(**Source:** *adapted from Crompton 1993*)

Not all the criteria noted by Crompton (1993) will be used in the assessment of each sponsorship proposal, or by every company, as a different range of outcomes or benefits will operate in each instance. Nonetheless, the example provided in figure 9.3 of AMP, an Australian financial services and insurance firm, clearly shows how complex the screening criteria used by large firms can be.

■ **Figure 9.3**
AMP
sponsorship
assessment
criteria

Overall fit with corporate objectives — e.g. development of new market segments

Brand — strategic fit with AMP positioning, prestige and unique value of property, representation of brand values

Target audience — appropriateness of audience, size/quality of audience, capacity to communicate with directly or indirectly

Exposure/visibility — media broadcast or coverage, on-site and total reach

Exclusivity — ownership of property, ability to differentiate from competitors, ambush potential

Cost — cost of sponsorship, marketing support investment required, staff requirements, opportunity costs, media costs/spend to receive similar outcomes

Ability to measure outcomes — e.g. media exposure, increased sales

Sufficient time exists to leverage involvement in event — time will vary with nature of event, cost of sponsorship

Meets company guidelines — e.g. blood sports are not to be sponsored

Geography — fits with AMP 'footprint', number of locations impacted and how

Business unit needs — appeal across business units, and built-in benefits as opposed to those that need to be created

Revenue generation — ease of developing marketing programs focused on generating incremental revenue, opportunity for on-site activities and cross-promotional activities

Sponsorship frequency — one-time event versus ongoing, opportunity to develop equity in event, fits with existing AMP event sponsorships

Employee impact — potential for positive impact on employees, ability to establish and unify corporate culture.

Hospitality options — access for VIPs, ability to host customers

(**Source:** *AMP 2000*)

WHEN SHOULD AN EVENT SEEK SPONSORSHIP?

Many event managers assume sponsorship is an appropriate source of income for their event and set about seeking to obtain it, later running into a range of difficulties, not the least of which is being unable to attract any sponsors. Geldard and Sinclair (1996) identify a number of questions that an event manager should ask before seeking to develop sponsorship as a revenue stream so that they can avoid wasting time and resources for little or no gain. These questions are:

• **Does the event have rights or benefits that can be offered to sponsors?** Organisations must see in an event opportunities to achieve specific promotional objectives such as image enhancement or development of stronger relationships with suppliers/buyers. If such benefits are not present, an event manager would be wasting his or her time in seeking income from this source. A better alternative in such instances may be to seek a donation, which by its nature does not require benefits to be given in return. In this regard it is not uncommon for corporations, particularly large corporations, to provide an allocation of funds specifically for this purpose. Commonly these funds are made available to events of a community or charitable nature

- **Are major event stakeholders likely to approve of commercial sponsorship?** It is not hard to conceive of situations in which, for example, the members of a particular association, or the potential audience for an event, would view commercial sponsorship negatively. For example, a conservation body may avoid seeking sponsorship for its annual conference because it might be seen as inappropriate by many within its membership. Under such circumstances, the broad support necessary for sponsorship to be successful would be absent.
- **Are there companies that are not suitable as sponsors?** Event managers need to identify organisations from which it would be inappropriate to seek sponsorship. For example, a charity event aimed at raising funds for a children's hospital is unlikely to be willing to accept sponsorship from breweries or tobacco companies.
- **Does the event have the resources necessary to sell and operate a sponsorship?** A considerable amount of time and effort is required to research, develop and sell sponsorships to those organisations identified as offering potential in this area. Additionally, sponsors must be serviced in that all promises made in the proposal need to be fulfilled. This will mean allocating staff and other resources to the sponsorship area.

*T*HE VALUE OF A SPONSORSHIP POLICY

Geldard and Sinclair (1996) strongly recommend that all managers of events seeking sponsorship develop a sponsorship policy to guide their actions, and those of their employees. They suggest that such a policy should:
- state the event's objectives for seeking sponsorship
- set the rules for entering into sponsorship, e.g. no sponsorships are to be accepted from organisations or individuals who are party to significant tendering processes associated with the event, and all sponsorships are to be in the form of written agreements
- ensure a uniform approach is taken to sponsorship, e.g. all proposals are to follow a particular format, and each sponsorship is required to have a business plan developed for it (see later discussion)
- state levels of accountability and responsibility, e.g. all sponsorships are to be signed off and overseen by a designated person.

IDENTIFYING APPROPRIATE SPONSORS

The key to identifying potential sponsors for an event is to identify organisations that want access to the same audience the event attracts (or a significant component of it), or who have a specific problem that the event may assist in solving. To identify such organisations an event manager needs to engage in some measure of research. At one level, this research can involve keeping abreast of business developments through such means as the financial press. This form of research allows the event manager to identify organisations that might, for example, be seeking to reposition themselves, expand into new markets or introduce new products or services. Once identified, and depending on the nature of the event, such organisations can become a sponsorship target. For example, an organiser of a garden festival may notice that a horticultural company has just launched a new range of fertilisers. This development may represent a sponsorship opportunity if the firm can be convinced that the event offers scope to increase awareness and sales of its new product line.

Event managers can also seek to develop insights into potential sponsors by reading, for example, their annual reports or viewing their Web sites. These sources may indicate broad strategies the organisation is pursuing, indicate what sponsorships they have in place and whether they have any specific requirements for sponsorships (see figure 9.4 on page 234). This information will provide insights into whether an opportunity exists to pursue a sponsorship arrangement with the organisation concerned.

Still another means of identifying potential sponsors is simply to determine who has sponsored similar events in the past. This can be done by examining programs/promotional material/Web sites of these events, or contacting the event organiser(s) responsible for their conduct.

Once organisations that potentially might act as sponsors are identified, a more detailed examination of each may be warranted. Additional information that might be sought includes the types of events the organisation is willing to sponsor, whether the organisation is tied to particular causes (for example, charities), and when in their planning cycle they allocate their sponsorship budget (a sponsorship proposal would need to arrive some months before this time). Information, such as this last item, is likely to require direct enquiry.

Once a final list of potential sponsors has been arrived at, the next challenge for the event manager is to determine the person within the organisation to whom completed sponsorship proposals should be directed. This question may already have been answered if, in the process of researching the organisation, the person/area responsible for sponsorship was identified and/or spoken to. In smallish companies this person is likely to be the CEO or managing director. In firms of moderate size, the marketing or PR manager may make such decisions while in large corporations a section that is dedicated to sponsorship might exist within the marketing, public relations or corporate affairs areas. Once sent, it is sound practice to follow up proposals within a reasonable period (say, three to four weeks) to determine their status (e.g. yet to be considered, under review, rejected). Avoid, however, ringing so often that you become a 'pest'.

*T*HE SPONSORSHIP PROPOSAL

A formal proposal document is commonly the means through which sponsorship is sought. This document, according to Geldard and Sinclair (1996), must answer three basic questions.
- What is the organisation being asked to sponsor?
- What will the organisation receive for its sponsorship?
- What is it going to cost?

The length and level of detail of a proposal that sets out to answer these questions will depend on the amount being sought. However, a comprehensive treatment of these areas would mean the following would appear in the proposal:
- overview of the event including (as applicable) its mission/goals; history; location; current and past sponsors; program/duration; staff; past or anticipated level of media coverage; past or predicted attendance levels; and actual or predicted attendee profile (e.g. age, income, sex, occupation)
- sponsorship package on offer and its associated cost. Here a number of options face the event organiser. They may, for example, create a number of identical 'packages' (as is the case with the Olympics), develop a hierarchical structure cascading down through a principal naming rights sponsor, major sponsor, minor sponsor and official supplier, or opt to go for a sole sponsor. In pricing the offering it should be remembered that an organisation has available to it alternative promotional tools (such as advertising) that can achieve similar outcomes.
- duration of agreement
- strategic fit between the proposal and the needs of the organisation. Discussion here will be based on research conducted using the sources noted earlier.
- contact details.

Many large corporations, in order to assist sponsorship seekers, have developed proposal guidelines or criteria. In figure 9.4 on the following page an example of such guidelines has been provided. You will also note from this example that this company, Country Energy, requires a lead time of at least 60 days. This is because time is required to leverage involvement in the event through such means as advertising and merchandising.

SPONSORSHIP CRITERIA

To help Country Energy evaluate your sponsorship request, your proposal should include/cover relevant points from the list below.

Event details
■ Concise description of the event or activity
■ Objectives of event
■ The geographic location, as well as local, State or national extensions
■ A brief background of the applicant, listing experience, mission statement and long-term goals for the organisation or event
■ Staffing of the event/organisation
■ Date and times of the event or activity
■ Other critical deadlines
■ How you will judge the success of your event.

Financial details
■ How much money is requested?
■ How will it be spent?
■ Are there other sponsors involved? If so, who?
■ Will you be seeking other sponsors?

Target audience
■ How many people will be present at the event? (e.g. attendance)
■ How many people will be participating in the event? (e.g. number of volunteers, committee, etc.)
■ Who are the target audiences for your event? (e.g. age, gender, employment status, etc.)

Publicity
■ How will the event be promoted? (e.g. TV, radio, print)
■ What, if any, media coverage do you expect? Is this an aim?
■ What are the benefits for Country Energy in sponsoring this event? Can you offer exclusivity or signage opportunities to Country Energy?

History of the event or activity
■ Has the event been conducted in the past?
■ If yes, how did you evaluate it and what were the results?
■ Please attach examples/copies of promotional items, publicity, advertising from previous events.

The future
■ Do you intend repeating this event?
■ Is there potential for Country Energy to continue to be involved in the future?

Assessment of applications
■ Applicants will be advised in writing of the outcome of their proposal.
■ It should be noted that Country Energy receives many applications for sponsorship and is unable to fund all those requests. Sponsorships will be selected on the basis of criteria offering strong community links and participation.

Submission of applications
■ All applications for sponsorship are to be submitted in writing.
■ Applications for sponsorship must provide a lead time of at least 60 days.

(**Source:** *Country Energy 2001*)

From the previous discussion it is possible to gain some insights into what makes a successful proposal; however, it is worth addressing this matter specifically to try to ensure time and effort are not wasted on preparing documents of this nature that simply end up in the waste paper basket. According to Ukman (1995), there are six attributes of a successful proposal:

1. **Sell benefits, not features**. Many proposals describe the features of the event, such as the artistic merit of the festival, rather the benefits to sponsors. Sponsors buy promotional platforms so that they can reach their market(s) in an effort to sell products/services.
2. **Address the sponsor's needs, not sponsored's**. Many proposals emphasise the event's need for money, rather than the sponsor's needs such as market access.
3. **Tailor proposals to the business category**. Benefits will not have equal meaning to each potential sponsor. For example, an insurance company might be interested in an event's mailing list, while a soft drink bottler is likely to be concerned with on-site sales opportunities.
4. **Include promotional extensions**. There are two types of sponsorship benefits. First, automatic ones, such as identification in collateral materials and on-site signage, come with the deal and do not require the sponsor to do anything. The second comes from a sponsor's leverage of the event through trade, retail and sales extensions. These include competitions, redemption offers (e.g. free ticket offers for the customers of a sponsor's wholesalers) and the handing on of benefits (such as hospitality) to retailers for them to use as 'giveaways' in their promotions. It is not enough to give sponsors a check list of direct benefits; proposals also should include an 'exploitation menu' showing them how to leverage their investment.
5. **Minimise risk**. Risk can be reduced through such means as making guaranteed media coverage part of the package and listing reputable co-sponsors.
6. **Include added value**. The proposal should be presented in terms of its total impact on achieving greater sales rather than focusing on one aspect such as media. The combination of one plus one should equal more than two in terms of overall benefit.

*P*RESENTATION, NEGOTIATION AND CONTRACTS

An organisation that has received a sponsorship proposal will act in several possible ways. After scanning the proposal it will
- dispose of it
- request further information
- seek to negotiate in an attempt to have the sponsorship offering better meet its needs
- accept the offering as is.

Given that many of the organisations that are targeted by events as potential sponsors receive large numbers of proposals each week, an effort should be made to ensure, first, that the proposal provides sufficient information on which a decision can be made. In addition, if an organisation produces guidelines for sponsorship seekers to follow, it must be evident from the contents page and/or a quick scan that these matters have been addressed. Some attempt to make a proposal stand out can also be useful. For example, a food and wine festival might print a brief version of the proposal on a good bottle of wine, as well as submitting the fuller version.

Time is increasingly crucial in business. If a proposal is too long, does not contain adequate information, or leaves out key elements (such as to whom to respond), the chances of the proposal being discarded are high. As a general rule the length of a sponsorship proposal should be commensurate with the amount sought, and must be as succinct as possible. If the amount asked for is substantial and the proposal is to be over, say, five pages, consideration should be given to providing an executive summary that overviews its key elements, and a contents page.

On occasions the proposed sponsorship package may be of interest to an organisation but the organisation may wish to 'customise' it further. If this is the case negotiation will need to be entered into. Under such circumstances the sponsorship seeker should have a clear understanding of the minimum payment it is prepared to accept, determine the extent to which it can move in negotiations in an effort to create a 'win–win' situation (particularly if multiple sponsors are being sought) and avoid the temptation to promise too much.

Once agreement has been reached between the sponsoring organisation and the event organiser, a contract will need to be entered into (see chapter 11). Although a contract can take the form of a verbal agreement, it is sound business practice to commit such agreements to paper to avoid misunderstandings regarding the benefits being offered, their costs, payment terms, and the responsibilities of each party to the agreement.

CONSTRUCTING A SPONSORSHIP BUSINESS PLAN

Once a sponsorship has been secured, it must be effectively managed in order to ensure the benefits that were promised are delivered. To this end, it is useful to prepare a sponsorship business plan, as is suggested by Geldard and Sinclair (1996). At its most basic this document should identify what the sponsorship is to achieve for the sponsor, the benefits that have been promised, costs associated with providing specified benefits, review and evaluation approaches to be used and a time line detailing the activities that need to be conducted to deliver on the sponsorship and when they are to take place. These planning elements are discussed below.

Objectives associated with any given sponsorship will obviously differ, but they should be specific, tangible, realistic and measurable. For example, the sponsor's key objective in the TAC Wangaratta Jazz Festival was to create awareness of the 'If you drink, then drive, you're a bloody idiot' message.

Additionally there were subsidiary objectives relating to the establishment of community relationships. In order to achieve these objectives, the event organiser, in combination with the sponsor, established specific objectives on which their performance was to be assessed. These related, among other things, to minimum numbers of promotional spots on television and radio featuring recognition of the TAC.

The groups that are impacted by the sponsorship also need to be noted as they are the focus of actions undertaken to achieve sponsorship objectives. These groups may include attendees, members of the broader community in which the event is taking place, staff of the sponsoring organisation and general or specific media.

All benefits and associated actions need to be clearly identified, along with the group(s) they are specific to and any costs (financial or otherwise) that are associated with them. These costs might include signage manufacture and erection, supporting advertisements, promotional material, prize money, sponsor hospitality costs, professional fees, labour costs associated with hosting sponsors on-site, tickets, postage and preparation of an evaluation report. It is sound practice to prepare a budget that encompasses these costs and places them in the context of the value of the sponsorship received. Figure 9.5 provides a check list of items to be included in a sponsorship budget (see chapter 10 for more information on preparing budgets). It should also be remembered that sponsorship (both in-kind and cash) attracts GST, and as such this must be factored into any bottom line calculations.

■ **Figure 9.5**
A check list of items to be included in a sponsorship budget

ITEMS THAT WILL INCUR CASH OUTLAYS OR PERSON HOURS TO SUPPORT THE SPONSORSHIP	COST ($)
❑ Event programs	
❑ Additional printing	
❑ Signage production	
❑ Signage erection	
❑ Support advertising	
❑ Hospitality — food and beverage	
❑ Telephone, Internet and fax	
❑ Public relations support	
❑ Tickets for sponsors	
❑ VIP parking passes	
❑ Cost of selling sponsorship (staff time at $ _____ per hour)	
❑ Cost of servicing sponsorship (staff time at $ _____ per hour)	
❑ Legal costs	
❑ Travel costs	
❑ Taxis and other transport	
❑ Evaluation research/report	
❑ Media monitoring	
Total costs	
Profit margin	
Minimum sponsorship sale price	

A list of the actions necessary to fulfil the sponsorship should be made, specifying what is to be done and when. Additionally the individual or committee responsible for each deliverable needs to be identified.

An evaluation and review process needs to be built into the sponsorship plan. The review process should be ongoing and act to identify and address problems that might affect the achievement of sponsorship outcomes. Evaluation is concerned with providing a clear understanding of how the sponsorship performed regarding the objectives that were set for it. Evaluation seeks to answer questions such as: did the promised media coverage eventuate, did the attendee profile match that given in the proposal document and what was the overall quality of implementation of the sponsorship like? Evaluation also allows fine tuning of the sponsorship to occur if it is to continue into the future.

In general terms the development of the sponsorship business plan should be viewed as a creative and rewarding task that also serves to communicate to the sponsor that their investment is being managed in a professional manner.

MAKING SPONSORSHIP WORK

To ensure that the event does satisfy the sponsor's marketing needs listed in the sponsorship agreement, it is essential that the event organisation services (i.e. looks after) the sponsor. This can include everything from maintaining harmonious relationships between the sponsor's staff and the staff of the event organisation, to ensuring sponsor's signage is kept in pristine condition. Following is a list of suggestions and actions, adapted from Geldard and Sinclair (1996), that will greatly assist in ensuring positive and enduring relations are developed with sponsors.

- **One contact:** One person from the event organisation needs to be appointed as the contact point for the sponsor. That person must be readily available (a mobile phone helps), have the authority to make decisions regarding the event, and be able to forge harmonious relationships with the sponsor's staff.
- **Understand the sponsor:** A method of maintaining harmonious relationships is to get to know the sponsor's organisation, its staff, its products and its marketing strategies. By doing this, it becomes easier to understand the needs of the sponsor and how those needs can be satisfied.
- **Motivate an event organisation's staff about the sponsorship:** Keeping staff informed of the sponsorship contract, the objectives of the sponsorship and how the sponsor's needs are to be satisfied will help ensure that the sponsorship will work smoothly and to the benefit of both parties.
- **Use of celebrities associated with the event:** If the event includes the use of artistic, sporting, or theatrical celebrities, ensure that sponsors have an opportunity to meet them in a social setting. Most people enjoy immensely the opportunity to tell anecdotes about their brush with the famous!

- **Acknowledge the sponsor at every opportunity:** Use all available media to acknowledge the sponsor's assistance. Media that can be used include the public address system, newsletters, media releases, the annual report and staff briefings.
- **Sponsorship launch:** Have a sponsorship launch to tell the target market that brand X is to sponsor the event. The style of the launch depends on the type of sponsorship and the creativity of the event director.
- **Media monitoring:** Monitor the media for all stories about the event that include mention of the sponsor (a media monitoring firm may be contracted to perform this task). This shows the sponsor that the event takes an interest in the sponsorship and is alert to the benefits the sponsor is receiving.
- **Principal sponsor:** If the event is such that it has many sponsors, ensure that the logo of the principal sponsor (i.e. the sponsor who has paid the most) is seen on everything that the event does. This includes stationery, uniforms, flags, newsletters, stages, and so on.
- **Naming rights:** If the event has given naming rights to a sponsor, it has an obligation to ensure that these rights are used in all communications emanating from the event organisation. This includes making every endeavour to ensure that the media are aware of, and adhere to, the name of the event. Sometimes this is difficult, but must be attempted.
- **Professionalism:** Even though volunteers manage many events, this does not mean that staff can act like amateurs. Sponsors expect to be treated efficiently and effectively, with their reasonable demands met in a speedy manner. Sponsorship is a partnership. Loyalty to that partnership will be repaid.
- **Undersell and over-deliver:** Do not promise what cannot be delivered. Be cautious in the proposal and then ensure that the expectations raised by the cautious proposal are met and, ideally, exceeded.

SUMMARY

Sponsorship has increasingly become a mainstream component of the promotional mix of many corporations and public sector organisations. The reasons for this can be found in a variety of changes that have occurred in the business environment, as well as in the range of benefits that sponsorship offers.

From an event's perspective, sponsorship often (but not always) represents a significant potential revenue stream. To develop this income source this chapter has shown that a variety of practices and procedures need to be adopted. These include the development of a sponsorship policy, the use of formal proposals based on research and an understanding of the full range of benefits organisations seek through sponsorship use, and the employment of business plans to ensure commitments to sponsors are met. Additionally, this chapter has provided insights into how to identify, approach and work with sponsors in order to develop long-lasting relationships.

Questions

1. Drawing on the definitions provided in this chapter, develop your own definition of sponsorship.

2. Identify forces or changed environmental conditions, other than those mentioned in this chapter, that might explain the expanded use of sponsorship as a promotional medium.

3. Identify a public sector organisation that is sponsoring one or more events and contact the person responsible for sponsorship in this organisation. Ask them what they are trying to achieve through the sponsorship and how they intend to assess the outcomes.

4. Name an event for which sponsorship may be inappropriate and list the reasons for this.

5. Obtain several non-current sponsorship proposals from event organisers/corporate sponsorship managers. Review the content and presentation of these documents in the light of suggestions made in this chapter.

6. Identify an actual event and indicate how you would go about identifying potential sponsors for this event.

7. Investigate a specific recurring event with a view to identifying the potential benefits it might be able to offer sponsors. Are all of these benefits currently being offered to sponsors? If not, what reasons are there for not doing so?

8. Select three events and contact their organisers with a view to determining if they have developed sponsorship policies or sponsorship business plans. Establish why they have, or have not, acted in this way. If they have developed one, or both of these documents ask about their broad content.

9. Contact the event organiser of a community festival in your area. Ask if you can be of assistance in preparing sponsorship proposals for next year's event. As human resources are often scarce in the context of such events, the answer is likely to be 'yes'. Use the guidelines for proposal preparation discussed in this chapter to guide your efforts.

EDS and the
Arundel Festival

Pairing scheme award winner

Electronic Data Systems Ltd (EDS) has been a leader in the global information services industry for over 35 years, delivering systems expertise, management consultancy, and electronic business solutions to more than 9000 businesses, and government clients in about 50 countries. In the UK, EDS employs more than 13 000 people at over 140 locations. Its UK clients include Vauxhall, BP, the DSS and the Inland Revenue.

EDS' Inland Revenue division in Worthing, West Sussex, represents a highly successful public/private sector partnership, which employs 400 people. Here, EDS provides IT services for Inland Revenue specialist offices throughout the UK. At Worthing the company also develops and supports IT systems for other EDS customers.

EDS is not new to sponsorship (the company sponsored the last two Flora London Marathons, the World Cup '98 competition, and also sponsors Premier Division Derby County Football Club), or indeed arts sponsorship, having partnered the Academy of St Martin in the Fields and Shropshire's Weston Park Foundation in recent years. EDS is also a Founder of Lowry, the National Landmark Millennium project for the arts in Salford — the second largest Millennium project in the UK. However, EDS Worthing sponsored the arts for the first time in 1999. Following three years of negotiations, the company signed a substantial three-year contract with Arundel Festival.

EDS Worthing sponsored a concert by the English Classical Players, which took place in the open air theatre at Arundel Castle on 29 August, and a recital by Wayne Marshall in the Castle's Baron's Hall on 4 September. As a result of winning an award of £20 000 under the Government's Pairing Scheme (managed by Arts & Business), which aims to encourage business to sponsor arts events through cash incentives and Government endorsement, EDS also sponsored the Festival's Street Theatre day. The company entertained 400 Worthing employees and their families at this totally free public event, which would not have taken place without EDS' involvement, and the Pairing Scheme award.

Frank Mullin, Group Communications Manager with EDS explained how the partnership with Arundel Festival developed over several years. In 1996, with a brief to develop community based activities for the company, Mr Mullin encouraged EDS Worthing to establish a number of projects locally, including a mentoring project with Worthing High School. These projects were very successful and worthwhile, and EDS retains its commitment to local education projects. Based on this success, EDS made a strategic decision to expand its activities in the community by seeking an appropriate partner.

Through membership of Sussex Enterprise, EDS met Judith Buckland, the dynamic Chair of Arundel Festival, and discussions began as to how the Festival could best help EDS to raise their profile. Mr Mullin comments that although 'branding' was central to the discussions, EDS was also 'keen to add in the "people" factor'. As a major local employer, the company wanted to raise awareness of its name particularly for recruitment purposes, and to involve their existing staff in any chosen project.

At this stage, locally based senior managers were brought in to the discussions with Judith Buckland and Jan Billington, the Festival's Development Manager. The relationship developed over three years, and ideas were exchanged and benefits negotiated until the three year contract described earlier was agreed as the best way to meet the needs of both parties.

Sharman Walker, Public Relations Manager with EDS is clear that this sponsorship represents part of a wider sponsorship strategy for the company, and its national and international sponsorships of sports and other arts events confirms this. The breadth and range of sponsorship activity reinforces EDS' position as a global, national, but also a very community-orientated company.

Ms Walker highlights the fact that EDS chose the events within the Arundel Festival on the basis of 'the need to address various objectives'. These included profile raising for recruitment purposes, employee involvement, community support, and profile raising amongst the wider business community. Clearly the high profile events selected provided both branding and hospitality opportunities, as well as the chance for EDS to state publicly their commitment to the local community.

Both Frank Mullin and Sharman Walker are delighted with EDS Worthing's first venture into arts sponsorship. Ms Walker said 'the attention to detail demonstrated by Arundel was exceptional. The Festival were concerned about the needs of EDS all through the program'. This partnership has been a model of good practice and professionalism, which certainly seems to have paid off from the perspective of the company's employees, who are delighted with their level of involvement in the project. Obviously, the impact of the sponsorship in terms of profile raising within the wider community will take longer to assess. More research will be carried out, but anecdotal evidence to date suggests that this objective was also met very effectively. For example, the company feels that it has already substantially raised its profile with several local authorities through the project. Councillor Tim Dice, Leader of Worthing Borough Council, said 'these local activities demonstrate a long-term commitment to the area. We are already looking into a number of other joint initiatives that will benefit both the local community and EDS.'

The future for this partnership looks very promising. EDS is keen to consolidate and improve upon the success of year one, and is looking at opportunities within next year's Festival which may offer a slightly different emphasis, whilst enabling the company to retain its commitment to the local community.

Sharman Walker feels that EDS has taken risks with this project. However, when sufficient research is carried out and both arts organisation and sponsor work together to meet each other's needs, then the risks are calculated ones, and the likelihood of failure minimised. Sharman Walker reflects this when she says that 'partnership is the key. As an IT provider, or as a sponsor, we believe it is essential that we work closely with our partners'.

Jane Chambers, Arts Services Manager with Arts & Business South East said 'that this partnership has proved so successful to date is due to the commitment and high degree of professionalism of both parties. It represents a model of good sponsorship practice which Arts & Business is always happy to promote.'

Source: Arts & Business Week, (http://www.aaandb.org.uk accessed 3 September 2001)

Questions

1 What objectives were EDS seeking to meet through their sponsorship of the Arundel Festival?

2 What does Sharman Walker mean when she states that 'partnership is the key'?

3 Why do you believe EDS sought a long term (three year) contractual relationship with the Arundel Festival?

4 Why did EDS choose to sponsor the three events that it did from the range of events taking place under the umbrella of the Arundel Festival?

5 Would the 'Pairing Scheme' mentioned in this case have application in an Australian context? If so, what benefits would it offer business and the organisers of arts festivals?

REFERENCES

AMP 2000, *Sponsorship Assessment Guidelines* (internal document).

Crompton, J. 1993, 'Understanding a business organisation's approach to entering a sponsorship partnership', *Festival Management and Event Tourism*, vol. 1, pp. 98–109.

Crompton, J. 1994, 'Benefits and risks associated with sponsorship of major events', *Festival Management and Event Tourism*, vol. 2, pp. 65–74.

Geldard, E. & Sinclair, L. 1996, *The Sponsorship Manual*, The Sponsorship Unit, Victoria, Australia.

Getz, D. 1997, *Event Management and Event Tourism*, Cognizant Communication Corporation, New York.

IPSOS RSL 2000, *UK Sponsorship Statistics*, available from: http://www.sponsorshiponline.co.uk (accessed 31 January 2001).

Smart Marketing Street Wise Workshops 2001, available from http://www.smsw.com/contacti.htm (accessed 25 April 2001).

Sponsorship Business Review, Edition 1, September 1999, pp. 32–34.

Sunshine, K., Backman, K. & Backman, S. 1995, 'An examination of sponsorship proposals in relation to corporate objectives', *Festival Management and Event Tourism*, vol. 2, pp. 159–166.

Ukman, L. 1995, *Successful Proposal*, available from: www.sponsorship.com/forum/success.html (accessed 25 April 2001).

LEARNING OBJECTIVES

After studying this chapter, you should be able to:

- understand the use of control by management
- identify the control systems used in special events and festivals
- analyse the factors that create successful control mechanisms
- identify the key elements of budgetary control and explain the relationship between them
- understand the advantages and shortcomings of using a budget.

INTRODUCTION

After planning the festival or event, the central function of management is controlling. This chapter introduces the various methods that the festival or event management can use to recognise that the event is going to plan and respond to any changes. The event budget is perhaps the most important control plan. The chapter then outlines tips on increasing revenue and decreasing expenditure.

WHAT IS CONTROL?

Control consists of making sure that what happens in an organisation is what was supposed to happen. The control of an event can range from the event manager simply walking the site and discussing daily progress with staff to implementing and monitoring a detailed plan of responsibilities, reports and budgets. The word 'control' comes from the Latin *contrarotulare*, meaning 'against the roll': in ancient Rome, it meant comparing something to the official records, which were kept on paper cylinders or rolls. In modern times, the word has retained some of this meaning, and the control of any business activity involves comparing the progress of all key functions against a management plan to ensure that projected outcomes are met.

Event planning can be effective only if the execution of the plan is carefully controlled. To do this, it is necessary to develop proper control mechanisms. These are methods which are designed to keep a project on course and return it to plan if it wanders. Control affects every aspect of the management of events, including:
- logistics
- human resources
- administration

and its basic nature remains the same in every area.

The nature of control is described by Beniger (1986), who identified two complementary activities:
- **Information processing:** This is necessary for all planning. When it is goal-directed, it allows the continual comparison of an organisation's stated goals against reality.
- **Reciprocal communication, or feedback:** There must be a constant interchange between the controller and the areas being controlled.

These two activities depend on an effective communication system.

This chapter explores control in the context of festivals and special events. It will demonstrate that the choice of workable control mechanisms is central to the success of an event, and discuss budgets, which are the main control system used in event management.

ELEMENTS AND CATEGORIES OF CONTROL

The process of control involves establishing standards of performance and ensuring that they are realised. This can be a complex process, but consists of three main steps:

- **Establishing standards of performance:** These can come from several sources, including standard practices within the event management industry; guidelines supplied by the board of management of the event; specific requirements of the client and sponsors; and audience or guest expectations. Standards must be measurable.
- **Identifying deviations from standards of performance:** This is done by measuring current performance and comparing it with the established standards. Since the event budget is expressed in measurable terms, it provides an important method of highlighting areas that are straying from the plan and which require attention.
- **Correcting deviations:** Any performance that does not meet the established standards must be corrected. This can entail the use of many types of problem-solving strategies, including renegotiating contracts and delegating.

These three steps are also called the control cycle (Burke 1993) and are central to the successful delivery of an event. Such a cycle would be applied with varying frequency, depending on the size and complexity of the event itself.

Generally, events are characterised by two types of controls: operational and organisational. Operational controls are used for the day-to-day running of the event. Organisational controls relate to the overall objectives of the event organisation, for example whether the event is profitable and satisfies the client's brief. Hicks (1976) suggests a further category of controls according to when they are applied:

- **Predictive control** tries to anticipate and identify problems before they occur. Predicting cash flows for an event is an important area because expenses are not concurrent with income. For example, venue hire is usually paid in advance of the event. Similarly, for an event with a small budget, briefing a lawyer is another example of predictive control. Some companies, for instance, may be less likely to pay promised fees to a small company than they would to a larger, more powerful company. Also, the organisers of a small one-off event are not in a position to threaten a defaulting company with withdrawal of further work opportunities. In these, and similar situations, a swift letter from a solicitor who has been briefed beforehand can often hasten payment. Another term for predictive controls is feedforward.
- **Concurrent control** measures deviation from the standards as they occur. The event manager's informal question of 'How's it going?' falls into this category. The monitoring of food stalls during an event for instance is essential to ensure that health and safety regulations are being followed.

It may be difficult to predict just how a food provider will deviate from the guidelines. (At one festival, for example, tea and coffee urns were placed against a canvas dividing wall. On the other side, a children's play group was in operation.)

- **Historic controls** are mostly organisational controls and can include analysis of major deviations from an event plan so that the next event runs more closely to plan. Such controls review the concluded event and are concerned with the question: 'How were objectives met?'

In order to compare actual and planned progress in managing an event, points of comparison are necessary. These include the following:

- **Benchmarks** are identifiable points in the organisation of the event where a high standard is achieved. Benchmarks emphasise quality and best practice. For example, catering of a high standard could be a benchmark for a corporate party. Attaining a benchmark is often a cause for celebration by the event company.
- **Milestones**, or key dates, are intermediate achievement dates that stand as guideposts for monitoring an event's progress. They mark particularly critical completion times. For example, the arrival of the headline performers at the venue is a critical time, and the submission date of a grant proposal is a key date.

■ **Figure 10.1**
The control process

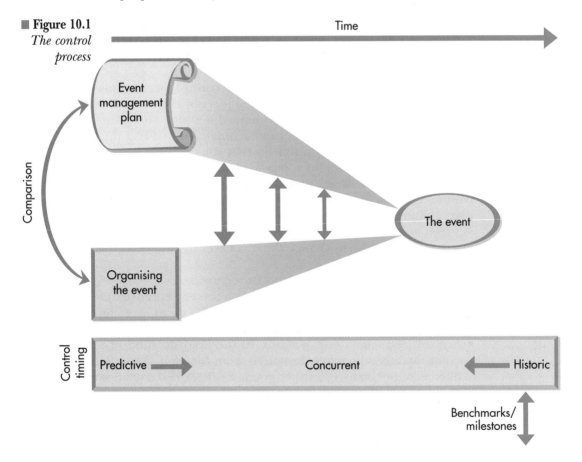

Event control can be expensive in time and money. Its cost and effectiveness depend on the choice of the control mechanisms that make up the control system. Control mechanisms must be:

- **meaningful and efficient:** They should be directed only at those areas that contribute to the success of the event. These significant areas have to be identified in advance, and addressed in the event plan. A limited amount of time is available for measuring and comparing — this process must be streamlined so it does not become an end in itself.
- **simple:** Controls should not be any more complicated than is necessary. Their aim is practical and they have to be able to be communicated to many levels within an event. An excessively complicated system of controls can alienate a broadly based festival committee.
- **relevant:** Controls must be prepared to match each area of event management, and they should be distributed to those who have the responsibility of carrying them out. For example, there is no point in the publicity section having data that concern the budget of the performers.
- **timely and flexible:** Deviations from the plan should be identified early and addressed before they develop further. Concurrent controls should allow sufficient time to correct any gaps with the plan. Flexibility is essential, as the controls may need to respond to revision of the event plan up until the last moment. Sometimes, milestones must be moved to accommodate changes in the event. For example, a benchmark may be an attendance of 1000 people, but if only 800 chairs were delivered, it is no longer a best practice benchmark and must be dropped lest it create a logistical problem.
- **able to suggest action:** The most useful control mechanisms provide corrective actions to be taken when members of the event team find a gap between the plan and reality. Without these suggestions for action, inexperienced staff or volunteers can become confused and the festival manager can be swamped by problems that could readily have been solved by others if guidance had been provided.

When deviations or gaps are identified, the event manager can make a reasoned choice — either to close the gap, or leave it alone and revise the plan. Historic organisational controls, for example, may show a gap between the festival objectives and what actually happened. The festival manager can choose to change the objectives themselves or change aspects of the event instead.

Examples of gaps that can be measured are:

- *Ticket sales targets versus actual sales.* For the entrepreneur the amount of sales of tickets is the 'make or break' of the event. Any deviations from the schedule may cause a cash flow problem.
- *Supplier compliance versus contracts.* In the fluid situation of setting up an event there can be many deviations from the plan. In particular the supplier may not send the exact goods as described in the contract. This needs to be anticipated and pre-empted.
- *The 'buzz' or event awareness versus the marketing/promotion plan.* If the promotion of the event is not creating at least an interest, the plan may have to change.

- *Actual logistics versus the operation plan.* A small deviation from the plan can create major problems throughout the event. For example, if the delivery trucks to an exhibition arrive at the wrong docks the delay and confusion can be magnified in a short time.
- *Entertainment versus crowd response.* If the crowd are not responding as expected then it may be time for quick managerial action.

CONTROL METHODS

Some of the control methods used in events are very straightforward, while others are complex and require a high level of financial reporting skills. However, they all have the same aim: to highlight areas that have strayed from the plan so that management can take appropriate action.

■ Reports *and meetings*

Reports that evaluate the progress of an event are perhaps the most common control method. The reports are presented at management or committee meetings. The frequency of these meetings will depend on the proximity of the event date. Many event management companies hold weekly meetings with reports from the teams (or subcommittees) and individuals responsible for particular areas. The meetings are run using standard meeting rules, such as those described in Renton (1994), with a time for subcommittee reports. The aim of these reports is to assist the meeting in making decisions.

Typically, an annual community festival would have monthly meetings throughout the year leading up to the event, and increase these to weekly meetings two months before the festival is scheduled to begin. For example, the Broome Shinju Matsuri Festival of the Pearl has weekly meetings that alternate between the festival committee and those of the general community (which discuss major decisions by the festival committee). In this way, the public has some control over the planning of the festival. At the committee meetings, the subcommittees dealing with publicity, sponsorship, entertainment, youth and community relations report their actions. The reports expose any gaps so that the event coordinator can take action to close them. This is also called management by exception, because it assumes everything is flowing well, that routine matters are handled by the subcommittee and that the event coordinator need step in only when significant deviations from the plan demand it.

■ Delegation *and self-control*

The use of subcommittees at a festival is an example of delegating activities to specialist groups. Part of the responsibility of each subcommittee is to solve problems before they report. Since it is impossible for the event manager to monitor all the areas of an event, this method is valuable because it allows delegated groups to control their own areas of specialisation. However, the subcommittee must confine its actions to its own event area and the event manager must be aware of possible problems arising across different subcommittees. For example, solving a problem in the entertainment part of an event could give rise to problems in the sponsorship areas.

■ Quality

There are various systems to control the quality of an event and the event company itself. In particular, quality control is dependent on
• gaining and responding to customer feedback
• the role played by event personnel in delivering quality service.

Integrating the practical aspects of controlling quality with the overall strategy of an event is called total quality management (TQM). Total quality management seeks to create an event company that continually improves the quality of its services. In other words,
• feedback
• change and improvement
are integral to the company's structure and operations.

Various techniques of TQM are used by event companies. One technique is finding and rewarding quality champions — volunteer programs often have awards for quality service at an event. Different professional organisations, such as the International Special Events Society (ISES) and the International Festivals and Events Association (IFEA), share the same aim: to strive to improve the quality of festivals and events. They do this by disseminating information and administering a system of event evaluation and awards for quality.

■ The break-even *chart*

This simple graphic tool can highlight control problems by finding the intersection of costs and revenue. Figure 10.2 on the opposite page shows a simple but effective break-even chart for an event that is dependent on ticket sales. For example, a Neil Cameron Fire Event (Cameron 1993) would have fixed costs of stage, pyrotechnics and administration. But the greater the attendance, the larger the cost of security, seating, cleaning, toilets and so forth. However, at one point the revenue from ticket sales exceeds the costs. At this point, the break-even point, the event starts making a profit.

If a fixed cost such as venue hire is increased, the extra number of people needed 'through the door' can quickly be calculated. How would the organisers attract those extra people to the event? One means might be increased promotion.

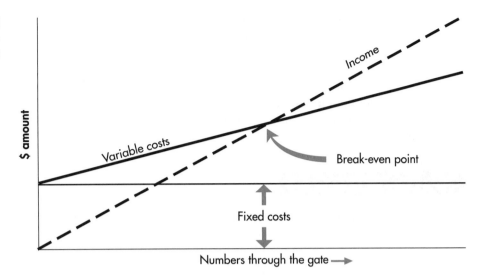

■ **Figure 10.2**
The break-even chart

■ **Ratio** *analysis*

There are several ratios that can be used to identify any problems in the management of an event. They can also be used for predictive control as in the earlier example. Their main function is as indicators of the health of the event organisation. In particular the ratio of

$$\frac{\text{Current assets}}{\text{Current liabilities}}$$

indicates the financial strength of the organisation. However, calculation of assets can be difficult, since special events by their nature have few current assets except those intangible qualities: goodwill and experience. In a similar way to a film production company, an event company may be formed to create and manage a one-off festival where every asset is hired for the duration of the event.

Return on investment is a significant ratio for any sponsors or investors in an event. This is expressed as:

$$\frac{\text{Net revenue}}{\text{Investment}}.$$

The revenue for a sponsor may be expressed in advertising dollars. For example print press exposure can be measured by column centimetres and approximated to the equivalent cost in advertising. This ratio is most often used for events that are staged solely for financial gain. An entrepreneur of a major concert performance must demonstrate a favourable return on investment to potential investors to secure financial backing.

Other ratios can provide valuable data. As Brody and Goodman (1988) explain in their discussion of fundraising events, the ratio between net and gross profit is important in deciding the efficiency of an event for fundraising and provides a means to compare one event to another. This ratio is called the percentage of profit or the profit margin. Another useful ratio is that of free publicity to paid advertising, particularly for concert promoters.

By performing a series of appropriate ratio analyses, an event management company can obtain a clear picture of the viability of the organisation and identify areas requiring more stringent control.

THE BUDGET

A budget can be described as a quantified statement of plans (in other words, the plan is expressed in numerical terms). The budget process includes costing and estimating income and the allocation of financial resources. The budget of an event is used to compare actual costs and revenues with projected costs and revenues. In particular, maximum expenditure for each area of the event's operation is estimated. To achieve this efficiently, a budget can take many forms. For instance, it may be broken into sub-budgets that apply to specific areas of a complex or large event such as the staging, logistics, merchandising and human resources. Budgets are of particular importance to the management of events because most aspects of the event incur costs requiring payment before the revenue is obtained. Cash flow needs special attention. Most funding or sponsorship bodies need to see a budget of the proposed event before they will commit their resources. This second part of the chapter expands on these points and provides an example to illustrate them.

CONSTRUCTING THE BUDGET

Two types of budget process can be used in event management. The line-item budget, as the name suggests, focuses on each cost and revenue item of the total event, and the program budget that is constructed for a specific program element (Getz 1997). An example of the latter is a budget devised for a festival that concerns only the activities of one of the performance areas or stages. Such a budget effectively isolates this area of the event from the general festival finance. In this way individual budgets can be used to compare all the performance areas or stages. The line-item budget is illustrated in figure 10.3. The line-items are venue costs, artist fees and so on.

The creation of a budget has the advantage of forcing management to establish a financial plan for the event and to allocate resources accordingly. It imposes a necessary financial discipline, regardless of how informally an event may be organised. In a similar way to the Gantt chart, it can be used for review long after the event is over.

HUNTER VALLEY FESTIVAL

Musica Viva Australia

Budget
Income and expenditure

Income		$	Expenditure		$
Box office		26 000	Artist fees and expenses		21 752
Subscription — 5 concerts					
80 @ $150		12 000	*Venue costs*		
Single sales			Stage and lighting		13 600
40 @ $35 Adult	1 400		Booking charges		2 602
30 @ $15 Concession	450		Marketing and publicity		15 000
	1 850		Front of house staff		5 600
× 5 concerts		9 250			
Sale of merchandise		5 000			
Sponsorship		7 500			
Total income		**59 750**	**Total expenditure**		**58 554**

SURPLUS/DEFICIT	**1196**

■ **Figure 10.3** *Hunter Valley Festival 1991*

Preparing a budget is illustrated by figure 10.4 on page 255. The process begins by establishing the economic environment of the event. The economics of the region and the nation (and even world economics) may impinge on the event and significantly change the budget. An example of this is the effect of the fall in the value of the Australian dollar on the major arts festivals. Within a week the cost of the entertainment imported for the festivals rose by over 10 per cent. To determine the economic environment, it is useful to ask the following questions. What similar events can be used as a guide? Will changes in the local or State economy affect the budget in any way? If it involves international performers or hiring equipment from overseas, will there be a change in the currency exchange rates? These, and many more questions, need to be answered before constructing a budget that will result in reasonable projections of costs and revenue.

The next step is to obtain the guidelines from the client, sponsors or event committee. For instance, a client may request that only a certain percentage of their sponsorship be allocated to entertainment, with the rest to be allocated to hospitality. Guidelines must fit with the overall objectives of the event and may require constructing sub-budgets or program budgets. This is both an *instructive phase*, in that the committee, for example, will instruct the event manager on the content of the budget and a *consultative phase* as the event manager would ask the advice of other event specialists and the subcontractors.

The third step is to identify, categorise and estimate the cost areas and revenue sources. The categories become the line items in the budget. A sample of the categories is given in table 10.1. This is a summary, or a first-level budget, of the cost and revenue areas. The next level down expands each of these line items and is shown in tables 10.2 and 10.3. The use of a computer-generated spreadsheet enables a number of levels in the budget to be created on separate sheets and linked to the first-level budget. Cost items take up the most room on a budget and are described below.

■ **Table 10.1**
Generic budget — first level

INCOME	AMOUNT	EXPENDITURE	AMOUNT
Grants		Administration	
Donations		Publicity	
Sponsorship		Venue costs	
Ticket sales		Equipment	
Fees		Salaries	
Special programs		Insurance	
Concessions		Permits	
TOTAL		Security	
		Accounting	
		Cleaning	
		Travel	
		Accommodation	
		Documentation	
		Hospitality	
		Community groups	
		Volunteers	
		Contingencies	
		TOTAL	

Once the costs and possible revenue sources and amounts are estimated, a *draft budget* is prepared and submitted for approval to the controlling committee. For example, this may be the finance subcommittee of a large festival. The draft budget is also used in grant submissions and sponsorships. The Federal Government funding bodies, including the Australia Council and Festivals Australia, have budget guidelines and printed forms that need to be completed and included in the grant application.

The final step involves preparation of the budget and financial ratios that can indicate deviations from the initial plan. An operating business has a variety of budgets including capital expenditure, sales, overheads and production. Most special events will require only an operation budget or cash budget.

Note the similarity between the classification system used for the budget and the work breakdown structure described in chapter 13 (Logistics). The work breakdown structure is often used as a basis of a budget. The costs of the lower levels are added to give the overall costs — called 'rolling up'. This means that many aspects of the event can be coded. A simple coding system can be used to link the work breakdown structure, the budget, the task sheets and risk analysis. For example the artwork (A) for the publicity (P) can use the code PA. This can be cross-referenced to the company or person who is responsible, to possible risks and to the amount budgeted.

■ **Figure 10.4**
The budget process

CASH FLOW

The special nature of events and festivals requires close attention to the flow of cash. Goldblatt (1997), Getz (1997), and Catherwood and Van Kirk (1992) all emphasise the importance of the control of cash to an event. Goldblatt (1997) stresses that it is imperative for the goodwill of suppliers. Without prompt payment the event company faces immediate difficulties. Payment terms and conditions have to be fully and equitably negotiated. These payment terms can ruin an event if they are not given careful consideration beforehand. To obtain the best terms from a supplier Goldblatt suggests the following.

• Learn as much as possible about the suppliers and subcontractors and the nature of their business. Do they own the equipment? What are the normal payment terms in their business? Artists, for instance, expect to be paid immediately, whereas some information technology suppliers will wait for 60 days.

• Be flexible with what can be offered in exchange — including sponsorship.

- Try to negotiate a contract that stipulates a small deposit before the event and full payment after it is over.
- Suggest a line of credit, with payment at a set time in the future.
- Closely control the purchasing.
- Ensure that all purchases are made through a purchase order that is authorised by the event manager or the appropriate finance personnel. A purchase order is a written record of the agreement to supply a product at a prearranged price. All suppliers, contractors and event staff should be informed that no purchase can be made without an authorised form. This ensures that spending is confined to what is permitted by the budget.
- Obtain a full description of the product or service and the quantities required.
- Itemise the price to a per unit cost.
- Calculate any taxes or extra charges.
- Determine payment terms.
- Clarify delivery details.
- Consider imposing penalties if the product or service delivered is not as described.

As figure 10.5 shows, the ability of an event coordinator to effect any change diminishes rapidly as the event draws closer. The supply of goods and services may, of necessity, take place close to or on the actual date of the event. This does not allow organisers the luxury of reminding a supplier of the terms set out in the purchase order. Without a full written description of the goods, the event manager is open to all kinds of exploitation by suppliers and, as the event may be on that day, there may be no choice but to accept delivery.

■ **Figure 10.5**
Control, cost and time

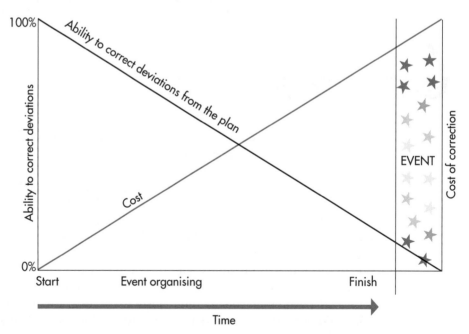

(**Source:** *Burke, R. 1993, Project Management: Planning and Control, John Wiley & Sons, New York, 2nd edn*)

When considering cash flow, the advantage of the ticketing strategies of events such as the Port Fairy Folk Festival are obvious. As tickets are sold months before the event, the management is able to concentrate on other areas of planning. A similar advantage is obtained by event companies that specialise in the corporate area. Generally they are paid up-front. This allows the event manager or producer the freedom to negotiate terms and conditions with the suppliers without having to worry about the cash flow. A cash flow timing chart similar to the Gantt chart is often helpful in planning events. This shows the names of the suppliers and their payment requirements. It includes deposit dates, payment stages, payment on purchase, monthly fixed cost payments and 30, 60 or 90 day credit payments.

COSTING

The cash flow at an event is heavily dependent on the cost of goods and services. These are estimated for the construction of the budget. The prediction, categorisation and allocation of costs is called the costing. In relation to the break-even chart (see figure 10.2) two types of costs have been identified. These are described in the following text.

Fixed costs or overheads are costs associated with the event that occur regardless of how many people come to the event. They include the unchanging expenses concerned with the operation of the event management company, for example rent, staff salaries, telephone and other office expenses. At a large festival these expenses may include rates, land tax and interest on loans. When deciding on a budget, these costs should be apportioned reasonably to the various event areas. This process is called absorption of the overheads by the cost centres. Cost centres, for example, include entertainment, catering, staging or travel. The publicity costs of the Hunter Valley Festival included a part cost of the general publicity for the work of the event company, Musica Viva. If the fixed costs are incorrectly absorbed the cost centre will be wrongly described. For a correct financial picture of the future event, the overheads have to be reasonably spread to all areas. The aim of an event company is to reduce the fixed costs without affecting the quality of the event.

Variable costs are expenses that pertain solely to the event and are directly related to the number of people who attend the event. Food and beverage costs are linked directly to the number of people attending an event. If more people attend an event more tickets need to be printed, more staff may need to be hired, and certainly more food provided.

This division of costs is not as clear-cut in the event industry as in other industries. It is sometimes clearer instead to talk in terms of direct costs (the costs directly associated with the event, whether variable or fixed) and overheads (costs associated with the running of the event company). In this case the direct costs are the major costs — and the aim of the event company is to control these costs. Table 10.2 lists the detailed budgeted costs of a one-off event.

Table 10.2
Projected costs — second level

		$			$
Administration	Office rental			Communication	
	Fax/photocopy			First aid	
	Computers			Tents	
	Printers			Tables and chairs	
	Telephone			Wind breaks	
	Stationery			Generators	
	Postage			Technicians	
	Office staff			Parking needs	
	SUBTOTAL			Uniforms	
Publicity	Artwork			SUBTOTAL	
	Printing		Salaries	Coordinator	
	Poster and leaflet distribution			Artists	
	Press kit			Labourers	
	Press ads			Consultants	
	Radio ads			Other	
	Programs			SUBTOTAL	
	SUBTOTAL		Insurance	Public liability	
Venue	Hire			Workers' compensation	
	Preparation			Rain	
	SUBTOTAL			Other	
Equipment	Stage			SUBTOTAL	
	Sound		Permits	Liquor	
	Lights			Food	
	Transport			Council	
	Personnel			Parking	
	Toilets			Childcare	
	Extra equipment			SUBTOTAL	

		$			$
Security	Security check		Documentation	Photo/video	
	Equipment			SUBTOTAL	
	Personnel		Hospitality	Tent	
	SUBTOTAL			Food	
Accounting	Cash and cheque			Beverage	
	Audit			Personnel	
	SUBTOTAL			Invitations	
Cleaning	Before			SUBTOTAL	
	During		Community	Donations	
	After			SUBTOTAL	
	SUBTOTAL		Volunteers	Food and drink	
Travel	Artists			Party	
	Freight			Awards and prizes	
	SUBTOTAL			SUBTOTAL	
Accommodation			Contingencies		
	SUBTOTAL			SUBTOTAL	

Catherwood and van Kirk (1992) divide the costs of an event into four main categories:

- operational or production costs including hiring of event staff; construction; insurance and administration
- venue/site rental
- promotion — advertising, public relations, sales promotion
- talent — costs associated with the entertainment.

To obtain the correct cost of each of the elements contained in the budget categories (sometimes called cost centres) there is a common costing process involved. The steps are described in the following text.

Conceptual estimate or 'ball park figure': This would be used in the conceptual development stage of the event to give management an idea of what costs are involved. Generally this would have an accuracy of +/− 25 per cent.

Feasibility study: This includes comparing costs in similar events. For example the cost of headline speakers varies according to their popularity and type of career. Asking other event managers about current speaker fees gives the event producer a basis for negotiating a fair price and a more realistic budget estimation.

Quote or definitive estimate: This is the cost quote in reply to the tender. The larger festivals will put out to tender many of the elements of the event including sound, lights and security. A near-correct estimate can be made on this basis. For small events, the quote may be obtained by phoning a selection of suppliers and comparing the costs. However, it is rarely the case that the costs are comparable, as there are so many unusual features or special conditions. Once an event company has built up a relationship with a supplier, it tends to stay with that supplier.

TIPS ON REDUCING COSTS

With careful and imaginative planning, costs can be reduced in a number of areas. They are discussed below.

Publicity: An innovative event may need a large publicity budget that is based on revenue from ticket sales. The event manager's aim should be to reduce this wherever possible. Established festivals may need very little publicity as 'word of mouth' will do all the necessary work. For instance, the annual Woodford Folk Festival with a budget of $2.3 million spends very little on publicity because it has built up a strong reputation with its target audience. The more innovative the event the greater the possibility for free publicity. The Tropicana Festival of Short Films in Sydney, for example, gains enormous free publicity as it attracts film stars to the event.

Equipment and supplies: Suppliers of products to events have down times during the year when their products may be hired cheaply. In particular, theatrical productions at the end of their run are a ready source of decoration and scenery. Annual events like the Sydney Gay and Lesbian Mardi Gras often have equipment in storage that can be hired.

In-kind gifts: Many organisations will assist events to achieve cross-promotional advantages. Entertainment can be inexpensive if there is a chance that an organisation can promote a performance or product at the event. For instance, at the Macquarie Marshes concert the boutique wine company, Bloodwood, agreed to supply their wine freely to the party for the media and friends held prior to the event — in exchange for the rights to sell their product at the concert.

Hiring charges: The hire costs of large infrastructure components such as tents and generators and headline acts can be reduced by offering work at other festivals and events. For example, the large cultural festivals around Australia, including the Melbourne International Festival and the Adelaide Festival of the Arts, can offer a festival circuit to any overseas performer. Costs are amortised over all the festivals.

Priorities cost centres: At some time it will be necessary to cut costs. You will need to anticipate the effect on the overall event if one area is significantly changed or eliminated. In project management this is called sensitivity analysis (Burke 1993). Estimates are made of the effect of cost changes on the event and the costs centres are placed in a priority list according to the significance of the effect. For instance, a sensitivity analysis could be applied to the effect of imposing a charge on a program that was previously available free. While this could significantly increase revenue, it may produce a negative effect in sponsorship and audience satisfaction, which may well be translated into the reduction of revenue.

Volunteers: Costs can be reduced by using volunteers instead of paid staff. It is important that all the skills of the volunteers are fully utilised. These skills should be continually under review as new skills may be required as the event planning progresses. For charitable functions, volunteers will often absorb many of the costs as tax deductible donations.

REVENUE

Anticipating potential sources of revenue should be given as much attention as projecting expenses. The source of the revenue will often define the type of event, the event objectives and the planning. A company product launch has only one source of revenue — the client. Company staff parties, for example, are paid by the client with no other source of revenue. The budget then has only one entry on the left-hand side. A major festival, on the other hand, has to find and service a variety of revenue sources such as sponsors and participants. This constitutes a major part of festival planning.

Revenue can come from the following sources:
- Ticket sales — most common in entrepreneurial events
- Sponsorship — common in cultural and sports events
- Merchandising
- Advertising
- 'In-kind' arrangements
- Broadcast rights — an increasingly important source of revenue in sport events
- Grants — federal, State and local government
- Fund-raising — common in community events
- The client — the major source for corporate events.

Table 10.3 features an expanded list of revenue sources. For many events, admission fees and ticket prices need careful consideration. The revenue they generate will impact on the cash flow and the break-even point. The ticket price can be decided by one or more of three methods:

1. **Covering costs:** All the costs are estimated and added to the projected profit. To give the ticket price, this figure is then divided by the expected number of people that will attend the event. The method is quick, simple and based on knowing the break-even point. It gives a 'rule of thumb' figure that can be used as a starting point for further investigations in setting the price.

2. **Market demand:** The ticket price is decided by the prevailing ticket prices for similar or competing events. In other words, it is the 'going rate' for an event. Concert ticket prices are decided in this way. In deciding on the ticket price, consider elasticity of demand. For instance,

if the ticket price is increased slightly will this affect the number of tickets sold?

3. **Perceived value:** The event may have special features that preclude a price comparison to other events. For instance, for an innovative event the ticket price must be carefully considered. By its nature this kind of event has no comparison. There can be variations in the ticket price for different entertainment packages at the event (at many multi-venued events the ticket will include admission only to certain events), for extra hospitality or for special seating. Knowing how to grade the tickets is an important skill in maximising revenue. There are market segments that will not tolerate differences in pricing, whereas others expect it. It can be a culturally based decision and may be part of the design of the event.

■ **Table 10.3**
Revenue sources — second level

INCOME		$	INCOME		$
Grants	Local		Ticket sales	Box office	
	State			Retail outlets	
	Federal			Admissions	
	Arts			SUBTOTAL	
	Other		Merchandise	T-shirts	
	SUBTOTAL			Programs	
Donations	Foundations			Posters	
	Other			Badges	
	SUBTOTAL			Videos	
Sponsorship	In kind			SUBTOTAL	
	Cash		Fees	Stalls	
	SUBTOTAL			Licences	
Individual contributions				Broadcast	
	SUBTOTAL			SUBTOTAL	
Special programs	Raffle		Advert sales	Program	
	Auction			Event site	
	Games			SUBTOTAL	
	SUBTOTAL		Concessions		
				SUBTOTAL	

■ Ticket *scaling*

There are many ticketing strategies that strive to obtain the best value from ticket sales. The most common strategy is to vary the pricing, according to seat position, number of tickets sold and time of sale. Early-bird discounts and subscriptions series are two examples of the latter. Another strategy involves creating a special category of attendees. This could include patrons, special clubs, 'friends of the event', people for whom the theme of the event has a special meaning or those who have attended many similar events in the past. For example, for a higher ticket price, patrons are offered extra hospitality, such as separate viewing area, valet parking and a cocktail party.

■ In-kind support *and bartering*

One way to increase income is to scrutinise the event cost centres for areas that could be covered by an exchange with the supplier or bartering. For example, the advertising can be expanded for an event with a program of 'give-aways'. These are free tickets to the event given away through the press. Due to the amount of goodwill surrounding a fund-raising event, bartering should be explored as a method of obtaining supplies.

■ Merchandising

The staging of an event offers many opportunities for merchandising. The first consideration is 'Does the sale of goods enhance the theme of the event?'. The problems of cash flow at an event, as stated earlier in this chapter, can give the sale of goods an unrealistic high priority in event management. It is easy to cheapen a 'boutique' special event with the sale of 'trinkets'. However, the attendees may want to buy a souvenir. For example, a large choir performing at a one-off spectacular event may welcome the opportunity to purchase a video of their performance. This could be arranged with the choir beforehand and result in a guaranteed income. As a spin-off the video could be incorporated into promotional material for use by the event management in bidding for future events.

■ Broadcast *rights*

An increasingly important source of revenue, particularly in sporting events, is the payment for the right to broadcast. A live television broadcast of an event is a lucrative area for potential — but it comes at a price. The broadcast, rather than the needs and expectations of the live audience, becomes master of the event. Often the live audience becomes merely one element in the televising process. At the ARIA (Australian Record Industry Association) Awards the audience includes 'fillers' — people who fill any empty seats so that the camera will always show a capacity audience.

If the entire event is recorded by high-quality video equipment, future broadcast rights should also be investigated. For instance, in many countries there is a constant demand for worthwhile content for pay television (cable or satellite). At the time of writing, Internet broadcast is in its infancy. There have been a number of music and image broadcasts but they are limited by the size of the bandwidth. There can be no doubt that this will become an important medium for the event industry.

■ Sponsorship *leverage*

Leverage is the current term for using event sponsorship to gain further support from other sponsors. Very few companies or organisations want to be the first to sponsor a one-off event. However, once the event has one sponsor's support, sufficient credibility is gained to enable an approach to other sponsors. For example, gaining the support of a major newspaper or radio station allows the event manager to approach other sponsors. The sponsors realise that they can obtain free publicity.

■ Special *features*

When an event is linked to a large population base, there are many opportunities for generating income. Raffles, for example, are frequently used to raise income. At a concert dance in England, all patrons brought along a prize for a raffle to be drawn on the night. Everyone received a ticket in the raffle as part of the entry fee to the event. The prizes ranged from old ties to overseas air tickets. Every person received a prize and the raffle became part of the entertainment of the evening.

Holding an auction at an event is also an entertaining way to increase income. Prior to the Broome Fringe Festival (held in June 1998), the event manager organised an innovative auction. The items auctioned included haircuts, 'slave for a day', body work and massages. The sale of players' jerseys, complete with the mud stains, after a major football match has also proved a lucrative way of raising revenue.

REPORTING

The importance of general reporting on the progress of event planning has already been described in this chapter. The budget report is a means of highlighting problems and suggesting solutions. It is an effective form of communication to the event committee and staff and should be readily understood. It is important that appropriate action is taken in response to the report's suggestions. Figure 10.6 is a list of guidelines for a straightforward report.

■ **Figure 10.6**
Reporting
guidelines

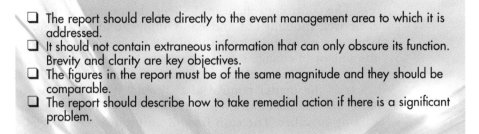

❑ The report should relate directly to the event management area to which it is addressed.
❑ It should not contain extraneous information that can only obscure its function. Brevity and clarity are key objectives.
❑ The figures in the report must be of the same magnitude and they should be comparable.
❑ The report should describe how to take remedial action if there is a significant problem.

The most common problem in an event is the cost 'blow out'. Special event planners often encounter unforeseen circumstances that can cost dearly. For example the subcontractor who supplies the sound system can go bankrupt; the replacement subcontractor may prove far more expensive. One of the unwritten laws of project management is that the closer the project is to completion the more expensive any changes become. Appropriate remedial action may be to use cheaper catering services or to find extra funding. This could take the form of a raffle to cover the extra costs. Figure 10.5 graphically shows how the cost of any changes to the organisation of an event escalate as the event date nears.

A major problem associated with a budget, particularly for special events, may involve blind adherence to it (Hicks 1979). It is a tool of control and not an end in itself. The elegance of a well laid-out budget and its mathematical certainty can obscure the fact that it should be a slave to the event objectives, not its master. A budget is based on reasonable projections made within an economic framework. Small changes in the framework can effect large changes in the event's finances. For instance, extra sponsorship may be found if the right products are added to the event portfolio. A complicated, highly detailed budget may consume far more time than is necessary to make the event a success.

Time is a crucial factor in special event management. Keeping rigidly within budgetary standards can take up too much time and energy of the event management, limiting time available for other areas.

Finally, a budget that is constructed by the event management may be imposed on staff without adequate consultation. This can lead to losing valuable specialist staff if they find themselves having to work to unreasonable budgetary standards. In particular, an innovative event requires the creative input of all the staff and subcontractors. At these events, informal financial control using a draft budget is often far more conducive to quality work than strict budgetary control.

It needs to be remembered that a budget is only an approximation of reality, and not reality itself. It will need to be adjusted as the event changes and new information comes to hand. However, it is a vital part of the control mechanism for events.

SUMMARY

There is little point in expending effort in creating a plan for an event if there is no way to closely monitor it. The event plan is a prerequisite for success. The control mechanisms to keep the project aligned to the plan need to be well thought out and easily understood by the management team. When the event strays from the plan there needs to be ways to bring it back into line or to change the plan.

An estimate of the costs and revenues of an event is called the budget and it acts as the master control of an event. With a well-reasoned budget in place, all sections of an event know their spending limits and can focus on working together. The cash flow of an event needs special considerations. When is the cash coming in? Moreover, when does it need to go out? An event that does not have control mechanisms, including a well-planned budget, is not going to satisfy its stakeholders. Not only will it fail, but organisers will never know the reason for its failure. A sound budget gives management a solid foundation on which to build a successful event.

Questions

1. What controls do you use to get from home to work or school?

2. List the milestones for a Rough Water Swim event involving at least 1000 competitors.

3. Identify the best practices for a corporate conference dinner.

4. Identify the cost centres and revenue sources for:
   (a) a corporate staff party
   (b) a concert (include a break-even chart)
   (c) a wine and food festival
   (d) the Sydney Olympics.

5. If it was necessary to cut costs at the above events, which areas would be the first to feel the effects?

6. What 'economies of scale' can be expected from multi-venued festivals?

7. Anticipate the possible cash-flow problems at a large cultural festival in a State capital.

....

Sydney Gay and
Lesbian Mardi Gras

Sydney Gay and Lesbian Mardi Gras is a community-based organisation that has just reached its 20th anniversary. Our organisation was formed from the diverse lesbian and gay communities of Sydney to enable us to explore, express and promote the life of our combined community through a cultural focus. We affirm the pride, joy, dignity and identity of our community and its people through events of celebration.

Mardi Gras provides resources and opportunities for our community — for creative expression and the development of cultural and political skill. It enhances the potential of both.

There is a volunteer Board of 14 that is elected by the membership, a full-time staff of 14, volunteer committees and thousands of volunteers who work on the Parade, in the office, in the workshop and at our numerous events.

The organisation has a budget of over $4 million. The main sources of income are the two parties, the Sleaze Ball and the Mardi Gras Party, as well as membership fees from over 8000 members. Sponsorship contributes approximately five per cent in cash to the budget and a further five per cent 'in-kind' arrangements.

Committees are chaired by board directors and it is these directors, along with relevant members of staff, who are responsible for events and activities, such as marketing, coming in on budget. With the size of the organisation growing at a rate of 15 per cent per annum, keeping budgets under control is a challenge.

For all expenditure, purchase orders are raised and are kept in check with the budget figures and the cash flow projections. Regular reviews occur to ensure projections are accurate and realistic.

Mardi Gras has found it invaluable to have accounts presented at board meetings once a month, that include income and expenditure, cash flow and cash at bank information. This ensures that decisions in regard to extraordinary expenditure can be made using the most accurate and up-to-date information.

An administration committee has been in operation for some years. It deals with all staff issues, the general management of the company and the administration budget that includes membership, wages, ticketing, maintenance, capital costs and other general costs.

Sydney Gay and Lesbian Mardi Gras is a not-for-profit organisation that is limited by guarantee. However, the company has established cash reserves to maintain the future of the organisation.

Overall the financial structure of the Mardi Gras is secure, due mostly to the strong income base the parties provide the organisation.

Prepared by Bev Lange, former President, Sydney Gay and Lesbian Mardi Gras

Questions

1 As a fast-growing organisation and major event, the Sydney Gay and Lesbian Mardi Gras has had to develop its budget and financial control systems as it has evolved. From what you have been told in the case study, do you think these systems are adequate for the event? What changes, if any, would you suggest to these systems?

2 How would you describe the organisational framework of the Sydney Gay and Lesbian Mardi Gras? What other organisational structures could it employ? Do you think it has the best structure for its needs?

3 The Sydney Gay and Lesbian Mardi Gras is one of the largest internationally known events in Australia. What factors do you think have led to its rapid growth and success?

REFERENCES

Beniger, J. 1986, *The Control Revolution*, Harvard University Press, Cambridge.

Bennett, R. 1994, *Managing: Activities and Resources*, 2nd edn, Kogan Page Limited, London.

Brody, R. & Goodman, M. 1988, *Fund-Raising Events: Strategies and Programs for Success*, Human Sciences Press Inc., New York.

Burke, R. 1993, *Project Management: Planning and Control*, 2nd edn, John Wiley & Sons, New York.

Cameron, N. 1993, *Fire on the Water*, Currency Press, Paddington, Australia.

Catherwood, D. & Van Kirk, R. 1992, *The Complete Guide to Special Event Management*, John Wiley & Sons, New York.

Getz, D. 1997, *Event Management and Event Tourism*, Cognizant Communications, New York.

Goldblatt, J. 1997, *Special Events: Best Practices in Modern Event Management*, 2nd edn, Van Nostrand Reinhold, New York.

Hicks, H. & Gullet, C. 1976, *The Management of Organisations*, McGraw-Hill Kogakusha Ltd, Tokyo.

Renton, N. 1994, *Guide for Meetings and Organisations: Volume 2, Meetings*, 6th edn, The Law Book Company Ltd, Sydney.

CHAPTER 11

Legal and
risk management

LEARNING OBJECTIVES

After studying this chapter, you should be able to:

- explain the central role of event ownership in event administration

- identify the necessary contracts for events and their components

- construct a risk management plan

- understand the variety of rules and regulations governing events

- describe the process of gaining insurance.

INTRODUCTION

Underpinning all aspects of an event are risk management and legal issues. This chapter introduces the concepts of event ownership and the all important duty of care of the event management. The contract is the documentation of the relationship between the event and the various stakeholders. It is therefore important that event and festival management be familiar with the key terms used. Finally the standard procedures of risk analysis are introduced.

LEGAL ISSUES

A key question in event administration is: 'who owns the event?' The legal owner of an event could be the event coordinator, the committee, a separate legal entity or the sponsors, but it is important to recognise that the ownership of the event entails legal responsibility and therefore liability. The members of an organising committee can be personally held responsible for the event. This is often expressed as 'jointly and severally liable'. The structure of the event administration must reflect this, and the status of various personnel, such as the event coordinator, the subcontractors and other stakeholders, must be clearly established at the outset. Likewise, sponsorship agreements will often have a clause as to the sponsor's liability, and therefore the extent of their ownership of the event. All such issues need to be carefully addressed by the initial agreements and contracts.

The organising committee for a non-profit event can become a legal entity by forming an incorporated association. Such an association can enter into contracts and own property. The act of incorporating, under the relevant association incorporation act in each State, means that the members have limited liability when the association incurs debts. It does not grant them complete exemption from all liability such as negligence. By law, an association must have a constitution or a list of rules. Such documents state the procedures and powers of the association, including auditing and accounting matters, the powers of the governing body and winding-up procedures. In many cases, community and local festival events do not form a separate incorporated association as they are able to function under the legal umbrella of another body such as a local council. This gives the event organising committee considerable legal protection as well as access to administrative support. For a one-off event, this administrative support can save time and resources, because the administrative infrastructure, such as fax machine, phone lines, secretarial help and legal and accounting advice, is already established.

Establishing an appropriate legal structure for an event management company is an exercise in liability minimisation. Several structures are possible for an event company, which could operate as a sole trader, partnership or a company limited by liability. Each of these legal structures has different liability implications. Legal advice may be required to determine the most appropriate structure for a particular circumstance.

CONTRACTS

A contract is an agreement between two or more parties that sets out their obligations and is enforceable by law. It describes the exchange to be made between the parties. A contract can be a written or an oral agreement. In the world of event management, an oral contract is of little use if problems occur in the future. Therefore, it is appropriate to put all contractual agreements in writing. This may frequently take the form of a simple letter of agreement, not more than a page in length (see figure 11.1). However, when large amounts of money and important responsibilities are involved, a formal contract is necessary.

As Goldblatt (1997) explains, a typical event industry contract will contain:
- the names of the contracting parties, their details and their trading names
- details of the service or product that is offered (e.g. equipment, entertainment, use of land, expert advice)
- the terms of exchange for such service or product
- the signature of both parties indicating understanding of the terms of exchange and agreement to the conditions of the contract.

■ **Figure 11.1**
An example of a letter of agreement

Festival copy (sign and return)

Date:
To:

PERFORMER AGREEMENT

This agreement is between the Folk Federation of South Australia Inc (hereafter referred to as the Festival) and _____ (hereafter referred to as the Performer).
The Festival and Performer(s) agree that:

1. **Performances:** The Festival engages the Performer(s) for the following days and times to perform at the 1998 Victor Harbor Folk Festival):
(See Timetable attached)

and the Performer(s) accept the said engagement.

2. **Payment:** Provided that the Performer(s) fulfil the obligations set out in the agreement, the Festival shall pay the Performer(s) an agreed fee of $ _____ .

3. **Time of payment:** Payment will be made *by cheque* within 10 days of the Festival (unless otherwise arranged).
Cheque to be made out to: _____ name of person/company

(continued)

4. **Other commitments:** to the Performer(s) include the following: *(n/a denotes not applicable)*
   Number of passes to performers: _____
   Travel: _____
   Transit: _____
   Accommodation: _____
5. **Travel arrangements** made by the Festival are final and the cost of any changes not agreed to during the negotiations of this contract shall be borne by the Performer(s).
6. **Outside performances:** The performer shall inform the Festival of any other engagements taken during the period 2–5 October within 50 km of the Victor Harbour Folk Festival.
7. **Cancellation:** If any performances by the Performer(s) are cancelled or prevented for any reason, including but not limited to, public calamity, strike, lockout, Act of God or due to reasons beyond the control of the Festival, the Festival shall not be liable to the Performer(s) for fees, costs, expenses or damages of any kind.
8. **Publicity:** The Performer(s) agree to allow *short* takes of their performances to be photographed, recorded or video taped by the Festival or by Festival approved media to assist in promotion of the Festival and Performer(s) may obtain copies of such recordings or photography at their own expense. The Performer(s) shall provide the Festival as requested with the necessary materials required to adequately promote the Festival and the Performer. This may take the shape of recordings, photographs, biography and appearances or media interview subject to availability of such materials.
9. **Deductions:** The Festival shall have the right to deduct or withhold from the Performer(s) any amounts required to be deducted by law. The Festival does not take responsibility for the payment of any taxes and any amounts payable under superannuation guarantee legislation relating to the artists' income from this engagement.
10. **Merchandise:** The artist agrees that any merchandise items offered for sale by the artist at the Festival shall be sold solely through the Festival shop operated on behalf of the Festival. The artist further agrees that a 15% commission will be deducted from the reconciled gross sales.
11. **All notices:** regarding this agreement shall be in writing and served by mail, email, telegram, or facsimile addressed to the parties at their respective addresses.
12. **In the event of a dispute:** this agreement shall be governed by and construed in accordance with the laws of the province of South Australia.
13. **Alterations:** This agreement may not be changed without consent of both parties; however, the Festival shall have the power to make changes to Performer(s) program times under special circumstances.

Please sign **BOTH** copies of this agreement and **RETURN ONE** to the Festival office.

* A signed copy of this contract is required for issue of cheque to the performer(s).

Signed for the Festival _____ 1998

Signed for the Performer(s) _____ 1998

To make this mutual obligation perfectly clear to all parties, the contract would set out all key elements. These would consist of the following: financial terms, including a payment schedule; a cancellation clause; delivery time; the rights and obligations of each party; and an exact description of the goods and services being exchanged.

Event management companies may need a wide range of contracts to facilitate their operation. Some of these are shown in figure 11.2.

■ **Figure 11.2**
Contracts required by an event management company

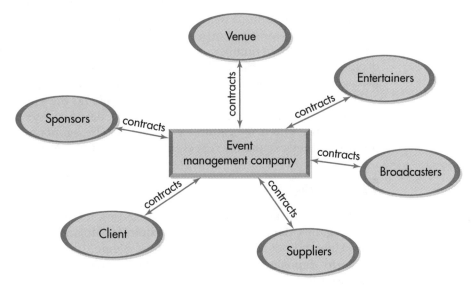

An event of medium size would require a set of formal contracts covering:
• the event company or coordinator and the client
• the entertainers
• the venue
• the suppliers (e.g. security, audiovisual, caterers)
• the sponsor(s).
For smaller events these may be arranged by letters of agreement, without going into too much detail.

Different contracts have different 'styles' and the event manager must be familiar with them. Some of these contracts are discussed in the following text.

■ Entertainment

A common feature of entertainment contracts is the 'rider'. This is an attachment to the contract, usually on a separate piece of paper. Hiring a headline performer may necessitate signing a 20 to 30 page contract. The contract often contains a clause requiring the event company to provide the goods and services contained in the rider, as well as the performance fee. The rider can list such things as food, extra accommodation, transport and set-up assistance. The event company ignores this at its peril. The rider can be used by the entertainer's agent as a way of increasing the fee in real terms, which can have serious consequences for the budget of an event. For example, a university student union that employs a well-known rock group at a minimal fee for a charity function would find its objectives greatly damaged by a rider stipulating reimbursal of food, accommodation and transport costs for 30 people.

Another important clause in any entertainment contract is exclusivity. For example, a headline act may be the major attraction for an event. If the act is also performing nearby this could easily detract from the uniqueness of the event. A clause to prevent this is therefore inserted into the contract. It indicates that the performer cannot perform within a specified geographic area during the event or for a certain number of days prior to and after the event. The intricacies of entertainment contracts led Freedman and Smith (1991) to suggest that event managers obtain legal advice about contracts when planning a celebrity concert.

The contract must contain a clause that stipulates the signatories have the right to sign on behalf of the contracting parties. An entertainment group may be represented by a number of agents. The agents must have written proof that they exclusively represent the group for the event.

■ Venue

The venue contract will have specialist clauses, including indemnifying the venue against damages, personnel requirements and provision of security staff. The contract can also contain these elements:

- **security deposit:** an amount, generally a percentage of the hiring fee, to be used for any additional work such as cleaning and repairs that result from the event.
- **cancellation:** outlining the penalty for cancellation of the event and whether the hirer will receive a refund if the venue is rehired at that time.
- **access:** including the timing of the opening and closing of the doors, and actual use of the entrance ways.
- **late conclusion:** the penalty for the event going overtime.
- **house seats:** the free tickets reserved for venue management.
- **additions or alterations:** the event may require some changes to the internal structures of the venue.
- **signage:** this covers the signs of any sponsors and other advertising. Venue management approval may be required for all promotional material.

When hiring a venue, it is important to ascertain exactly what is included in the fee. For example, just because there were chairs and tables in the photograph of the venue does not mean that they are included in the hiring cost.

■ Sponsor

The contract with the sponsor would cover issues related to quality representation of the sponsor such as trademarks and signage, exclusivity and the right of refusal for further sponsorship. It may specify that the sponsor's logo be included on all promotional material, or that the sponsor has the right to monitor the quality of the promotional material. Geldard and Sinclair

(1996) advise that the level of sponsor exclusivity during an event will need to be reflected in the contract between the event committee and the sponsor. Possible levels are sole sponsor, principal sponsor, major or minor sponsor and supplier. The contract would also describe hospitality rights, such as the number of complimentary tickets supplied to the sponsor.

■ Broadcast

Broadcast contracts can be very complex, due to the large amounts of money involved in broadcasting and the production of resultant merchandise such as videos and sound recordings. The important clauses in a broadcast contract address the following key components:

- **territory or region:** The broadcast area — local, State or international — must be defined. If the attached schedule shows the region as 'World', the event company must be fully aware of the rights it is bestowing on the broadcaster, and their value.
- **guarantees:** The most important of these is the one stating that the event company has the rights to sign for the whole event. For example, some local councils require that an extra fee be paid for broadcasting from their area. Also, performers' copyright can preclude any broadcast without written permission from their record and publishing companies. Comedy acts and motivational speakers are particularly sensitive about broadcasts and recordings.
- **sponsorship:** This area can present difficulties when different levels of sponsorship are involved. Sometimes the rights of the event sponsor and the broadcaster's sponsors can clash.
- **repeats, extracts and sub-licences:** These determine the allowable number of repeats of the broadcast, and whether the broadcaster is authorised to edit or take extracts from the broadcast and how such material can be used. The event company may sign with one broadcaster, only to find that the rights to cover the event have been sold on for a much larger figure to another broadcaster. In addition, a sub-licence clause may annul many of the other clauses in the contract. The sub-licensor may be able to use its own sponsors, which is problematic if they are in direct competition with the event sponsors.
- **merchandising:** The contract may contain a clause that mentions the rights to own products originating from the broadcast. The ownership and sale of such recordings can be a major revenue source for an event. A clause recently introduced in these sorts of contracts concerns future delivery systems. Multimedia uses, such as CD-ROMs, cable television, and the Internet are all relatively recent, and new communications technologies continue to be developed. It is easy to sign away the future rights of an event when the contract contains terms that are unknown to the event company. It is wise to seek out specialist legal advice.
- **access:** The physical access requirements of broadcasting must be part of the staging and logistic plan of the event. A broadcaster can easily disrupt

an event by demanding to interview performers and celebrities. It is important to specify how much access the broadcaster can have to the stars.

- **credits:** This establishes, at the outset, the people and elements that will be listed in the titles and credits.

The broadcaster can offer all kinds of assistance to the event company. It has an interest in making the event presentable for television and will often help decorate the site. The level of assistance will depend on its stake in the event. For example, Channel Ten's involvement in the Uncle Toby's Iron Man series has led to many kinds of synergies between the event, the sponsors and the broadcaster.

CONSTRUCTING A CONTRACT

The process of constructing a contract is shown in figure 11.3 and comprises five main steps: the intention, negotiation, initial acceptance, agreement on terms, and signing. This process can be facilitated if the event management has standard contracts, where the name of the supplier and any special conditions can be inserted. This saves the event company going through unfamiliar contracts from sponsors, suppliers and entertainers, which can be very time consuming.

■ **Figure 11.3**
The process of constructing a contract

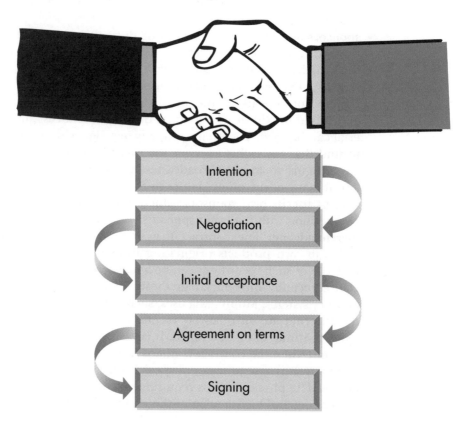

Intention

Negotiation

Initial acceptance

Agreement on terms

Signing

For large events and more complex contracts a 'heads of agreement' is sent after the negotiations are completed. This is a summary of any important specific points, listing the precise service or product that is being provided. The contract can be renegotiated or terminated with the agreement of all parties. The final should contain a clause that allows both parties to go to arbitration in the event of a disagreement.

TRADEMARKS AND LOGOS

Another kind of ownership issue for event management is the ownership of trademarks and logos. Recently, a federal court order was granted to the Sydney Organising Committee for the Olympic Games preventing another party from using an image that was deemed similar to their own logo. This illustrates the importance of the ownership of event symbols.

The event company must also be aware of the risks of misrepresenting its event. There is a danger, when promoting an event, of exaggerating its benefits. Descriptions of the product must always be accurate, as disgruntled consumers may and do take legal action to gain punitive damages when they feel that advertising for an event has made false claims. The Trade Practices Act can be used to argue such cases.

■ Part V of the *Trade Practices Act 1974* (Cth) prohibits 'unfair practices' within the marketplace and has, in certain instances, been effectively used to protect those involved in events marketing.

The sections most often relied on are section 52, which prohibits 'misleading or deceptive' conduct and section 53(c) and (d) which concern representations made by a corporation that it has, or its goods and services have, sponsorship approval or affiliation that it in fact does not have.

These sections are of obvious benefit to individuals and associations alike as they provide the means by which effective action can be taken against those who wish to associate themselves with an event when they have no right to do so.

Section 52 states 'a corporation shall not, in trade or commerce, engage in conduct that is misleading or deceptive or is likely to mislead or deceive.' Section 52 has often been used to restrain the unauthorised use of 'personalities' in advertising and marketing strategies. An instance where section 52 was used to protect the rights of a sporting personality in an advertising and market campaign was in the case of World Series Cricket Pty Ltd v Parish (1977) 17 ALR 181. A claim was made alleging a breach of section 52 of the Trade Practices Act in relation to the holding of an event. In this case, it was the first year that World Series Cricket was to be held. The Australian Cricket Board commenced proceedings because the Board claimed that the public would be misled through the various advertisements in believing that the particular event has been endorsed by the Board. The claim was upheld (Fewell 1995). ■

DUTY OF CARE

A fundamental legal principal is that of taking all reasonable care to avoid acts or omissions that could injure a 'neighbour'. This is called duty of care, and is covered by an area of law known as torts. A tort is a breach of duty owed to other people and imposed by law, and in this it differs from the duties arising from contracts, which are agreed between contracting parties. Unlike criminal law, which is concerned with deterrence and punishment, the law of torts is concerned with compensation.

For event management, duty of care means taking actions that will prevent any foreseeable risk of injury to the people who are directly affected by, or involved in, the event. This would include event staff, volunteers, performers, the audience or spectators and the public in the surrounding areas.

RISK MANAGEMENT

Special events are particularly susceptible to risks. Risk, in the event context, may be defined as the likelihood of the special event or festival not fulfilling its objectives. A unique venue, large crowds, new staff and volunteers, movement of equipment and general excitement are a recipe for potential hazards. The event manager who ignores advice on risk prevention is courting disaster and foreshortening his or her career in the event industry. The sensible assessment of potential hazards and preventative action is the basis of risk management.

Risk is not necessarily harmful. One reason that an event company wins the job of organising an event is that other companies perceive it to be too risky. Risk is the basis of the entrepreneur's business. Without risk there can be no competitive advantage. Without risk there can be no tightrope walking or Xtreme games. Part of what makes an event special is the risk — it has not been done before.

According to Standards Australia, '[r]isk management is the term applied to a logical and systematic method of establishing the context, identifying, analysing, evaluating, treating, monitoring and communicating risks associated with any activity, function or process in a way that will enable organisations to minimise losses and maximise opportunities. Risk management is as much about identifying opportunities as avoiding or mitigating losses' (http://www.standards.com.au).

Every part of event management has potential risks. Berlonghi (1990) categorises the main areas of risk as follows:

• administration: The organisational structure and office layout should minimise risk to employees.
• marketing and public relations: The promotion section must be aware of the need for risk management. By their nature, marketeers are optimistic about the consequences of their actions and tend to ignore potential risks.

- health and safety: A large part of risk management concerns this area. Loss prevention plans and safety control plans are an important part of any risk management strategy. The risks associated with food concession hygiene and sanitation require specific attention.
- crowd management: Risk management of crowd flow, alcohol sales and noise control. (See the chapter on logistics, chapter 13.)
- security: The security plan for an event involves careful risk management thinking.
- transport: Deliveries, parking and public transport contain many potential hazards that need to be addressed.

A good risk management strategy will also cover any other areas whose operations are crucial to the event and which may need special security and safety precautions, such as ticket sales and other cash points and communications.

In every area the risks must be identified and pre-empted, and their management fully integrated into the event plan.

As with many aspects of event management, risk management can be represented as a cycle. This cycle has four components, which are discussed below.

■ Identification

Pre-empting problems requires skill, experience and knowledge. Something that appears safe to some of the event staff may well contain hidden dangers. A sponsor's sign at an event may look securely mounted when examined by the marketing manager, but it would require the specialist knowledge of the stagehands to be assured that it is secure. Since the event manager cannot be expert in every field, it is best to pool the experience of all the event staff and volunteers by convening a risk assessment meeting. Such a meeting should aim to gather risk management expertise. For large events a consultant may be hired. The meeting is also an opportunity to train and motivate event staff in the awareness, minimisation and control of risks.

Identification techniques

Several techniques assist in identifying risks:
- **Work breakdown structure:** Breaking down the work necessary to create an event into manageable parts can greatly assist in the identification of risks. It provides a visual schema as well as the categorisation of the event into units associated with specific skills and resources. Isolating the event areas in this way gives a clear picture of the possible problems. However this analysis may not reveal the problems that result in a combination of risks. For example a problem with the ticketing of an event may not be severe on its own. If it is combined with the withdrawal of a major sponsor the result may require the event to be cancelled.
- **Test events:** Large sporting events often run smaller events to test the facilities, equipment and other resources. The Olympic test events were

effectively used to iron out any problems. Such a test is a self-funded rehearsal. The pre-conference cocktail party is used to test some aspects of the conference. Many music festivals will run an opening concert on the night before the first day of the festival as a means of testing the equipment.

- **Internal/external:** To assist the analysis it is useful to have a classification according to the origin of the risk. Internal risks arise in the event planning and implementation. They may also result from the inexperience of the event company. These risks are generally within the abilities of the event company to manage. External risks arise from outside the event organisation and may need a different control strategy. This technique focuses on mitigating the impact of the risk. For example, the impact of the cancellation of a soccer star player may be minimised by allowing free entry to the event.
- **Fault diagram:** Risks can also be discovered by looking at their impact and working backwards to the possible cause. This is a *result to cause* method. For example a lack of ticket sales would be a terrible result. The fault diagram method would go back from this scenario through the various aspects of the event to postulate its cause. The list of causes is then used to manage the risk.
- **Incident report:** Almost all large public events have an incident report document. These may be included in the event manual and are meant to be filled out by the event staff when there is an incident.
- **Contingency plan:** An outcome of the risk analysis may be a detailed plan of viable alternative integrated actions. The contingency plan contains the response to the impact of a risk and involves decision procedure, chain of command and a set of related actions. An example of a contingency planning was the response to the Y2K threat. On the south coast of NSW the New Year's Eve events required an emergency plan. If the Y2K adversely affected the computer system at the local Navy airfield, then the emergency services would be called to the navy base. This could pose a major problem for any event in the local area, particularly as that time of year is a time of high fire danger in the region.

■ Evaluation

Once the risks are identified they can be listed in order of importance. They are given priority according to the probability of their occurrence and the severity of their results. Risk assessment meetings often reveal the 'prophets of doom' who can bring an overly pessimistic approach to the planning process. This is itself a risk that must be pre-empted. It is important that the meeting be well chaired and focused, since the time needed for risk assessment must always be weighed against the limited time available for the overall event planning. An effective risk assessment meeting will produce a comprehensive and realistic analysis of the potential risks.

■ Control

After the potential risks have been evaluated, the event manager needs to create mechanisms to control any problem that can arise. Many different strategies are possible.

In his comprehensive manual on risk management for events, Berlonghi (1990) suggests the following risk control strategies:

- **Cancel and avoid the risk:** If the risk is too great it may be necessary to cancel all or part of the event. Outdoor concerts that are part of a larger event are often cancelled if there is rain. The major risk is not audience discomfort, but that of electrocution.
- **Diminish the risk:** Risks that cannot be eliminated need to be minimised. For example, to eliminate all possible security risks at an event may require every patron to be searched. This solution is obviously unworkable and instead a risk minimisation strategy will need to be developed. This might mean installing metal detectors or stationing security guards in a more visible position.
- **Reduce the severity of risks which do eventuate:** A major part of safety planning is preparing quick and efficient responses to foreseeable problems. Training staff in elementary first aid can reduce the severity of an accident. The event manager cannot eliminate natural disasters but can prepare a plan to contain the effects. For example, see the Woodford Disaster Plan referred to in the chapter on logistics (chapter 13).
- **Devise back-ups and alternatives:** When something goes wrong the situation can be saved by having an alternative plan in place. For example, in case the juggler does not turn up to the children's party, the host has organised party games to entertain the children. On a larger scale, back-up generators are a must at big outdoor events.
- **Distribute the risk:** If the risk can be spread across different areas, its impact will be reduced if something does go wrong. One such strategy is to spread the cash-taking areas, such as ticket booths, so that any theft is contained and does not threaten the complete event income. Having a variety of sponsors is another way to distribute risk. If one sponsor pulls out, the others can be approached to increase their involvement.
- **Transfer the risk:** Risk can be transferred to other groups responsible for an event's components. Subcontractors may be required to share the liability of an event. Their contracts generally contain a clause to the effect that they are responsible for the safety of their equipment and the actions of their staff during the event. In Australia, most performing groups are required to have public liability insurance before they can take part in an event.

■ Specific *event risks*

Crowd management

There are many factors that impinge on the smooth management of crowds at an event. The first risk is correctly estimating the number of people who will attend the event. No matter how the site is designed too many attendees can put enormous strain on the event resources. Even at free events, too few attendees can significantly affect the event objectives. The launch of the Paralympic mascots in the Domain in Sydney saw an audience of only 500 when the site was designed for thousands. It gave a spacious look to the event site. Crowd risk management is also a function of the type of audience and their standards of behaviour. A family event will have different priorities in risk management to a rock festival. The expectations of the crowd can be managed with the right kind of information sent out before the event.

Alcohol

Events can range from a family picnic with the audience sipping wine while watching a show to New Year's Eve mass gatherings of youth and the heavy consumption of alcohol. Under the law both events are treated the same. The results of the later can cause an event to be cancelled. The alcohol risk management procedures can permeate every aspect of some events including limiting ticket sales, closing hotels early, increased security, and roping off areas.

For the New Year's Eve celebrations in Darling Harbour the management also identified the major risks resulting from broken glass. In the past the site needed a large and expensive clean up and the safety issue was paramount. After consultation with all the stakeholders, their risk management procedure included:
- erecting a perimeter fence around the site
- alcohol allowed only in licensed premises
- alcohol- and glass-free policy for all public areas
- rearranging the entertainment so that there were areas that appealed to families and senior citizens
- publicising the new policy in all advertisements.

Communication

The risks involved in communication are varied as it concerns both the organising of the event and the reporting of any risks. Setting up a correct computer and paper filing system for the event office can prevent future problems. Easy access to relevant information is vital to good risk management. A standard, yet customised, reporting procedure can also reduce the risk of ineffective communication. Communication can include how the public is informed of the event. It includes signage and keeping the attendees informed when they are at the event site. The event manual is an excellent communication device for the procedures, protocol and general event information for the staff and volunteers. There can be a risk of too much data obscuring the important information. It needs to be highly focused.

Environment

Of increasing concern to the general community is the risk to the environment posed by modern businesses. There are both dangerous risks such as pollution, spills and effluent leakage and the more indirect risks minimised by waste recycling, water and energy conservation. The impacts and therefore the priorities for their control will vary over the event project life cycle.

Emergency

An awareness of the nearest emergency services and their working requirements is mandatory for the event management. The reason for calling in the outside emergency service is that the situation is beyond the capabilities of the event staff and needs specialist attention. It is important to understand the chain of command when emergency services arrive. They can be outside the control of the event management who would act purely in an advisory capacity. They may be called in by any attendee at an event.

■ Review

Evaluating the successes and failures of the risk control strategy is central to the planning of future events. The event company must be a 'learning organisation'. The analysis of and response to feedback is essential to this process.

EVENT PROFILE

When things go wrong

Event managers plan for months to ensure that nothing goes wrong at the event. The unfortunate reality is that something will always go wrong.

For outdoor festivals and events, rain can create havoc. Two separate major Australia Day ceremonies faced cancellation due to torrential rain in 1997. Contingency plans were implemented for each ceremony. The call was made that the first event, Lord Mayor's Citizenship Ceremony, would remain in Hyde Park. Unfortunately the rain returned and the event was rather damp. By the time the second evening State Ceremony was due to commence, it had already been moved inside, so there was even time for rehearsal and the event was a great success.

The international Tall Ship Fleet set sail from Sydney on Australia Day 1998 to commemorate the bicentenary of the circumnavigation of Tasmania by Bass and Flinders. Just as the Parade of Sail was commencing on the harbour the captain of the huge Mexican tall ship *Guathemoc* hoisted sail and proceeded to collide with the wharf of Goat Island. Hearing of the incident on the marine radio the Waterways and Sydney Ports moved in to provide assistance. In a very short period the ship was pulled clear by tugs, inspected and pronounced seaworthy. She proceeded to rejoin the commemorative race to Tasmania and, other than some very bruised egos, no-one was injured.

Be it wet weather or running aground, elements in every event remain outside the event manager's control. The key to a quick recovery when things go wrong is to have identified possible problems and their solutions in advance, and have the necessary slack resources on standby just in case.

Warren Pearson
Arts and Events Manager
Australia Day Council of New South Wales

INSURANCE

Central to any strategy of liability minimisation is obtaining the correct insurance.

The Community Festival Handbook (1991) contains helpful suggestions regarding insurance. These include the following:

- Allow enough time to investigate and arrange the correct insurance. This may include asking for quotes and professional advice. Finding the right insurance broker is the first priority.
- Make sure that the event committee or company is fully covered for the whole time. That is, from the first meeting.
- Require all the suppliers of products and services to show they have liability cover.
- Be prepared to give the insurance broker all information concerning the event and the companies involved. They may require a list of possible hazards such as pyrotechnics.
- Be prepared to record the details of any damage or injury. Photographs and videos are a help in this.
- Keep all records, as a claimant has six years to formulate a claim.
- Do not accept the transfer of liability of the suppliers to the event management.
- Look at what is included and excluded in the insurance document. For example, rain insurance is specific about the amount and time of the rain. Are the event volunteers covered by the insurance?
- Are there any additional stakeholders insured? These are companies or individuals that are covered by the insurance but not the named insured. For example, the sponsors and the venue may benefit from the insurance policy.

There are many kinds of insurance that can be taken out for events. These include weather insurance; personal accident insurance for the volunteer workers; property insurance, including money; workers' compensation insurance; public liability; directors' and officers' liability. The choice of the particular insurance cover is dictated by the risk management strategy developed by event management.

REGULATIONS, LICENCES AND PERMITS

There are long lists of regulations that need to be satisfied when staging a simple event. The bigger and more innovative the event, the larger the number of these regulations. The correct procedure in one State may be completely different in another. The principal rule is to carry out careful research, including investigating similar events in the same area and seeking advice on what permits and licences are necessary to allow an event to proceed.

It is always the responsibility of an event company to find out and comply with all pertinent rules and regulations. For example, a street parade through Sydney can come under a wide range of government authorities. The Paddington Festival Parade along Oxford Street required a series of long meetings with the two local councils, police and traffic authorities. The event itself was over in two hours. In Victoria a special licence is required to erect tents over a certain size. This includes tents that are used for only one night. Local noise regulations can change within the same city within the jurisdiction of different councils. Not only that, but event management must make it a practice to pay particular attention to workplace health and safety regulations.

Figure 11.4 describes some of the permits, licences, insurances and regulations with which a community festival must comply to take place on the south coast of Victoria. It is evident that an event manager may need to seek legal advice to ensure that all relevant regulations are taken into account.

■ **Figure 11.4**
Legal requirements for the Port Fairy Folk Festival

Insurance:
(a) Public liability insurance of $5 000 000. Excess $500. Property damage claims only.
(b) Personal accident insurance covering 550 volunteers
    $600 — weekly benefits
    $60 000 — death benefits
The policy also covers the committee, charitable and school organisations that provide the food stalls.
(c) Occasionally special insurance is taken out to cover tents with specific risks, for example the Circus Oz tent.
(d) Car parks are covered against damage to vehicles.
(e) Insurance against theft, fire and other damage to the equipment owned by the festival committee. Equipment includes storage sheds, staging, electrical equipment, tables and chairs.

Legislation to be aware of:
1. Liquor licensing for alcohol.
2. Health — food vans, smoking, toilets.
3. Victorian building regulations — tent construction, people in arena. Tent construction workers must be licensed.
4. Country Fire Authority — fire reels and hoses, extinguishers.
5. Security personnel are governed by a licence.
6. Police Act — vehicle access along streets, crowd control.
7. (a) Local Government Act — leasing of municipal property.
   (b) By-laws of the Moyne Shire Council — drinking alcohol in the streets, fence erection, signage, street closure, planning permits, craft stall permits.
8. Banking Act — control of finances.
9. Insurance legislation.
10. Residential tenancies and caravan parks legislation — accommodation of performers, ticket holders, and guests.
11. Associations Incorporation Act — governing the organising Committee.
12. General contract law — agreements with performers, printing, agreement with the Australasian Performing Rights Association (APRA).
13. Environmental Protection Authority (EPA) noise levels.

(**Source:** *Bruce Leishman, of Conlan and Leishman Pty Ltd, solicitors*)

Permits and licences allow special activities during an event such as the handling of food, pyrotechnics, sale of liquor and road closures. They can even cover the performances. The Australasian Performing Rights Association (APRA) issues licences for the performance of its members' works. APRA functions as a collection society, monitoring and collecting royalties on behalf of its members (music composers and their publishers). So when an event company decides to set fireworks to music, it is not just a matter of hiring a band.

Many regulations, permits and licences change with each local government area and State and new regulations and reinterpretations of the old rules are proclaimed regularly. For example, at the time of writing the complex regulations relating to workers' compensation are under review in NSW. Also, workers' compensation regulations are different in each State. The Public Halls Act is administered by local councils and often its interpretation will vary from council to council. Local councils are also responsible for issuing entertainment licences and open air permits for events. Even event accounting may need permits, and an event company must register a business name before opening an account at a bank.

This complex area needs the close attention of event management. Companies must undertake detailed research into all regulations affecting their event and should allocate time to deal with the results of that research. Government agencies can take a long time to respond to requests. Therefore it is imperative to begin early in seeking any permits and licences, and to factor delays and difficulties with obtaining them into the time frame of the event planning process.

EVENT PROFILE

Corroboree 2000 and risk management

Closing the Sydney Harbour Bridge for the fourth time in history for 250 000 people to walk in support of reconciliation required significant resources to reduce the risk to the public to an acceptable level. Representatives of affected stakeholders and government agencies met every four weeks for nine months leading up to the event to plan and coordinate their involvement. Identification and evaluation of the area's risk was a critical element of the planning process.

City Rail planned to manage North Sydney station as a one-way operation to account for the huge numbers they carried to the start of the walk. They implemented their contingency plan of unloading trains a station earlier at Milson's Point when North Sydney became overcrowded. Without this risk minimisation contingency, full trains could have arrived and been unable to unload onto the already full platform.

The Roads and Traffic Authority installed over five kilometres of barricades on the deck of the bridge to keep walkers clear of the train tracks, clear of unprotected areas open to the water hundreds of metres below, and clear of the emergency vehicle's access lane. The RTA also had to plan for motorists not attending the walk. The Harbour Tunnel toll was waived for the day to keep traffic flowing, and they erected over 2000 special event clearway signs and 35 variable message signs around the Sydney road network to minimise impact on the travelling public. This avoided frustrated motorists driving unsafely and causing additional public risk.

In five hours 250 000 citizens walked for reconciliation. A few people sprained their ankles and one of the ambulances became a de facto breast-feeding unit. Sound risk management ensured a smooth and safe event.

Warren Pearson, Arts and Events Manager
Australia Day Council of New South Wales

$\int$UMMARY

Event managers have a duty of care to all involved in an event. Any reasonably foreseen risks have to be eliminated or minimised. The process of doing this is central to a risk management strategy. Liability minimisation is part of this strategy. This includes identifying the ownership of the event, careful structuring of the event management, taking out insurance and adhering to all the rules and regulations pertaining to the event. Specific legal issues of concern to the event management team include contracting, trademarks and trade practices. Legal matters can be complex and differ from State to State. It is recommended that any event company seek legal advice when unsure of these matters.

Questions

1. List the areas covered by the contract between the event company and supplier of audiovisuals.

2. What are two methods of minimising liability?

3. Contrast the risks involved in staging an outdoor concert to those involved in producing an indoor food fair. What risk management strategy could be used to reduce or eliminate these risks?

4. What actions can be taken to reduce the cost of overall liability insurance? Should the event company be insured for patrons to be covered after they leave the event?

5. What licences and permits are needed for a street party?

The Shakespeare Festival
Australia

The Shakespeare Festival Australia began as a 12-day festival in April 1997, celebrating the works of William Shakespeare. It is presented by the Southern Highlands Institute for the Performing Arts, a non-profit, incorporated association formed to build a performing arts centre in the southern highlands district of New South Wales. This area has declining rural and manufacturing sectors, shrinking blue-collar industries and increasing youth unemployment. A thriving tourism industry will assist the area's economy.

Most of the information on which the committee based its decision to hold such a festival was sourced from the experience of Shakespeare festivals overseas, especially those held in the USA and Canada. The example of the Shakespeare Festival in Stratford, Ontario was considered especially relevant as it was held in a rural area like the southern highlands — scenically beautiful and about two hours drive from a large population centre. This festival grew from small beginnings in a tent in 1953 to a six-month-long festival with three theatres and a budget of millions of dollars. From the beginning, the Shakespeare Festival Australia was intended to develop into a major national festival like its Canadian predecessor.

The festival was developed with two goals: firstly, as a new arts event to highlight the need for a performance and educational centre and, secondly, to attract visitors to the region during autumn. We decided to hold the first festival to coincide with Shakespeare's birthday on 23 April.

School halls were used for indoor performances. Outdoor performances were held in public spaces and in the grounds of some of the larger hotels. Our limited budget prevented us from producing our own plays, so we brought in productions that had already had a season, or were currently in production. The festival involved the local community through a street parade. Local amateur theatre companies and film and music practitioners also participated. Funding came from cash sponsorship of events by local businesses, as well as in-kind sponsorship. We obtained significant amounts of media coverage, both locally and nationally, as the event captured the imagination of the public. The box office takings reflected this enthusiasm. Capacity audiences attended most events, except those with a high ticket price (which usually involved food).

In its second year the festival was expanded to a month-long event incorporating five weekends, and moved forward to commence in early March. Theatre companies from Victoria and Queensland, as well as Sydney and regional New South Wales, travelled to the highlands to participate. The program was expanded to include mid-week as well as weekend performances and a number of new elements were added.

Despite overall attendance and box office figures being up on the first year, the extra expenses involved in running a much bigger festival did not cover the costs. The earlier timing also clashed with the Sydney Gay and Lesbian Mardi Gras and the Adelaide Festival, which affected non-local media coverage and, surprisingly, the weather was generally too hot. However, the audience feedback was very positive.

Letters of agreement confirmed most of the planning and contractual arrangements for the festival. Two board members with expertise in the area handled all negotiations and agreements for the hire of equipment. All negotiations with performers began with telephone calls to assess their availability. Performance fees and travel and accommodation arrangements were discussed. Accommodation for the performers was arranged at one guesthouse. When agreement was reached with the performers, the performance fee, travel and living expenses, technical requirements and rehearsal facilities were confirmed in a letter of agreement. There was no common agreement document.

Formal contracts were drawn up between the festival and the ticketing agencies. These were standard agreement forms specifying such details as commission, performance dates, times and cancellation of shows. Similar arrangements were made with the supplier of merchandising. The contract covered details including sale or return, commission on sales and payment details.

The sponsorship committee sourced cash sponsorship, which was receipted and documented by the treasurer. In-kind sponsorship was generally agreed upon with a verbal agreement. The only government funding came from Tourism New South Wales. A contract between Tourism New South Wales and the festival was signed.

The event general manager and the local council were kept fully informed about all plans and arrangements. Permission was obtained from the Highway Patrol, the council's traffic manager and the traffic committee for the street closure. A supporting letter was obtained from the Bowral Chamber of Commerce indicating that there would be no opposition to the closure from traders.

The council also gave permission for the use of Corbett Gardens, a formal park in the centre of Bowral. The local Rotary Club, who also ran a food stall during the performances, supplied security during performances. Garbage collection and access to toilets that were normally locked at night were issues we had to consider when using the park as a performance venue.

Milton Park, a large country-style resort hotel, was also used as a site for events during the festival. No council permission was required to use this site as it came under existing usage guidelines. Milton Park donated the use of their outdoor amphitheatre and conference room. The festival provided a port-a-loo at the amphitheatre site. Milton Park arranged for the removal of garbage.

Bradman Museum Theatre is a licensed venue under the Public Halls Act and therefore had all of the facilities we required on site. A staff member was in attendance at every performance to provide security.

The most challenging venue was the Renwick Festival Centre. It is in a remote location, so a lot of signage was needed to direct patrons to the site. Using the

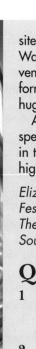

site involved negotiation between the Highlands Soccer Club and the New South Wales Department of School Education, who recently purchased the site. The venue is a poorly maintained multipurpose gymnasium. However, it was transformed with hired seating, a complete lighting rig, masses of black drapes and a huge stage built for the room.

Although we did not achieve all of our goals in the second year of the Shakespeare Festival Australia, we have learned invaluable lessons that will be applied in the following years until Shakespeare becomes synonymous with the southern highlands in the same way that country music is with Tamworth.

Elizabeth Rogers
Festival Director
The Shakespeare Festival Australia
Southern Highlands Institute for the Performing Arts, New South Wales

Questions

1 What characteristics of the southern highlands of New South Wales led to it being chosen as the location for the Shakespeare Festival Australia?

2 Draft an appropriate mission statement and key objectives for the festival.

3 What contracts and permissions were considered necessary by the organisers for the conduct of the festival? From what you know of the festival, do these measures seem adequate? If not, what other areas of the event might usefully have been covered by written agreements?

4 What lessons regarding the program and timing have been learned from the first two festivals, and how would you apply these lessons if you were organising the next festival?

5 Create a marketing plan for the festival designed to exploit its potential to attract tourists and maximise their length of stay and expenditure.

REFERENCES

Berlonghi (1990), *Special Event Risk Management Manual*, Bookmasters, Mansfield, Ohio.

Fewell, Mark 1995 (ed.), *Sports Law: A Practical Guide*, LBC Information Services, Sydney.

Freedman, H. & Smith, K. 1991, *Black Tie Optional*, Fund Raising Institute, Rockville, Maryland.

Geldard, E. & Sinclair, L. 1996, *The Sponsorship Manual*, The Sponsorship Unit, Olinda, Vic.

Goldblatt, J. 1997, *Special Events: Best Practices in Modern Event Management*, 2nd edn, Van Nostrand Reinhold, New York.

Neighbourhood Arts Unit, City of Melbourne 1991, *Community Festival Handbook*, Neighbourhood Arts Unit, City of Melbourne, Melbourne.

12
Information technology
and events

LEARNING OBJECTIVES

After studying this chapter, you should be able to:

■ understand the importance of information technology in the
event life cycle and to the event company

■ recognise the advantages and limitations of software in these event
management areas

■ realise the changing nature of the event environment and the
importance of technology

■ establish a draft information technology software/hardware
requirement list for events

■ understand and describe the use of the Internet in event
management

■ understand the basis of recently developed event management
software.

INTRODUCTION

This chapter first surveys the current use of information technology in special events and festivals. Event management is divided into the areas of event design, planning, marketing and implementation. The second section looks at the use of the World Wide Web to assist management. Finally, the method of Web-enabling an event is outlined.

CHANGE

Heraclitus said, 'You cannot step twice into the same river'. One of the certainties about the future of technology in special events and festivals is that it will change — the technology will change and so will the way events are managed and marketed. A number of commentators regard the current state of affairs as similar to the European Renaissance, a paradigm shift. Interestingly the event industry is not only subject to technological change, it is also being used as a harbinger and carrier of that change. Whether it is the release of a new software package or a retraining session for the staff of a company, it is the event manager who is called on to assist the process.

A snapshot of the state of technology and event management would show a spectrum of digital technology use. At one end of the spectrum is the event company that is just getting used to e-mail and thinking of putting up a Web site, while at the other end are companies that create, manage and promote only on-line events. In between are events that are managed by a mixture of digital and analogue — paper and screen. The spread of Internet literacy has produced a pressure for events to be up on the Web. Along with the 'magic' Web site go the high and perhaps unrealistic expectations of the client, sponsor and other stakeholders. Many event managers have regretted this decision after doing a post-event return on investment (ROI) study analysis.

A major variable in the strategic decisions made by the event stakeholder is the direction of this change. How will technology impact on the future of events? Will events become fully virtual? Will this result in a need for a 'real' experience? The event company in a highly competitive field has to ask if it has the competitive advantage by using its current software systems. Have we chosen Beta instead of VHS? Will the current systems we are using serve our future needs?

It is a basic premise that the computer is more than just a tool in event management. It can encompass so many aspects of the event, from planning to evaluation to scenario building to communication. It is all-pervasive and can redefine the event, the event management process and the event company.

This section is concerned with the business support provided by digital technology. So many of the functions of business have been changed by computer use that many of these functions will already be familiar to the reader. Each of the sections of the event life cycle are considered, from design to implementation. Often digital technology has crept into these areas as a requirement of the stakeholders such as the banks, suppliers or government. The event management field is realising that a comprehensive information technology (IT) plan is integral to the planning process and not just an afterthought. Without planning, any introduction of new software or hardware can be traumatic to the event staff and have a negative effect on the profitability of the event. Such a 'rejigging' of the business can take the focus away from the event to 'getting the new computer system working'. Once again, as has been emphasised throughout this text, planning is vital to event success. In particular, planning all the elements of management that can be planned allows the event management the freedom to focus on the success of the event.

■ Design

Event designing is a combination of form and function, aesthetics and practicality. It is more that just creating the event idea or theme and fitting in the various staging elements. It involves presenting the design to a client or sponsor. For the stakeholders the event has to 'work'. It also concerns the feasibility of the event and answering such questions as: Will this design work and are there alternatives? All the elements of event design are computer compatible. The World Wide Web, in particular, is a rich source of event ideas. Search engines on the Web can uncover a plethora of workable concepts. In addition, there are sites such as TRIZ, devoted to methods of creating new ideas.

The visual theme of the event, also called the 'look' of the event, lends itself to standardisation through digital technology. This includes the logo, signage, banners, decorations, uniforms and other event identification. By the use of templates all aspects of the management, such as event documentation, can be visually themed. This visual theme can then be digitally passed on to the subcontractors such as the site designer, printers, sign writers and publicists.

The layout of the site or venue can also be assisted by computer. A full CAD (computer aided design) suite may not be necessary. Some event management programs carry simple graphics program to help with site design and map creation.

Perhaps the most widespread area for computer technology has been in the presentation of the event design to the stakeholders. Graphically representing both the event idea and draft functionality through presentation software such as PowerPoint is an important role for digital technology. A visual presentation can give the client and other stakeholders a straightforward view of the event. Although not at the level of specialised presentation software, a Web browser such as Netscape can also be used as a presentation tool. The advantage of using a Web browser is that the presentation can be simply placed on the Web as well as used in the face-to-face office presentation. This is another aspect of the Web-enabled event outlined in the next section of this chapter.

Using some CAD software, the stakeholders can be presented with a 'three dimensional' (3D) view of the proposed event, called a 'virtual event'. Three dimensional visualisation with software can give the corporate client an idea of the set-up of a venue. It can include the venue set-up seen from various angles. Different design scenarios can be created on the computer to allow a choice of themes.

The practicality of the event ('Will this design work?') is generally communicated through a feasibility study. By the use of templates, spreadsheets and graphs the event variables, constraints, and parameters can be demonstrated. The basic three-choice concept in the feasibility study can be effectively represented though simple spreadsheet modelling and comparison tables (see www.epms.net for an in-depth look at event feasibility studies).

Such presentation software as PowerPoint can help to visualise the event and impart the excitement.

■ Planning

The most important aspect of computing to event management is the relational database. As discussed in the chapter on logistics, an event can be seen as a system of interrelated parts. A change in one area can reverberate through the event. It is essential that the management knows the results of any change or new information. In other words it enables the event manager to assess the relationship between event variables. The major variables are time, cost and event content. The latter is also called the scope, the event product or simply 'what's on'. Within the event, the relationship between each of these variables can be ascertained and linked to other event areas. Currently the simplest relational database is the spreadsheet. The data, such as finances, are entered into a field (or cell) and the relationship to other fields is created through linkages (or equations). Any new data, or changes to the existing data, result in a change in the other fields. The spreadsheet is one of the oldest software products and is used extensively for other business functions. This means that the spreadsheet is understood by most of the event stakeholders, in particular the client or sponsor. As pointed out by Neil Timmins (see the case study on p. 313), it was the easiest way to communicate the reports generated by the Primavera software program for the Sydney Olympics.

The scheduling side of event planning and control is often taken care of by the various project management software products. The advantages of these products are that they are readily available off the shelf and possibly already in use in other parts of the organisation. Many of the products are fully integrated into other software suites. For example, MS Project can import data from Word and Excel. The user interface is familiar to those who use Microsoft products. All project management software can produce reports, charts and graphs, and this information is a slave to the schedule. The software revolves around the work breakdown structure that can be delivered in outline or broken down into fine detail. An assessment of many of the commercially available products is found in the PMI publication, *Project Management Software Survey* (1999).

A major limitation of project management software is that it has been developed for the construction of a definite object such as a building or a piece of software. Many aspects of these projects do not correspond to event management. In particular the volatile environment of special event management does not translate well to this software. The linking of tasks in the event planning is also not as certain as is needed by the software. This can lead to the event management loosing focus, creating a linked schedule that does not correspond to the actual event.

The work of volunteers can be difficult to quantify as a definite resource. The amount of work that they will do can depend on what the project management profession calls 'soft' variables. In particular these soft variables include intangibles such as charismatic leadership and self-esteem.

Both spreadsheets and scheduling software can assist in the risk management and scenario building necessary for event management. Using the cash flow analysis ability of the spreadsheet can be a quick and easy way to create financial scenarios. These assist urgent decision optimisation and indicate any possible problems. The importance of the spreadsheet method to the decision process is explained in detail in Kirkwood (1997).

The two important features of the software — the relational database and scheduling — discussed so far in this chapter can be found in the one software package. The specialist event software packages are discussed in the last section of this chapter. The quick development in information technology and software development means that only a snapshot of the present situation can be presented.

■ Marketing

Almost every aspect of marketing, from researching needs analysis to designing a promotional leaflet, has been affected by digital technology. Market research can now be undertaken by e-mail and analysis by sophisticated computer generated algorithms. The first use of data collection in the USA census was collated by computer and used to identify target markets. For the correct collation of the raw data a model of the event attendee can be established. This rich data can be used in all the four Ps of marketing.

■ Implementation

With the correct software and staff skills, the computer can be used to track the progress of implementation of the plan. The promotion of the event, for example, can be created using scheduling software and the daily activity reports checked against the schedule. The ability of the software to generate reports is vital in the control process. The reports must be in a form that is legible to the event staff and volunteers and it must highlight the problem areas. The 'data smog' is a real risk with reports. Too much data can easily obscure important variations from the plan. Due to the changing nature of the event environment, clarity is an essential characteristic of all event reports.

Another important area of event implementation is the creation of accurate time-activity sheets. These are fundamental to large events. They indicate to the staff who is responsible for what and when it needs to be completed. Currently in project management software these task sheets are a standard output of the software. They are simply a mixture of the schedule and the database and are only as accurate as the quality of the input data. To assist in the process some project management software programs have a system of e-mail triggers. These are e-mail messages sent at a predetermined time to remind an individual of their task responsibility.

Valid reporting will only work, however, if the data are continually updated — hence the need for an information technology plan that is fully integrated into the event plan. Questions such as 'How often will the data be updated?', 'Who is responsible for this task?' and 'Is there a contingency plan for data loss?' need to be fully answered at the start of the information technology implementation plan.

EVENT PROFILE

The Sydney Festival and EventWorks partnership — the need for new software, FestivalWorks

Over a number of years, the Sydney Festival had tried to adapt various generic planning programs to our own particular scheduling requirements.

Festival planning and scheduling is distinct from that in any other industry, so we encountered great difficulty and enormous frustration trying to adapt our requirements to the parameters of existing programs that could not schedule and report as flexibly as we needed.

We reached the conclusion that if we wanted a program that could satisfy our scheduling requirements in totality, then we would have to design one ourselves. Consequently, in collaboration with two computer programmers over a period of about a year, we created what would eventually become FestivalWorks.

These were the things that we needed most in the program:

1. Simplicity
We wanted a system that replicated the thought processes that operate when creating a schedule. These were:

- date
- start time
- stop time
- activity
- location
- detail
- supplier
- event
- company
- crew
- people
- comments.

2. Data input all done on the one 'page'

Another important requisite was to be able to input and manipulate all information on a 'page' in front of us. This way you can think creatively and sequentially while working, rather than going back into different windows to change particular pieces of information.

3. Program event-based

Our other main requirement was that the program be 'event-based'. For example *Elektra: The Opera* would be the basis from which all the scheduling information for that production would come.

4. Reporting flexible

Within the apparent simplicity of the system we had very complex scheduling stipulations that required the program to have great reporting flexibility. We had to be able to track any activity or combination of activities that related to:

- a single event/all events
- a single artist/an entire company
- any venue/all venues.

In other words, we had to track the range of activities from the arrival of an artist or company in the country until their departure; for example, arrival, transfer, check in, media calls, rehearsals, performances, check out, and departure. Production activities relating to the event would also be incorporated: bump in/out, lighting, sound, dress rehearsals, opening performance and so on.

As an example, in our database we have assembled a list of about 165 venues and 120 different activities relating to all aspects of mounting an event, including all production, accommodation and travel, media and hospitality activities.

We may be working in 15 different rehearsal and performance venues across the city on a particular day, with companies arriving in the country, some leaving, VIP functions in the evening for certain festival staff members, and a TV media call which airs on the evening news.

Reports needed to be produced by selecting:

- a single activity in a date range (for example, a list of check ins at a particular hotel)
- all activities relating to an event/company/venue/supplier/carrier (for example, a bus company), or any specific combination of activities that may be required

As activity combinations are not predictable, flexibility in reporting is essential. For example, a particular artist comes to Australia, and is doing solo concerts as well as playing in an opera orchestra. The concerts are in three different venues. We needed to produce a schedule for that artist.

Alternatively, all activities related to a particular event can be reported on by simply choosing the event required.

(continued)

For venues, the schedule of activities programmed for the event to be performed would be listed.

A complete printout of all activities happening on a particular date, including all artist arrivals, production work in all venues, media calls, a list of functions and who is attending, must be easily reported to the festival director. The publicity manager would require a full list of media calls, the program manager needs to know all company and artist movements, and the operations manager needs to know all production activities in all venues.

Different people require different categories of information, but it all is inputted into the same schedule pulled up under the designated event header. This also means that the publicity department can read a schedule, and input media calls accordingly, and likewise with travel and accommodation. Each department within an organisation can input its own requirements, and the rest of the organisation can read it, but not adjust it.

5. Double bookings on resources/suppliers avoided

Avoiding double bookings on resources — for example, festival transport vehicles — was another of the motivations for designing our own scheduling program.

We also have a large list of suppliers. A pick up and delivery list for any of the suppliers across all the events is very useful, particularly when a number of people are scheduling separately within the organisation!

Our requirements were rather specific. It took a lot of work on our part and the programmers to eventually arrive at the current version of FestivalWorks, which incidentally is still evolving.

Annette Alderson
Production Manager, Sydney Festival

WEB-ENABLED EVENTS

A Web-enabled event is an event that incorporates the use of the Web throughout the event life cycle, from feasibility to the event shutdown. A number of factors have created the need for the Web-enabled event. The growth of the use of the Web and the features of the latest software have created both the need and the preconditions for Web-enabling.

When the World Wide Web originally came in use, many special events and festivals regarded a Web site in a similar way to an advertisement. However it was soon apparent that there was little inducement for the public to go to an event Web site, regardless of its 'bells and whistles'.

With the upgrading of software, event documents are almost Web-ready. Microsoft programs have a 'save as HTML' feature, for example. This means that the capabilities for Web-enabling are already easily accessed by the common software programs.

The combined result is that it is almost mandatory for an event to have a well-thought-out and targeted Web site. This does not mean that the event manager is burdened with another task, just as in every aspect of event management the manager does not have to be an expert in this area. However he or she does need to know the terms used and the possibilities. Figure 12.1 shows a few questions that the event manager must consider when developing a Web page. All these questions need to be answered and placed into the brief given to the Web developer.

■ **Figure 12.1**
Web development considerations

- Is the content cleared with copyright, and relevant licences assigned?

- Who owns the computer code and is it transparent? That is, can another Web developer easily use this code — or will your event be always tied to the one developer?

- What is the schedule for development, upgrading and integrating with other event management functions? There is no point in having the site ready only on the day of the event.

- Will the Web page have a life after the event? Who will remove it?

- How will the Web page interface with other event documentation and management functions?

- What will the finished product be? Are there to be alpha, beta and gamma versions, and who will sign off? Will there be a need for staff training?

E V E N T   P R O F I L E

Setting up an event information Web site for Australia Day 2000 in Newcastle

The Australia Day events in Newcastle provided the event management with an opportunity to use the Web as a method of organising the event. The participants included 12 choirs from the Hunter Valley, two highland pipe bands, a military band, a scrap steel orchestra and a lantern parade. The aim was to compose and perform a specially commissioned music piece with all these participants. The Hunter Valley education department insisted on all schools being computer-literate. As most of the groups came from the schools the major hurdle of training and Web literacy had already been overcome. The popular Internet service provider (ISP) in the area, Hunterlink, had sponsored previous events. The event thus had both an ISP and a source of expertise.

The Web site was planned to contain all the information about the event of interest to the participants, attendees and suppliers. Part of this planning was to allow for the growth of the Web site and the addition of extra events. In this way it was a simple matter to add the Webcast to the page. This was mapped out as in figure 12.2. Although not all the participants were Web-literate, only a small percentage of the key participants were needed to use the Web to save time and communication costs. The costs of creating such a simple Web page structure were very small and its creation was an integral part of the whole event planning process. The Web page is shown in figure 12.3.

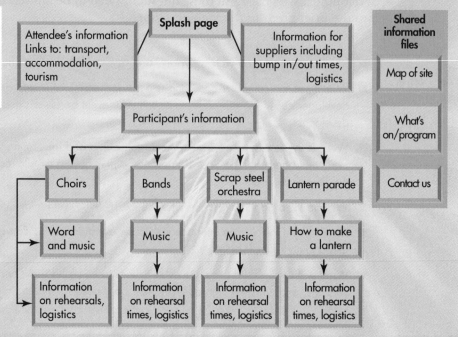

■ **Figure 12.2**
Map of Web site for Australia Day 2000 events in Newcastle

■ **Figure 12.3**
Web page for Australia Day 2000 events in Newcastle

■ Marketing

The initial euphoria for the Web as a major promotional tool quickly dissipated when it did not return the expected results. Although there are similarities to TV advertising, the Web is not a broadcast medium. The closest likeness is to a TV with 10 million channels. The aim of promotion moves from capturing the attention of the viewer to actually getting them to tune in at all, hence the move towards adding value to a visit to a Web site. This can be done by prizes, discounts, information, ease of registration or ticket buying. The latter two are common methods of both ticket distribution and information gathering.

Advertising on Web sites and cross-linking sites are also common methods of capturing attention. The possible success rate can be indicated through the number of visits and the length of the visit. These are measured as hits, impressions and click throughs. For actual advertising on the Web, a common measure is the click-through ratio: the number of click throughs divided by the number of impressions.

■ Information *distribution*

The fundamental use of the Web in today's configuration is for the distribution of information to participants, potential attendees, sponsors, organisers and suppliers. It is perhaps the most important, yet understudied, area of the Web-enabled event. The pervasiveness of the Web in advertising is an indication of the use of the Web and the extent of Web literacy. A volunteer may not know how to use a spreadsheet or use project management software, but it is more than likely that they have used the World Wide Web. This means that the major constraint of lack of training, as pointed out by 90 per cent of event managers at a recent conference, has been overcome without the need for training sessions. For example, if a client is not able to use email to receive a feasibility study created for a large event, the solution could be to place it on a Web site. The client, and all other stakeholders, can therefore access this information. It is important to realise that higher management, and this includes clients, may be as computer-illiterate as the staff and volunteers and much less likely to admit it.

Many suppliers have Web sites and are familiar with the process of seeking and downloading information. This means that the Web can be an efficient method of transferring information to the suppliers. Such essential information as the logistics schedule and the map are easily placed on the Web site. This transfers both the responsibility and some of the cost of obtaining event-relevant information to the supplier.

This section deals specifically with the World Wide Web, but a company's internal 'web' or intranet is often used to distribute event information. Corporations with an extensive intranet, such as IBM, often use it to distribute information about upcoming events. Another use is for the distribution of the event manual within international event management companies.

■ Information *gathering*

The Web is a very useful tool for researching an event. As an inducement to visit their site, suppliers are increasingly offering real information. Initially many of the sites were just promotion sites or 'brochureware'. The viewer was paying to be the recipient of biased information. The more successful sites incorporate as much information about their products as possible. Quite a few sites have tips that event managers and information users need to know if they are to get the most out of using the service. It is now possible for venue Web sites to include a map of the venue together with photographs. Caterers can now include menu selections and tips on catering. Some of the staging and lighting companies include a complete 'how to' to assist planners to design their event. With the development of Java scripts it will not be long before the user can set up a virtual event on the Web site and have it assessed by the suppliers.

Other research over the Web can include
- weather conditions
- other events of a similar nature
- risk management standards
- rules and regulations
- traffic conditions.

Many of the funding bodies now allow applications over the Web.

One of the most common areas of Web use is in conference and exhibition registration. Many of the event software packages mentioned in this chapter have this capability.

■ Communication

With the notable exception of e-mail, the various communication capabilities that may be assessed on the Web (for example, Internet relay chat) are only now becoming apparent.

E-mail
E-mail is, of course, almost taken for granted now as it is so essential to event management communication. It is important because:
- costs are minimal and integrated into the general event administration costs
- it provides a single protocol for communication which can be in point form and succinct
- it is 'threaded' so that all correspondence can be easily traced
- it is integrated with all other aspects of event management and, in particular, event documentation
- there is little or no training necessary as so many people are familiar with it
- distance is not a problem
- graphic, text or sound files can be transferred simply.

Internet relay chat

Internet relay chat (IRC), or just 'chat', is only just starting to be used in event management. The ICQ ('I seek you') software, with its user number, like a telephone number, is occasionally used to assist event management. In these situations meetings can be held without the costs of telephone conferencing and with a record of the proceedings as they occur. Conferencing over the Internet, with its capabilities of whiteboards and images, can be used. This shrinkage of distance is important to places like Australia as a virtual event team can be created, no matter how large the geographical spread. The IRC can also be used as a promotional tool for the event. If there are any stars at the event they may be available for a chat over the Internet. The time for this can be advertised and used to help promote the event.

Other communication groups

Other communication groups include newsgroups, lists and Web rings. There are a number of event management lists on the Web. Currently they are mainly concerned with the study of events rather than the practice of event management. All these are in their infancy compared to other management disciplines such as civil engineering project management. They seem to be following the same path, however. In civil engineering the project portal is the latest development. This is a Web site that acts as a virtual terminal to a server computer. All the software resides on the server's computer and the company rents time and use of this software. This means that, rather than buying specialised or off-the-shelf software package, with the expense of training and possible new equipment, the project manager rents the software and pays for the access time. As many aspects of the event industry seem to be following closely other project-based industries, this will probably be the next direction.

■ Webcast

Sending images and sound live over the Web is an ideal way to promote an event and contact a completely new audience. However, just as the Web is not a television, at this point in time the Internet is not a broadcast medium. It is 'narrowcasting' in the true sense of the word. The number of viewers who can be reached by any material sent over the Internet is restricted by the bandwidth. The bandwidth is a measure of the amount of data that can be transmitted in a given period of time.

The 'eventcam' is another method of information distribution. In some cases a correctly placed camera can give the suppliers, attendees and participants a real-time knowledge of the event. These Webcams are used extensively around the world and are carefully placed to give Web users a particular view. The most common are the surf and ski cams, as they target the right audience. An eventcam can show the traffic conditions, the type of people at the event and the weather.

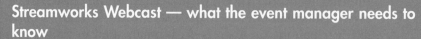

Streamworks Webcast — what the event manager needs to know

Webcasting, or Netcasting as it is sometimes known, is the process of transmitting your event as a video file over the Web. It can be viewed by many thousands of people over the Internet anywhere in the world for a fraction of the cost of using satellite technology. The types of function using Webcasting include awards nights, annual general meetings, parades, product launches, company announcements, even big, high-society weddings.

When going to a Webcasting supplier you will need to give them particular details so that they can give you a cost estimate. These are:
- When is the event?
- Where is the event?
- Are there existing ISDN or higher-speed telephone lines that can be used to send the signal off the site to the transmission servers?
- Does your client have a budget in mind?

This last question is important. Some Webcasts can be done cheaply for $2000 to $3000 dollars and some for as much as $50 000, depending on what is wanted. An average cost for a three-camera Webcast with a broadcast standard tape archive of the event is around $10 000 (May 2000, pre-GST). You get a number of extras for this kind of budget, but this is too complex to go into here.

There are also a number of questions you should ask your Webcasting supplier:
- Is all their equipment broadcast standard? It should be, as you should start with the highest grade picture possible, although you are going to a small screen on some computers. In addition, the client will very often require a tape copy of the event and broadcast standard is the minimum standard you should aim for.
- Does your supplier Webcast in all the Webcast formats? This will keep your options, and those of your client, open.
- Are the partners with all the propagated networks? This will give viewers, and therefore your client, the highest rate of transmission.

Mark Muggeridge
Head of Production, Streamworks

Due to its narrow bandwidth requirements, audio Webcasting is more common than the full Webcast. The technology required by both the client (user/viewer) and the server is well within the normal event budget. Most of the sound equipment will already be used by the event and it may be just a matter of taking a sound output cable (a 'line') from the audio desk. This is fed into a computer with the capabilities of digitising the sound and uploading the information to a Web site. If this is done in 'real-time' (i.e.

instantaneously), then it is called audiostreaming. The 'listener' can find the right Web site and, assuming they have compatible equipment, they can listen to the audiocast of the event. It is much cheaper and easier to upload the audio file at a later time. The file can be accessed after the event, rather than being simultaneous with the event. However, this misses the 'wow' of an audiocast and its promotional possibilities.

EVENT PROFILE

Festival of the Southern Ocean

Research is probably the most common use for the Web for our festival. For example, someone working on the Sunset Ritual just walked into the office and asked if I could help him find a copy of the South African flag on the Internet. It took about five minutes to find it. He has what he needs. In the last year, I have used it countless times for things like:

- downloading grant application forms
- downloading other people's and organisations' strategic plans and guiding principles so we can have some help creating our own
- networking with other arts workers for help with specific and general arts-related problems.

In addition, our Web site helps us promote the festival and this year we have had a lot of enquiries through this avenue.

Another aspect of digital technology is our use of the digital camera. We take pictures of events as they happen and this enables us to get images to newspapers very quickly. We have had a couple of pictures in major metropolitan papers in the lead up to this festival as a result, plus many in regional papers. During the festival, the digital camera allows us to get a press release and photo out virtually 'as it happens'. The Web site enables us to deal with incoming enquiries more easily. We suggest people look up our program on the Web rather than receiving information in the post, which is expensive for us. E-mail also reduces phone costs and paper costs.

Lindy Bartholomew
Festival Administrator

IMPLEMENTING A SYSTEM

With the pervasiveness of digital technology we are not so much introducing a system as changing the current system. Moore's law, that microchip density and therefore computing power will double every 18 months, leads to a reticence for change as there may be a better system coming out soon and the current one will be cheaper. This is a risk that has to be considered. However, introducing new hardware and software can take the focus away from the management of the event. There has to be a certain amount of good guesswork as to what the event may require and whether the current software and hardware can service those requirements.

■ Hardware *considerations*

The first task before any implementation is to know exactly what resources are already owned by the event organisation. In particular, a list of the hardware and its capabilities can be compiled. This hardware audit needs to include the possibility of upgrading, rather than replacing the whole or parts of the present system. As the hardware needs to service the requirements of the event, the scope of the event would be used to measure the requirements and matched to the hardware. This process is illustrated in figure 12.4. For example, if part of the scope of work is promoting the event to the press, then a scanner is probably necessary.

■ **Figure 12.4**
Web
implementation
plan

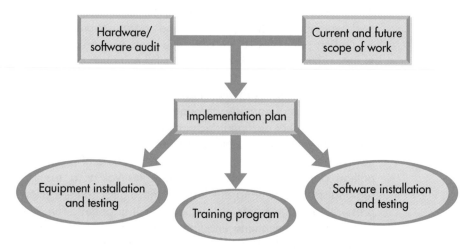

From a hardware audit and the scope of work, a list of new hardware requirements can be compiled. The new hardware should be assessed according to:

- its ability to meet the technical specifications of the proposed event software
- its compatibility with current software and hardware
- the need for staff training
- its ability to upgrade easily
- its compatibility to current service contracts
- the agreement with the event sponsors
- its adaptability to the growth of the event, increasing use and the expansion of work
- its ability to survive the rigours of intense use in less then perfect conditions.

The work required by a piece of equipment in use during the event life cycle varies from being idle for long periods to sudden intense use. A printer that carefully produces perfect documents inside the airconditioned showroom may not last long on a crate in an on-site tent. It is during these periods of intense activity that the event management requires a perfectly functioning piece of equipment. Other issues for consideration are whether the equipment needs to be portable, and if it needs to be compatible with on-site equipment.

A software audit should be completed at the same time as the hardware audit. The software requirements of the special event will determine a number of the hardware characteristics, in particular the size of the memory required and the type of processor. If any of the necessary programs are memory intensive (such as graphics for mapping and promotion), this can be a considerable cost. It is also necessary to determine whether the hardware and software needs to interface with any event staging and production equipment such as audiovisual equipment, scoring equipment and on-site ticketing.

■ Integration

Once the suitable software and hardware have been identified, the next decision is the method of integrating the new system with the current management practice. There are three ways to do this:

1. **Test:** Run the new system, or a smaller version of it, on one aspect of the event as a test. A good example of this is the test events for the Sydney Olympics. These also act as tests for the IT systems for planning, controlling and staging. The complete system can then be phased in gradually. The risk associated with this is the confusion of using two different systems and possible compatibility problems.
2. **Parallel:** Run the system in parallel with the existing computer system. This decision is a trade-off between the advantages of testing and comparing the system against the time and resources necessary to do it.
3. **Complete replacement:** The current system is dropped and the new one implemented. The risk of failure is higher and is traded against the savings made when running just one system.

Compatibility with existing systems is perhaps a primary consideration for software/hardware integration. The obvious differences between Apple and IBM are compounded with Unix and Linux. A clash of micro-programs such as printer drivers can cause tasks to suddenly arrive on the critical path. The well-thought-out event schedule can easily be destroyed by software incompatibility. These types of problems are not often mentioned by the software vendors, or written on the software box.

The software licence has to be considered. It may be licensed to only a few users. This may be suitable for the early stages of event planning but, as the event grows, will the licence cover extra users? The lesson to be learned here is that an IT system is not just an assistant to event management — it is an integral and capricious part of management and requires continuous checks, controls, reports and evaluation.

■ Limitations

There are basic risks associated with using IT in event planning and control, apart from the all too common crashing of the system. Assessing these risks is part of the event management's role.

As the results of an IT system should be tangible, a return on investment analysis needs to be performed. However, it is difficult to do this in an ever-changing environment. Many of these types of decisions require an extrapolation based on past conditions. Unfortunately the decision about the necessary software and hardware will require an amount of guesswork. A number of events are organised without the use of any IT — just with paper and commitment.

The one salient fact that comes from all the literature on IT systems implementation is that the company has to change its current system to fit in with the new one before it arrives. This preparation needs to permeate all aspects of the event management. In particular it will affect the reporting procedures and event documentation. Staff will have to be trained in the new system and this has to fit in with their current responsibilities. The retraining can be a major item in the ultimate cost of the system.

One method of limiting the risks involved is to provide for a backup system. This is an unavoidable cost. Information loss through crashing, theft, mistakes, incompatibility or viruses can disable the event management. This is most likely to happen during the time of intense activity. It is the time when the system is being used to full capacity, new features are being accessed and new combinations of software are in use.

There can be no doubt that IT influences the method of event management. It can refocus the event itself. For example the Web and e-mail when embraced by the event management can blind it to the fact that there are still many people — including senior management — who get their information through the traditional channels. Computer jargon can stifle communication within the event organisation. It can also change the power relationships as those who are more comfortable with systems thinking will have the intellectual keys to the event organisation.

Another limitation of IT is the security issue. Securing the information and yet making it easily available to the right people is a problem for all computer systems. Password access and other methods of limiting access can restrain the free flow of necessary information. The security that may be essential during the bidding process at the beginning of the event life cycle may become a restriction while the event is being planned.

In this section a number of event software packages are briefly outlined. They are chosen because they are the most popular at the time of writing.

■ Events *Perfect*

Events Perfect is particularly suitable for the conference and meeting industry. It is a relational database that allows users to track and record each individual event booking and all related details within a user-friendly interface. Events Perfect also has seamless integration with Microsoft Office programs, including Visio for CAD floor plans and room layouts.

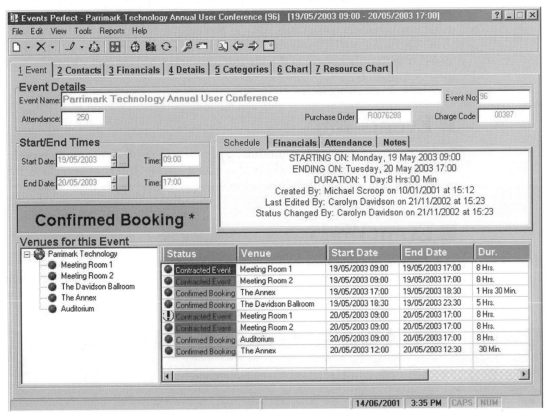

■ **Figure 12.5** *Events Perfect screen page*

■ Event Business *Management System*

Event Business Management System is a 20-piece modular system including sales and marketing, event management, operations management and attendance management. This modular management system is used on both corporate and public events. The company has developed an international focus with user groups worldwide.

■ Summit *Event Management*

Summit Event Management is primarily for the exhibitions and meetings industry. It is a relational database with registration, name badges and programming as central features. There is also an inexpensive, 'light' edition.

■ MS *Project*

MS Project is perhaps the most common piece of project software used in the event management industry. Unlike the other, more comprehensive event management programs, this is basically a function scheduling software. This means that individual delegates or exhibitors are not the prime focus. It is mainly concerned with the allocation of resources to tasks and their completion.

■ Events *Pro*

Events Pro from Amlink is a modular approach to conference management and associated exhibition. Events Pro has a strong Internet interface for registering and gathering information.

■ Event*Works*

EventWorks was developed in consultation with the Sydney Festival. It is a scheduling software that can handle a variety of stages and venues and their necessary resources.

EVENT PROFILE

The future from USI

The following is an excerpt from a recent Ungerboeck Systems Inc. (USI) technology forecast:

1. While the Internet has now been around (as far as event management is concerned) for at about five years, its use will continue to be substantially expanded in transaction processes such as event bookings, exhibit booth sales, service orders, registration, ticketing, billing, etc.

2. Core software components such as database activities will be pulled back from the desktop computers into server machines. Two powerful but fundamentally unrelated forces ('thin-client' networks or 'server-centric' network architecture) are pulling in that direction:
   (a) Internet software relies primarily on server resources and utilises client machines only for communications and presentation
   (b) cost management: 'thin-client' computing helps manage the capital cost of hardware rejuvenation, reduces the labour cost of network administration, and facilitates the increased use of low-cost portable computing devices.
3. The trend towards focusing 'thin clients' on communications and presentation will be amplified with speech recognition; this, in turn, will utilise the processing cycles vacated by 'server-centric' applications. Speech recognition will also drive another wave of global productivity boosts.
4. Hand-held computers and wireless communications will be used by mobile workers to view messages, work orders, floor plans, pictures, inventory status, and so on, and to report work order completion, time and attendance, and so on.
5. There will be tighter interface of management systems and process systems; for example, access security; time and attendance; heating, ventilation and airconditioning; escalators; turnstiles and so on. Perhaps, handwriting recognition may be part of the action — but only temporarily — until fully eclipsed by the inherently more productive concept of continuous speech recognition.

$\mathcal{S}$UMMARY

As in every facet of modern management, IT is becoming an imperative and at the same time it is changing the management process itself. Currently event management is benefiting from this. The very nature of the event industry, with its periods of quiet and then intense activity, creates an ability to take up new technology very quickly. The use of technology in the event gives the event manager a hands-on experience with digital technology. This use of IT has to be planned as much as any other aspect of management. In particular the event management has to plan for change. The major change has been the growth of the World Wide Web. Event management can benefit from this but it needs to be done in an all-encompassing way. The Web is not just an addition to the marketing and communication mix. The event needs to be Web-enabled.

Questions

1 Choose an event from the list below and map out a draft event management information system:
- Mining equipment exhibition
- Regional wine and food festival
- A large rock concert.

2 What techniques could an event manager use to successfully implement a new software system for the event company?

3 Design — on paper or in HTML — a Web site for the events in question 1. Could each of these events use the same template? How would you attract people to the site?

4 How can the Web be used in regional Australia to assist event management in remote regions? What are the preconditions and the constraints?

5 Choose a particular event and construct an information technology assessment grid or matrix. The column headings could be the areas of event management and the row headings could be software functions.

Project managing
The Dream

On the GamesForce 2000 T-shirts adorning the (debatably) more fashionable staff buzzing around Sydney 2000 headquarters was the slogan 'Delivering The Dream'.

The successful delivery of this dream (the Olympic and Paralympic Games) to the customers and project stakeholders such as the competing athletes, the IOC, NOCs, spectators, media and the great Australian public totally depends on the seamless integration and project management of the 'big five' Sydney 2000 organisations: SOCOG (including sponsors and service providers), SOBO, OCA, ORTA and OSCC.

SOCOG's Project Management division had the central responsibility for understanding, scoping, integrating, recording and reporting the sub-projects of all four key organisations to the SOCOG Board and executive sub-groups, plus the IOC Executive Board and IOC Coordination Commission. In essence they had the responsibility for coordinating the master project — project managing The Dream.

Getting across the Games

Understanding the relationships (or dependencies) between organisational sub-projects demands a willingness to work away from your desk; this is essential for building relationships. Initially, many of the venue teams with which I interacted showed a reluctance to share key information and project direction, naturally triggering my suspicion. I felt like a private detective hired by SOCOG to report venue management shortfalls and critical issues (which was not wholly true!) and not their achievements.

The difficulty in translating micro-level detail into macro-level reporting is in maintaining the meaningfulness of summarised information, without misrepresenting the accountable party. For instance, a summary bar may roll up 20 activities — 15 may have been achieved by the deadline, and five may be either pending completion or require an extension of time. The summarised status on completion is 75% — in work management terms it may be 99.9% — with five signatures required from a single source on five outstanding documents!

It became increasingly important to maintain a regular presence within the venue teams — to be proactive, but not too obtrusive. The key to gaining trust was to provide a range of services which benefited the venue teams (e.g. providing user-defined reports, chasing problematic program areas on their behalf, sharing information) — in essence, becoming a part-time extension of their team.

To give you an understanding of the complexity of the SOCOG project management task, you only have to look at the key statistics pertaining to SOCOG's organisational breakdown structure, which are listed on the next page.

- Six 'groups', e.g. Games Coordination
- 19 'divisions', e.g. Project Management and Special Tasks
- 84 'programs', e.g. Project Management
- 30 competition venues
- major non-competition venues — MPC, IBC, OLC, HAAC, UDAC
- three villages — Olympic, Media and Technical Officials
- training venues, hotels, arts festivals, and so on
- a Games-time workforce of 110 000 (paid, volunteers and contractors).

The sheer size of the multi-organisational Sydney 2000 with its multiple projects and multiple dependencies made managing and reporting the status of the master project at varying (hierarchical) levels extremely challenging.

Thoughts into action

There is no blueprint for the Olympic Games (as for many other unique events) and although two years ago when I joined SOCOG we had on board many people who had experienced the highs and lows of Olympic Games, World Cups and other large events, the need to speed up the 'conceptual' phase and turn thoughts into structured directives and future actions became the immediate objective.

Working hand-in-hand with operational integration program area project management, the concept of the 'Games coordination time line' was devised to communicate the importance of project managing the events while continually focusing Sydney 2000 on the delivery of the two final stages of the Games project delivery.

The strategy behind the two-stage approach was to bring the Games closer in the minds of the organisation ('only two stages to go!') and make the achievement of these stages more tangible to the responsible delivering parties.

The two stages of the Games coordination time line can be seen in table 12.1.

■ Table 12.1
The two stages of the Games coordination time line

STAGE	NAME	DATES	FOCUS
One	Venue project plan	01-01-99– 31-01-00	'How we're going to get there', off-site activity planning, documentation and approvals
Two	Day-by-day plan	01-08-00– 31-11-00	'What we're going to do when we get there', on-site activity installation, training, rehearsal, operation space-specific — CPA

'Venuisation' — building the team

The promotion of the Games coordination time line was strategically launched in line with Sydney 2000's arguably most important organisational restructuring. This organisational metamorphosis was referred to as *venuisation*.

Venuisation in basic terms is the shift of organisational focus from program-based delivery to venue-based delivery. The venue structure was created, multi-organisational venue teams began to develop, and Sydney 2000 organisations began to interact with each other on a day-to-day, face-to-face basis in a singular office environment.

Venuisation immediately began to improve communications between formerly remote organisations and instil an empathy in each organisation's individual agenda, an empathy which was previously either unrecognised or in some cases not acknowledged.

Project managing the event managers

In my humble and biased opinion SOCOG recruited well. The knowledge, professionalism and dedication of the Games work force was quite astounding.

However, in many organisations positive personal attributes do not always guarantee the possession of project management focus and skills. For example, a good event operations manager may not necessarily make a good event project manager.

The key management issues SOCOG project management had to successfully overcome with the implementation of the Games coordination time line are briefly outlined in table 12.2.

■ **Table 12.2** *Key management issues*

ISSUE	DEFINITION	SOLUTION	OUTCOME
Technofear	Fear of the autonomous use of SOCOG's adopted project management software — Primavera P3	Utilisation of a spreadsheet approach — deemed more user-friendly. Facilitated by P3's e-mail friendly post office system. Centrally managed by SOCOG project management.	Excellent response record to deadlines imposed by the monthly project management cycle. Clarity and ownership of information. On-line ownership and updates.
Empathy	Lack of understanding of the dependencies inherent in the delivery of the venue-based project	Pilot project developed before global release — evolution of the 'pilot' communicated to the venue teams	Consistency in information reported: – level of content – activity descriptions – project structure
Multiple definitions	Key words and project phases meant different things to different people	Joint OCA & SOCOG definitions of overlay, logistics and operations phases developed by project management/ OCA, adopted by Sydney 2000 organisations	Clear and global understanding of delivery phases, dependencies and project documentation, improved understanding of project management principles.
Adoption	Lack of/fear of ownership of the plan — fear of incriminations through transparency and subsequent elevation of information	Venue readiness meetings organised on a monthly basis as part of the project management cycle — chaired by the venue manager — plan owned by the team	Venue team ownership of information

Another 'positive' problem SOCOG project management had to overcome in establishing the Games coordination time line was Sydney 2000's focus on test events. Although a distraction from developing the plans, the lessons learnt and the essential team building gained through working on these high-profile, international standard events added a greater integrity to the information being reported for the Games.

Managing the software

SOCOG consciously adopted Primavera P3 software as its primary project management tool for controlling the delivery of the Olympic and Paralympic Games. P3 is a high-end software application which is more than capable of managing multiple projects with multi-level sub-projects. By comparison with its off-the-shelf competitors it has an advanced suite of standard functions, including EVR (earned value report), user-defined reporting, post office and remote data entry.

For an experienced project manager this tool has the flexibility and 'grunt' to generate scenarios and reports reliably and speedily. For example, SOCOG has extracted information from the core day-by-day project plan to generate the logistics 'bump in' and the site management 'overlay transition' schedules, setting the parameters for program area task-level activity.

In my opinion, another plus for P3 is the fact that it is a code-driven application, which encourages the project manager to scope the project and sub-projects prior to developing the plan. The work breakdown structure becomes the framework and control mechanism for the project (see table 12.3).

■ Table 12.3
The Games work breakdown structure

LEVEL	CODE-FIELD	DESCRIPTION
1	Master project (1)	The Games coordination time line
2	Project (2)	Venue project plan and day-by-day plan
3	Event (2)	The Olympic Games and the Paralympic Games
4	Precinct (4)	Geographical areas, e.g. Sydney West
5	Venue (30)	Specifi venues allocated to precincts, e.g. Sydney International Equestrian Centre, Sydney West
6	Space (multiple)	Specific (predominantly) room locations within the venue
7	Cluster (multiple)	Logistical delivery and resupply area within the venue — cluster of spaces
8	Activity/task	Action description
9	Responsibility	Notification of who is delivering the action and who is receiving the action
10	Reporting	Activities tagged to user-defined reports

The drawbacks for P3 as an event project management tool are few, as long as the event manager understands the software and project management principles that drive the creation of the work breakdown structure coding structure and interdependencies.

For medium level projects P3 might be considered a bit expensive (about $7000 off the shelf), but if you believe Primavera is the way to go there is an offspring of the parent product called Suretrak which has most of the 'whistles and bells' without the sting in the pocket.

You do not have to manage all aspects of a project or multiple projects through a single software application. SOCOG project management did not fully utilise the P3 suite. For instance, cost planning and analysis and resource levelling is owned by the venue manager but controlled via a quantity surveyor/finance manager and venue staffing manager respectively. The quantity surveyor uses specially developed in house software, and the venue staffing manager uses an off-the-shelf spreadsheet package.

Project managing a 'medium-size' event

Many of the principles discussed in this paper can be applied to a medium-sized event. Whatever the scope and budget of your project I would encourage you to do the following:

- Adopt a two stage (off-site and on-site) focus.
- Project manage space-specific, on-site activities using CPA.
- Utilise mid-range PM software, such as Primavera Suretrak or MS Project.
- Be proactive — work away from your desk.
- Regular PCGs are essential — the key players are the event manager, quantity surveyor/finance/commercial manager, architect and local government agencies.
- Establish common project terminology.
- Develop your deployment and recruitment plans early — evolve the plan.
- Use the project plan in a positive way, highlight achievements and incorporate key performance indicators.
- If inexperienced or constrained by time, utilise the services of an experienced project management consultant to set up and administer the project.

Neil Timmins
Manager, Programming & Planning
Sydney Olympic Park Common Domain

Questions

1 Identify the key management issues in these events. Define the issues, provide a solution and describe the outcome for each of the events:
   (a) an Australian overseas trade exhibition in the Philippines, including a festival of Australian culture.
   (b) an international agricultural exhibition in Brisbane
   (c) Pan-Indian Ocean Music Festival in Kalgoorlie
   (d) world trade conference in Melbourne.

2 Construct a lexicon of event terms that may cause confusion at events. This would include terms such as bump in, shut down, set up and staging.

3 Why did the Olympics organisation structure change from program-based to venue-based? Was there an alternative way to organise the Olympics?

4 Why did the author use the term 'autonomous' in describing the fear of software?

5 Compare the use of software by the Sydney Festival and the Sydney Olympics. Why didn't the Olympics use the program set up by the Sydney Festival?

6 Discuss the constraints of webcasting the Olympics. Some of these will be technical, political and financial.

FURTHER READING

Collins T. 1998, *Crash: Learning from the World's Worst Computer Disasters*, Simon & Schuster, London.

Cooper A. 1999, *The Inmates are Running the Asylum*, Macmillan Computer Publishing, Indiana.

Kirkwood C. 1997, *Strategic Decision Making: Multiobjective Decision Analysis with Spreadsheets*, Duxbury Press, New York.

Project Management Institute, 1999, *Project Management Software Survey*, Project Management Institute, Pennsylvania.

PART 4

EVENT
COORDINATION

This final part looks at the practical implementation of the event. It examines the logistics of the flow of people, supplies and information on site, and at the staging process which is at the heart of events. It also examines the evaluation and reporting process so vital in gauging and communicating the success of the event, and the vital feedback process that facilitates the continuous improvement of events.

CHAPTER 13

13 Logistics

LEARNING OBJECTIVES

After studying this chapter, you should be able to:

- define logistics management and describe its evolution

- understand the concept of logistics management and its place in event management

- construct a logistics plan for the supply of customers, event products and event facilities

- use event logistics techniques and tools.

INTRODUCTION

This chapter adapts the science of business and military logistics to events. The management of an event is divided into supply, setting up and running the event on site, and the shutdown process of the event. Communication, flow and supply are the three elements of event logistics treated in this chapter. The process and terms of project management are introduced. Various check lists are outlined which can assist in the management of event logistics.

WHAT IS LOGISTICS?

'One of the hardest tasks, for logisticians and nonlogisticians alike, is to look at a list and spot what's not there' (Pagonis 1992, p. 73).

Placing the word 'logistics' into its historical context provides an understanding of its use in present event management. Logistics stems from the Greek word *logistikos*, 'skilled in calculating'. The ancient Romans used the term for the administration of their armies. The term evolved to refer to the practical art of the relocation of armies. Given the complexity of modern warfare, logistics became a science that included speed of operations, communications and maintenance of the armed forces. After World War II, modern businesses applied the experience and theory of logistics as they faced similar problems with transport and supply to those faced by the military.

The efficient movement of products has become a specialised study in the management discipline. Within large companies, especially international companies, a section can be devoted to coordinating the logistics requirements of each department. Logistics has become a discipline in its own right. This has led to consolidation into a separate independent function in companies, often called integrated logistics management. Coyle, Bardi and Langley (1988) describe logistics as the planning, implementing and control of the flow and storage of products and their related information from production to the point of consumption, according to consumer requirements.

The value of a company's product can be improved by the efficient coordination of logistics in the company. Gilmour (1993) argues that, due to the special conditions and widespread distribution of customers, services and products in Australia, logistics takes on an importance not found in many other countries. He emphasises that the logistic practices developed in the USA and Europe are not good enough for Australian conditions and, to be competitive in world markets, Australia needs to pay attention to overcoming the disadvantages of vast geographic distances.

For a complete understanding of event logistics, this chapter is divided into sections dealing with the tasks of event logistics and the role of the logistics manager.

The various elements of event logistics can be organised into the logistics system shown in figure 13.1. This system is used to organise the logistic elements of an event.

Whereas most logistics theory concerns the supply of products to customers, event logistics includes the efficient supply of the customer to the product, and the supply of facilities to and from the event site. In this sense, it has more in common with military logistics than modern business logistics. Business logistics is an ongoing activity and is part of the continual management of a company. Military and event logistics often concern a specific project or campaign rather than continuing management. There is a defined preparation, lead up, execution and shutdown. As well, issues such as inventory control and warehousing that are the basis of business logistics are not as important to a one-off event.

■ **Figure 13.1**
Elements of the logistics system

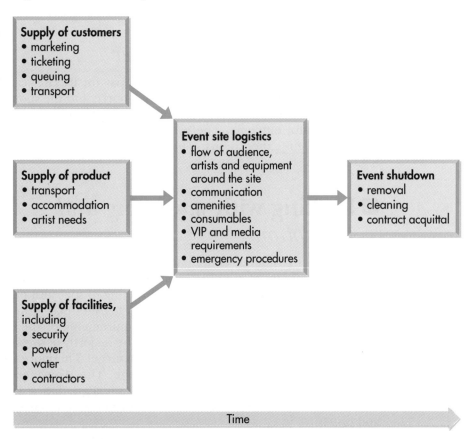

Supply of customers
• marketing
• ticketing
• queuing
• transport

Supply of product
• transport
• accommodation
• artist needs

Supply of facilities,
including
• security
• power
• water
• contractors

Event site logistics
• flow of audience, artists and equipment around the site
• communication
• amenities
• consumables
• VIP and media requirements
• emergency procedures

Event shutdown
• removal
• cleaning
• contract acquittal

Time

The areas of importance to event logistics can be categorised as:
• *Supply*: this is divided into the three areas of customer, product and facilities. Supply also includes the procurement of the goods and services.

- *Transport*: in Australia, as pointed out by Gilmour (1993), the transport of these goods and services can be a major cost to an event and requires special consideration.
- *Linking*: logistics is part of the overall planning of an event and is linked to all other areas. With large multi-venue events, the logistics become so complex that an operations or logistics manager is often appointed. The logistics manager functions as part of the overall network management structure outlined in this chapter.
- *Flow control*: this refers to the flow of products, services and customers during the event.
- *Information networks*: the efficient flow of information during the event is generally a result of efficient planning of the information network. This concept is expanded in the section about on-site logistics.

All these areas need to be considered when creating a logistics plan. Even for small events, such as a wedding or a small product launch, a logistics plan must be incorporated in the overall event plan. For these sorts of events, logistics comes under the title 'staging', which is described in chapter 14.

■ Supply of *the customer*

The customers of an event are those who pay for it. They can be the audience (concerts and festivals), spectators (sport), and the sponsors or clients (corporate events). The customers have expectations that have to be met for a successful outcome. The way the event is promoted will particularly influence their expectations. These expectations will include aspects of logistics.

■ Linking with *marketing and promotion*

The supply of customers is ultimately the responsibility of marketing activities. The numbers, geographical spread and expectations of the customers will affect the logistics planning. The targeting of specialist markets or widespread publicity of an event will require a logistics plan with very different priorities. For example, the transport requirements of the customers will vary according to the distance travelled. The majority of the audience of the Port Fairy Folk Festival drives from Melbourne. Therefore, vehicle access and parking is a priority at the festival site. The Womadelaide festival in Adelaide, with its nationwide publicity campaign, has a large interstate audience. This offers opportunities for special negotiations with the airlines and hotels.

If the publicity of an event is spread nationwide, the logistics will be different to a product launch that concerns only the staff and customers of a company. In this way the logistics are closely linked to the marketing of an event.

■ Ticketing

Ticketing is important to events whose primary income is from the entrance fee. Most corporate events, including office parties and product launches, and many public events are free. However, for other events, such as sports events, the extent of ticket sales can determine success or failure (Graham, Goldblatt & Delpy 1995). Ticket distribution is regarded as the first major decision in event logistics.

The pricing and printing of the tickets is generally not a logistics area. However, the distribution, collection and security are of concern. In Australia, tickets for events can be sold through various distributors like Ticketek for a fee, or they can be sold by mail. The Port Fairy Folk Festival sells out all its tickets at least four months in advance. Selling tickets at the gate gives rise to security problems in the collection, accounting and depositing of funds. The ticket collectors need training to deal with the public, as well as efficiently moving the public through the entrance. The honesty of the staff may also be a security concern. In larger venues, an admission loss-prevention plan is used to minimise the possibility of theft.

It is not unusual in Australia to sell tickets through retail outlets. For the Macquarie Marsh Project, an environmental concert in the wetlands of central New South Wales, the organiser used local tourism information centres as a distribution channel to sell tickets. Inventory control and cash receipts are two areas that require special attention when using retail outlets for ticket distribution. Numbering of the tickets and individual letters of agreement with each outlet are the most efficient methods of control. The letter of agreement would include the range of ticket numbers, level of the tickets (discount or full price) and the method of payment. Depending on the size of the event, the ticketing can be crucial to the event's success and take up a significant amount of the event director's time. Figure 13.2 is a check list of the logistics of ticketing an event.

An innovative method of ticketing for festivals is to use the hospital-style wristbands called crowd control bands. These are colour coded to indicate the level of the ticket — a day ticket, a weekend ticket or a special performer's ticket. The use of these wristbands introduces a visual method of control during a large event, as the sale of food and drinks is allowed only if the wristband is shown. In this way, the food vendors become part of the security for the event.

The Internet is increasingly used for the distribution of tickets for large events, concerts and conferences. This use of the Internet illustrates the linking of logistics and marketing. Originally the World Wide Web (WWW) was used to market events by advertising them through a Web site. The introduction of encrypted data enabled an increase in the privacy and security of payment methods and the sale of tickets from a site. The site collaborates with the existing ticketing system and can also be connected to travel agencies.

Does the artwork on the ticket contain the following?
❏ number of the ticket
❏ name of the event
❏ date and time of the event
❏ price and level of the ticket (discount, complimentary, full price, early bird)
❏ seating number or designated area (ticket colouring can be used to show seating area)
❏ disclaimer (in particular, this should list the responsibilities of the event promoter)
❏ event information, such as a map, warnings and what to bring
❏ artwork so that the ticket could be used as a souvenir (part of the ticket could be kept by the patron)
❏ contact details for information

Printing schedule
❏ When will the tickets be ready?
❏ Will the tickets be delivered or do they have to be collected?
❏ If there is an error or a large demand for the tickets, will there be time for more to be printed?

Distribution
❏ What outlets will be used — retail, Ticketek, Internet, mail or at the gate?
❏ Has a letter of agreement with all distributors, setting out terms and conditions, been signed?
❏ What method of payment will be used (by both the ticket buyer to the distributor and in the final reconciliation) — credit card, cash, direct deposit?
❏ Are schedule of payment and reconciliation forms available?
❏ Does the schedule of communications referring to ticket sales indicate sales progress and if more tickets are needed?

Collection of tickets
❏ How will the tickets be collected at the gate and transferred to a passout?
❏ How experienced are the personnel and how many will there be? When will they arrive and leave?
❏ Is a separate table for complimentary tickets needed at the ticket collection site?
❏ What security arrangements are in place for cash and personnel?
❏ How will the tickets be disposed of?

Reconciliation of number of tickets with revenue received
❏ What method of reconciliation will be used? Is an accountant being used?
❏ Is the reconciliation ongoing, at the conclusion of the event, or at the end of the month?
❏ Has a separate account been set up just for the event to assist the accountancy procedure?

■ Queuing

Often the first experience of a customer at an event is queuing for tickets or parking. Once inside the event, customers may be confronted with queues for food, toilets and seating. An important aspect of queue theory is the 'perceived waiting time'. This is the subjective time that the customers feel that they have waited. There are many rules of thumb about diminishing the customers' perceived waiting time. In the catering industry, queuing for food can affect the event experience. An informal rule is one food or beverage line for every 75 to 100 people. Figure 13.3 lists some of the factors to consider in the logistics of queuing.

■ **Figure 13.3**
Queuing —
factors to
consider

- How many queues and possible bottlenecks will there be?
- Have an adequate number of personnel greeters, crowd controllers, ticket collectors and security staff been allocated?
- Is signage (including the estimated waiting time) in place?
- When will the queues form? Will they form at once or over a period of time?
- How can the perceived waiting time be reduced (for example, queue entertainers)?
- What first aid, access and emergency procedures are in place?
- Are the lighting and sun and rain protection adequate?
- Are crowd-friendly barricades and partitions in place?

At the Atlanta Olympics the perceived waiting time at the entrance queues was diminished by the use of entertainers. Exit queuing can be the last experience for the customer at an event and needs the close attention of the event manager. At Darling Harbour's New Year's Eve celebrations in Sydney, the authorities use 'staggered entertainment' to spread the exit time of the crowds.

The oversupply of customers at a commercial event can give rise to a number of security and public safety problems that should be anticipated in the logistics plan. Only presale tickets will indicate the exact number of the expected audience. When tickets are sold at the entrance to an event, the logistics plan has to include the possibility of too many people. Oversubscription may be pleasing for the event promoter, but can produce the logistical nightmare of what to do with the excess crowd.

■ Customer *transport*

Transport to a site is often the first physical commitment by the audience to an event. The method and timing of arrival — public or private transport — is important to the overall logistics plan. The terms used by event managers are 'dump', when the audience arrives almost at once, and 'trickle', when they come and go over a longer period of time. Each of these needs a different logistics strategy. The first impression of the event by the audience can influence all subsequent experiences at the event. For this reason, it is the most visible side of logistics for customers. In their work on sports events, Graham et al. (1995) comment on the importance of spectator arrivals and departures. They stress that arrival and departure is a part of the event hospitality experience. The first and last impression of an event will be the parking facility and the traffic control.

The organisation of transport for conferences takes on a special importance. In a handbook for conference organisers by CIM Rostrum (n.d.), the linking of transport and the selection of the venue is emphasised. The selection of the conference venue or site has to take into account the availability and cost of transport to and from the site. As well, the transport to other facilities has to be considered. A venue that involves a 'long haul' will increase overall costs of a conference or event, as well as adding to the organisational confusion. CIM further points out that it can make the conference seem less attractive to the delegates and therefore impact on delegate numbers.

For large events, festivals and parades, further logistic elements are introduced to the transport of the customer to the event. In particular, permission (council, main roads departments, police) and road closures need to be part of the logistics plan. Figure 13.4 lists the elements of customer transport that need to be considered for an event.

An innovative way of solving many logistics problems (parking, etc.) and enhancing the audience experience was used by the organisers of the Australian Music Festival in Glen Innes, New South Wales. The festival took place at the old Glen Innes railway station and the audience arrived by steam train with the performers. By the time the passengers arrived from Central Station (Sydney) on the Great Northern train, the festival experience had already begun.

The Glen Innes festival also demonstrates how the transport arrangements for the customer (audience) can be linked to the transport of the product (musicians). This can be taken much further and include sponsorship deals with transport companies. In particular, the transport of equipment can be offset against the large number of tickets required to transport the audience. Australian domestic airlines will often negotiate a discount for excess baggage charges incurred by performers if the event account is large enough.

The lack of transport facilities can be used as part of the event experience. As Nick Rigby, Head Ranger at Cape Byron, New South Wales, describes:

■ For our inaugural environmental heritage concert at the Pass we did not allow cars near the site as it would have spoilt the feeling of the evening. The audience had to park a kilometre away and walk along the beach to the Pass. This little journey was part of the environmental experience. We had volunteers steering people in the right direction and welcoming them to Cape Byron. It was quite a sight, over a thousand adults and children strolling along the beach with their picnic 'eskies' and blankets. ■

❑ Have the relevant authorities (e.g. local council, police, Department of Main Roads) been contacted for information and permission?

❑ What public transport is available? Are timetables available?

❑ Has a backup transport system been organised (in case the original transport system fails)?

❑ Is the taxi service adequate and has it been informed of the event? (Informing the local taxi service is also a way of promoting the event.)

❑ What quality is the access area? Do weight and load restrictions apply? Are there other special conditions that must be considered (e.g. underground sprinkler systems under the access area)?

❑ Is there adequate provision for private buses, including an area large enough for their turning circle, driver hospitality and parking?

❑ Is there a parking area and will it be staffed by trained personnel?

❑ Is a towing and emergency service available if required?

❑ Has transport to and from the drop-off point been organised (e.g. from the parking station to the site or venue entrance and back to the parking station)?

❑ At what rate are customers estimated to arrive (dump or trickle)?

❑ Is there adequate access and are there parking facilities for disabled customers?

■ Supply of product — *product portfolio*

Any event can be seen as the presentation of a product. Most events have a variety of products and services — a product portfolio — all of which help to create the event experience for the customer. The individual logistic requirements of the various products need to be integrated into a logistics plan.

For a large festival the product portfolio may include more than 200 performing groups from around Australia and overseas. For a small conference the product may be a speaker and video material. It should be remembered that the product can also include the venue facilities. This is why the term 'the event experience' is used to cover all of the aspects of the customers' experience. It can include, for example, the audience itself and just catching up with friends, in which case the people become part of the product portfolio.

■ Transport

If the product portfolio includes products coming from overseas, the logistics problems can include issues such as carnet and customs clearance. A carnet is a licence issued by Customs that allows the movement of goods across an international border. A performing artist group coming into Australia is required to have clearance for all its equipment, and needs to pay any taxes on goods that may be sold at the event, such as videos or compact disks.

A large account with an airline can allow the event manager an area of negotiation. Savings, discounts, free seats or free excess charges can be granted by an airline company in exchange for being the 'preferred airline' of the event.

The transport requirements for the performers should be forwarded to the logistics manager by the artistic director well before the event. This illustrates the linking of the various functional areas of a large event.

Importing groups from overseas or interstate provides the logistics manager with an opportunity to communicate with these groups. The 'meet and greet' at the airport and the journey to the site can be used to familiarise the talent with the event. Such things as site map, rehearsal times, accommodation, dressing-room location, equipment storage and transport out can be included in the artist's event or festival kit.

■ Accommodation

The accommodation requirements of the artists must be treated separately from the accommodation of the audience. The aim of the event manager is to get the best out of the 'product'. Given that entertainers are there to work, their accommodation has to be treated as a way of increasing the value of the investment in entertainment. Substandard accommodation and long trips to the site are certain ways of reducing this value. Often these requirements are not stated and need to be anticipated by the logistics manager.

■ Artists' needs *on site*

A range of artists' needs must be catered for, including transport on site, storage and movement of equipment, stage and backstage facilities, food and drink (often contained in the contract rider), sound and lights. All these have a logistic element, but are described in detail on pages 376–7 in chapter 14.

As with accommodation, an efficient event manager will anticipate the on-site needs of the artists. Often this can only be learned from experience. In multicultural Australia, the manager needs to be sensitive to requirements that are culturally based, such as food, dressing rooms (separate) and appropriate staff to assist the performer.

*S*UPPLY OF FACILITIES

The supply of the infrastructure to an event site introduces many of the concepts of business logistics. The storage of consumables (food and drink) and equipment, and the maintenance of equipment become particularly significant. For a small event taking place over an evening, most of the facilities will be supplied by the venue. The catering, toilets and power, for example, can all be part of the hiring of the venue.

Larger festivals or more innovative events require the sourcing of many of the facilities. Some of these are discussed in detail in chapter 14. An inaugural outdoor festival will need the sourcing of almost all the facilities. To find the best information about the availability and cost of the facilities, the event manager should look for a project in the area that required similar facilities. For example, earth moving equipment, toilets, generators, fencing and security are also used by construction and mining companies. Some facilities can be sourced through film production companies. Many of the other facilities travel with the various festivals. Large tents and sound systems need to be booked in advance.

Figure 13.5 is an order sheet listing some of the facilities used for the 1997–98 Woodford Folk Festival in southern Queensland. Note the need for steps and the number of site offices.

Innovative events, like a company-themed Christmas party in an abandoned car park, will require a long lead-time to source the facilities. For example, it may take months to source unusual and rare props and venues for an event. These lead times can significantly affect the way the event is scheduled.

ON-SITE LOGISTICS

The site of an event may vary from an old woolshed for a bush dance to an underground car park for a Christmas party, to a 50 hectare site for a festival. Logistic considerations during the event become more complex with the size of the event. The flow of materials and people around the site and communication networks become the most important areas of logistics.

■ Flow

With larger festivals and events, the movement of the audience, volunteers, artists and equipment can take a larger part of the time and effort of the logistics manager than the lead-up to the event. This is especially so when the site is complex or multi-venued and there is a large audience. During the lead-up to an event, many of the elements of logistics can be taken care of by the subcontractors. For example, the movement of the electricity generators to the site is the responsibility of the hire company. However, when the facilities are on site, it becomes the responsibility of the logistics manager for their positioning, movement and operation.

■ **Figure 13.5** *Woodford Folk Festival order sheet*

VENUES	Hoecker	Marquee	Shade	Backstage	Floors	Site office	Stage size	Extensions
Big top		160' × 110'		12' × 12'			9.6 × 4.8 × 0.9 m	(2) PA wings 3.6 × 2.
Concert	20 × 30 m			12' × 12'			9.4 × 4.8 × 0.6 m	
Folkloric theatre	20 × 30 m			6 × 9 m 3 × 6 m	6 × 9 m 3 × 6 m		9.6 × 4.8 × 0.6 m	Foldback risers at 0.4
Forum	15 × 20 m						5 × 4 × 0.45 m	
Blues	20 × 20 m			24' × 24'			8.4 × 4.8 × 0.6 m	
Dance	15 × 20 m				12 × 9.6 m		7.2 × 4.8 × 0.6 m	
Murri	10 × 20 m						8.4 × 4.8 × 0.6 m	
Children's festival Workshop Cafe		40' × 60' 24' × 36'	(2) 13 × 15 m	12' × 12' (7) 12' × 12'	4 × 4 m		6 × 4.8 × 0.3 m	
Cooroboree ground			13 × 18 m	12' × 12'				
Talking circle				12' × 12'				
Visual arts				(12) 4 × 4 m TT (2 sides each)	3.6 × 3.6 m	Penny to organise		
Greenhouse		48' × 60'					5.6 × 3.6 × 0.45 m	
Fire event		(3) 36' × 36'	8 × 10 m			2.4 × 4.8 m 2.4 × 3.6 m		
Amphitheatre	20 × 15 m			5 × 10 m 12' × 24'	18 × 13 m			
Troubadour		40' × 60'					4.8 × 2.4 × 0.3 m	
The Wok House							5.4 × 3.6 × 0.3 m	
Bim Bamboo!!								
Lantern factory		36' × 36'						

FACILITIES

Administration		36' × 36'				2.4 × 6 m A/C		
Signology		15' × 15'						
Green room		(2) 30' × 36'						
Street theatre		(2) 12' × 12'						
Sponsors' lounge	10 × 10 m				10 × 10 m			
Front gate	5 × 10 m					2.4 × 4.8 m A/C		
Camping gate	6 × 6 m					JS caravan		
Welcome tent		4 × 4 m TT						
Organisers' green room	10 × 15 m							
Treasury						3.4 × 6 m A/C		
Cashiers						2.4 × 4.8 m A/C		
Security						2.4 × 4.8 m A/C		

BARS

Guinness		48' × 60'		10 × 10 m		2.4 × 4.8 m	4.8 × 3.6 × 0.3 m	
Session		48' × 48'						
Carnival		(2) 30' × 36'						
The Club		48' × 60'					5.4 × 3.6 × 0.4 m	
The Cafe		30' × 36'	8 × 10 m					
Blues		(2) 30' × 36'						

MURRI CAMP

Kitchen		30' × 36'	8 × 10 m					
Accommodation		(3) 6 × 9 m			(3) 6 × 9 m			
		(3) 6 × 9 m			(3) 6 × 3 m			

TOTALS

s	Chrs	8'T	3' Rnd	6' Rnd	Cold room	Cool cube	Tubs	Electricity	Plumbing	Pickets	Hessian	Extras
450 mm	1100	4										
600 mm	500	3										
600 mm	350 40	2 3	6									small fridge small urn
450 mm	300	2										
800 mm	350	2										
	150	2										
600 mm	250	2										
	150 60 48	2 12 4	12		small fridge							4 tiered seats/2 fans 4 × 4 m sandpit 12 hay bales
		1										
	100	40						1 switchboard	1 tap			
	200	4										
	30	10										
	10 20	4 4	3									fridge
	140	6	15	2								
		2								60 (20 × 4'3"s)	80 m	
	12	6										
	20	15										
	2	2										
	40	60										
	12	2						caravan		6	30 m	2 floods in punchbowl
	20		6									fridge
	10	10										
	5	4										
	4	4										
	100	15										
	10	8										
	4	3										
	200	4	20	2	1	1	6					
	120	4	20		1	1	6					
	120	3	20		1	1						
	200	4	20		1	1	6					
	120	3	20		1	1	4					
	150	4	25		2	1	6					
	120	3	20		1 (small)	1	4					gas BBQ
												gas rings
	150	4	25		2	1	6					
	3847	256	167	4	7	6	28					
ЭER	5000	280	180									

The access roads through a large festival and during the event have to accommodate:

- artist and equipment transport
- garbage removal
- emergency fire and first aid access and checking
- stall set up, continual supply and removal
- security
- food and drink supplies
- staging equipment set up, maintenance and removal, and
- site communication.

As illustrated by figure 13.6, even during a straightforward event, many factors of the traffic flow must be considered. The performers for an event will need transport from their accommodation to the stage. Often the performers will go via the equipment storage area to the rehearsal rooms, then to the stage. At the conclusion of the performance, the performers will return their equipment to storage, then retire for a well-earned rest in the green room. For a community festival with four stages, this to-ing and fro-ing can be quite complex.

At the same time as the performers are transported around the site, the media, audience and VIPs are on the move. Figure 13.6 does not show the movement of the food vendors' suppliers, water, security, ambulances and many more. When any one of the major venues empties there is further movement around the site by the audience. This results in peak flow times when it may be impossible to move anything around the venue except the audience. These peaks and lows all have to be anticipated in the overall event plan.

■ **Figure 13.6**
Some of the traffic patterns to consider when planning an event

1. Performers' accommodation → equipment storage area → rehearsal area → stage → equipment storage area → social (green room)
2. Media accommodation → media centre → stages → social area
3. VIP accommodation → stages → special requests
4. Audience pick-up points → specific venue

Each event contains surprising factors in traffic flow. For the Easter Show which was formerly held at the Sydney Showground, for example, the narrow gate that allowed entrance to the performers was also the gate that was used for the various animals. Each day of the two-week show had a queue that contained a mix of school orchestras, dancers, bands, sound equipment, Brahmin bulls, sheep trucks, camels and horses moving in both directions. This flow was coordinated by one gatekeeper.

■ Communication

On-site communication for the staff at a small event can be with the mobile phone or the loud hailer of the event manager. With the complexity of larger events, however, the logistics plan must contain an on-site communications plot (CP). The Woodford site communications plot (figure 13.7) shows the complexity of communications at a festival that attracts 90 000 admissions.

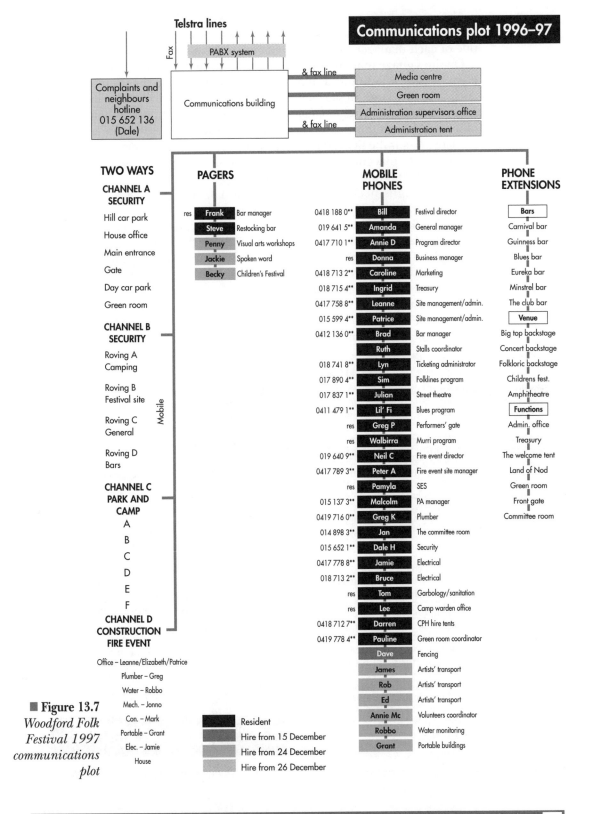

Telstra lines

PABX system

Communications plot 1996–97

Complaints and neighbours hotline 015 652 136 (Dale)

Communications building

& fax line — Media centre
Green room
Administration supervisors office
& fax line — Administration tent

TWO WAYS

CHANNEL A SECURITY

Hill car park
House office
Main entrance
Gate
Day car park
Green room

CHANNEL B SECURITY

Roving A
Camping

Roving B
Festival site

Roving C
General

Roving D
Bars

CHANNEL C PARK AND CAMP

A
B
C
D
E
F

CHANNEL D CONSTRUCTION FIRE EVENT

Office – Leanne/Elizabeth/Patrice
Plumber – Greg
Water – Robbo
Mech. – Jonno
Con. – Mark
Portable – Grant
Elec. – Jamie
House

PAGERS

res	Frank	Bar manager
	Steve	Restocking bar
	Penny	Visual arts workshops
	Jackie	Spoken word
	Becky	Children's Festival

MOBILE PHONES

0418 188 0**	Bill	Festival director
019 641 5**	Amanda	General manager
0417 710 1**	Annie D	Program director
res	Donna	Business manager
0418 713 2**	Caroline	Marketing
018 715 4**	Ingrid	Treasury
0417 758 8**	Leanne	Site management/admin.
015 599 4**	Patrice	Site management/admin.
0412 136 0**	Brad	Bar manager
	Ruth	Stalls coordinator
018 741 8**	Lyn	Ticketing administrator
017 890 4**	Sim	Folklines program
017 837 1**	Julian	Street theatre
0411 479 1**	Lil' Fi	Blues program
res	Greg P	Performers' gate
res	Walbirra	Murri program
019 640 9**	Neil C	Fire event director
0417 789 3**	Peter A	Fire event site manager
res	Pamyla	SES
015 137 3**	Malcolm	PA manager
0419 716 0**	Greg K	Plumber
014 898 3**	Jan	The committee room
015 652 1**	Dale H	Security
0417 778 8**	Jamie	Electrical
018 713 2**	Bruce	Electrical
res	Tom	Garbology/sanitation
res	Lee	Camp warden office
0418 712 7**	Darren	CPH hire tents
0419 778 4**	Pauline	Green room coordinator
	Dave	Fencing
	James	Artists' transport
	Rob	Artists' transport
	Ed	Artists' transport
	Annie Mc	Volunteers coordinator
	Robbo	Water monitoring
	Grant	Portable buildings

PHONE EXTENSIONS

Bars
Carnival bar
Guinness bar
Blues bar
Eureka bar
Minstrel bar
The club bar

Venue
Big top backstage
Concert backstage
Folkloric backstage
Childrens fest.
Amphitheatre

Functions
Admin. office
Treasury
The welcome tent
Land of Nod
Green room
Front gate
Committee room

Legend:
- Resident
- Hire from 15 December
- Hire from 24 December
- Hire from 26 December

■ **Figure 13.7**
Woodford Folk Festival 1997 communications plot

The communications plot includes fax, two-way radios, pagers, mobile phones and landline extensions. The Woodford communications plot also contains the title of each manager, as well as the complaints and neighbours' hotline.

On-site signage is an important part of communicating to the attendees of an event. It may be as simple as messages on a whiteboard in the volunteers' dining area, or involve large on-site maps showing the public the location of facilities. Two important issues in on-site signage are position and clarity. A direction sign that is obscured by such things as sponsors' messages diminishes its value to the event. For large events the signage may need a detailed plan. The issues to consider are:

- overall site placement of signs — at decision points, danger spots, so that they are integrated into the event
- types of signs needed, such as directional, statutory (legal and warning signs), operational, facility and sponsor
- the sign literacy of the attendees — what sort of signs are they used to reading?
- actual placement of signs — entrance, down the road, height
- supply of signs, their physical maintenance and their removal
- maintaining the credibility of the signs — if a facility is moved then the signs may need to be changed.

The most effective way of communicating with the audience at an event is to have the necessary information in the program. Figure 13.8 shows information for the audience for a small festival in northern New South Wales.

~Festival Information~

Staying at the festival Limited on-site camping is available at a flat rate of $10 per person. N.B. this fee is not for profit, it's to cover the costs of providing facilities.

Other accommodation There are three caravan parks in Lismore, delightful rural cabins, B&Bs, hotels, motels and backpacker accommodation. You can book your stay in or around Lismore through the Lismore Tourist Information Centre, 1300 369795 (no booking charge). Please tell them you are coming to the festival.

People with disabilities Facilities are provided for people with disabilities. If you have special needs please contact us first and we will do our best to help you.

Volunteers Our heartfelt thanks to all the wonderful folk who have given their time and energy to create this very special event.

This festival is run entirely by volunteers, who appreciate a helping hand! If you can put in a couple of hours to help it would be great, just check in at the festival office.

Festival workers put in even more time. If you would like to help with setting up or clean-up, etc., please call us on 02 66 217 537.

The bars The festival is a licensed event, run strictly according to licensing regulations! Under 18s and anyone who seems intoxicated will not be served. No BYO. Photo ID required.

First aid The Red Cross will be on site throughout the festival.

Car parking We welcome back the **Tuncester Bush Fire Brigade** to take care of the car park.

(Donations to these two essential voluntary services would be appreciated.)

Lost and found care for children and things — located in the club house.

Tickets Please bring your ticket to exchange for a wristband which must be worn throughout the festival. Spot checks will happen!

We suggest you bring your own mug for soft drinks, etc. to save on disposables. Sunscreen and hats are strongly recommended and you may need a jumper for the cool spring nights.

The Lismore Folk Trust Inc.

A not-for-profit organisation run solely by volunteers, the Trust produces this annual festival, the Lismore Lantern Festival and other events throughout the year. Membership entitles you to concessions at all Folk Trust events, newsletters (vacancy for an editor!) and is essential support for the festival. You can find out more about the Trust, and how to join, at the festival office.

Proudly supporting Summerland House, Alstonville

■ **Figure 13.8** *Festival information from the Northern Rivers Folk Festival program, 3–5 October 1997*

■ **Amenities and** *solid waste management*

For large festivals and events, the layout of the amenities is always included in the logistics site map. Figure 13.9 is an example of a large festival logistics site map that shows the layout of amenities.

■ **Figure 13.9**
*Victor
Harbor
logistics site
map*

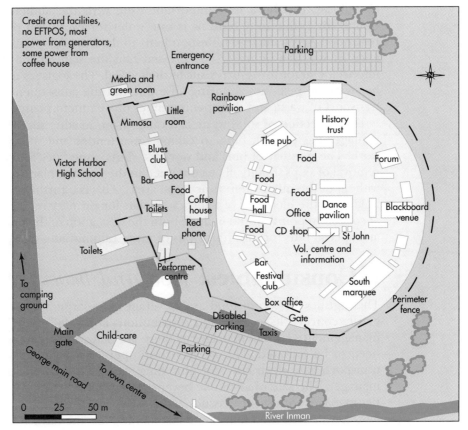

The site map is an indispensable tool for the event manager and is described in more detail later in this chapter. The schedules for the maintenance and cleaning of the amenities are part of the plan. For smaller events, these areas may be the sole responsibility of the venue management and part of the hiring contract.

Responsibility for cleaning the site and restoring it to its original condition is of particular importance to an event manager, as it is generally tied to the nature of the event. For example, the Sound Cloud event in 1988 at Sydney's Royal Botanic Gardens attracted a huge audience to a delicate area. The mere movement of the audience severely damaged the grass and resulted in the Gardens administration being suspicious of any further events in their area. If a national park is used as the site for an event, a Review of Environmental Factors (REF) is mandatory. The REF is a list of criteria the activity must meet to be permitted under various acts and regulations. These include the *National Parks and Wildlife Act 1974* (NSW), the *Endangered Fauna (Interim Protection) Act 1991* (NSW) and the *Threatened Species Conservation Act 1995* (NSW). As well, the REF has to contain descriptions of the future implications of the activity, its impact on the existing environment and land use, and its significance to the local Aboriginal community.

Well maintained toilets, in particular their number, accessibility and cleanliness, can be a very important issue with the audience. A rule of thumb for community festivals is one toilet for every 150 people (Neighbourhood Arts Unit 1991). Respondents to the Port Fairy Folk Festival audience survey (see figure 13.18) stressed that the state of the toilets was an important factor for return visits to the festival. The logistics manager has to be aware of 'peak flows' during an event and the consequences for vehicle transport of waste and the opening times of treatment plants.

The collection of solid waste can range from making sure that the venue manager has enough bins, to calling for a tender and subcontracting the work. The number of bins and workers, shifts, time lines for collection and removal of skips should all be contained in the logistics plan, as it interrelates with all of the other event functional areas. This is a further example of the linking of the elements of logistics. A plan for primary recycling (recycling at collection point) would include both the education of the public (signage) and special bins for different types of waste (aluminium, glass, paper).

■ Consumables: *food and beverage*

The logistics aspects of food and beverage on a large, multi-venue site primarily concern its storage and distribution. Food stalls may be under the management of a stall manager as there are State and local regulations that need to be followed. The needs of the operators of food stalls, including transport, gas, electricity and plumbing, are then sent on to the logistics manager. The sale of alcoholic beverages particularly can present the logistics manager with security issues.

At a wine and food fair, the 'consumables' are the attraction. The collection of cash is often solved by the use of presale tickets that are exchanged for food and wine samples. The tickets are bought at one place on the site, which reduces possible problems with security, cash collection and accounting.

Figure 13.10 lists some of the main factors to consider when including food and beverage outlets at an event.

As well as feeding and watering the public, logistics includes the requirements of the staff, volunteers and performers. The catering area for the staff and performers, often called the green room, provides an opportunity to disseminate information to the event staff. At the Northern Rivers Folk Festival, a strategically placed, large whiteboard in the green room was used to communicate with volunteers.

Last, but not least, is the catering for sponsors and VIPs. This generally requires a separate plan to the general catering. In some festivals, a hospitality tent is set aside for special guests. This aspect of events is covered in chapter 14.

■ Have local and State liquor licences been granted?

■ What selection criteria for stall applicants (including the design of the stall and menu requirements) will be used?

■ What infrastructure will be needed (including plumbing, electrical and gas)?

■ Does the contract include provisions for health regulations, gas supplies, insurance and workers' compensation?

■ What position on the site will the stalls occupy?

■ Have arrival, set up, breakdown and leaving times been set?

■ What cleaning arrangements have been made?

■ Do stallholders understand the need for ongoing inspections, such as health, electricity, plumbing, garbage (including liquids) disposal and gas inspection?

■ Are there any special security needs that must be catered for?

■ How and when will payment for the stalls be made?

■ Will the stallholder provide in-kind support for the event (including catering for VIPs, media and performers)?

■ VIP and *media requirements*

The effect on event logistics by media coverage of the event cannot be over-estimated. Even direct radio broadcasts can disrupt the live performance of a show, both in the setting up and the actual broadcast. The recording or broadcast of speeches or music often requires separate microphones or a line from the mixing desk. This cannot be left until just before the performance. Television cameras require special lighting, which often shines directly into the eyes of the audience. The movement of a production crew and television power requirements can be distracting to a live performance, and need to be assessed before the event.

Media organisations work on very short time lines and may upset the well-planned tempo of the event. However, the rewards in terms of promotion and even finance are so large that the media logistics can take precedence over most other aspects of the event. These decisions are often made by the event manager in consultation with event promotions and sponsors. This is an area that illustrates the need for flexible negotiations and assessment by the logistics manager.

The requirements of VIPs can include special security arrangements. Once again it is a matter of weighing up the benefits of having VIPs with the amount of extra resources that are needed. This, however, is not the logistic manager's area of concern; the event manager or event committee should deal with it. Once the VIPs have been invited, their needs have to take precedence over the public's.

■ Emergency *procedures*

Emergency procedures at an event can range from staff qualified in first aid, to using the St John Ambulance service, to the compilation of a comprehensive disaster plan. The location of first aid should be indicated on the site map and all the event staff should be aware of this. Large events require an emergency access road that has to be kept clear. These issues are so important that a local council may immediately close down an event that does not comply with their regulations about emergencies.

Festivals in the countryside can be at the mercy of natural disasters, including fires, storms and floods. Figure 13.11 shows just one page of the disaster plan of the Woodford Folk Festival 1997.

■ **Figure 13.11**
Extract from the Woodford Folk Festival 1997 disaster plan

Authority
This plan is written under the authority of the *State Counter Disaster Organisation Act 1974–78*.

Aim
The aim of this plan is to set out the policies and procedure to be followed by State Emergency Service personnel in times of major incidents, disasters or emergencies that may occur during the Woodford Folk Festival.

In matters where this document is silent, then the Caboolture Shire Disaster Plan will come into effect and be enacted.

Objectives
To establish the general guidelines to be followed for all incidents and/or emergencies.
To set the guidelines to be followed in the event of a fire.
To set the guidelines to be followed in the event of a multicasualty incident.
To set the guidelines to be followed in the event of a lost person.
To set the guidelines to be followed in the event of a flood in the festival site.
To set the guidelines to be followed in the event of a severe storm causing damage.
To set the general guidelines to be followed for any other event that may occur.

Command and control
The control organisation for emergencies and searches is the Queensland Police Service.

The control organisation for fire incidents is the Queensland Fire and Rescue Service.

The control organisation for medical and multicasualty incidents is the Queensland Ambulance Service.

The support and management organisation for the above is the Queensland State Emergency Service.

The control organisation for storm damage operations is the Queensland State Emergency Service.

The Maleny State Emergency Service Group activities at the Woodford Folk Festival are overseen by the training officer and are conducted as training.

In the event of an incident or emergency occurring, the Maleny training officer or delegate must be informed immediately, regardless of the time of day.

The lines of authority and necessary procedures are stressed in the disaster plan. These procedures include the partial evacuation of the festival site in the event of a disaster (particularly prolonged, heavy rain). It notes that rescuers should concentrate on personnel in immediate danger when conducting an evacuation.

SHUTDOWN

As Pagonis (1992) points out, military logistics is divided into three phases:
- deployment
- combat
- redeployment.

Redeployment often takes the most effort and time. The amount of time and effort spent on the shutdown of an event are in direct proportion to the size of the event and its uniqueness. Repeated events, like many of the festivals mentioned in this chapter, have their shutdown schedule refined over many years. Shutdown can run quickly and smoothly. All the subcontractors know exactly how to get their equipment out and where they are placed in the order of removal. The event manager of a small event may only have to sweep the floor and turn off the lights.

Most difficulties arise in inaugural events, large events and muti-venued events. In these cases, logistics can be as important after the event as at any other time and the need for planning most apparent. An event shutdown check list is provided in figure 13.12 on the following page. The breakdown and removal of site structures, the collection of equipment and the exits of the various traders should all be part of the schedules contained in the logistics plan. The plan for the breakdown of the event is part of the initial meeting and negotiation with contractors. A major part of working out a Gantt chart (see pages 345–7) or a critical path is the acquittal of equipment, which includes removing, repairing and cleaning the equipment.

As emphasised in the Port Fairy example in the case study at the end of this chapter and by Catherwood and Van Kirk (1992), the shutdown of an event is the prime security time. The mix of vehicles, movement of equipment and general feeling of relaxation provides a cover for theft. The smooth flow of traffic leaving an event at its conclusion must also be considered. Towing services and the police may need to be contacted.

Very large events may require the sale of facilities and equipment at a post-event auction. Some events in Australia find that it is more cost effective to buy or make the necessary equipment and sell it after the event. Finally, it is often left to the person in charge of logistics to organise the final thank-you party for the volunteers and staff.

Crowd dispersal
❑ Exits/transport
❑ Safety
❑ Related to programming
❑ The dump and staggered entertainment

Equipment
❑ Bump out schedule including correct exits and loading docks
❑ Shut down equipment using specialist staff (e.g. computers)
❑ Clean and repair
❑ Store — number boxes and display contents list
❑ Sell or auction
❑ Small equipment and sign off
❑ Schedule for dismantling barricades

Entertainment
❑ Farewell appropriately
❑ Payments — cash
❑ Thank-you letters/awards/ recommendations

Human resources
❑ The big thank you
❑ Final payments
❑ Debrief and next year
❑ Reports
❑ Celebration party

Liability
❑ Records
❑ Descriptions
❑ Photo
❑ Video

On-site/staging area
❑ Cleaning
❑ Back to normal

❑ Environmental assessment
❑ Lost and found
❑ Idiot check
❑ Site/venue hand-over

Contractors
❑ Contract acquittal
❑ Thank you

Finance
❑ Pay the bills
❑ Finalise and audit accounts — best done as soon after the event as possible — the following day or week
❑ Thank you to donor and sponsors

Marketing and promotion
❑ Collect press clippings/video news
❑ Reviews of the event — use a service
❑ Market research on community reaction

Sponsors and grants
❑ Acquit grants: reports — don't be placed on the D list of funding bodies
❑ Meet sponsors and enthuse for next time

Government and politics
❑ Thank services
❑ Reports to council and other government organisations

Client
❑ Glossy report, video, photos
❑ Wrap up and suggestions for next time

TECHNIQUES OF LOGISTICS MANAGEMENT

We will now consider the role of logistics managers and their relation to the other functional areas and managers of an event.

■ The event *logistics manager*

As mentioned throughout this chapter, the logistics manager has to be a procurer, negotiator, equipment and maintenance manager, personnel manager, map maker, project manager and party organiser. For a small event, logistics can be the direct responsibility of the event manager. Logistics becomes a separate area if the event is large and complex. Multi-venued and multi-day events usually require a separate logistics manager position.

Part of the role of the logistics manager is to efficiently link all areas of the event. Figure 13.13 shows the lines of communication between the logistics manager and various other managers for a large, complex, multi-venued event. It is a network diagram because, although the event manager or director has ultimate authority, decision-making authority is usually devolved to the various submanagers who work at the same level of authority and responsibility as the event manager.

The information required by the logistics manager from the other festival managers is shown in table 13.1 on the next page. The clear communication between managers in this network is also partly the responsibility of the logistics manager.

■ **Figure 13.13**
The lines of communication between the logistics manager and other managers for a multi-venued event

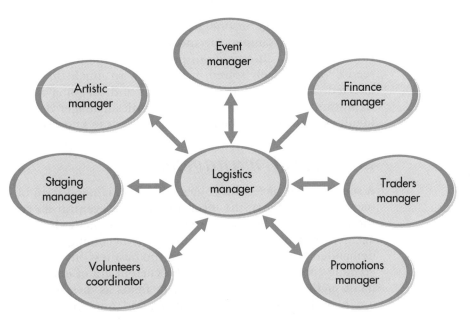

■ Table 13.1 *Information required by the logistics manager from the other festival managers*

POSITION	GENERAL ROLE	INFORMATION SENT TO LOGISTICS MANAGER
Artistic director	Selection of and negotiation with artists	Travel, accommodation, staging and equipment requirements
Staging manager	Selection of and negotiation with subcontractors	Sound, lights and backstage requirements and programming times
Finance director	Overseeing budgets and contracts	How and when funds will be approved and released and the payment schedule
Volunteers coordinator	Recruitment and management of volunteers	Volunteers selected to assist Requirements of the volunteers (e.g. parking, free tickets)
Promotions manager	Promotion during the event	Requirements of the media and VIPS
Traders manager	Selecting suitable traders	Requirements of the traders (e.g. positioning, theming, electricity, water, licence agreements)

*L*OGISTICS TECHNIQUES

The tools used in business and military logistics can be successfully adapted to event logistics. Because an event takes place at a specific time and specific place, the tools of scheduling and mapping are used. The dynamic nature of events and the way that the functional areas are so closely linked means that a small change in one area can result in crucial changes throughout the event. For example, the incorrect placement of an electric generator can lead to a mushrooming of problems. If the initial problem is not foreseen or immediately solved, it can grow so much that the whole event is affected. This gives initial negotiations and on-going assessment a special significance in event logistics. The logistics manager needs to be skilled in identifying possible problem areas and needs to know what is *not* on the list.

■ Project *management*

A special event or festival comes under the general term of a project. As it has a life expectancy, the term used for the event, from cradle to grave, is the event project life cycle. Almost all of the methodology of project management can be applied to events. It is becoming more common as it is demanded by the stakeholders and the business environment as a means of creating common standards. In the current era of change, project management methodology is being used in fields as diverse as software development, business change management and now in event management. As pointed out in the chapter on information technology, the language of project management is the modern language of business. The first step in this methodology is to scope the work; that is, list the amount of work necessary for the event. This may be helped along by deciding what does not have to be done. Fundamental to project management is the ability to break all the work involved in a project into manageable units. The graphic representation of this decomposition or analysis is called the work breakdown structure (WBS). The units are assigned necessary resources so that there are outcomes or deliverables. For example, the work involved in promoting a festival may be divided first by paid advertising and publicity. This can be further subdivided according to the media used — TV, Web, print. Each unit in this subdivision is assigned resources such as money, time, staff, equipment and supplies. The WBS is used as a basis of costing and risk management. The costs of each unit are 'rolled-up' to give the total cost of the work to create the event. An outcome of the WBS process is the responsibility or task sheets that communicate to the event staff their responsibilities and when they need to complete them. Once the work has been decomposed in this way, the schedule of work is created.

■ **Figure 13.14**
Event project management process

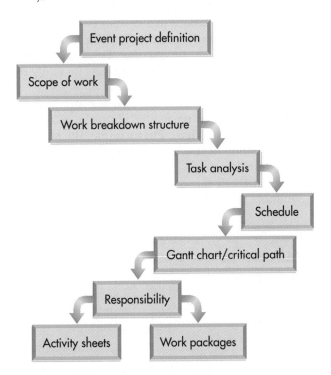

■ **Scheduling:** *bar chart*

One of the most important tools used in logistics is the bar chart or time line, or the Gantt chart. Gantt charts are bar charts that are used in project management as a visual representation of the schedule. The steps in creating a Gantt chart are now described.

- *Tasks*: break down the logistics of the event into manageable tasks or activities. For example, one of the tasks of the security for the event is the erection of the perimeter fence. This can be further broken down into the arrival of the fencing material, the arrival of volunteers and equipment, and the preparation of the ground.
- *Time lines*: set the time scale for each task. Factors to consider are the starting and completion times. The availability, hiring costs, possible delivery and pick-up times and costs are other considerations in constructing a time scale. For example, a major factor in the arrival of large tents is their hiring costs. These costs can depend on the day of the week on which they arrive, rather than the amount of time they are hired for.
- *Priority*: set the priority of the task. What other tasks need to be completed before this task can start? Completing this priority list will create a hierarchy of tasks or a work breakdown structure.
- *Grid*: draw a grid with the days leading up to the event across the top and a list of the tasks down the left-hand side of the grid. A horizontal bar that corresponds to each task is drawn across the grid. For example, the task of preparing the ground for the fencing is dependent on the arrival of materials and labour at a certain time and takes one day to complete. The starting time will be when the prior tasks are completed and the length of the time line will be one day. The horizontal bars or time lines are often colour-coded so that each task may be easily recognised when the chart is completed for all activities.
- *Milestones*: as the chart is used for monitoring the progress of the event, tasks that are of particular importance are designated as milestones and marked on the chart. For example, the completion of the security fence is a milestone as it acts as a trigger for many of the other event preparation activities.

Figure 13.15 shows an example of a simplified Gantt chart. This chart is common to most small rural Australian festivals.

■ **Figure 13.15**
Simplified Gantt chart of a small festival

Tasks	F	S	S	M	T	W	T	F	S	S	M	T	W	T	F	S	S
Clear and prepare site		▐	▐	▐	▐						opening night			◇			
Generators arrive						▐											
Lighting on site								▐	▐	▐	▐	▐	▐	▐			
Tents arrive										▐	▐	▐	▐				
Stages arrive and set up												▐	▐				
Site security														▐	▐	▐	▐
Sound system arrives															▐		

◇ **Milestone:** start of festival

In his work on the human factors in project management, Dinsmore (1990) stresses that this display of project tasks and time requirements has high communication value to an event. It forestalls unnecessary explanations to the staff and sponsors and gives a visual representation of the event. Time lines are used in events no matter what their size. The arrival of goods and services on time even at a small event can add significant value to the event.

The advantages of a Gantt chart are that it:

- visually summarises the project or event schedule
- is an effective communication and control tool (particularly with volunteers)
- can point out problem areas or clashes of scheduling
- is readily adaptable to all event areas
- provides a summary of the history of the event.

For the Gantt chart to be an effective tool, the tasks must be arranged and estimated in the most practical and logical sequence. Underestimation of the time needed (length of the time line) can give rise to cost blow out and render any scheduling ineffective. As Lock (1988, p. 89) points out:

> ■ Extended schedules produced in this way are an ideal breeding ground for budgetary excesses according to Professor Parkinson's best-known law, where work is apt to expand to fill the time available. ■

■ Network analysis: *critical path*

One important aspect of any logistic plan is the relationship of tasks to each other. This can be difficult to show on a chart. With larger events, the Gantt chart can become very complex, and areas where there is a clash of scheduling may be obscured by the detail of bars and colours. A vital part of logistics is giving tasks a priority. For example, the arrival and set-up of the main stage in an event is more important than finding an extra extension cord. However, on a Gantt chart all of the tasks are given equal importance. The tool of network analysis was developed to overcome these problems.

Network analysis was created and developed during defence force projects in the USA and UK in the 1950s and now has widespread use in many project-based industries. The basis of network analysis is critical path analysis, which uses circles to represent programmed events and arrows to illustrate the flow of activities. Thus, the precedence of programmed events is established and the diagram can be used to analyse a series of sub-events. From the diagram, the most efficient scheduling can be found. This is known as the critical path. Figure 13.16 illustrates a network derived from the Gantt chart shown in figure 13.15. The critical path is shown as an arrow. This means that, for example, if the generator did not arrive on time, everything along the critical path would be directly affected. The lights would not be put up and, without evening light or electricity to run the pneumatic hammers, the tents could not be erected. Without the protective cover of the tents, the stage could not be constructed and so the sound system could not be set up. The critical path is indeed critical.

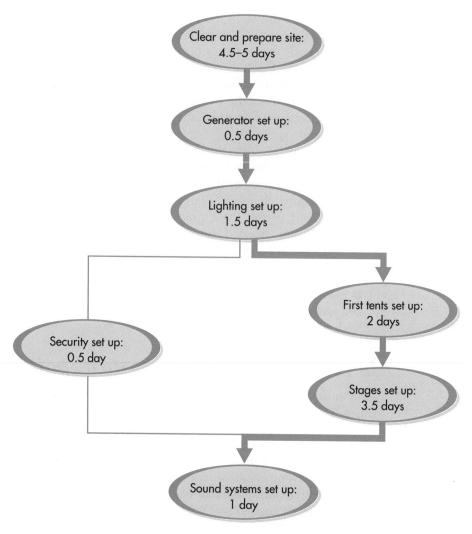

■ **Figure 13.16**
Gantt chart represented as a network

Clear and prepare site:
4.5–5 days

Generator set up:
0.5 days

Lighting set up:
1.5 days

First tents set up:
2 days

Security set up:
0.5 day

Stages set up:
3.5 days

Sound systems set up:
1 day

There are a number of software packages available to help create the Gantt chart and critical path. These are project management programs, which are usually used in the construction industry. Unfortunately, most of these packages are based on a variable completion time or completion within a certain time. In the event industry, the completion time (i.e. when the event is on) is the most important factor and every task has to relate to this time. The event manager cannot ask for an extension of the time to complete all of the tasks.

Time charts and networks are very useful as a control and communication tool; however, like all logistics techniques, they have their limitations. Graham, Goldblatt and Delphy (1995) describe how the Los Angeles Olympic Organising Committee gave up on the critical path chart as it became too unwieldy. There were 600 milestones. Rather than assisting communication and planning, it only created confusion. The solution was for the committee to return to a more traditional method of weekly meetings.

■ Site or *venue map*

A map of the event site or venue is a necessary communication tool for the logistics manager. For small events, even a simple map can be an effective tool that obviates the need for explanations and can quickly identify possible problem areas. The map for larger festivals can be an aerial photograph with the logistic features drawn on it. For smaller events, it may be a sketch map that shows only the necessary information to the customer. The first questions to ask are 'what is the map for?' and 'who will be reading it?'. A logistics site map will contain very different information than the site map used for promotional purposes. The map needs to filter information that is of no interest to the logistics plan. Monmonier (1996, p. 25), in his highly respected work on mapping, summarises this concept thus:

> ■ A good map tells a multitude of little white lies; it suppresses truth to help the user see what needs to be seen. Reality is three-dimensional, rich in detail, and far too factual to allow a complete yet uncluttered two-dimensional scale model. Indeed, a map that did not generalize would be useless. But the value of a map depends on how well its generalized geometry and generalized content reflect a chosen aspect of reality. ■

The three basic features of maps — scale, projection and the key (showing the symbols used) — have to be adapted to their target audience. Volunteers and subcontractors, for example, must be able to clearly read and understand it. The communication value of the site map also depends on where it is displayed. Some festivals draw the map on the back of the ticket or program.

The check list for items to be included on a site map can be very detailed. Figure 13.17 shows a standard check list of the logistics for a small festival.

■ **Figure 13.17**
Check list for the logistics site map

❑ scale and direction (north arrow)	❑ food and market stalls
❑ a list of symbols used on the map (key)	❑ tents and marquees
❑ entrance and exits	❑ equipment storage areas
❑ roads and parking	❑ off-limit areas and danger spots (e.g. creeks, blind corners)
❑ administration centre	❑ green room
❑ information booths	❑ maintenance area
❑ first aid and emergency road access	❑ pathways
❑ lost children area	❑ telephones
❑ electricity and water outlets	❑ ATMs
❑ toilets	❑ media area

As the Macquarie Marshes are in outback New South Wales, a sketch map on the ticket showed how to find the site, parking and the location of facilities. Next to the map was a list detailing the behaviour expected of event participants. The festival site map shown in figure 13.9 would be used by volunteers, staff, performers and all other personnel at the event. The promotional map for the audience, on the other hand, would be in colour and display points of interest to the public.

For corporate events, a simple map of the venue at the entrance, showing the location of seating, toilets, food areas and the bar, can relieve the staff of having to answer a lot of questions!

NEGOTIATION AND ASSESSMENT

No matter what the size of the event, mutual agreement on supply and conditions is vital. In particular, the special but changing nature of one-off events requires the techniques of dynamic negotiation to be mastered by the logistics manager. In his work on negotiation and contracts, Marsh (1984, p. 1) defines negotiation as:

■ a dynamic process of adjustment by which two parties, each with their own objectives, confer together to reach a mutually satisfying agreement on a matter of common interest. ■

Logistical considerations need to be covered by the initial negotiations with subcontractors. Agreement on delivery and removal times are an indispensable part of the time lines, as they form the parameters of the critical path.

It needs to be stressed that the management of special events in Australia is a dynamic industry. The special nature of many events means that many aspects cannot be included in initial negotiations. Decisions and agreements need to be continually reassessed. Both parties to the agreement have to realise that the agreement needs to be flexible. However, all possible problems have to be considered at the beginning, and there are logistics tools to enable this to happen.

Having prepared the schedules and site map, an important tool to use is what Pagonis (1992, p. 194) describes as the skull session:

■ Before implementing a particular plan, I usually try to bring together all of the involved parties for a collective dry run. The group includes representatives from all appropriate areas of the command, and the goal of the skull sessions is to identify and talk through all the unknown elements of the situation. We explore all possible problems that could emerge, and then try to come up with concrete solutions to those problems. Skull sessions reduce uncertainty, reinforce the interconnection of the different areas of specialisation, encourage collaborative problem solving, and raise the level of awareness as to possible disconnects [sic] in the theatre. ■

Goldblatt (1997) calls this gap analysis. Gap analysis is studying the plan in an attempt to identify gaps that could lead to a weakening in the implementation of the logistics plan. Goldblatt (1997) recommends using a critical friend to review the plan to look for gaps in your logical thinking.

The identification of risk areas, gaps and 'what ifs' is important in the creation of a contingency plan. For example, at the Woodford Folk Festival that takes place in the hottest months of the year in Queensland, the supply of water was identified as a priority area and a contingency plan created for a viable alternative. This included having water carts on call and making sure the nearest water pipe was available to the general public.

CONTROL OF EVENTS LOGISTICS

The monitoring of the logistics plan is a vital part of the overall control of an event. An important part of the plan is the identification of milestones — times when crucial tasks have to be completed. The Gantt chart can be used to compare projected performance with actual performance by recording actual performance times on the chart as the tasks occur. It is a simple monitoring device.

The aim of the logistics manager is to create a plan to enable the logistics to flow without the need for active control. The use of qualified subcontractors with experience in events is the only way to make this happen. This is where the annual festival, with its established relationship with suppliers, has an advantage over the one-off, innovative event. For example, the objective of the director of the Port Fairy Folk Festival was to enjoy the festival without having to intervene in any on-site problems!

EVALUATION OF LOGISTICS

The ultimate evaluation of the logistics plan is the success of the event and the easy flow of event supply and operations. However, the festival committee, event director and/or the sponsors may require a more detailed evaluation. The main question to ask is if the logistics met their objectives. If the objectives as set out in the plan are measurable, then this task is relatively straightforward. If the objectives require a qualitative approach, then the evaluation can become imprecise and open to many interpretations.

An evaluation enables the logistics manager to identify problem areas that enables improvement and therefore adds value to the next event. Techniques used in evaluation are:
- quantitative — meeting measurable objectives; sometimes called benchmarking
- qualitative — discussion with stakeholders.

The term 'logistics audit' is used for a systematic and thorough analysis of the event logistics. Part of the audit concerns the expectations of the audience and whether they were satisfied. The Port Fairy Folk Festival carried out an audience survey that identified areas of infrastructure for improvement and expansion for the growth of the festival. Figure 13.18 is an extract from a detailed survey of the attending audience of the Port Fairy Folk Festival.

For very large events, the evaluation of the logistics may be contained in the overall evaluation that is put out to tender. In 1997 the Australian Department of Foreign Affairs and Trade launched a multidimensional promotion of Australia in India. It included a series of events throughout India, ranging from trade shows to cultural activities. The logistical problems of such a varied event spread over a large area in a foreign country with a huge population are many. The evaluation report of this promotion was mostly concerned with the business outcomes. However, large sections of the 90-page Buchan Communications Group (1997) report were concerned with the logistics. Areas such as travel, communication and accommodation were evaluated by the participants. Other areas of logistics were 'evaluated' by the fact that they were unseen by the participants and therefore deemed a success. For example, as a result of the security measures put in place as part of the logistics planning, there were no terrorist activities during the promotion. (The day after the promotion had finished a train was blown up.)

■ **Figure 13.18**
Extract from the Port Fairy Folk Festival 1996 audience survey

2.9 Standard of toilet services in camping areas

	Count	Percentage	1994(%)	1995(%)
Good	116	43	46	46.7
Reasonable	114	42	44	44
Poor	41	15	10	9.3
TOTAL	271	100%	100%	100%

2.10 Standard of toilet services in arena

	Count	Percentage	1994(%)	1995(%)
Good	141	35	47	46
Reasonable	196	49	45	46
Poor	65	16	8	8
TOTAL	402	100%	100%	100%

2.11 Respondents' comments about facilities

Category of comment	Count	Percentage
More showers	31	14
Toilets smell/dirty	39	18
Excellent	21	10
Toilets are clean	1	0.5
More ladies toilets	40	18
Better than 1995	14	6
More cleaning needed	16	7
Very clean	7	3
Facilities not large enough	6	3
Food variety needed	22	10
Too crowded	9	4
Table and chairs are good	8	4
More rubbish bins	2	1
Toilets for handicapped inadequate	2	1
TOTAL	218	100%

(Source: Port Fairy Folk Festival 1996, Audience Survey, p. 9)

THE LOGISTICS PLAN

Whether the event is a school class reunion or a multivenued festival, a written logistics plan needs to be part of the communication within the event. It could range from a one-page contact list with approximate arrival times, to a bound folder covering all areas. The folder for a large event would contain:

- a general contact list
- a site map
- schedules, including time lines and bar charts
- the emergency plan
- subcontractor details, including all time constraints
- on-site contacts, including security and volunteers
- evaluation sheets (sample questionnaires).

All of these elements have been described and discussed in this chapter.

These elements can make up the event manual that is used to stage the event. The manual needs to be a concise document as it may need to be used in an emergency. An operation manual may be used only the once but it has to be able to withstand the rigours of the event itself. Some organisations, in particular in the exhibition industry, have a generic manual on their intranet that can be adapted for all their events in any part of the world.

Although this text emphasises the importance of planning, over-planning can be a significant risk, particularly with the special event as there is often a need to respond and take opportunities when they arise. Artistry and innovation can easily be hampered by a purely mechanical approach to event creation. As pointed out in the Marine Corps Doctrinal Publication no. 4, *Logistics*:

> ■ To deal with disorder, the logistics system must strive for balance. On the one hand, it must estimate requirements and distribute resources based on plans and projections; otherwise the needed support will never be available where and when it is required. On the other, a system that blindly follows schedules and procedures rapidly loses touch with operational realities and inhibits rather than enables effective action. ■

SUMMARY

Military logistics is as old as civilisation itself. Business logistics is a recent science. Events logistics has the advantage of building on these areas, using the tools of both and continually improving on them as the events industry in Australia grows.

The event logistics system can be broken down into the procuring and supply of customers, products and facilities. Once on site, the logistics system concerns the flow around the site, communication and requirements of the event. At the conclusion of the event, logistics concerns the break-down of structures, cleaning and managing the evacuation of the site or venue.

For small events, logistics may be the responsibility of the event manager. However, for larger events a logistics manager may be appointed. Their role within the overall event management was described and their relationship with other managers is vital. The logistics of an event needs to be treated as any other area of management and have in-built evaluation and ongoing control. All of these elements are placed in a plan that is a part of the overall event plan.

Logistics is an invisible part of events. It enables customers to focus completely on the event without being distracted by unnecessary problems. It becomes visible only when it is looked for or when there is a problem. It enables the paying customer, the public, client or sponsor to realise and even exceed their expectations.

Questions

1 What are the logistics areas that need to be contained in initial agreements with the event suppliers?

2 Set out an emergency plan for a small event.

3 List the logistics tasks for (a) a street parade, (b) a product launch and (c) a company party.

4 Create a Gantt chart for a street parade or another event. Identify the critical path.

....

The Port Fairy
Folk Festival

From a small folk festival specialising in amateur music sessions or get-togethers in 1977, the Port Fairy Folk Festival on the south coast of Victoria has grown to an event that attracted 34 000 people to Port Fairy in 1996. The festival has won many awards, including the Hall of Fame Award and the Australian Tourism Award in 1993, 1994 and 1995. The festival, which is under the management of the Port Fairy Committee, showcases more than 300 international, national and regional artists in 30 venues around town, including the main stages within the festival arena. It is estimated that the festival pumps more than $3 million into the Port Fairy township each year.

The Port Fairy Folk Festival has three advantages over one-off events:
1. a stable and well-connected organising committee
2. a regular venue that is improved each year
3. a well-maintained relationship with the various participating artists and the town.

The festival is managed by a committee of 14 volunteers. The volunteers are local citizens, with professional people and businesses well represented. The members include a health surveyor, a real estate agent, a local shopkeeper, the local fish co-op representative, a retired factory manager, a school principal and a lawyer. The festival director coordinates the festival's content, marketing, staging and performers. The chairman of the festival has a long background in building contracting and project management.

The festival site is the parklands, playing fields and camping ground of Port Fairy. The site is surrounded by a high fence with two entrances. Venues in the township are also used for festival activities. The festival includes free events and a ticketed area called the arena. The arena takes up the area of the local sportsgrounds and contains the four main stages and many smaller venues, including the folk circus which is an area dedicated to children's entertainment. The programming of the stages is the responsibility of the festival director.

In 1997 the PFFF spent only $8000 on publicity. Tickets are sold out four months prior to the start of the three-day festival, which gives the festival a good working capital. The organisers are very conscious of the feedback from participants. For many years an informal feedback sheet from the audience indicated the level of satisfaction with the festival. In 1995 the festival committee commissioned an audience survey on the facilities and program of the festival. The survey also provided demographic information about the audience.

The minimal use of advertising and the complete presale of tickets indicates an audience that has either already attended the festival or has been told about it by friends. This means that the audience is familiar with the festival and is already educated about the logistics that concerns it. For example, people attending the festival will know about how to get there, parking, accommodation, food, toilets, seating and water availability through friends who have been to a previous festival or from attending themselves. One consequence of this is that minimal signage is needed on-site compared to other festivals.

The festival 'product portfolio' contains more than 450 performances, including processions through the town, a craft fair, story telling, instrument making, dancing, competitions and awards. The headline acts come from overseas and are transported by road from Melbourne. Interstate artists generally find their own way to Port Fairy.

The gradual growth of the festival has allowed the organising committee to introduce new facilities and improve them. This improvement has been used as a benchmark for each year. For example, the 1986 festival is noted as the year when the hoeckers were introduced. These large tents are internally supported and do not need the external ropes and pegs that are so dangerous when large crowds are moving around a site. In 1992 the Guinness and wine bars were started, which secured a major sponsor and produced a new source of funds.

Security and rubbish collection, including 80 wheelie bins, are put out to tender. Most of the infrastructure is built up during the year in preparation for future growth. The electricity, water, sewerage and phone lines are all underground. Four large lights were erected by the festival committee in the arena area. The lights have the dual purpose of lighting the festival, allow for night construction work and help the local sports teams who use this area for the rest of the year. This close relationship between the festival and the local community is central to the philosophy of the festival. Many areas of the festival's logistics reflect this relationship. For example, the hoeckers are erected each year by the local farming community of Yambuk. In exchange, the festival provides funds to be distributed as grants to benefit the community.

The festival's critical path is worked out through experience rather than theory. The use of volunteers, community groups and contra deals has resulted in a very personal management style.

The festival has a similar on-site schedule to many of the festivals around Australia. For example, the Northern Rivers Folk Festival, although smaller, is set up and broken down over the same period as the Port Fairy Folk Festival. The following time line is not exhaustive; however, it highlights the milestones that must occur before the next step can happen.

Note how long the festival takes to set up — two weeks — compared to the shut down period — two days. Also note how the security arrives the day before the event begins.

Timing	Day of the week	Milestone task or event	Notes
Fortnight before the festival begins		• pegs set out and surfaces marked	Position of each venue indicated with marking paint. Position of underground power lines are marked on the surface.
Week before the festival begins	Saturday	• marquees and smaller tents arrive	All of the tents are hired and transported from Melbourne.
	Sunday	• tents are erected • electrician constructs power boxes at each venue	Power boxes are needed for on-site construction, particularly for the hydraulic hammers for the hoeckers.
	Monday, Tuesday, Wednesday	• stages, lighting bars, more tents and tables are set up • specially-made fire extinguishers and hoses are set up • the mobile hot water unit arrives • toilets are joined to the sewerage	The extensive underground power is tapped into and the power boards for sound and lighting are connected. This is an advantage of creating an infrastructure for the festival at one site.
	Thursday	• security arrives	Minimal security guards the site Thursday night.
		• Port Fairy Folk Festival events begin at 8.00 p.m.	Full-strength security team on site by 6.00 p.m.
Post-festival	Monday	• flags are taken down • traders leave on Monday night • barbeque dinner, security leaves	The local cycling club organises a barbeque dinner for 5.00 p.m. for all of the workers.
	Wednesday	• committee inspects site	The construction crew have already inspected all equipment, reported any damage and packed the equipment away.

William O'Toole has worked as an entertainment consultant to the Port Fairy Folk Festival supplying performers and event concepts. He has also performed at the festival with the group Sirocco.

Questions

1 Create a Gantt chart that displays the logistics of the Port Fairy Folk Festival.

2 What aspects of the logistics of the festival are 'sensitive' (i.e. a small change in one area will have a large effect on the festival)?

3 Imagine the festival had to change locations to a nearby town. What elements of the logistics would remain the same and what would need changing?

4 Create a risk management list for the festival that would be used as the basis of a 'skull session'.

REFERENCES

Buchan Communications Group, May 1997, *Australia–India New Horizons Evaluation Report*, Department of Foreign Affairs and Trade, Canberra.

Catherwood, D. W. & Van Kirk, R. L. 1992, *The Complete Guide to Special Events Management*, John Wiley & Sons, New York.

CIM Rostrum n.d., *The Comprehensive Convention Planner's Manual*, vol. 32, Rank Publishing Company, St Leonards.

Coyle, John J., Bardi, Edward J. & Langley Jnr, C. John 1988, *The Management of Business Logistics*, 4th edn, West Publishing Company, St Paul.

Dinsmore, P. C. 1990, *Human Factors in Project Management*, AMACOM, New York.

Gilmour, Peter 1993, *Logistics Management, An Australian Framework*, Addison Wesley Longman, Melbourne.

Goldblatt, J. 1997, *Special Events: Best Practices in Modern Event Management*, 2nd edn, Van Nostrand Reinhold.

Graham, S., Goldblatt, J. & Delpy, L. 1995, *The Ultimate Guide to Sports Event Management and Marketing*, Richard Irwin, Chicago.

Lock, Dennis 1988, *Project Management*, Gower Press, Aldershot, England.

Marine Corps Doctrinal Publication no. 4, Logistics 1997, http://www.doctrine.quantico.usmc.mil/mcdp/mcdp4.html

Marsh, P. D. V. 1984, *Contract Negotiation Handbook*, 2nd edn, Gower Press, Aldershot, England.

Monmonier, Mark 1996, *How to Lie with Maps*, 2nd edn, University of Chicago Press, Chicago.

Neighbourhood Arts Unit 1991, *Community Festival Handbook*, City of Melbourne, Melbourne.

Pagonis, Lt General William G. 1992, *Moving Mountains: Lessons in Leadership and Logistics from the Gulf War*, Harvard Business School Press, Boston.

Queensland Folk Federation Incorporated 1997, *Operational and Site Management Plan 1997*.

CHAPTER 14

Staging *events*

LEARNING OBJECTIVES

After studying this chapter, you should be able to:

■ analyse the staging of an event according to its constituent elements

■ demonstrate how these elements relate to each other and to the theme of the event

■ understand the safety elements of each aspect of staging

■ identify the relative importance of the staging elements for different types of events

■ use the tools of staging.

The term 'staging' originates from the presentation of plays at the theatre. It refers to bringing together all the elements of a theatrical production for its presentation on a stage. Most events that use this term take place at a single venue and require organisation similar to that of a theatrical production. However, whereas a play can take place over a season, a special event may take place in one night. Examples of this type of event are product launches, company parties and celebrations, awards ceremonies, conference events, concerts, large weddings, corporate dinners and opening and closing events.

Staging can also refer to the organisation of a venue within a much larger festival. A large festival may have performance areas positioned around a site. Each of these venues may have a range of events with a distinct theme. At the Sydney Royal Easter Show, there are a number of performance areas, each with its own style. Because it is part of a much larger event, one performance area or event has to fit in with the overall planning of the complete event and has to fit in with the festival programming and logistics. However, each performance area is to some extent its own kingdom, with its own micro-logistics, management, staff and individual character. For example, at one of the stages of Sydney's Royal Easter Show the theme was world music and dance. The venue had its own event director, stage manager and light and sound technicians. Although it was part of the overall theme of the Royal Easter Show, it was allowed a certain amount of autonomy by the Show entertainment director.

The main concerns of staging are as follows:
- theming and event design
- choice of venue
- audience and guests
- stage
- power, lights and sound
- audiovisuals and special effects
- catering
- performers
- crew
- hospitality
- the production schedule
- recording the event
- contingencies.

This chapter analyses the staging of an event according to these elements. It demonstrates how these elements revolve around a central event theme. The type of event will determine how important each of these elements is to the others. However, common to the staging of different events are the tools: the stage plan, the contact and responsibility list and the production schedule.

THEMING AND EVENT DESIGN

When staging an event, the major artistic and creative decision to be made is that of determining what the theme is to be. The theme of an event differentiates it from other events. In the corporate area, the client may determine the theme of the event. For example, the client holding a corporate party or product launch may want medieval Europe as the theme, or Australiana, complete with native animals and bush band. Outside the corporate area, the theme for one of the stages at a festival may be blues music, debating or a children's circus. Whatever the nature of the event, once the theme is established, the elements of the event must be designed to fit in with the theme. This is straightforward when it comes to deciding on the entertainment and catering. With the medieval corporate party, the entertainment may include jongleurs and jugglers and the catering may be spit roasts and wine. However, audiovisuals may need a lot of thought in order to enhance the theme. The sound and lights must complement the entertainment or they may not fit in with the period theme. Figure 14.1 is a breakdown of the elements of staging, and it emphasises the central role of the theme of the event.

■ **Figure 14.1**
The elements of staging revolve around the theme

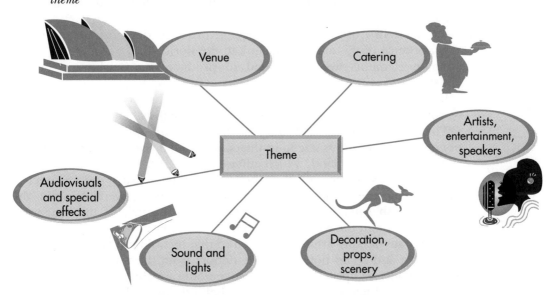

The director of the Port Fairy Folk Festival expresses the importance of staging in the following way:

> ■ A great concert experience begins with the excitement built by the advertised program and venue facilities. The audience must be given reasonable comfort and have their expectations met. You must deliver the advertised act, at the advertised place and time and leave them wanting more. This means that the staging will look good, preferably great, the sound production and lighting will be of high quality, the overall presentation will be dignified and professional. ■

■ An example of event theme and design: *Macquarie Marshes*

The Macquarie Marshes are a wetland system on the Macquarie River in central New South Wales. The marshes filter the river and are a major bird habitat.

As a way of drawing the attention of the public to this area, the music group Sirocco and the local National Parks and Wildlife officers organised an innovative event in the wetlands. The event consisted of:

- a concert of original compositions by Sirocco describing the area in music
- various performances, including a dance by stilt-walkers dressed as sacred ibises
- overnight camping
- a guided walk through the wetlands.

The concert was broadcast live on radio around Australia, Asia and the Pacific by satellite. As the event occurred in a wildlife heritage park not normally open to the public, only 1000 people were allowed into the area.

The three components of the theme decided by the event organisers were:

- the beauty of the Australian environment and the need to conserve it
- high quality cultural performance taking inspiration from the environment
- the latest in Australian technology, in order to demonstrate the world importance of this area and its link to the world.

These elements were combined to produce the Celebration of the Marshes.

It was also important that the event include all the local farming interests — cotton and beef — as well as the environmentalists.

The site was chosen and laid out in accordance with the theme components. The event was staged in the coolabah and river red gum woodland adjacent to the wetland, which allowed ample dry camping space but retained a sense of being within the wetlands. The clear water was next to the stage and the sounds of the bird life enhanced the event. At night, the double splash (one from the legs followed by the tail) of the kangaroos jumping through the wetlands could be clearly heard.

A separate parking area was situated so that it could not be seen from the event area and could not, therefore, detract from the venue environment. The stage was set up so that the audience would see the performers in front of the trees, which were lit from below. Behind this, and quite visible to the audience, was the large ITERRA satellite dish pointing to the stars. At one point in the evening, two four-metre high sacred ibises (stilt-walkers in full costume) came out of the wetlands, to the surprise of the audience, and performed a dance choreographed to the music.

The promotional campaign had to reflect all the elements of the design. The chosen logo was a stunning colour photograph of the wetland plant, nardoo. All the artwork was high quality, environmentally friendly and recyclable. An unintended consequence of this was a high demand for the posters of the event. Recycled paper was used for the tickets. (See figure 14.2.)

The music used high quality digital recordings of the sounds of the birds and other wildlife in the wetlands. The media launch, one month before the event, was staged in an urban rainforest in Sydney.

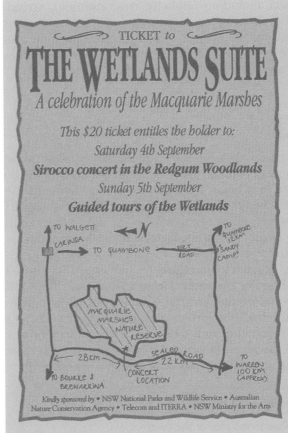

Program
- Saturday 4th September: 7pm Sirocco concert.

8pm Broadcast by ABC–FM and ITERRA Satellite to Asia and the Pacific

Overnight camping (bring a tent)
- Sunday 5th September: tours of the Wetlands every half hour from 8.30am.

Camping suggestions and regulations
- Parking and camping directions provided on entry
- Bring your own tent and camping gear
- Water and toilet facilities provided
- Food and wine on sale
- NO fires
- NO pets
- Beware of snakes
- This is a wildlife sanctuary and the purchase of the ticket implies that you act safely and responsibly — the organisers accept NO responsibility.

The Marshes

The Macquarie Marshes make up a diverse and extensive wetland on the Macquarie River in North West NSW. The Marshes begin where the River breaks into smaller distributive streams. These rejoin and divide many times before the river emerges as a single channel. It then flows into the Darling River and finally into the Southern Ocean.

Prolific in wildlife including a stunning range of waterbirds like the brolga, magpie goose, sacred ibis and spoonbill. The Marshes were a well known meeting place for the Aboriginal tribes.

The Wetlands acts as a filter for the river and has been identified as integral to the health of the inland river systems.

It is VITAL that the Marshes be preserved.

■ **Figure 14.2** *The Wetlands Suite — a sample ticket for the event*

Food was provided by the local farmers and the profits went to the local schools. To minimise any possible impact on the natural environment, water was brought in by truck and portable toilets were hired. An important design element was that the site be left in pristine condition. The choice of generators was made according to strict guidelines — the latest silent generator was driven up from Sydney. Even the helicopter that was used to film the event for television enhanced the high technology aspect. Indirectly, its presence stressed that the wetlands are of world interest and are not just a local swamp. The audience accommodation was in the bushwalking tradition of small tents scattered through the river red gum woodland. In one sense, the lack of facilities was an element in the event's design.

On the Sunday, the National Parks and Wildlife officers guided small groups through the wetlands. This involved the audience wading waist deep through the clear water. This was an unforgettable part of the event experience.

The products from the event — a video and CD — were themed in much the same way. The nardoo picture was used on the CD cover and the video showed the beauty of the Australian wetlands. It ended with footage of the event.

Designing the event around the theme enabled the audience to be enveloped by the event. All aspects, including publicity, entertainment, arrival, accommodation, food and merchandise, were arranged using the theme as the guide. The sensitive nature of the project, which involved possible conflicting interests, meant that every aspect of the event had to be well thought out in order to celebrate an area that is, ultimately, owned by the world.

CHOICE OF VENUE

The choice of venue is a crucial decision that will ultimately determine many of the elements of staging. Figure 14.3 lists the major factors in the choice of a venue. The venue may be an obvious part of the theme of the event. A corporate party that takes place in a zoo is using the venue as part of the event experience. However, many events take place within 'four walls and a roof', the venue being chosen for other factors. It can be regarded as an empty canvas on which the event is 'painted'. Cameron (1993), in his work on community theatre, describes the events he has staged in disused factories, forests and stages floating on water. He describes how the event manager can utilise the atmosphere and natural beauty of open-air performances. In these situations, the traditional roles of stage manager and event manager become blurred. When the audience and the performers mix together and where they and the venue become the entertainment package, the delineation between stage and auditorium is no longer appropriate.

■ **Figure 14.3**
The factors in venue selection

- Matching the venue with the theme of the event
- Matching the size of the venue to the size of the event
- Venue configuration, including sight lines and seating configuration
- History of events at that venue, including the venue's reputation
- Availability
- What the venue can provide
- Transport to, from and around the venue; parking
- Access for audience, equipment, performers, VIPs, staff and the disabled
- Toilets and other amenities
- Catering equipment and preferred caterers
- Power (amount available and outlets) and lights
- Communication, including telephone
- Climate, including microclimate and ventilation
- Emergency plans and exits

A special event that uses a purpose-built venue, such as an entertainment centre, will find that much of the infrastructure will be in place. However, because there are so many factors in an event that are dependent on the venue or site, an inspection is absolutely necessary. For conference events, *Rostrum* (vol. 32) suggests that the event manager attends a function at the venue and tests the facilities. They recommend placing a long distance telephone call, trying the food and staying in the approved accommodation.

Two documents that are a good starting point for making an informed choice about the venue are the venue map and the list of facilities. However, *Rostrum* (vol. 32) recommends that the event manager meet with the venue management before making any commitment to hire the venue. The principal purpose of this meeting is to check the accuracy of the two documents, since the map, and the list of facilities and the photographs can often be out of date or aimed at promoting the venue rather than imparting detailed information. The photograph of the venue, for example, may be taken with a wide-angle lens so that all the facilities are included. Such a photograph may not give a realistic view of the site if it is being used for event design.

As with many aspects of supplier selection, the World Wide Web has had a significant effect on venue choice. Using a search engine on the Web is often the first action in the investigation of a suitable venue. Some Web sites display a choice of venues once the information, such as size of audience, approximate location and type of event, has been entered. The major hotels, conventions and exhibition centres, universities and purpose-built venues have Web sites to enable the matching of event requirements to venue characteristics, However, this method faces the same limitations as the use of photos and brochures to assess a venue. The Web sites are a tool of selling the venue, not a technical description. In addition, many suitable venues may not have a Web presence. The Web will only show venues that expect to host events. If the event is truly special, the event venue may be part of that theme. A car park or a rainforest will not appear in a search for event venues.

AUDIENCE AND GUESTS

The larger issues of audience (customer) logistics have been described in chapter 13. The event staging considerations concerning the audience are:
* position of entrances and exits
* arrival times — dump or trickle
* seating and sight lines
* facilities.

Goldblatt (1997) emphasises the importance of the entrance and reception area of an event in establishing the event theme, and suggests that the organiser should look at it from the guest's point of view. It is in this area that appropriate signage and meeting and greeting become important to the flow of 'traffic' and to the wellbeing of the guests. An example of a carefully planned entrance area was at the 1998 Woodford Folk Festival, where the children's area was entered through the mouth of a large papier-mâché dragon.

Once the guests have entered the event area, problems can occur that are specific to the type of event. In the case of conferences, audiences immediately head for the back rows. Interestingly, Graham et al. (1995, p. 65) mention the opposite problem occurs at sports events, where the front rows are rushed as soon as the gates open. The solution, therefore, is in the type of admission. For example, organisers can adopt reserved seating methods, using ticket numbers or roped-off sections and a designated seating plan. The style of seating can be chosen to suit the event; theatre, classroom and banquet type seating are three examples. Ultimately, the seating plan has to take into consideration:

• type of seating — fixed or moveable
• the size of the audience
• the method of audience arrival
• safety factors, including emergency exits and fire regulations
• placement and size of the aisles
• sight lines to the performances, speakers or audiovisual displays
• disabled access
• catering needs.

The facilities provided for the guests will depend on the type of event. Referring to figure 14.4, the corporate event will focus on particular audience facilities as they relate to hospitality and catering, whereas a festival event will concentrate on audience facilities as they relate to entertainment. For example, there are no chairs for the audience in some of the Port Fairy Folk Festival performance areas but, because of the nature of the festival, spectators are happy to bring their own or sit on the ground. At the other end of the spectrum, the 1998 Australian Petroleum Production and Exploration Association Conference Dinner, organised by Sing Australia in the Great Hall at Parliament House, Canberra, had high quality furnishings and facilities.

THE STAGE

A stage at an event is rarely the same as a theatrical stage complete with proscenium arch and auditorium. It can range from the back of a truck to a barge in a harbour. It is important to note that, in event management, the term 'stage' can be applied to the general staging area and not just to a purpose built stage. However, all stages require a stage map called the stage plan. The stage plan is simply a bird's-eye view of the performance area, showing the infrastructure, such as lighting fixtures, entrances, exits and power outlets. The stage plan is one of the staging tools (as shown in figure 14.11) and a communication device that enables the event to run smoothly. For large events, the stage plan is drawn in different ways for different people, and supplied on a 'need-to-know basis'. For example, a stage plan for the lighting technician would look different from the plan for the performers. The master stage plan contains all these different plans, each drawn on a separate layer of transparent paper. Other plans that are used in event design are the front elevation and side elevation. In contrast to the bird's-eye view that the stage plan gives, these plans show the staging area as a ground-level view from the front and side, respectively. They assist in establishing the audience's sight lines; that is, the audience's view of the staging area and performers.

An example of when a large stage plan for a special event was used was for the conference of the Société Internationale d'Urologie in Sydney in 1996. The 3000 guests were treated to three streams of entertainment that reflected modern Australia: 'multicultural', including a lion dance and middle eastern dancers; 'land and sea', including a large sailing boat and Aboriginal and Australiana entertainers; and 'cities', with fashion parades and modern dancers.

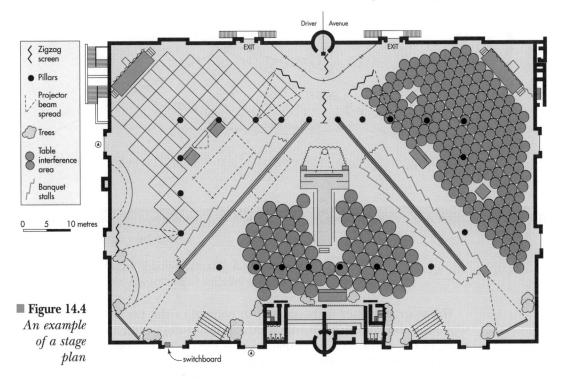

Figure 14.4
An example of a stage plan

Roger Foley, of Fogg Production, the creator of the Australian Multicultural Show, described the stage plan:

■ The stage plan is 100 per cent accurate. I went to the building's architects to get an exact drawing and we used that as the master stage plan. The accuracy of having all the building's peculiarities on a plan allowed all the sub-contractors to anticipate any problems in setting up. [There were] one-metre markings on the building's circumference. All these little things enabled the whole show, including 13 stages and 21 food stalls, to be set up and bumped out in 24 hours. A stage plan for each of the individual stages was created by enlarging that section from the master plan and filling in the necessary information. ■

When the staging of an event includes a large catering component, the stage plan is referred to as the venue layout or floor plan. This is the case in many corporate and conference events, where hospitality and catering become a major part of the staging. Figure 14.5 illustrates how the focus on the elements of staging changes according to the style of event.

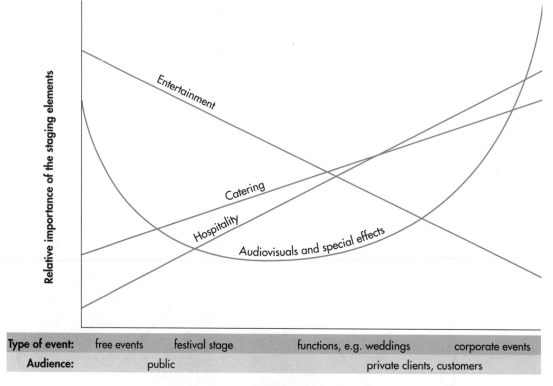

The stage manager is the person in control of the performance and for signalling the cues that coordinate the work of the performers. The scheduling of the event on a particular stage is generally the responsibility of the event manager. The stage manager makes sure that this happens according to the plan. The public face of the event may be called the master of ceremonies (MC) or compere. The compere and the stage manager work closely together to ensure that all goes according to the plan. The compere may also make public announcements such as those about lost children and program changes.

The combination of electric wiring, hot lights, special effects and the fast movement of performers and staff in a small space that is perhaps two metres above ground level makes the risk management of the staging area particularly important. At the event, stage safety is generally the responsibility of the stage manager. Figure 14.6 on the opposite page lists a selection of safety considerations.

■ There must be a well-constructed stage, preferably done professionally by a company with adequate insurance.

■ There must be clear well-lit access points to the stage.

■ All protrusions and steps should be secured and clearly marked.

■ Equipment and boxes should be placed out of the way and well marked.

■ There should be work lights that provide white lighting before and after the event.

■ All electric cabling must be secured.

■ A first-aid kit and other emergency equipment should be at hand.

■ There must be clear guidelines on who is in authority during an emergency.

■ A list of all relevant contact numbers should be made.

The director of the Port Fairy Folk Festival gives this advice for stage managers:

■ Make sure you anticipate the many little things that can ruin an otherwise great concert experience. Watch out for distracting buzzes or cracks in the sound (e.g. from powerful fridges); settle out of control children or noisy audiences; ensure all small stage requirements are there (e.g. chair, stool, table, water); ensure you have competent MCs who are well prepared; stop delays before they start. ■

The backstage area is a private room or tent near the performance area and is set aside for the performers and staff. It provides the crew with a place to relax and the performers with a place to prepare for the performance and wind down afterwards. It can be used for storage of equipment and for communication between the stage manager and performers, and it is where the food and drink are kept.

*P*OWER

Staging of any event involves large numbers of people and to service this crowd electricity is indispensable. It should never be taken for granted. Factors that need to be considered concerning power are:
• type of power — three phase or single phase
• amount of power needed, particularly at peak times
• emergency power
• position and number of power outlets
• types of leads and distance from power source to device
• the correct wiring of the venue, since old venues can often be improperly earthed
• the incoming equipment's volt/amp rating
• safety factors, including the covering of leads and the possibility of electricity earth leakage as a result of rain
• local and State regulations regarding power.

IGHTS

Lighting at a venue has two functions. Pragmatically, lights allow everyone to see what is happening; artistically, they are integral to the design of the event. The general venue or site lighting is important in that it allows all the other aspects of staging to take place. For this reason, it is usually the first item on the check list when deciding on a venue. Indoor lights include signage lights (exit, toilets etc.) as well as those illuminating specific areas such as catering and ticket collection. Outside the venue, lighting is required for venue identification, safety, security and sponsor signs.

Once the general venue or site lighting is confirmed, lighting design needs to be considered. The questions to ask when considering lighting are both practical and aesthetic. They include the following.

- Does it fit in with and enhance the overall event theme?
- Can it be used for ambient lighting as well as performance lighting?
- Is there a back-up?
- What are the power requirements (lights can draw far more power than the sound system)?
- Will it interfere with the electrics of other systems? For example, a dimmer board can create an audible buzz in the sound system.
- Does it come with a light operator, that is, the person responsible for the planning of the lighting with the lighting board?
- What light effects are needed (strobe, cross fading) and can the available lights do this?
- What equipment is needed, (e.g. trees and cans), and is there a place on the site or in the venue to erect it?
- How can the lighting assist in the safety and security of the event?

The lighting plot or lighting plan is a map of the venue that shows the type and position of the lighting. As Reid (1995) points out, the decisions that the event manager has to make when creating a lighting plan are:

- placement of the lights
- the type of lights, including floods and follow spots
- where the light should be pointed
- what colours to use.

OUND

The principal reason for having sound equipment at an event is so that all the audience can clearly hear the music, speeches and audio effects. The sound system also is used to:

- communicate between the sound engineer and the stage manager (talk-back or intercom)
- monitor the sound
- create a sound recording of the event

- broadcast the sound to other venues or through other media, including television, radio and the Internet.

This means that the type of equipment used needs to be designed according to the:

- type of sound to be amplified, including spoken word and music
- size and make-up of the audience. An older audience, for example, may like the music at a different volume from a younger audience.
- acoustic properties of the room. Some venues have a bad echo problem, for example.
- theme of the event. A sound system painted bright silver may look out of place at a black tie dinner.

The choice of size, type and location of the sound speakers at an event can make a difference to the guests' experience of the sound. Figure 14.7 shows two simplified plans for speaker positions at a venue. The speakers may all be next to the stage, which is common at music concerts, or distributed around the site. They may also be flown from supports above the audience. At a large site, with speakers widely distributed, the sound engineers need to take into account the natural delay of sound travelling from the various speakers to the members of the audience.

■ **Figure 14.7**
Two examples of audio speaker layout

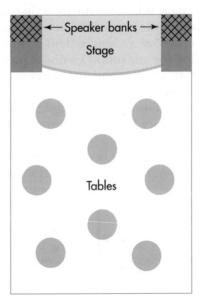
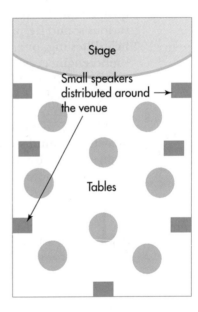

For small events, a simple public address (PA) system may be used. This consists of a microphone, microphone stand and one or two speakers. It is basically the same as a home stereo system with a microphone added, and generally has only enough power to reach a small audience. The quality of sound produced makes such systems suitable for speeches only.

For larger events that have more complex sound requirements, a larger sound system is needed. This would incorporate:

- microphones, which may include lapel mikes and radio mikes
- microphone stands

- cabling, including from the microphones to the mixing desk
- mixing desk, which adjusts the quality and level of the sound coming from the microphones before it goes out the speakers
- amplifier
- speakers, which can vary in size from bass speakers to treble speakers, and which enhance the quality of the sound within a certain sound spectrum
- sound engineer or sound technician, who looks after all aspects of the sound, particularly the sound quality that is heard by the audience
- back-up equipment, including spare leads and microphones.

The next step up from this type of system includes all of the above as well as:
- foldback speakers (are also called monitors) that channel the sound back to the speakers or performers so they can hear themselves over the background sound
- foldback mixing desk
- foldback engineer who is responsible for the quality of sound going through the monitors.

If an event needs a sound system managed by a sound engineer, time must be allocated to tune the sound system. This means that the acoustic qualities of the venue are taken into account by trying out the effect of various sound frequencies within the venue. This is the reason for the often-heard 'testing, one, two, one, two' as a sound system is being prepared. The sound engineer is also looking for any sound feedback problems. Feedback is an unwanted, often high-pitched sound that occurs when the sound coming out of the speakers is picked up by the microphones and comes out of the speakers again, thereby building on the original sound. To avoid the problem of feedback, microphones must be positioned so that they face away from sound speakers. The tuning of a large sound system is one of the main reasons for having a sound check or run-through before an event. Figure 14.8 shows a simplified sound run-through prior to an event.

■ **Figure 14.8**
A simple flow chart for sound systems

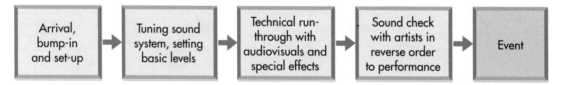

Volume and sound leakage during an event can become a major problem. Local councils can close an event if there are too many complaints from residents. At some venues, for example, there are volume switches that automatically turn off the power if the sound level is too high. At multi-venue events, sound leakage between stages can be minimised by:
- thoughtful placement of the stages
- careful positioning of all sound speakers (including the monitors)
- constant monitoring of the volume level
- careful programming of the events on each stage in a way that avoids interference.

AUDIOVISUAL AND SPECIAL EFFECTS

Many event managers hire lighting and sound from separate companies and integrate their services into the overall design of the event. However, there are suppliers that provide both lighting and sound equipment and act as consultants prior to the event. These audiovisual companies can supply a fully integrated system of film, video, slides and often special effects. However, most audiovisual companies are specialists in flat-screen presentations, and the special effect area is often best left to specialists in this field. For example, pyrotechnics obviously require different skills and licences from ice sculptors. Complex events that use a variety of special effects and audiovisuals require a coordinator who is familiar with the event theme and knows how to link all the specialist areas to each other. This coordinator is called the event producer. Although the terms 'event manager', 'stage manager' and 'event producer' are confusing, they are terms that are used in the industry. The position of event producer is created when there are many different specialists involved in the event. Organisers of corporate events, including product launches and conferences, often sub-contract the audiovisual elements, because the specialist knowledge required means an expert is needed to operate these systems effectively. The decision to use an audiovisual company for an event depends on:

• how the audiovisual presentation fits in with the overall event design
• the budget allocated to the event
• the skills of the audiovisual company, including its technical hardware, software and the abilities of the audiovisual producer and writer.

For large-budget events, the audiovisual company will act as a consultant, with the producer and writer researching and creating a detailed audiovisual script.

Roger Foley of Fogg Production is an expert in the area of 'illuminating art as entertainment and performance'. He regards the essence of an event as the special effects. His aim is to make the event itself a special effect. 'A special effect is anything that is not anticipated or expected. It must heighten the awareness of the viewers and increase their anticipation, sensitivity and receptiveness. The result is to make it easy to get across the message of the event.' Roger emphasises the need to take command completely of all the elements of the special effect. The event producer must know exactly what they are getting when hiring specialists. Fireworks, for example, must be individually listed, fully integrated into the event and not just left to the specialist. The timing of setting off the various devices must be exact, without any gaps.

According to Goldblatt (1997), special effects at an event are used to attract attention, generate excitement and sustain interest. In larger festivals, such as the opening of the Melbourne Festival on the Yarra River, the pyrotechnics become part of the overall logistics planning. Event managers and planners must fully realise the importance of event decoration, scenery and appropriate props as an enhancing tool for the staging of any event.

Because much of the audiovisual and special effects technology is highly complex, it is often 'preprogrammed'. This means that all lighting, audiovisual and sound 'presets' (technical elements positioned prior to the event), including the changing light and sound levels and the cueing of video and slide presentations, can be programmed into the controlling computer. The computer control of much of the audiovisuals means that the whole presentation can be fully integrated and set up well in advance. Because these aspects are prearranged, including all the cue times, the advantage is that few technicians are needed to control these operations during the event. The disadvantages are that spontaneity can be taken from the event and, the more complex the technology, the more things can go wrong. Moreover, the technology becomes the master of the cue times and it is nearly impossible to take advantage of any unforeseen opportunities.

PROPS AND DECORATION

Some events are similar to operatic productions in the use of scenery, stage properties (props) and decoration. By skilled use of these elements the attendees can feel as though they are in an imaginary world. The audience can often enhance this by dressing the part and therefore becoming part of the entertainment. Themed parties, festivals and dinners are a significant part of the event industry. The way these staging elements are combined and their relative emphasis at the event often reflects the personal style of the event company. Lena Malouf (1999) in her book, *Behind the Scenes at Special Events*, devotes over two-thirds of the content to theming in events, in particular the use of flowers, lights and colour to create a sense of wonder.

CATERING

Catering can be the major element in staging, depending on the theme and nature of an event. Most purpose-built venues already have catering arrangements in place. For example, Parliament House in Canberra contracts with catering companies. The conference dinners that take place in the Great Hall can only use the in-house caterers. Figure 14.9 illustrates some of the many factors to be considered in catering.

The event producer Reno Dal points out with regard to aspects of catering:

■ My rule for the staff to client ratio at a corporate function is:
silver service, 1 to 10 ratio;
five-star service 1 to 25 ratio;
general catering 1 to 50 ratio.

I emphasise that there should be 'waves of service'. This means that the main course and beverage arrive at the right time and then waiters leave the guests until the appropriate moment for the next course. I like to see each table as a stage, with the placements presented in the same manner as a theatrical stage. The waiters become the performers dressed to the theme. The waiters love it — after all, it's a difficult job at the best of times. ■

Figure 14.9
Issues to be considered when arranging catering for an event

In-house or contracted?

The advantage of in-house catering is the knowledge of the venue. The advantage of contract catering is that the event manager may have a special arrangement with the caterer that has been built up over time; the event manager can choose all aspects of the catering; and the catering can be tendered out and a competitive bid sought.

Quality control factors to consider

- Appropriateness and enhancement of the event theme
- Menu selection and design, including special diets and food displays
- Quality of staff and supervision
- Equipment, including style and quantity, and selection of in-house or hired
- Cleanliness
- Cultural appropriateness — a major consideration in a culturally diverse society
- Staff to guest ratio

Costs

- Are there any guarantees, including those against loss and breakages?
- What are the payment terms?
- Who is responsible for licences and permits: the caterer, the venue or event management?
- What deposits and up front fees are there?
- What is the per capita expenditure? Is each guest getting value commensurate with the client's expenditure?

Waste management

- Must occur before, during and after the event
- Must conform to health regulations and environmental concerns
- Must be appropriate to the event theme

As Graham et al. (1995) stress, the consumption of alcoholic beverages at an event gives rise to many concerns for the event manager. These include the special training of staff, which party holds the licence (venue, event manager or client), and the legal age for consumption. The possible problems that arise from the sale of alcohol, for example, increased audience noise at the end of the event and general behavioural problems, can affect almost all aspects of the event. The decision on whether to allow the sale or consumption of alcohol can be crucial to the success of an event and needs careful thought.

There are a variety of ways that the serving of alcohol can be negotiated with a caterer. The drinks service can be from the bar or may be served at the table by the glass, bottle or jug. A caterer may offer a 'drinks package', which means that the drinks are free for, say, the first hour of the catered event. A subtle result of this type of deal is that the guest can find it hard to find a drinks waiter in the first hour.

ERFORMERS

The 'talent' (as performers are often called) at an event can range from music groups to motivational speakers to specially commissioned shows. A performing group can form a major part of an event's design. The major factors to consider when employing artists are listed below.

- **Contact.** The event's entertainment coordinator needs to establish contact only with the person responsible for the employment of the artist or artists. This could be the artist, an agent representing the artist, or the manager of a group. It is important to establish this line of authority at the beginning when working with the artists.
- **Staging requirements.** A rock band, for example, will have more complex sound requirements than a folk singer. These requirements are usually listed on a document called the spec (specification) sheet. Many groups will also have their own stage plan illustrating the area needed and their preferred configuration of the performance area.
- **Availability for rehearsal, media attention and performance.** The available times given by the artists' management should include the time it takes for the artists to set up on stage as well as the time it takes to vacate the stage or performance area. These are referred to as the time needed for 'set-up' and 'pull-down'. These times need to be considered when, for example, scheduling a series of rehearsals with a number of performing groups.
- **Accompanying personnel.** Many artists travel with an entourage that can include technicians, cooks, stylists and bodyguards. It is important to establish their numbers, and what their roles and needs are.
- **Contracts and legal requirements.** The agreement between the event manager and the performers is described in chapter 9. Of particular importance to the staging are union minimum rates and conditions, the legal structure of the artists and issues such as workers' compensation and public liability. Copyright is also important as its ownership can affect the use of the performance for broadcast and future promotions.
- **Payment.** Most performing groups work on the understanding that they will be paid immediately for their services. Except for 'headline' acts that have a company structure, the 30-, 60- or 90-day invoicing cycle is not appropriate for most performers, who rarely have the financial resources that would allow them to wait for payment.

Performers come from a variety of performance cultural backgrounds. This means that different performers have different expectations about the facilities available for them and how they are to be treated. Theatre performers and concert musicians, for example, expect direct performance guidelines — conducting, scripting or a musical score. Street and outdoor festival performers, on the other hand, are used to less formal conditions and to improvising.

Supervision of performers in a small theatre is generally left to the assistant stage manager, whereas a festival stage may not have this luxury and it may be the stage manager's responsibility. Regardless of who undertakes it, supervision cannot be overlooked. The person responsible needs to make contact with the artists on arrival, give them the appropriate run sheets, introduce them to the relevant crew members and show them the location of the green room (the room in which performers and invited guests are entertained). At the end of the performance, the artists' supervisor needs to assist them in leaving the area.

THE CREW

The chapter on leadership (chapter 6) discussed the role of staff and volunteers at an event. While a large festival or sport event will usually rely on the work of volunteers, staging tends to be handled by professionals. Dealing with cueing, working with complex and potentially dangerous equipment and handling professional performers leaves little room for indecision and inexperience. Professionalism is essential when staging an event. For example, the staging of a concert performance will need skilled sound engineers, roadies, security staff, stage crew, ticket sellers and even ushers. (The roadies are the skilled labourers that assist with the set up and breakdown of the sound and lights.) The crew is selected by matching the tasks involved to the skills of each crew member and ensuring that they all have the ability to work together.

The briefing is the meeting, before the event, at which the crew members are given the briefs, or roles, that match their skills. The names and jobs of the crew members are then kept on a contact and responsibility sheet.

Neil Cameron, the organiser of many events and lantern parades around Australia and overseas, stresses the importance of being 'brief' at the briefing. His events involve large numbers of performers moving near fire sculptures. These sculptures can be over three storeys high and take weeks to build. He first briefs the support organisations, such as St John Ambulance and the Fire Brigade, and emphasises the importance of communication and chain of command. At the crew briefing, Neil is conscious of not overloading the leaders with too much information.

The event producer should also not forget that the crew comes with an enormous amount of experience in staging events. They can provide valuable input into the creation and design of the event.

It is also interesting to note that the changes in the events industry, particularly in the audiovisual area, are reflected in the make-up and number of crew members. As event producer Mark Cavanagh points out:

■ Events in 1998 compared to those as recently as the early 90s require [far fewer] technical staff. When we produced the launch of the Good Food Guide for 800 guests, the entire presentation, including rapidly evolving imagery in sync with a variable sound score, only needed two technical staff on the night. ■

HOSPITALITY

A major part of the package offered to sponsors is hospitality (Catherwood & Van Kirk 1992). What will the sponsors expect event management to provide for them and their guests? They may require tickets, food and beverages, souvenirs and gifts. As well as the sponsors, the event may benefit in the long term by offering hospitality to stakeholders, VIPs and others, including politicians, media units, media personalities, clients of the sponsor, potential sponsors, partners and local opinion leaders. They are all referred to as the guests of the event.

The invitation may be the first impression of the event that the potential guest receives, and it therefore needs to convey the theme of the event. It should create a desire to attend as well as impart information. Figure 14.10 is a check list for making sure the various elements of hospitality are covered.

In their informative work on sports events, Graham et al. (1995, p. 84) describe the four stages for achieving success in the provision of hospitality to guests. Stage 1 is to know the guests' expectations. Stage 2 is to exceed the guests' expectations, particularly through providing extra amenities. Stage 3 is to be responsive to changes in the guests' needs during the event. Stage 4 is to evaluate the hospitality at the event so that it can be improved next time.

Corporate sponsors may have a variety of reasons for attending the event and these have to be taken into account in hospitality planning. Graham et al. (1995) suggest networking opportunities for business, an incentive for a high sales performance, an opportunity for entertaining possible clients, or just the creation of goodwill from their customers.

The hospitality experience is of particular importance at corporate events. In one sense, such an event is centred around hospitality (see figure 14.5). As it is a private function, there is no public and the members of the audience are the guests. Most of the items on the hospitality check list, from the invitations to the personal service, are applicable to staging these events. For the guests, the hospitality experience is fundamental to the event experience.

■ Figure 14.10
*Looking
after
corporate
sponsors —
a hospitality
check list*

HOSPITALITY CHECK LIST

Invitations

❑ Is the design of high quality and is it innovative?

❑ Does the method of delivery allow time to reply? Would hand delivery or e-mail be appropriate?

❑ Does the content of the invitation include time, date, name of event, how to RSVP, directions and parking?

❑ Should promotional material be included with the invitation?

Arrival

❑ Has timing been planned so that guests arrive at the best moment?

❑ What are the parking arrangements?

❑ Who will do the meeting and greeting? Will there be someone there to welcome them to the event?

❑ Have waiting times been reduced? For example, will guests receive a welcome cocktail while waiting to be booked into the accommodation?

Amenities

❑ Is there to be a separate area for guests? This can be a marquee, corporate box (at a sporting event) or a club room.

❑ What food and beverages will be provided? Is there a need for a special menu and personal service?

❑ Is there a separate, high-quality viewing area of the performance with good views and facilities?

❑ Has special communication, such as signage or an information desk, been provided?

Gifts

❑ Have tickets to the event, especially for clients, been organised?

❑ What souvenirs (programs, pins, T-shirts, CDs) will there be?

❑ Will there be a chance for guests to meet the 'stars'?

Departure

❑ Has guest departure been timed so that they do not leave at the same time as the rest of the audience?

THE PRODUCTION SCHEDULE

The terms used in the staging of events come from both the theatre and film production. A rehearsal is a run-through of the event, reproducing as closely as possible the actual event. For the sake of 'getting it right on the night', there may also need to be a technical rehearsal and a dress rehearsal. A production meeting, on the other hand, is a get-together of those responsible for producing an event. It involves the stage manager and the event producer, representatives of the lighting and sound crew or audiovisual specialists, representatives of the performers and the master of ceremonies. It is held at the performance site or stage as near to the time of the event as possible. At this crucial meeting:

- final production schedule notes are compared
- possible last-minute production problems are brought up
- the flow of the event is summarised
- emergency procedures are reviewed
- the compere is introduced and familiarised with the production staff
- the communication system is tested (Neighbourhood Arts Unit 1991, p. 50).

The production schedule is the main document for staging. It is the master document from which various other schedules, including the cue or prompt sheet and the run sheets, are created. Goldblatt (1997, p. 143) defines it as the detailed listing of tasks, with specific start and stop times occurring from the set-up of the event's equipment (also known as 'bump-in') to the eventual removal of all the equipment (bump-out or load-out). It is often a written form of the Gantt chart (see page 346, chapter 13) with four columns: time, activity, location and responsibility. Production schedules can also contain a description of the relevant elements of the event.

Two particularly limited times on the schedule are the 'bump-in' and 'bump-out' times. The bump-in is the time when the necessary infrastructure can be brought in, unloaded and set up. The bump-out is the time when the equipment can be dismantled and removed. Although the venue or site may be available to receive the equipment at any time, there are many other factors that set the bump-in time. The hiring cost and availability of equipment are two important limiting factors. In most cases, the larger items must arrive first. These may include fencing, tents, stage, food vans and extra toilets. Next could come the audiovisual equipment and finally the various decorations. Supervision of the arrival and set-up of the equipment can be crucial to minimising problems during the event. The contractor who delivers and assembles the equipment often is not the operator of the equipment. This can mean that once it is set up, it is impossible to change it without recalling the contractor.

Bump-out can be the most difficult time of an event, because the excitement is over, the staff are often tired and everyone is in a hurry to leave. Nevertheless, these are just the times when security and safety are important. The correct order of bump-out needs to be on a detailed schedule. This is often the reverse of the bump-in schedule. The last item on the checklist for the bump-out is the 'idiot check'. This refers to the check that is done after everything is cleared from the performance area, and some of the staff do a search for anything that may be left.

The run sheets are lists of the order of specific jobs at an event. The entertainers, for example, have one run sheet while the caterers have another. Often the production schedule is a loose-leaf folder that includes all the run sheets. The cue sheets are a list of times that initiate a change of any kind during the event and describe what happens on that change. The stage manager and audiovisual controller use them.

RECORDING THE EVENT

By their very nature, special events are ephemeral. A good quality recording of the event is essential for most event companies, as it demonstrates the ability of the organisation and can be used to promote the event company. It can also help in evaluating the event and, if necessary, in settling later disputes, whether of a legal or other nature. The method of recording the event can be on video, sound recording or as photographs. Making a sound recording can be just a matter of putting a cassette in the sound system and pressing the record button. However, any visual recording of the event will require planning. In particular, the correct lighting is needed for depth of field. Factors that need to be considered for video recording are:

- What is it for — promotion, legal purposes or for sale to the participants?
- What are the costs in time and money?
- How will it affect the event? Will the video cameras be a nuisance? Will they need white lighting?
- What are the best vantage points?

Recording the event is not a decision that should be left to the last minute; it needs to be factored into the planning of the event. Once an event is played out there is no going back.

CONTINGENCIES

As with large festivals and hallmark events, the staging of any event has to make allowances for what might go wrong. 'What if' sessions need to be implemented with the staff. A stage at a festival may face an electricity blackout; performers may not arrive; trouble may arrive instead. Therefore, micro-contingency plans need to be in place. All these must fit in with the overall festival risk-management and emergency plans. At corporate events in well-known venues, the venue will have its own emergency plan that needs to be given to all involved.

SUMMARY

The staging of an event can range from presenting a show of multicultural dancers and musicians at a stage in a local park, to the launch of the latest software product at the most expensive hotel in town. All events share common staging elements including sound, lights, food and beverages, performers and special effects. All these elements need to create and enhance the event theme. The importance of each of these elements depends on the type of event. To stage an event successfully a number of tools are used: the production schedule, the stage plan and the contact and responsibility list, all of which are shown in figure 14.11 on the following page.

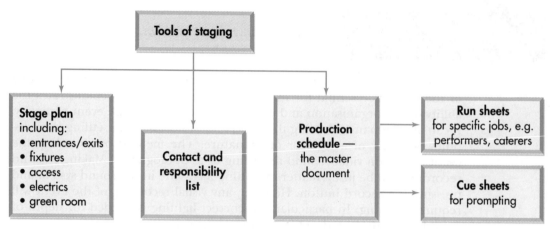

Figure 14.11 *A summary of the tools necessary for staging an event*

Questions

1 Analyse an event into its staging elements and discuss the relationships between each of these elements.

2 Choose a theme for a company's staff party. How would you relate all the elements of staging to the theme?

3 Compile a stage plan, contact responsibility list and production schedule with the relevant run sheets for:
(a) a corporate party for the clients, staff and customers of a company
(b) a fun run with entertainment
(c) a large wedding
(d) one of the stages for a city arts festival.

Engineering Excellence Awards, *Sydney Town Hall*

The Engineering Excellence Awards is an annual event that draws over 800 people to the Sydney Town Hall each September to witness the presentation of citations for excellence, both for projects and individual achievement. Because the event celebrates excellence in engineering, the design and engineering of the event must be of a high standard.

From the initial briefing, it was decided that the ceremony had several purposes. We had to produce an event that provided:
- the right level of dignity
- a way of honouring the entrants and winners
- recognition of the sponsors
- a sense of warmth that would appeal to the 400 partners attending the night
- a reflection of the professional values of the Institution of Engineers and an enhancement of its public image, both for members and the general public.

To satisfy these goals, it was necessary to develop a strategy of shifting emphases while still keeping the main goal in sight — the presentation of the awards. Thus we developed a sequence for the night that offered each of the stakeholders recognition, value and enjoyment.

The following production schedule for the awards night outlines the basic sequence of events for the rehearsal and the actual show.

PRODUCTION SCHEDULE

SET-UP AND REHEARSAL SCHEDULE

Time	Location/Items	Duration
7:00	Town Hall lighting staff on call (2 people)	
7:00	Load in data projectors and computer systems.	2:00
7:30	Town Hall lighting staff de-rig bar for screen and Sony 1270 data projector.	2:00
8:00	Town Hall staff do room lighting while screen is set	2:00
	NB Screen position: Bar 3	
	NB Screen size: 30 × 40 feet	
	Staging: two lecterns onstage — steps in middle	
	Install follow spots.	1:00
10:00	Install video-camera system.	2:00

Time	Location/Items	Duration
10:30	Tables put in place in main hall.	
11:00	Lighting: general focus lighting — front bars	1:00
11:00	Town Hall staff — sound set-up	1:00
12:01	Lighting break	1:00
12:01	Focus data projectors.	2:00
12:01	Focus video projector.	1:00
14:00	Banquet tables in place	0:30
15:00	Technical rehearsal (with follow spots) and full sound & lighting system operational	1:00
16:00	Dress rehearsal (with MC) Step through entire awards script.	1:00
16:30	Centrepieces in place	0:30
17:00	End dress rehearsal; technical staff meal break (60 mins)	1:00
18:00	Dress rehearsal with finalists	0:30
18:15	Stand by for guests	
	Linear duration in hours — sum:	19:30
	Duration available:	11:15

SHOW SCHEDULE

	Main Hall	
18:00	Stand by for guests	0:01
18:00	Dress rehearsal for finalists (100 pax [people])	0:30
18:25	The organ plays quietly.	
18:30	**Guests arrive** Official party greets guests (till 6:40 p.m.).	0:30
18:30	Caterers serve drinks in vestibule. Entrées *mise en place* [entrées preset]	0:10
18:40	Open Main Hall doors. Caterers open hall doors and cease vestibule service.	0:01
18:41	Quartet plays background music. Caterers stop serving drinks in foyer. Caterers commence drink service in main hall.	0:18
18:45	VIP arrives, greeted by officials. Proceed to separate reception room.	0:15
19:00	MC: (video) 'Ladies & gentlemen, please be upstanding.' Arrival of the official party	0:01
19:01	Play the national anthem. MC: 'Ladies & gentlemen, the Awards Chairman'	0:01
19:02	Awards Chairman welcomes official guests.	0:03
19:05	MC: 'Back soon for Awards of Personal Achievement'	0:01
19:06	Dinner served	0:20
	Caterers note: serve official table first. Video: roll sponsor video (20 min).	
19:20	Young engineers to stand by backstage	

Time	Location/Items		Duration
19:26	**After officials finish their main course**		
19:26	Organ concludes with fanfare.		0:02
	Stage brightens for MC's entry.		
19:28	MC thanks organist and welcomes/settles guests.		0:02
	Invites Sydney Division President onstage.		
	(He comes from his table, as does VIP.)		
	Official proceedings commence.		
19:30	Sydney Division President		0:05
	who asks VIP onstage		
19:35	VIP speech		0:05

PERSONAL ACHIEVEMENT AWARDS

Time	Location/Items		Duration
19:40	MC introduces four engineering students who enter from rear of stage.	1P*	0:01
	MC explains Student Engineer award.		
19:41	Sponsor announces winner.		0:01
19:42	Young Student Engineer speech		0:01
19:43	MC introduces Community & Environment Award.	2P	0:00
19:43	Sponsor announces winner.		0:01
19:44	Winner to lectern		0:01
19:45	Winner speech		0:01
19:46	MC introduces Bachelor of Engineering Final Project Award.	3P	0:00
19:47	Sponsor announces winner.		0:01
19:48	Winner to lectern		0:01
19:49	Winner speech		0:01
19:50	MC introduces B. Tech & FE Project Award.	4P	0:00
19:50	Sponsor announces winner.		0:01
19:51	Winner to lectern		0:01
19:52	Winner speech		0:01
19:53	MC introduces Young Assoc. Engineer Award.	5P	0:00
19:54	Sponsor announces winner.		0:01
19:55	Winner to lectern		0:01
19:56	Winner speech		0:01
19:57	MC introduces Young Professional Engineer Award.	6P	0:01
19:58	Sponsor announces winner.		0:01
19:59	Winner to lectern		0:00
19:59	Winner speech		0:01
20:00	MC introduces journalists' award for best media engineering report.	7P	0:01
20:01	Sponsor announces winner.		0:01
20:02	Winner to lectern		0:00
20:03	Winner speech		0:01
20:04	MC introduces Professional Engineer of the Year Award.	8P	0:01
20:05	Sponsor announces winner.		0:01

Time	Location/Items		Duration
20:06	Winner to lectern		0:00
20:06	Winner speech		0:01
20:07	MC introduces Hollows Award.	9P	0:01
20:08	VIP announces winner.		0:01
20:09	Winner to lectern		0:00
20:10	Hollows Award & speech		0:01
20:11	Awards Chairman thanks VIP etc.		0:02
20:13	MC: 'Thanks, please enjoy meal...'		0:00
20:13	Organ plays (20 min).		0:00
20:13	Clear main course (20 mins).		0:20
20:33	Organ ends.		0:01
20:34	MC welcomes comedian.		0:01
20:35	Entertainment: comedy/music		0:30
21:05	MC thanks; announces dessert, 'back soon with...'		0:20
21:05	Dessert served, coffee cups set in place.		0:20
	Caterers make sure every table has a red and a white wine bottle on it.		
21:25	MC: 'Ladies & gentlemen please take your seats... The awards are about to commence.'		

PROJECT AWARDS SEQUENCE

Time	Location/Items		Duration
21:25	Opening animation		0:01
21:26	Opening video (3 min)		0:03
	Bring up house lights at end.		
21:29	MC: Intros		0:02
	Asks Sydney Division President & VIP to to present awards.		
21:31	Awards commence	A1 to A11*	
21:31	Intro & finalists (1 min)		
21:31	Finalists av. 7 = 1 min		
21:31	Sponsor speech (1)		
21:31	Winner and text (1)		
21:31	Winner's speech (1)		
21:31	13 awards × 4 mins = 52 mins		0:52
22:23	Introduce Bradfield Award		0:01
22:24	Bradfield video		0:02
22:26	Bradfield award sequence		0:05
22:31	Sydney Division President thanks VIP (Governor of NSW)		0:02
22:33	Credits video (3 mins) & animation (1 min)		0:04
22:37	Awards end		
22:37	MC concludes & introduces organist (or Tina Turner again).		0:01
	Raise screen on his cue to reveal organist.		
22:38	Organist's recital during dessert service		0:20
22:58	Caterers: serve coffee & beverages as organ plays.		

Time	Location/Items	Duration
22:58	Taped music till midnight	0:57
23:55	Lights gradually brighten, music fades...	0:05
0:00	End	0:00
	Pack up immediately after function	

* Annotations such as 1P and A1 are sequence codes.

Reno Dal, B.A. Hons (Sociology)
Executive Producer, Special Event Reno Dal Pty Ltd
© Reno Dal Pty Ltd

Questions

1 Why do you think it is necessary to use sequence codes?

2 From the production schedule, make a list of the major elements in the staging, then devise two back-up plans in case equipment does not arrive at the venue or breaks down. For example, what would you do if the data projector does not arrive?

3 Why was the event set up on the day of the event and not the night before?

4 Why did the guests arrive at 6.30 p.m. and doors open at 6.40 p.m.?

5 What is the benefit of the entrées being preset?

6 Why do event producers use terms such as 'pax' instead of 'people'? Would such a term be understood by everyone in the event industry?

7 Does a production schedule give you a complete picture of an event?

REFERENCES

Cameron, N. 1993, *Fire on the Water*, Currency Press, Sydney.

Catherwood, D. & Van Kirk, R. 1992, *The Complete Guide to Special Event Management*, John Wiley & Sons, New York.

Goldblatt, J. 1997, *Special Events: Best Practices in Modern Event Management*, 2nd edn, Van Nostrand Reinhold, New York.

Graham, S., Goldblatt, J. & Delpy, L. 1995, *The Ultimate Guide to Sports Event Management and Marketing*, Richard Irwin, Chicago.

Malouf, Lena 1999, *Behind the Scenes at Special Events*, John Wiley & Sons, New York.

Neighbourhood Arts Unit 1991, *Community Festival Handbook*, City of Melbourne.

Reid, F. 1995, *Staging Handbook*, 2nd edn, A & C Black, London.

Rostrum, vol. 32, *The Comprehensive Convention Planner's Manual*, Rank Publishing Company, Sydney.

15
Evaluation
and reporting

LEARNING OBJECTIVES

After studying this chapter, you should be able to:

- understand the role of evaluation in the event management process
- know when to evaluate an event
- understand the evaluation needs of event stakeholders
- create an evaluation plan for an event
- apply a range of techniques, including the conducting of questionnaires and surveys, in evaluating events
- describe and record the intangible impacts of events
- measure the expenditure of visitors to an event
- prepare a final evaluation report
- use event profiles to promote the outcomes of events and to seek sponsorship
- apply the knowledge gained by evaluation to the planning of a future event.

INTRODUCTION

Event evaluation is critical to the event management process. Event management is still a young industry, and in some areas is still struggling to establish legitimacy and acceptance as a profession. One of the best means for the industry to gain credibility is for events to be evaluated honestly and critically, so that their outcomes are known, their benefits acknowledged, and their limitations accepted. However, event evaluation serves a much deeper purpose than just 'blowing the trumpet' for events. It is at the very heart of the process where insights are gained, lessons are learnt and events are perfected. Event evaluation, if properly utilised and applied, is the key to the continuous improvement of events, and to the standing and reputation of the event industry. As such, it should be a high priority for all event managers to properly evaluate their events, and to disseminate this evaluation to their stakeholders and interested groups. If done well, this will not only enhance the reputation of their events, but also their own reputation as true professionals.

WHAT IS EVENT EVALUATION?

Event evaluation is the process of critically observing, measuring and monitoring the implementation of an event in order to assess its outcomes accurately. It enables the creation of an event profile that outlines the basic features and important statistics of an event. It also enables feedback to be provided to event stakeholders, and plays an important role in the event management process by providing a tool for analysis and improvement.

The event management process is a cycle (see figure 15.1) in which inputting and analysing data from an event allow more informed decisions to be made and more efficient planning to be done, and improve event outcomes. This applies to individual repeat events, where the lessons learnt from one event can be incorporated in the planning of the next. It also applies to the general body of events knowledge, where the lessons learnt from individual events contribute to the overall knowledge and effectiveness of the event industry.

Tamworth, for example, has learnt to cope with an influx of visitors, which doubles the population of the town during the Tamworth Country Music Festival, by applying the lessons learnt each year to the logistics planning of the next year's festival. As discussed in chapter 2, New Year's Eve celebrations in Sydney have also been developed and refined over a period by intelligently feeding back information from one year's celebrations into the planning for the next.

Lessons learnt from one event can also be applied to other events or to the whole event industry. A Taste of Tasmania has solved many of its waste problems by using biodegradable containers, which have been adopted by other food festivals around the nation. The Sydney Royal Easter Show was used as a model to test the effectiveness of public transport systems going to and from Homebush Bay and, ultimately, the Sydney Olympics. Similarly, the Disney organisation, by perfecting quieter fireworks suited to the confines of Disneyland in the built-up area of Anaheim in California, has influenced the quality of pyrotechnics used in other markets. The Sydney Olympic Games has left a legacy of event knowledge and experience, which can be applied to future events in Australia and beyond. This transfer of knowledge was formalised in a project where 70 Greek students undertook a work placement with SOCOG supported by formal training at the University of Technology, Sydney. They will apply this knowledge and experience to the conduct of the Summer Olympic Games in Athens in 2004. Innovations in event communications, products and technologies are constantly spread and refined through the process of event evaluation, which leads to better event planning, implementation and further evaluation. This in turn leads to the improvement of individual events and to an ever-growing and more knowledgeable event industry.

■ **Figure 15.1**
Evaluation and the event management process

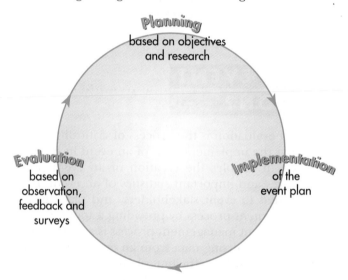

Planning
based on objectives and research

Implementation
of the event plan

Evaluation
based on observation, feedback and surveys

WHEN TO EVALUATE EVENTS

Evaluation is a process that occurs throughout the event management cycle. However, Getz (1997) and others have identified three key periods when it is useful to undertake evaluation.

■ Pre-event *assessment*

Some assessment of the factors governing an event usually takes place in the research and planning stage. This is sometimes called a feasibility study, and is used to determine what level of resources an event is likely to require, and whether or not to proceed with the event. Such a study may involve market research of the probable audience reaction to the event and some research into and prediction of attendance figures, costs and benefits. It will often compare the event with profiles and outcomes of similar previous events. The study may result in establishing targets, or benchmarks, against which the success of the project will be measured.

■ Monitoring *the event*

Event monitoring is the process of tracking the progress of an event through the various stages of implementation, and it enables factors governing the event to be adjusted. For example, ticket sales may be perceived as slow in the lead-up to an event, and this may result in increased advertising or a greater publicity effort. Monitoring the budget may result in the trimming of expenses or the freeing up of money for other areas of expenditure. Observation during the event may lead to changes which improve the delivery of the event, such as adjusting sound volume or altering the dispersal of security and cleaning staff to match changing crowd patterns. This process of monitoring is vital to quality control, and it will also provide valuable information for the final evaluation, and for future planning purposes.

■ Post-event *evaluation*

The most common form of evaluation is post-event evaluation. This involves the gathering of statistics and data on an event and analysing them in relation to the event's mission and objectives. Key Performance Indicators (KPIs) are sometimes used to translate the event objectives into measures that can be applied to gauge the success of the event. An important aspect is usually a feedback meeting of key participants and stakeholders, at which the strengths and weaknesses of the event are discussed and observations are recorded. Post-event evaluation may also involve some form of questionnaire or survey of the event participants or audience. Such surveys seek to explore participants' opinions of the experience and to measure their levels of satisfaction with the event. They often involve the collection of data on the financial expenditure of the participants, so that the cost can be compared with the revenue generated by the event. The nature of the evaluation will be determined largely by the purpose of the event and the audience for which it is intended.

*R*EPORTING TO STAKEHOLDERS

One of the prime reasons that event managers evaluate events is to report to stakeholders.
- The host organisation will want to know what the event achieved. Did the event come in on budget and on time? Did it achieve its objectives? How many people attended and were their expectations met? For future planning purposes, it might be useful to know where they came from, how they heard about it, and whether they intend to return next year.

- The event sponsor may have other measures. Was the level of awareness of the product or service increased? What penetration did the advertising achieve? What media coverage was generated? What was the profile of the people who attended?
- Funding bodies will have grant acquittal procedures to observe, and will usually require audited financial statements of income and expenditure along with a report on the social, cultural or sporting outcomes of the event.
- Councils and government departments may want to know what the impact was on their local or State economies.
- Tourism bodies may want to know the number of visitors attracted to the area and what they spent, not only on the event, but also on travel, shopping and accommodation.

Quantified event outcomes can be very helpful to event organisers in promoting the profile and acceptance of the event. The Sydney Gay and Lesbian Mardi Gras used the 1993 and 1998 studies of the economic benefits of the Mardi Gras very effectively in promoting support for and acceptance of the event. Similarly, the Adelaide Festival has used economic impact studies to underline the contribution of the event to the South Australian economy. Sydney New Year's Eve, the event that marked the start of the new millennium in Sydney, used statistics from the event in previous years to build the reputation of the event as part of a sponsorship strategy to raise funding for the staging of the events in 1999 and 2000.

*E*VALUATION PROCEDURES

In order to meet the many and varied reporting requirements of event stakeholders, it is necessary for the event manager to plan carefully the evaluation of the event. The evaluation will usually be more effective if it is planned from the outset and built into the event management process. Planning should include consideration of:
- what data is needed
- how, when and by whom it is to be gathered
- how it is to be analysed
- what format to use in the final reporting.

■ **Data** *collection*

The process of implementing the event may provide opportunities for useful data to be collected. For example, participants may be required to fill in an event entry form, which can be designed to provide useful information on numbers, age, gender, point of origin, spending patterns and so on. Ticketed events allow for a ready means of counting spectators, and the ticketing agency may be able to provide further useful information, such as the postcodes of ticket purchasers. For non-ticketed events, figures on the use of public transport and car parks and police crowd estimates can be used in calculating attendance figures. Event managers should look out for and make use of all opportunities for the collection of relevant data.

■ Observation

An obvious but critical source of data collection is the direct observation of the event. Staff observation and reports may provide information on a number of aspects of the event, including performance quality, audience reaction, crowd flow and adequacy of catering and toilet facilities. However, staff will provide more accurate and useful data if they are trained to observe and are given a proper reporting format, rather than being left to make casual and anecdotal observations. From the outset, staff should be made aware that observation and reporting on the event are part of their role, and they should be given appropriate guidance and benchmarks. They may be given check lists on which they are asked to evaluate items such as performance quality and audience reaction by using a scale of 1 to 5 or by ticking indicators such as below average, average, good, very good or excellent.

At Sydney's Darling Harbour, stage managers are required to complete a written report on each event, giving their estimates of attendance figures, weather conditions, performance standards and crowd reaction, and commenting on any unusual occurrences or features. Likewise, security staff are required to report on crowd behaviour, incidents, disturbances and injuries, and to estimate the size of crowds with the help of photographs taken at regular intervals by security cameras at strategic locations. By compiling these reports, by using statistics from attraction operators, and by assessing factors such as competition from other major events in the city, management is able to form profiles of individual events and to track trends over time.

Other key players in an event, such as venue owners, councils, sponsors, vendors, police and first-aid officers, can often provide valuable feedback from their various perspectives:

• Venue owners may be able to compare the performance of the event with their normal venue patterns and comment usefully on matters such as attendance figures, parking, access, catering and facilities.

• Police may have observed aspects such as crowd behaviour, traffic flow and parking, and may have constructive suggestions for future planning.

• Councils may be aware of disturbance to the local community or of difficulties with street closures or compliance with health regulations.

• Sponsors may have observations based on their own attendance at the event, or may have done their own surveys on audience reaction, awareness levels and media coverage.

• Vendors may have information on volume of sales, waiting time in queues and so on that will be valuable in planning future catering arrangements.

• First-aid providers may have statistics on the number and seriousness of injuries such as cuts, abrasions or heat exhaustion that will assist in future planning of safety and risk management.

All of these key stakeholders may have observations on general planning issues such as signage, access, crowd management, communication and the provision of facilities that will have implications for the improvement of the event. It is important that their observations are recorded and incorporated into the evaluation and planning stages of the event management process.

■ De-briefing *meetings*

All stakeholders should be made aware at the outset that they will be given an opportunity to provide feedback, and that this is a vital part of the event planning process. They should be encouraged to contribute their professional observations and assessment. This may be done at a single 'de-briefing' meeting or at a series of meetings, depending on the complexity of the event. It is often useful for the date and agenda of this meeting to be made known to all parties early in the process, so that if it is not possible for them to communicate their observations during the staging of the event, then they are aware that a suitable forum will be provided during the finalisation of the event. This meeting should ensure that neither congratulations nor recriminations overshadow the important lessons that are to be learnt from the event and the consequent changes to be incorporated in future planning. It is important that all parties are listened to and that their comments are taken into account in the future planning of the event.

The topics to be addressed at the meeting will be determined by the nature and size of the event. However, the check list in figure 15.2 is a useful starting point.

■ **Figure 15.2**
Event evaluation check list

CHECK LIST FOR EVENT EVALUATION			
Aspect	**Satisfactory**	**Requires attention**	**Comments**
• Timing of the event • Venue • Ticketing and entry • Staging • Performance standard • Staffing levels and performance of duties • Crowd control • Security • Communications • Information and signage • Transport • Parking • Catering facilities • Toilets • First aid • Lost children • Sponsor acknowledgement • Hosting arrangements • Advertising • Publicity • Media liaison			

Questionnaires *and surveys*

Questionnaires can range from simple feedback forms targeting event partners and stakeholders to detailed audience or visitor surveys undertaken by trained personnel. The scale of the questionnaire will depend upon the needs and resources of the event. Simple feedback forms can usually be designed and distributed using the event's own internal resources. They may seek to record and quantify basic data, such as the expenditure of event partners, the observations of stakeholders and their assessment of event management and outcomes.

Surveys are used to ascertain reliable statistical information on audience profiles and reaction and visitor patterns and expenditure. They may be implemented by direct interviews with participants or may rely on participants filling in written forms. They may be undertaken face to face, by telephone or by mail. Face-to-face interviews will usually generate a higher response rate, but techniques such as a competition with prizes as incentives for participation may improve the response rate of postal surveys. Undertaking effective surveys requires expertise and considerable organisational resources. For event organisers with limited in-house experience and expertise, professional assistance can be called upon for tasks, ranging from the design of survey forms to the full implementation of the survey process.

In the case of repeat events, a single well-designed survey may satisfy the basic research needs of the event. Some event organisers may wish to repeat the survey each year in order to compare successive events and to establish trends, or they may want to embark on more ambitious research programs in order to investigate other aspects of the event. Whatever the scale and approach that is decided on, experts such as Getz (1997), Veal (1997) and the publication by the National Centre for Culture and Recreation Statistics (1997) agree on certain basic factors that should be kept in mind. These are listed below.

- *Purpose.* Identify clearly the purpose and objective of the survey. A clearly stated and defined purpose is most likely to lead to a well-targeted survey with effective results.
- *Survey design.* Keep it simple. If too much is attempted in the survey, there is a danger that focus will be lost and effectiveness reduced. Questions should be clear and unambiguous, and should be tested by a 'trial run' before the actual survey.
- *Size of sample.* The number of participants must be large enough to provide a representative sample of the audience. The sample size will depend on the level of detail in the survey, the level of precision required and the available budget. If in doubt, seek professional advice on the size of the sample.
- *Randomness.* The methodology employed in the selection of participants must avoid biases of age, sex and ethnicity. A procedure such as selecting every tenth person to pass through a turnstile may assist in providing a random selection.
- *Support data.* The calculation of some outcomes will depend on the collection of support data. For example, the calculation of total visitor expenditure will require accurate data on the number of visitors to the event. Then the spending pattern revealed by the survey can be multiplied by the number of visitors to provide an estimate of the total visitor expenditure for the event.

Events have both tangible and intangible impacts. Surveys most commonly measure tangible impacts such as economic costs and benefits, because these can most easily be measured. However, it is also important to evaluate the intangible impacts of events, even if evaluation needs to be of a narrative or descriptive nature. Some intangibles that are hard to measure include the effect on the social life and wellbeing of a community, the sense of pride engendered by an event, and the long-term impact on the image of a place or a tourist destination.

The Survival Day concerts staged by Sydney's Aboriginal community on Australia Day have been a focus of Aboriginal identity and pride. The Festival of International Understanding at Cowra features a different national culture each year, and deliberately fosters racial tolerance. The South Pacific Festival, hosted by a different island nation every four years, has provided a strong focus for South Pacific national identity and independence. While all these events have undoubted social worth, it would be difficult, and perhaps even counterproductive, to quantify them in anything other than descriptive terms.

While the Sydney Gay and Lesbian Mardi Gras has been at the forefront of economic impact studies of events, their 1998 annual report contains a clear statement of the social and cultural values underpinning the event (1998, p. 2).

> ■ Sydney Gay & Lesbian Mardi Gras Ltd is an organisation formed out of the diverse lesbian and gay communities of Sydney to enable us to explore, express and promote the life of our combined community through a cultural focus.
>
> We affirm the pride, joy, dignity and identity of our community and its people through events of celebration.
>
> We are committed to serving our community.
>
> We seek to enable individuals and groups within our community to discover, express and develop their artistic, cultural and political skills and potential.
>
> We strive through our events of celebration to strengthen the lives and rights of gay and lesbian people both nationally and internationally. ■

In her report to Tamworth Council on the Tamworth Country Music Festival, Smyth (1998, p. 2) notes the impact of media reports on the long-term positioning of the city as Country Music Capital which:

> ■ re-inforce the 'this is where it's at' image of a sophisticated Festival which is now the accepted essence of the January event. The growing trend which sees urban dwellers in Australia desiring to embrace the image of their country's identity through clothing and lifestyle (cowboy culture), follows upon that of the United States ... urban Australia identifies the Festival (hence the city) as almost the heartland of rural Australia. ■

MEASURING VISITOR EXPENDITURE

All event managers should be familiar with constructing a simple financial balance statement of the income and expenditure of events. Until recent times, this form of reporting was considered sufficient, because most events were evaluated on the basis of their cost to the event organisers or their value to the local community. However, the growing involvement of governments, tourism bodies, corporations and sponsors has brought with it an increasing need to consider the wider impacts of events.

The impacts of events on the economy are based primarily on the expenditure of visitors to the event from outside the host community. The National Centre for Culture and Recreation Statistics (1997) has published simple guidelines for measuring the expenditure of festival visitors, which can be applied to most other public events. Their publication outlines a basic methodology, and includes sample questionnaires for visitor and resident surveys.

The visitors' survey form aims to identify expenditure on items such as accommodation, food, festival tickets, other entertainment, transport, personal services, films, books and souvenirs. This survey establishes an average expenditure which can then be multiplied by the number of visitors to obtain the total visitor expenditure. The methodology takes into account the complexity of estimating the number of visitors from outside the region. It seeks to distinguish those visitors attracted by the event or who have extended their visit because of the event from those who would have visited the region anyway.

In the case of a festival that extends for more than one day or that has multiple events, the survey also takes into account the need to identify the number of days or events attended, and to weigh this in calculating the results of the survey.

A residents' survey form is also provided to identify residents who 'holidayed at home' because of the event and 'switched' their expenditure, which can then be legitimately attributed to the event. Since it is difficult to determine what they would have spent if they had gone elsewhere, their expenditure is treated the same as that of visitors to the event.

Calculating the economic impact of events from the point of view of cities or governments is complex, involving many of the factors dealt with in detail in chapter 4. However, by applying the guidelines and the survey shown in figure 15.3, a simple snapshot of the economic impact of an event can be readily obtained.

■ Figure 15.3
Sample event participation survey

SAMPLE EVENT PARTICIPANT SURVEY

1. Gender: Male   Female
2. Age Group: Under 15   15–24   25–44   45–64   65+
3. Highest level of education:
   High School   Private College/TAFE   University
4. Employment status: Full time/Part time/Casual/Student/Unemployed/Senior
5. Household income (AUD):
   0–20 000   21 000–30 000   31 000–40 000   41 000–50 000   50 000+
6. Who are you travelling with today?
   Travelling alone   Adult couple   Family (parents and children)
   Friends or relatives   Club, Society   Business associates
   Other _____ specify
7. What means of transport did you use to come to the event from your home or place of accommodation?
   Car   Bus/coach   Taxi   Walked   Other _____ specify

(continued)

8. What was the primary means by which you found out about the event?
   Brochures/posters   Newspaper   Radio   TV   Internet
   Tourist Information Centre   Word of mouth   Other _____ specify

9. Have you attended this event in previous years?
   Yes   No   If yes, then which year did you last attend? _____

10. Do you intend to attend the event next year?   Yes   No
    If you answered no, is it because:
    Will not be in the area   Expenses/cost associated with event
    Like to do new things   Program too similar to previous years
    Event not particularly entertaining/enjoyable   Other _____

11. How would you rate the following aspects of the event?
    very poor   satisfactory   good   excellent
    (a)   Venue   (h)   Seating
    (b)   Parking   (i)   Toilets
    (c)   Value for money   (j)   Shade
    (d)   Quality of food   (k)   Overall presentation of event
    (e)   Variety of food   (l)   Crowd management
    (f)   Entertainment for adults   (m)   Signage/information
    (g)   Entertainment for children   (n)   Overall site presentation/layout

12. Were there any aspects of the event that you particularly enjoyed?
    _____

13. Were there any aspects with which you were particularly displeased?
    _____

14. Are there any additional comments that you wish to make about the event?
    _____

15. What is your usual place of residence?
    Local
    Elsewhere in Australia — list postcode
    Overseas — list country _____

16. Was your visit here today motivated by the event?
    Yes   No
    If not, what was the purpose of your visit?
    Holiday   Visit friends/relatives   Business   Other _____ specify

17. How long are you staying in the region?
    Less than 1 day   1–3 days   3–7 days   7–14 days   More than 14 days

18. If staying more than one day, what type of accommodation are you using?
    Hotel/motel/resort   Guest house/bed and breakfast
    Self catering cottage/apartment   Caravan park/camping ground
    Backpacker/hostel   Own or family property
    Other _____ specify

19. Please estimate how much you have spent or intend to spend on behalf of
    yourself or others during your visit including transport, food,
    accommodation, souvenirs and entertainment (AUD)
    0–50   51–100   101–150   151–250   251–300   301–500   500+

20. Other than the event, what activities/attractions did you or do you intend to
    engage in during your visit?
    _____

Media coverage is an important aspect of an event. This coverage can be either positive or negative depending on the event outcomes, the impact on the community and the kind of relationship built up with the media. It is important to monitor and record this coverage as part of the documentation of the event. If the event is local, it may be possible to do this by keeping a file of newspaper articles and by listening and looking for radio and television interviews and news coverage. For larger events, it may be necessary to employ a professional media-monitoring organisation that can track media coverage from a variety of sources. They will usually provide copies of print media stories and transcripts of radio interviews and news coverage. Audiotapes and videotapes of electronic coverage can be obtained for an additional charge. This coverage provides an excellent record of the event and can be used effectively in profiling the event for potential sponsors and partners.

A further issue is content analysis of the media coverage, as this is not always positive. Negative media coverage can impact on the reputation of the event, and by implication on stakeholders such as host organisations and sponsors.

Some media monitors attempt to place a monetary value on media coverage, usually valuing it at around three times the cost of equivalent advertising space, on the grounds that editorial is likely to be better trusted by consumers and is therefore worth more. Such valuations should be regarded as approximate only, but may provide a useful comparative assessment of media coverage.

Media coverage of the 1998 Greg Norman Holden International in Sydney was valued by ChangeData (1998) at $3.5 million. This included four days of national coverage by the Seven Network, sold on to international cable television, which opened with a shot of Greg Norman on top of the Sydney Harbour Bridge and included destinational promotion of Sydney in the form of video postcards.

EVENT PROFILE

Bureau of Tourism Research

The Bureau of Tourism Research (BTR) is a joint state and federal government agency which collects, analyses and disseminates information about the Australian tourism industry to the general public, government and industry (Bureau of Tourism Research 2000).

The BTR is a valuable source of statistical information for managers and researchers of tourism and events. Its research activities include both ongoing surveys such as the *International Visitor Survey* and the *National Visitor Survey* and one-off surveys and research topics such as the Olympics, cultural tourism, eco-tourism, wine tourism and the MICE industry.

(continued)

Survey data and research results are published and available from the BTR. It also provides a research service by telephone, fax or e-mail, and publishes select data on its Web site (www.btr.gov.au) such as *The Australian Tourism Datacard*, containing key statistics on the tourism industry. The datacard includes statistics from the *International Visitor Survey* such as tables of International Visitors by Main Purpose of Journey 1990–98, and International Visitor Expenditure in Australia by Item, 1996–98. It also includes statistics from the *National Visitor Survey* such as Domestic Visitors: Purpose of Visit by State or Territory Visited 1998, and Day Trips Undertaken by Australians 1998. The Web site also gives an overview of the impact of tourism on the Australian economy, including Estimated Tourist Expenditure, Estimated Employment due to Tourism Expenditure, and Estimated Contribution to Gross Domestic Product.

■ **Figure 15.4**
Home page of the Bureau of Tourism Research, www.btr.gov.au

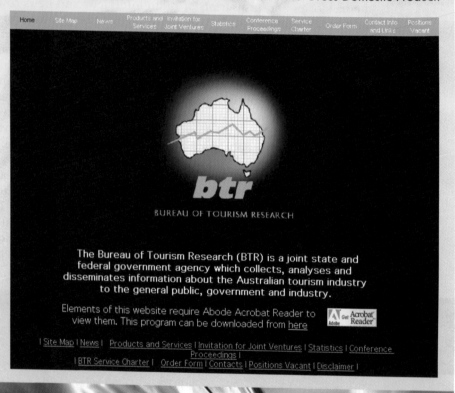

EVENT EVALUATION REPORTS AND PROFILES

Once information has been collated from data collection, observation, feedback meetings and surveys, a final event evaluation report should be completed and distributed to all stakeholders. The information should provide a profile of the event, which can be included in the executive summary of the report. This profile can form the basis of a media release promoting the outcomes of the event, and can be used to begin planning for the next event and approaching sponsors. Figure 15.4 provides an example of a media release based on the profile of an event.

■ **Figure 15.4**
Media release on economic impact of the 1999 Victorian Spring Racing Carnival

MEDIA RELEASE

SPRING RACING CARNIVAL WORTH $240 MILLION TO ECONOMY

Racing Minister Rob Hulls says the Victorian Spring Racing Carnival has once again confirmed its status as the most important sporting event for Victoria, generating a record breaking $238.2 million in 1999.

An economic impact study released today by Racing Victoria confirms the popularity of the carnival throughout Australia and overseas, as it attracts local, interstate and international visitors.

'It's the biggest tourist event of the year in terms of its worth to the Victorian economy,' Mr Hulls said. 'Once again it was an outstanding success.

'Melbourne IS the event city and today we are celebrating the achievements of Melbourne's biggest event — the Spring Racing Carnival.'

Speaking at a special luncheon at Parliament House, Mr Hulls said the carnival brought in more tourists than any other sporting event in the state and its economic benefit was a vital component of Victoria's economy.

The 1999 carnival broke record attendance figures with record crowds totalling almost 600 000.

Key findings of the economic impact study were:
- Record economic impact of $238.2 million, an increase of 6.4% over the 1998 total of $223.9 million
- Record direct spending of $140.1 million including accommodation, travel, shopping, souvenirs, food and beverages, entertainment, betting and fashions
- Fashion sales in Melbourne rose this year to $19.4 million with a strong growth in purchase of hats and shoes for visitors to the Carnival — more than 55 per cent of people surveyed brought something new to wear to the races
- Record Spring Racing Carnival attendances of 593 629
- At metropolitan Spring Racing Carnival racemeetings, 272 496 Melbourne residents spent an average of $84.40 each; country visitors (51 905) spent an average of $112.50; the 82 181 interstate visitors spent an average of $377; and the 25 951 overseas visitors to metropolitan racemeetings each spent an average of $354.
- The number of jobs created as a result of the Spring Racing Carnival was 2589 compared with 2433 in 1998.

(**Source:** *Minister for Racing, 6 December 1999*)

FINALISATION

Once the event is over and before administration is disbanded and preparation for the next event is begun, it is important to tidy up loose ends and to bring the event management process to a satisfactory conclusion. The following is a useful check list of tasks to be completed in finalising the event.

- Hold a debriefing meeting and provide an opportunity for feedback by all stakeholders.
- Settle accounts and prepare an audited financial statement.
- Fulfil all contractual and statutory obligations.
- Prepare a full report on event outcomes and distribute it to all key stakeholders.
- Make recommendations for future refinements and improvements to the event.
- Thank all staff, participants and stakeholders for their support of the event.

SUMMARY

Event evaluation is a process of measuring and assessing an event throughout the event management cycle. It provides feedback that contributes to the planning and improvement of individual events and to the pool of knowledge of the events industry.

Feasibility studies identify the likely costs and benefits of an event and help to decide whether to proceed with it. Monitoring the event establishes whether it is on track, and enables the event manager to respond to changes and adjust plans. Post-event evaluation measures the outcomes of the event in relation to its objectives. The exact nature of this evaluation will depend on the perspectives and needs of the stakeholders.

A range of techniques is used in event evaluation, including data collection, observation, feedback meetings, questionnaires and surveys. Good evaluation is planned and implemented from the outset of the event management process, with all participants being made aware of its objectives and methodology. As well as tangible impacts, events have intangible benefits that cannot always be quantified and may need to be recorded on a narrative or descriptive basis. These include social and cultural impacts on a community and the long-term profile and positioning of a tourism destination. A key factor in calculating the economic impact of an event is the measurement of visitor expenditure through the use of visitor surveys. The media coverage of an event should be monitored in-house or by using professional media monitors. Once information is gathered from all sources, an event evaluation report should be compiled and distributed to all stakeholders. This report can provide the basis of media releases that promote the outcomes of the event, and can be used in planning for the future and seeking sponsorship. In finalising the event, it is important to tidy up loose ends and apply lessons learnt from the event in future event management processes.

Questions

1   Identify an event that you are familiar with. Design an evaluation plan that will provide a profile of the event and form the basis of a report to key stakeholders.

2   Imagine that you are employing staff to work on a particular event. Design a report sheet for them to record their observations of the event. Decide what aspects you want them to observe and what benchmarks you want them to use.

3   Select an event that you are familiar with, and identify the stakeholders that you would invite to a final evaluation meeting. Write an agenda for the meeting that will encourage well-organised feedback on the event.

4   Imagine that you are a tourist officer for your region. Design a questionnaire for a major local event in order to evaluate the impact of the event on local tourism.

5   Obtain copies of three evaluation reports from libraries or from event organisations. Compare and contrast the methodology, style and format of these reports.

6   Choose an event that has a considerable impact, whether positive or negative, on its host community. Describe this impact, and evaluate the social costs and benefits to the community.

7   Using the same event as in question 6, design a brief requiring a professional organisation to carry out an economic impact study of the event.

8   Identify a high-profile event in your region, and monitor as closely as you can the media coverage of the event, including print, radio and television coverage.

9   Choose an event that you have been associated with, and assemble as much data as you can on the event. Using these data, create a written profile of the event. Using this written profile as a basis, draft a media release that outlines the outcomes of the event and the benefits to the local community.

How Tamworth became
the country music capital

Tamworth, NSW, is widely recognised, both in Australia and overseas, as Australia's 'Country Music Capital'. In January 2000 the city hosted the 28th anniversary of the Country Music Association of Australia's Toyota Country Music Awards of Australia, the event which was responsible for the birth of the Tamworth Country Music Festival and the development of Tamworth as our Country Music Capital.

So how did this relatively small inland country town acquire such a reputation and what has been the effect of this transformation on the modern town and its people? How did Tamworth manage to completely reverse the normal Australian tradition of heading for the beach in summer and, instead, influence thousands of people to flock to its sweltering streets at the hottest, most unpleasant time of year.

It is not a story of chance or good luck. It is about the conception and implementation by a group of country-based professionals, of an innovative, long-term, promotional and marketing project with the objective of creating an event and a brand which would generate commercial benefits for Radio 2TM, Tamworth and Australian country music. The story provides an object lesson for other entrepreneurs keen to develop their cities or towns in a similar way.

Earlier this century, in the 1930s, '40s and '50s, Tamworth, like most other country towns of the time, had a radio station with a long tradition of playing 'hillbilly' music in the early hours of the morning.

The modern story of country music, and Tamworth, does not begin until the late '60s when once-popular Australian country music had been relegated to the backblocks by the emerging and all-consuming 'rock'n'roll'. A few travelling showmen, like Slim Dusty and Buddy Williams, soldiered on, touring the country and preserving Australia's country music traditions.

At that time, commercial radio was smarting from the introduction of television (TV came to the bush later than the cities — in Tamworth's case, 1965). Radio's evening audiences were decimated, but in Tamworth the local station, 2TM, fought back by airing specialist programs such as drama, jazz, folk music and even the supposedly despised 'country and western' music, in night-time slots.

To everyone's amazement, the listener response to 2TM's country music program was huge. The radio station had (and still has) a clear transmission frequency which it did not share with other stations elsewhere, and at night its signal could be heard all over eastern Australia.

Hoedown (as it was known until 1996) with announcer John Minson, began to attract listeners from throughout the nation and became the catalyst for the entire Country Music Capital promotion.

In the late 1960s, a group of executives at 2TM conceived the idea of marketing Tamworth as an Australian centre for country music. In 1969, it was decided to nominate the city as 'Country Music Capital' in all promotional activity undertaken by the station. Despite the fact the only substance to the title was the *Hoedown* radio program, the name and concept caught on.

In 1972, plans were formulated for a national awards presentation to country music performing artists and songwriters and in January 1973 the first Australasian Country Music Awards were staged by 2TM.

Once the awards were consolidated, other activities were planned and initiated with the deliberate intention of developing a festival out of a single event. Gradually the period of the festival grew from two days to 10, with individuals and organisations staging a wide variety of events throughout the city and local district. In recent years a festival 'count down' has extended by another week.

During Tamworth's country music development period in the 1970s and '80s, several major factors strongly influenced its growth.

Country music capital as a marketing concept

The owners and promoters of the event were not 'fans'. 2TM was concerned only with the establishment of a national promotion which could be developed and marketed widely with financial and social benefits to the station and the City of Tamworth.

Professionalism of organisation

From the first, the awards and Country Music Capital campaign was run by marketing professionals. Every effort was made to present a highly professional event. This was reflected in everything from the publicity material and attitude to media to the organisation of the event, the quality and expertise of the people involved and the general approach to the entire promotion.

Centralised control

The entire country music promotion was tightly controlled and coordinated by the chief executive of the awards and festival, Max Ellis, who was also the manager of 2TM and, later, BAL Marketing (until 1984). All major decisions relating to any aspect of the promotion passed through his office.

While Tamworth City Council gradually became more involved with the festival as it grew, the centralised control continued, with council checking all its festival activities with BAL Marketing/2TM as a central reference point.

As other companies and organisations, such as talent quest organisers, registered club and hotel managers and outside entrepreneurs entered the festival, they voluntarily coordinated their activities through 2TM and BAL Marketing as unofficial, but very effective, festival coordinators. An example of how this worked was the sideshow operators who voluntarily stayed out of the city for a number of years because 2TM management believed the country music component had to be well established before other elements could safely be introduced into the festival.

Strong financial incentive

2TM undertook the entire organisation and promotion of the festival at its own expense, setting up and operating the overall activity as a major sales promotion, supported by numerous major national sponsors. Today, the awards are sponsored by Toyota, and the festival by Carlton, with dozens of other major sponsors involved in other events.

Continuity of management

One important facet was the continuity of supervision of the country music promotion, again by Max Ellis through 2TM and BAL Marketing over the period from its inception in the late '60s and the awards in 1973, until his departure in 1984. Many other key staff members were also deeply involved in setting up and running the promotion over these years, a period during which 2TM developed a close and personal relationship with artists, fans and the Australian music industry.

BAL Marketing continued its 'unofficial coordination' from 1986 through to the early '90s, finally handing its reduced role and responsibility to the city council in 1994. During the 1990s ex-BAL marketeers, including Max Ellis, again became active in the awards and festival management, particularly through their involvement with the Country Music Association of Australia, Prime Television (which telecasts the awards each year) and Rural Press Events, the successor to BAL Marketing.

Innovation

One of the most important factors in the expansion of the festival was innovation — the deliberate ongoing creation of complimentary new events by 2TM. These events provided the solid foundation of activity which encouraged others to participate. Most of the activities (such as Star Maker, Capital News and Pro-Rodeo) were created for commercial reasons but some (such as Hands of Fame, Roll of Renown and Cavalcade) were specifically started to enhance the overall drawing power of the festival.

Australian content

The Tamworth festival was always promoted strictly as an event for Australian country music and, while major overseas artists were encouraged to visit, they were discouraged from performing. This policy was formulated because 2TM believed its role was to encourage Australian music. Because it had relied on the ongoing support of Australian artists such as Slim Dusty to launch the concept, 2TM felt it had earned the right to top billing at the festival without the distraction of international stars. This approach obviously worked because the crowds keep coming back to hear Australian music and Australian artists. These days, international artists have become a regular part of the festival.

Publicity

The creation of a highly successful visual symbol, the Golden Guitar, provided a powerful public identity for the awards from the start. Publicity was handled by 2TM and its associated radio and TV stations in Tamworth, with the help of PR man Dave Douglas in Sydney and PR professionals in Melbourne and Brisbane.

Each year, awards executives, with the mayor, an alderman or prominent local business person, would visit each capital city and systematically canvas all available national media.

Over the years, articles appeared in virtually every paper and magazine published in those cities, together with countless appearances on radio, TV and news broadcasts. In addition to this promotional program, a few selected journalists were brought to Tamworth at 2TM's expense during the festival. Every effort was made to facilitate media involvement prior to and during the festival, and for some years 2TM flew parties of journalists to Tamworth before the event. Today, the council retains a PR firm to handle national publicity running a media centre in Tamworth during the festival with a December launch in Sydney.

Massive media coverage was achieved, with all the major TV networks and newspapers sending people to Tamworth for the awards.

From the very first awards in 1973, a live coverage was broadcast on commercial radio. From 1993, the ABC has been running a live three-hour coverage of the awards throughout their metropolitan and regional networks.

Prime Television covered the awards with news and specials until the late '80s when a telecast of the event was commenced. When the awards were taken over by the Country Music Association of Australia (CMAA) in 1993, Prime directed a massive regional Australian coverage, working with the CMAA and other regional operators.

In 1996, the awards became the first Australian awards presentations to be featured on national Australian pay TV.

Since 1997 the 7 Network has also carried a delayed broadcast of the awards nationwide.

Spreading the activity

Tamworth is unique in that there is no one venue which dominates the festival. This reflects the diversified nature of the event and is a major strength. From the beginning, 2TM worked hard to spread activity throughout the city rather than centralise it in one location. This meant that a vast diversity of music could be accommodated and it created a unique situation where virtually everyone who wished could become involved in one way or another. It also turned the entire city into an 'attraction' with benefits to all. Over the years various locations have gained a temporary prominence but generally this evens out as new developments occur.

The long weekend

One important factor in building crowds was the Australia Day long weekend which, up to 1988, was scheduled on the first Monday on or after 26th January. This enabled organisers and visitors to plan ahead and take advantage of this major cultural celebration.

Spin-offs

In tourism, an identity is the name of the game and country music has given Tamworth an identity second to none.

On the June long weekend in 2000 the CMAA staged its first highly successful 'Hats Off To Country' festival, a new annual event, capitalising on Tamworth's national branding. Local venues have given the CMAA major support and believe 'Hats Off' will develop into another different January for Tamworth.

Tourism is important to Tamworth. The Tourist Information Centre is shaped as a guitar, an obvious tribute to Tamworth's reputation. And the Roll of Renown, the Hands of Fame, the giant Golden Guitar, the Country Collection Wax Museum, the guitar-shaped pool and Walk a Country Mile Interpretive Centre are among dozens of other activities and tourist attractions utilising this famous theme.

Other spin-offs like recording studios and related activities, artists choosing Tamworth as a home base, printing, publicity, accommodation and so on have brought significant tangible benefits to the city. Tamworth remains a centre for country music promotion, through CMAA project office activities, broadcasting, various syndicated TV programs, artist management services and publishing, and as a base for touring artists. *Capital News*, started by BAL Marketing in 1975, is still Australia's major country music publication while *The Country Music Directory*, the industry's 'bible' is also published from Tamworth.

Since 1993 the CMAA (with EMI) has produced its *Winners* CD based on the awards finalists as well as the video coverage of the awards.

In 1997, the CMAA, with support from TAFE, established an annual College of Country Music in Tamworth in January, utilising today's top artists to help train tomorrow's country stars.

The Australian Country Music Foundation has been established in Tamworth to build a national archive and resource centre to preserve the heritage of Australian country music.

In 1998 the long-awaited Tamworth Regional Entertainment Centre was completed by Tamworth City Council with financial contributions from the country music industry, State and Federal governments and local business people. This provides a permanent home for country music in January and June, and Tamworth with a first class multifunction facility all year round.

Summary

It is now well over 25 years since the first awards were staged and over 30 years since the concept of Country Music Capital was born at 2TM. From the strong foundations laid in the 1970s and early '80s, the awards and festival have evolved and developed in many ways.

The CMAA Toyota Country Music Awards and Carlton Country Music Festival are an excellent example of a private enterprise event which has created enormous benefits for the community in which it takes place.

With no government assistance, Tamworth and country music have achieved a miraculous transformation of a country town from a summer backwater into a nationally — indeed internationally — recognised tourist destination.

The Tamworth Country Music Festival is also a rare example of a commercially based festival which runs itself. It has no single director but is shaped and driven by a number of major entrepreneurs and venues and many smaller operators, all with a common interest, each responsible for their own shows and each self-supporting through ticket sales and strong sponsorship. These activities take place

in a sophisticated, visitor-friendly environment, supported, maintained and professionally promoted by the local business community and the Tamworth City Council.

Max Ellis
Chief Executive, Australasian Country Music Awards and Festival 1973–84
Chief Executive, CMAA Country Music Awards of Australia 1993–99

Questions

1 From the case study, identify the main stakeholders in the Australasian Country Music Festival.

2 In evaluating the festival, what are the long-term benefits for the city of Tamworth?

3 How has Tamworth used the festival to create an identity for itself?

4 What role does the festival play in selling Tamworth as a tourism destination?

5 Write a brief requiring a consultant to prepare an economic impact study of the Australasian Country Music Festival.

REFERENCES

Bureau of Tourism Research 2000, www.btr.gov.au (accessed 21 September 2000).

ChangeData 1998, *Greg Norman Holden International Golf Sponsor Scores© Report*, Manly, NSW.

Getz, Donald 1997, *Event Management and Event Tourism*, Cognizant Communication Corporation, New York.

Goldberg, Joe Jeff 1997, *Special Events — Best Practices in Modern Event Management*, Van Nostrand Reinhold, New York.

National Centre for Culture and Recreation Statistics, Australian Bureau of Statistics 1997, *Measuring the Impact of Festivals: Guidelines for Conducting an Economic Impact Study*, Cultural Ministers Council, Statistics Working Group, Canberra.

Office of the Minister for Racing 1999, www.dpc.vic.gov.au/pressrel (accessed 21 September 2000).

Smyth, J. 1998, *1998 Foster's Tamworth Country Music Festival, file no. C25*, Business & Corporate Development Department Report no. 98/8 to Tamworth City Council.

Sydney Gay and Lesbian Mardi Gras 1998, *Annual Report*, Sydney.

Veal, A. J. 1997, *Research Methods for Leisure and Tourism: A Practical Guide*, Pitman Publishing, London.

INDEX